PROPERTY IN THINGS

IN THE COMMON LAW SYSTEM

Second Edition

BRUCE WELLING

SCRIBBLERS
PUBLISHING

**Property in Things
in the Common Law System**
Second Edition
© Bruce Welling 2008

Published by *Scribblers Publishing*
PO Box 501, Mudgeeraba
Gold Coast
Queensland 4213
AUSTRALIA
Fax/phone +61 7 5525 2528

National Library of Australia Cataloguing-in-Publication entry:

Author: Welling, Bruce, 1949-

Title: *Property in things in the common law system* / Bruce
             Welling.

Edition: 2nd ed.

ISBN: **9780980557008** (hbk.)

Subjects: Property--Great Britain.
             Things (Law)--Great Britain.
             Property--United States.
             Things (Law)--United States.
             Property--Canada.
             Things (Law)--Canada.

Dewey Number: 346.04

To
Ibid, Anon, and Trad

Without whom we would all be original, but weird

And to Kevin – long may he run

FOREWORD

Property law is straightforward, principled and interesting. Property cases tend to be complicated, irrational, and (occasionally) deadly dull and boring. Contradiction or paradox? I think it's the latter. Careless terminology is the cause. It isn't that hard to correct.

Judging by the judges, lawyers forget to keep it simple. Property is a first year subject. It doesn't get firmly imprinted on the average lawyerling. Law professors are partly to blame, but the basics get eroded later in the learning process. Clear concepts get mangled by commercial lawyers, who prefer the comfort of law French to the clarity of plain English.

This book is about the common law of property in things. I have tried to explain it in a straightforward and principled way, identifying and defining concepts before going on to the rules. Some readers' eyes may occasionally glaze over, but I hope it will be at the footnotes, not the text. The text should carry the theory and summarize the key historical developments. Healthy sceptics, and those curious for more detail, will find the footnotes useful.

The book evolved over several years. Large portions were written in Wolvercote, upstairs in a room overlooking Port Meadow. Any references to cows were inspired by the friendly herd that came round to visit my back gate most days: they're probably all mad now, poor things. Come to think of it, Jordan and I may have spotted the first one, pretending to be a sheep that day in the fog. Time elapsed and, back at Western, I reconsidered many conclusions. Much of it got re-written in Queensland, under the supervision of my editor who separated the wheat from the chaff and (unusually) published the wheat. To you, sir, a Guinness on my tab.

A few notes of thanks are due to a few people. Risa did her usual excellent work on some background details: she alone will recognize where I've gone wrong in changing her analysis. Bond University kept me for a year: I've rarely been better treated by an institution and I thank John Farrar for inviting me. Bernard McCabe and Jim Corkery, despite their political responsibilities on the Northwest Frontier, gave freely of their time, and we became good friends. Vicki Waye read the entire manuscript and made many helpful suggestions. Jan McDonald let me use her waves and never held it against me that she was a better surfer. Finally Emmy Lou and Amos never gave up on me, and took care of the house until my return.

I've tried to state the law accurately to mid-1996. Those who think I started off with a contradiction will disagree.

End of (Northern) Summer 1996

2nd Edition

This is an update. I stand by what I said in the opening paragraph of the Foreword to the first edition. The original theory has proved workable and remains intact. I am grateful to my student Alex Carr for helping to improve the details.

13 August 2008

Bruce Welling
London-Ontario-Canada

CONTENTS

PART III
THE LOST AND FOUND DEPARTMENT

PART IV
ACQUISITION AND DISPOSITION

CASES

PART I

NATURE AND TYPES

OF

PROPERTY IN THINGS

Property is a legal relationship. Legal relationships exist between people and are enforced by the state. Some, though not all, types of property are held in things.

Thing means a material object, a body; a being or entity consisting of matter, or occupying space.

A person who holds property in a thing can enlist the state to suppress another person's civil liberties to deal with the thing. Exactly what civil liberties will be suppressed varies with the type of property held in the thing.

CHAPTER 1

THE COMMON LAW CONCEPTION OF PROPERTY

A   THE NATURE OF PROPERTY

"Property" is a law word. We need a law-like system of rules and sanctions to make any sense of the concept. To say that property exists is to postulate a relationship among people within an already existing system. The idea of property is rooted in one of the most elementary of childhood experiences, the concept of "mine". From high court judge to highwayman, we all have played each of the roles in the following one-act play.

Vicky and Bobby are playing. Bobby picks up a teddy bear. Vicky says "mine".

There may be important sociological and economic issues hidden in this fact situation, but we are concerned with legal analysis. First, what options does Vicky have?

(i) Vicky might volunteer to share with Bobby, at least temporarily.
(ii) Vicky might threaten Bobby, or instigate physical violence.
(iii) Vicky might appeal to an authority figure.

The first option is frequently chosen but boring to analyze. It merely postpones action until either Vicky or Bobby loses interest in playing with the teddy bear, at which time the problem disappears. The second option is tempting, but Vicky soon learns that the advantages she may gain (removal of teddy bear from Bobby's arms) are outweighed by the disadvantages she may suffer (the ignominy of failure, or the infliction of physical pain, or punishment from an authority figure for resort to a forbidden form of self-help). The third option also has its down side. The authority figure might disagree with the substance of the "mine" claim[1] or might impose temporary sharing, regardless of the views of Vicky and other people as to the "mine" claim's merits.[2] Nevertheless, authority figures try to socialize people like Vicky and Bobby to select (iii) over (ii). The day to day running of the nursery depends on that socialization.

---

1 There could be many reasons for this. For example, Vicky's capitalist parents may have inadvertently consigned them to the Marx Day Care Center, thinking the proprietor was a disciple of Harpo. Alternatively, Vicky may have misidentified the teddy bear. Similar things happen in real-life law.

2 Clever people, and those with particularly nasty childhoods, will already have thought of some other options. Vicky or Bobby could blow up the bear. One child might be gunned down by the other. There are many ways of solving problems and law has no monopoly on dispute resolution. However, this is only a law book.

What does this have to do with property? Well, the nursery is a microcosm of everyday adult life. Imagine taller versions of Vicky and Bobby. Victoria and Robert, and the rest of their childhood cohort, interact on a scale they perceive to be somewhat grander. But is it? Now, if Robert drives off in a car that Victoria calls "mine", does Victoria have any more options than she had in the teddy bear affair? Not really.

In the grown-up world, the main differences are in degree - the degree of physical injury that either Victoria or Bobby can inflict; the degree of punishment that might be imposed for resort to violence - and in the identity of and ease of access to the authority figure. Now the authority figure is the state.

Just like the authority figures in the nursery and the Day Care Center, the state claims a monopoly on violence and provides a dispute resolution system, in an effort to keep the peace. The personalized appeals, the conventional (child-scale) warfare and low transaction costs of the nursery atmosphere have been replaced by lawyers, guns and money.[3]

However Victoria still has the same three choices. (i) Will she share, which may translate to lose in the long run? (ii) Will she resort to self-help, which may be dangerous in the circumstances? (iii) Will she invoke the judicial powers of the state?[4] If she chooses (iii) we get back to the problem of whether she can persuade a judge to agree with her statement that the car was "mine", and whether there is a legal remedy for her complaint. In short, will the authority figure recognize[5] and enforce[6] her claim?

"Mine" is an imprecise property word. To say "mine" is to assert a property claim. Victoria, in saying "that [teddy bear or car] is mine", is predicting that she will appeal to and will be assisted by greater authority[7] if the listener does not stop messing with the object described. The listener's reaction is likely to vary with the speaker's credibility about the consequences. Adult Victoria's credibility is enhanced because the state is the authority figure in the grown-up game of property.

---

3 Warren Zevon was neither the first nor the last to make use of this imagery.

4 I left out the police powers, although they are likely to be notified as well. The criminal (punishment of defendant) and civil (compensation of plaintiff) processes tend to be kept separate in common law systems. The police generally take a dim view of being used as stalking horses by a complainant seeking to coerce the settlement of a civil action.

5 Different people have different views of property. In a democracy we generally encourage the proliferation of varying views. Nevertheless, it is the state's view of property which matters when state assistance is invoked.

6 Sometimes a remedy will not be forthcoming, even though interference with property has been proved. More on that later.

7 It used to be fashionable to include extraterrestrial powers, and I sense that the fashion is being recycled. I mean to refer only to the types of earthly powers that I am fairly sure most people, whether they like it or not, accept as being backed by the police, the army, or some other organization generally conceded to have the most effective firepower in the neighbourhood.

2

The characters in the above scenarios were engaging in ordinary relationships. Some aspects of their relationships were legal in nature. Legal relationships are what property is all about. It works like this.

> *Property is a relationship. There are always three people in the relationship. The first person is the state.*
>
> *The second person is someone whom the state has concluded is the holder of a specified form of property. The third is any other person whom the state has not concluded is the holder of that specified form of property.*
>
> *The state will suppress the civil liberties of the third person to the extent they fall within the scope of the form of property held.*

The first proposition describes the nature of property. By definition, property is abstracted from the world of things. Property has more in common with familiar social relationships like friendship and club membership than with animals, vegetables and minerals. To use the word in a sentence is to predict how the people named or implied in the sentence will behave: no more than that. The prediction may turn out to be erroneous. For example, the simple prediction that most strangers will defer to a proprietor won't suffice to ward off thieves. However, a lawyer's work involves predicting the probable outcome of disputes. If the facts required to prove a particular form of property can be assembled, a predictable pattern of behaviour will usually follow.[8] The threat of coercion by the state ensures this.[9]

The second proposition indicates that property is an inter-personal relationship. A particular form[10] of property is held[11] by one person and not held by another.[12] The

---

8 "A statement that a legal relation exists between A and B is a prediction as to what society, acting through its courts or executive agents, will or will not do for one and against the other. ... The relation of A to his house is a physical relation." Corbin," Legal Analysis and Terminology" 29 Yale LJ 163 (1919) at 164-165

9 By the word "state" I mean to identify that group of individuals and legal institutions that at any particular time both claim and hold effective power to enact and enforce legal rules. In most common law countries these consist of groups of elected legislators and two other branches - executive and judicial - appointed by them. Law, in my view, tends to be whatever these people consistently say it is. For a criticism of this view of law, see Plucknett, *A Concise History of the Common Law* (5th ed, Butterworths London 1956) at 40-41, where the 20th century state is described thus.

> Instead of the mediaeval dominion based upon divine right and subject to law, we have the modern state based upon force and independent of morality. [Where] a mediaeval thinker would ultimately identify law with the will of God (sic), [now] it will be regarded as the will of the state.

For an interesting analysis of the derivation of the word, see Dowdall, "The Word 'State'"(1923) 39 LQR 98, suggesting a Latin root which conveys the message "the ... estate of an effectively sovereign prince, together with the rights and powers belonging thereto".

10 As we shall see, this legal relationship called property has sub-categories.

11 I have used the word "held" for two reasons. First, to describe the people in any property relationship I must have a verb to use in the sentence. Second, "held" has an attractive neutrality about it and is not

holder may be able to convince the third person of his superior legal position by asserting and documenting his claim. Doing so merely convinces the third person that the holder will win if a court battle is forced. Failing to do so invokes compromise or judicial resolution.

The third proposition is the key. Property is a dispute resolution mechanism. Disputes are likely to arise when one person wants to act in a way that another person does not want him to act. The other person may claim to be at liberty (or, in more popular though less exact terminology, to "have a right") to do it. Doing it, walking directly from point A to point B for example, may be ordinarily an exercise of civil liberty. It ceases to be so while "my" car is in the way. The actor's civil liberties will be suppressed if I am in a position to prove that the car is "mine". The suppressing[13] is done by the state.[14]

B   PROPERTY AND THINGS CONTRASTED

Property is as basic to a philosophy of the common law system as anatomy is to medical theory.[15] It is, therefore, curious that legal thought about property tends to be expressed in one of two ineffective ways.

Arcane terminology, incomprehensible to those who hadn't memorized a rigid tradition, used to be the major flaw. It still is in the sub-category of property in land. What works for doctors in bone labelling has turned out to be less easily manageable in a field where neither the number of working parts nor their potential interconnections are fixed in nature.

---

associated with any particular form of property as is the word "own".

12 This is not 100% accurate, as it is possible for two or more people to hold a form of property jointly. In such a situation, each of them can be viewed as *the property holder* in dealings with third parties. We can ignore the possibility in this introductory analysis.

13 It is the civil liberty that is suppressed, not the person. Suppressing a civil liberty involves using the threat, or imposition, of legal sanctions to inhibit the doing of what the person could otherwise do with legal impunity. It is not at all similar to suppressing dormice.

14 This tends to operate in an indirect way. Legal rules generally prescribe what the consequences will be if (i) the act is done and (ii) the property holder brings a formal legal action before the courts. The system would obviously not work if this were required in every case. Fortunately, it is not, as the threat of possible legal action is usually sufficient to either deter the act if interference or encourage a settlement of the dispute. This depends, of course, on the population being customarily respectful of the law and culturally acclimatized to the general nature of its rules.

15 By common law system I mean the system of law that evolved in England over some hundreds of years. The system was imposed on, or adopted by, other countries (notably Australia, Canada, the United States of America, Malaysia, India, and New Zealand) and continues to evolve along separate, but surprisingly similar lines in all of them. The evolution is usually characterized as proceeding through the interpretation of particular rules by individual judges in particular cases and the creation of new packages of rules by the various elected legislative bodies. This ignores the ongoing attempts by an army of philosophically diverse commentators in law reform commissions, local bar associations, and law schools to organize the history, judicial comments and legislation into cohesive and comprehensible packages.

Imprecise terminology was the tradition of the 19th and 20th centuries. Though superficially attractive, because it invokes common usage, it is fundamentally flawed by its lack of definition. A doctor's "broken ankle" diagnosis is fine for informing the patient, but would be insufficiently precise for correspondence between the doctor and an orthopaedic specialist. That is the diagnostic level of much legal argument. Common usage has its drawbacks in the field of law. Nevertheless, simplicity is attainable if some care is taken at the early stages of analysis.

Defining "property" was the first step. Property is a relationship between people. The next step is equally important. Property must never be confused with things.

The confusion of property and things has infected common lawyers for at least 200 years. It has complicated every area of property analysis and, surprisingly for such a simple point, has led to demonstrably erroneous decisions at the highest levels.[16] The habit is so entrenched in today's legal discourse that it may be impossible to eradicate. [17] What I propose to demonstrate, however, is the analytical advantage of adhering to this most basic of rules: never confuse property with things.

People held property in things in the early common law. Mostly those things were land and cattle. Who held property in land was critical to feudal politics. Consequently the common law of property in land developed early and became a specialist topic. Who held property in a cow or a sheep was rarely so involved a question. Simple rules could be phrased in simple ways. They could easily be adapted, as more things were discovered or created.

We measure wealth today, by computing the market value of "portfolios" of corporate shares, government bonds, pork belly futures and business "goodwill". These are concepts, not things. They were unknown to the early common law. Most early common

---

16 See, for example, *Winkfield (The)* [1902] P 42 (Eng CA) and *Wilson v Lombank* [1963] 1 WLR 1294 (Eng HC), leading to a proliferation of confusing academic and judicial discussions of *jus tertii* [the right of a third party?]. We shall deal with these cases in Chapter 10.

17 The following introductory comments written in a book on the law of property in 1918 (but by no means unusual terminology throughout the 20th century) illustrate the fundamental failure to maintain the distinction between property and things.

> By the word "things" is understood every object, except man, which may become an active subject of right. ... . It may therefore be considered as nearly or quite synonymous, at our later law with the word 'property'. [*Schouler on Personal Property* 5th ed (Matthew Bender & Co Albany 1918) at 19]

Lest I be accused of introducing an old and perhaps dated authority as a straw man, consider the following offering from 1973:

> *res corporales* include land as well as goods, and *res incorporales* include rights over land, such as rights of way and other easements and profits, which, though incorporeal, are treated by us not as choses in action but as incorporeal hereditaments, that is, as real property. [*Crossley Vaines Personal Property* 5th ed 1973 at 14]

I don't know what the Latin means. I don't know what the English means either. Note that, judging by the page numbers, these were meant to be introductory comments.

lawyers would have agreed with Yates, J. who opined in 1769: "[n]othing can be the object of property which has not a corporeal existence".[18] I agree with him, though probably not exactly as he meant it. The key is in the word "nothing" [no thing]. The reasoning is as follows.

The word "thing" is used ambiguously in the English language. One common usage is to refer somewhat vaguely to either an object or a concept. "The things we used to do" evokes nostalgia, but conveys little content, except among intimates. That won't do for legal analysis, if the objective is to make oneself clear to strangers. Alternatively, the word may denote an object, apparently of the material world, for which the speaker is unable to muster a descriptive label. The *thing* in UFO reports and monster movies is a good example of this second usage. I intend this second meaning whenever the word "thing" appears in this book.[19]

> *Thing means a material object, a body; a being or entity (excluding land) consisting of matter, or occupying space.*

Interestingly, this is precisely the position taken in the *German Civil Code*. Section 90 says unequivocally "[o]nly corporeal objects are things in the legal sense".[20]

Having thus distinguished property from things and defined each, we move to the question how to use the English language to verbalize our conception of property in things.

C   THE GRAMMAR OF PROPERTY IN THINGS

Boring though it might have seemed, what we learned about English grammar can be a valuable analytical tool. The study of grammar is the study of how we must phrase our ideas if we expect to convey them in an efficient manner. The structure of the English sentence is much neglected in basic property analysis: nouns become verbs; the object in one sentence becomes the predicate in the next. The shift from "X holds possession of that car" to "X possesses that car" seems harmless enough. Yet the shift from long to

---

18 *Millar v Taylor* (1769) 98 ER 201 at 232 *per* Yates J.

19 The inquisitive reader would find that the *Oxford English Dictionary* proposes the alternative meanings described in the text, but extends the second to include "a piece of property, an individual possession". I have excluded this extension, as it is an example of the confusion between property and things that I am attempting to expose and prevent.

20 The German Code goes on at some length to define such particulars as "fungible things", "component parts", "accessories", etc: *The German Civil Code* (as amended to January 1975: Eng translation) (Rothman & Co New Jersey 1975) ss 90-98. So far as I can make out, the only departure from linguistic purity occurs in s 96, which says "[r]ights which are connected with the ownership of a piece of land are deemed to be component parts of the land". I am unaware of any other code in which the basis for avoiding the confusion between property and things is so carefully set out, although it is possible that the confusion is peculiar to the English language.

short form too often becomes a lapse from precise terminology into jargon.

Consider the concept of ownership. Let us assume for the moment that ownership is a form of property.[21] That, according to the definition set out above, would indicate that ownership is being assumed to be a relationship between people whereby one person is by law entitled to state assistance in restricting the civil liberties of others. Let's call the former person "O".

Consider the concept of possession. Assume that possession is also a form of property. Let's use "P" to designate the person who is able to claim possession and restrict others' civil liberties.

Suppose the object of people's attention in this example to be a car. People want to drive the car. No permission from anyone would be required if there were no property in cars.[22] However, there is, and O or P might object if someone else drove the car. O could enlist state assistance to inhibit driving of the car without his permission; so could P. We are likely to explain this state of affairs in a short English sentence. "O owns the car." Similarly we might explain that "P possesses the car". Thus far there is no confusion.[23]

Now let's complicate the picture slightly. Assume the existence of a statutory form of property called "perfected security interest".[24] If we give "F" a perfected security interest

---

21 Strangely enough, the deeper one goes into the history of the common law, the less likely it seems that the concept of ownership played any meaningful role. Possession, not ownership, was what one ordinarily had to prove to get access to a common law remedy. See, on this point, Pollock and Wright, *Possession in the Common Law* (Clarendon Press Oxford 1888) at 5:

> Common Law never had any adequate process in the case of land, or any process at all in the case of goods, for the vindication of ownership ... . So feeble and precarious was property without ... possessory remedies ... that possession largely usurped not only the substance but the name of property ... .

Given the definition of property adopted in this book - which amounts to a prediction that the state will intervene (by remedy) to restrict the civil liberties of others - ownership without remedy would not seem to qualify. This, as we shall see, may have changed in more recent times.

22 Apart from the familiar concept of state licensing requirements, if the car is to be driven on a highway. This is not a property concept, but an example of direct state control of potentially dangerous behaviour.

23 There is no reason why two people like O and P can not hold property in the same thing at the same time. As will soon become clear, this is a quite common state of affairs. Each of O and P can enlist state support to inhibit the liberties of third parties *to the extent that the third party's actions constitute an interference with his property*. Each will be able to restrict the civil liberties of the other within the definition of his own form of property, but will find his own liberty restricted to the extent of the other's property. One of the simplest examples occurs as a result of a transaction called "bailment", dealt with later.

24 Despite the exotic name this too is a quite familiar concept, created under the *Uniform Commercial Code (UCC)* in the USA and under statutes in Canadian provinces usually called the *Personal Property Security Act (PPSA)*. Lending institutions create perfected security interests when lending money to borrowers who want to acquire ownership or possession of things like cars or farm machinery.

in the car, we must, in accordance with the propositions set out above, be saying that F is in a position to restrict the civil liberties of others in some way related to the use of the car. But how do we structure the simple sentence to explain this? Try the closest parallel to the above situations. "F perfected security interests the car." That sounds a bit unlikely, doesn't it?

The problem is that we have packed a lot of technical content into the familiar verbs "owns" and "possesses". The short form "P possesses the car" translates into the long form "P can enlist state support in restricting the liberty of others to use the car to the extent of the scope of the form of property called possession". That's prolix and unmanageable for verbal communication.

We can get rid of most of the words by agreeing (i) that we are talking about property, (ii) that possession is a form of property, and (iii) that property implies the ability to restrict civil liberty with state support. The sentence then reduces to a fairly straightforward assertion about a person called P, a form of property called possession, and a thing called a car. The reader gets a clear message that predicts state action should a stranger interfere with the car. What we want is an efficient way of conveying similarly structured messages about different forms of property.

PERSON	PROPERTY	THING
O	ownership	car
P	possession	car
F	perfected security interest	car

This is where English grammar comes in handy. We are missing a verb, a preposition, and a definite article to complete each sentence. Ideally these would be constants whereas the person, form of property, and thing would be variables. In short, we are looking for a formula. The preposition and the definite article are no problem: [form of property] *in* the car and [form of property] *of* the car" are equally acceptable.[25] "Ownership of the car", "possession of the car", and "a perfected security interest in the car" all make sense. The more difficult problem is what verb to use.

I recommend the verb "hold". The word can symbolize a host of meanings, not all of which are appropriate here[26] The sense in which it conveys the message we want is suggested by its synonym "maintain", as in maintaining a position that one has attained at some time in the past. Thus, one holds property if one has acquired it and maintains it, *ie*,

---

25 There seems no particular reason for the quirk of language that causes us to think that possession *of* a car sounds correct whereas a security interest *of* a car sounds odd. Having thought it over I concluded that no analytical difficulties would arise as a result of leaving the selection of preposition optional.

26 In particular, the pictorial ones that conjure images of a hand grasping something are not helpful, as it is the *property* that one holds, not a material thing. The most likely alternative verb is have (as in "X *has* property in the thing"), but that conveys a rather more passive image than I visualize for the role of a proprietor.

has not abandoned the holding of the property in some way.[27] Using the verb "hold" we can now complete the sentences to describe in proper, plain, and unambiguous English the relative legal positions of O, P, and F.

> O holds ownership of the car.
> P holds possession of the car.
> F holds a perfected security interest in the car.

The position of each person will be perfectly clear,[28] both in relation to other people and among themselves, once we understand what the property words ("ownership", "possession", "perfected security interest") mean.

D   PROPERTY OTHER THAN PROPERTY IN THINGS

The interpersonal relations of human beings are not restricted to dealing with objects of the physical world. The world of ideas, for example, is one in which we see people competing and earning a living. Most of us would predict that both the designer and the builder of the better mousetrap will make money. How is the legal system set up to realize this expectation?

When a stock of better mousetraps mysteriously disappears from the factory and reappears on the retail market in the next county, we have no difficulty finding legal remedies for the mousetrap builder. The analysis is based on the law of property in things: the builder had some form of property in the mousetraps and the legal system has no difficulty in restoring the property (ie, returning the relationship between builder and thief to its condition before the disappearance) or ordering the thief to pay compensation to the builder. The analysis of property in things has gone on for centuries.

Not so in the case of a claim based on property other than property in things. The designer probably has no property in the mousetraps. He may be able to secure court orders prohibiting their being made according to his design without his permission. He may be awarded compensation, if they are so made. But saying that this is so because he holds property in the mousetraps would be untrue. Some would say that the designer holds property "in the design". This makes no sense. The design is not a thing. Where the design is drawn on a sheet of paper, the "property in things" analysis will work if the paper is stolen. But if someone makes a photocopy of the original, or memorizes the drawing and specifications, it is not so easy to reason through to the conclusion that a property remedy is available. Two Canadian examples illustrate the difficulty.

---

27 Transfer, confiscation, losing and giving up hope of finding are but three different ways of ceasing to hold property. Acquisition and disposition, two key events in proving the existence of property in common law systems, are covered extensively later.

28 Assuming that we know the identity of each person and which car we are discussing.

R v *Stewart*[29] was a prosecution for theft under s 283(1) of the *Canadian Criminal Code*.[30] The defendant was hired to prepare a list of names, addresses and telephone numbers of hotel employees for union organization purposes. He did so from personnel files and computer payroll records. The evidence indicated that the employer had made security arrangements to limit access and would not have been willing to disclose the names. The question was whether the defendant's acts fell within the definition of theft. Section 283(1) of the *Criminal Code* said:

> Everyone commits theft who fraudulently and without colour of right takes, or fraudulently and without colour of right converts to his use or to the use of another person, anything whether animate or inanimate with intent ...
>
> (d)   to deal with it in such a manner that it cannot be restored in the condition in which it was at the time it was taken or converted"

A not guilty verdict at trial was reversed by the Ontario Court of Appeal.

R v *Offley*[31] was a similar case. The defendant was hired to do security checks on job applicants. He wanted to check for criminal offences through access to police computer records, but was told that access was restricted to law enforcement agencies. He asked a police officer to do the computer checks for him. The police entrapped him and charged him with counselling theft. The charge required proof that successful direct access would have constituted theft. He was convicted at trial, but acquitted by the Alberta Court of Appeal "on the ground that confidential information is incapable of being stolen".[32]

The Supreme Court of Canada resolved both cases along the Alberta line of analysis.

The section of the *Criminal Code* was badly written. Theft was a concept developed through the evolutionary process of the common law. At common law it meant intentional deprivation of possession. The concept of possession is one of the most basic and clearly understood in the common law system. First, it is a form of property. Second, it is a form of property *in things*: the statement "I have possession" is meaningless and would invoke the retort "you have possession of what?" At common law theft involved the intentional deprivation of a person's possession of a material object. Parliament could have written the *Criminal Code* to adopt or extend the common law meaning. Assuming that the words "fraudently and without colour of right" deal with the intention requirement, the words "takes, or ... converts to his use or to the use of another person, anything whether animate or inanimate" ... with intent ... (d) to deal with it in such a manner that it cannot be restored in the condition in which it was at the time it

---

29 *R v Stewart* (1983)149 DLR 3d 583, 42 OR 2d 225 (Ont CA), reversing (1982) 138 DLR 3d 73, 38 OR 2d 84.

30 RSC 1985 C 27.

31 *R v Offley* (1986) 45 Alta LR 2d 23, 11 CPR 3d 231 (Alta CA).

32 *Ibid.*

was taken or converted" must describe the criminal act. Is there any indication that these words mean "anything *or no thing*"? Does the concept of taking a "no thing" make any sense?

It does not. The legislative intent may have been to make it a criminal offence to intentionally deprive someone of any form of property. Given that most people think of property in things whenever the word property is mentioned, and that possession is not the only form of property in things, this seems a likely objective. Thus, if some strategic metal were thought sufficiently important to national security that the head of state (in Canada, Her Majesty the Queen), or the State itself (in republican countries) had been made by statute the owner of all supplies within national borders, someone found with a suitcase full at a border checkpoint could be charged with attempted theft even if he could not be proved to have disturbed anyone's possession of the metal. Further, given the tendency of English-speakers, including Parliamentarians, to confuse property with things, one would not be surprised to see the *Criminal Code* reference to "taking the thing" (whatever that means) interpreted to include depriving the Her Majesty, or the State, of its property in the thing.

Compare the similarly motivated legislative decision to monopolize the only known design for making bombs with the same strategic metal. We can't use the language of property in things, because the design is not a thing. Nor could someone who memorized the design be convicted of theft on the Criminal Code definition set out above. The act is simply not described by the words of the code. Her Majesty, or the State, might well hold a form of property, but it is not property *in something*. It might be possible to conceive of interference with the form of property as theft, but only if theft were redefined in terms of intentional interference with property, rather than inaccurately described in terms of things.

The point is that property - described above as a relationship whereby a property holder can enlist state support in restricting the civil liberties of a non-holder - need have nothing to do with what people do with things. The terminology of property in things remains the terminology of everyday conversation, partly because the most familiar forms of property dealt with restricting the use of things like teddy bears and cars. If someone says "I own some corporate shares", we have a generally accurate notion of what he means. So too could we understand the phrase "my friend broke his arm". However, an orthopaedic surgeon wouldn't tell a medical colleague "your patient broke his arm". For the same reason "your client owns some corporate shares" is not precise enough for dialogue between two legal analysis. The corporate share is itself a form of property, and people *hold* forms of property. Maybe that's why we call people who hold corporate shares "shareholders".

E   PROPERTY THEORY AND COMMON LAW PROCESS

Utopians talk about a time when "all property was common". They are not using the word "property" in today's sense. They refer to a time when *no one* held property in things and everyone was free to make use of them. There may have been such a time, but even if there was it isn't relevant to the study of property as we know it. Property limits the exercise of liberty by non-holders. A non-holder who wants to use a thing can (i) find someone who holds property in the thing and get permission, (ii) arrange with the holder to acquire the property by transfer, or (iii) just do it, and risk the legal consequences. A marketplace has evolved to handle the first two transactions. While some forms of property are not transferable and not all property has a market value,[33] it is assumed in the design of the system that most property has both attributes.

Property is part of the structure of the marketplace. If property as defined in this book did not exist a similar concept would probably evolve without legislative participation. Private enforcement mechanisms, backed by threats of violence from hired thugs, could no doubt provide the same security of transaction as judges and policemen paid out of tax revenues. However, most countries have seen fit to create a monopoly on violence, under which the State reserves to itself most forms of corporal punishment and incarceration. Self-help, while not ruled out, is limited in common law countries.

Common law countries provide a judicial process to resolve private disputes. Judges determine winners and losers in particular cases. Judging is a complex process. First the facts that led to the dispute must be ascertained. After that, legal rules must be applied. The rules aren't always written down and they aren't always obvious. In retrospect, the particular rule that determined the outcome in a particular case is usually discernible from a general theory of the area of law in dispute. More often than not, however, judges say they found a particular rule in the reasons for judgment of their judicial predecessors. Legal theories are found in books about law, not in law reports that chronicle the legal process.

The reason why is simple, if somewhat obscure. In the common law system, legal theory and legal process don't operate in exactly the same ways. I don't mean that legal theory and the common law process oppose one another. In fact, each relies on the other for its development. But their differences must be understood before their interaction can be appreciated.

The function of the common law process is to resolve disputes. This involves ascertaining what events occurred and assigning liability among the parties in the particular case. Over the centuries common law judges have recited and adapted general principles as they applied in the particular circumstances that came before them. Judicial

---

33 For example, some corporate shares can not be transferred, and I doubt that possession of (even a large quantity of) petrified buffalo dung would excite buyers at a commodities exchange.

theories of the common law evolved from the bottom up. Judging rarely involves the prediction of future events.

The function of a legal theory is to predict the future. Lawyers want to know what result the common law process is likely to produce if particular facts are proved. A good legal theory will also predict the past by explaining the results (but not necessarily the reasoning) in past cases.

The theoretician's objective is to organize the subject matter of research from the top down.[34] The general determines the specific. If a particular piece of data will not fit, the respectable theoretician rejects it as an aberration, a freak of nature. The clean logic lines of a good theory are not to be complicated and rearranged merely to account for one misfit. It is only when several aberrations occur, or a previously undiscovered colony of misfits is found, that the theory needs changing.

Consequently, developing and explaining a theory of some area of the common law is different from compiling a digest that organizes what judges have said. A theory imposes order on content. Academics enjoy the twin luxuries of reflecting upon what a wide range of judges have said while not having to focus on a particular dispute that requires immediate resolution. When an academic suggests that a particular judge was wrong in a particular case, the criticism is more often directed at the theory that was applied than at the judicial determination as to whether the plaintiff won or lost. When a judge suggests that an academic was wrong, the criticism is more often directed at a small sub-category of the academic's overall theory. Law, like modern science, progresses more smoothly and with greater good will when the practitioners and the theoreticians remember that their roles are complementary and make proper use of each others' material.

This book presents a *theory* of property in things. Its most likely use in the practical world of judges and lawyers is to suggest a different, simpler way of thinking through the resolution of future property disputes. For law students it offers a principled approach to discovering the property law hidden between the lines of centuries of common law cases.

F   A NOTE ON EQUITY

Equity is a much misunderstood concept. It has little to do with moral concepts like fairness, natural justice or good conscience. Equity is a system of law that grew out of political tensions and power struggles in the English Middle Ages. It evolved after, and to a large extent because of, the common law process.

---

34 "The business of the jurist is to make known the content of the law; that is, to work upon it from within, or logically, arranging and distributing it, in order, from its *summum genus* to its *infirma species*." Holmes, *The Common Law* at 173.

The common law process relied on precedent. Decisions were based on prior decisions. Prior to 1066, justice was administered by local courts.[35] The law varied according to district. After the Norman Conquest, power in England became more centralized.[36] A central court called the *Curia Regis*, made up of the King and his officials, was established.[37] At first the *Curia Regis* toured the realm with the King, but eventually the King began sending out judges on their own to dispense his justice.[38] The *Curia Regis* applied laws that were both predictable and common to all districts.

Predictability had its dark side. Common law actions were classified according to a system of forms called "writs" and every action had to be commenced by filing the appropriate writ. Writs were issued by the Chancellor,[39] who was a member of the *Curia Regis* and official keeper of the Royal Seal which was key to authenticating documents in a largely illiterate age. Prior to 1258 the system retained some flexibility through the Chancellor's power to create new writs as novel complaints arose. However, the Barons (powerful officials on whom the King depended for financial and military support) were wary of allowing the Chancellor too much influence over law and they negotiated the *Provisions of Oxford* whereby the Chancellor lost the power to create new writs.[40] Any new action subsequently had to be made to fit into an existing writ or it could not be commenced at all. Thus developed a system in which a limited number of rigid causes of action became more and more narrowly interpreted as the volume of precedent grew. Political reality also played a role: in many cases a common law remedy was not won, or was unenforceable, because of the military power of the defendant.[41]

Petitions regarding defects in the law were made to the King's council. The King, of course, had other matters to attend to and the Chancellor routinely presided over the council, and delivered the decisions.[42] Although it was not until 1474 that the Chancellor began to give decisions in his own name,[43] we can see in retrospect that the views reflected were generally his own, not the King's.

Prior to the 16th century the Chancellor had broad power to rule according to conscience. In the name of the King's conscience, a good deal of flexibility remained in early Chancellors' decisions.[44] The Chancellor was an ecclesiastic, so religious thinking

---

35 WH Holdsworth, *History of English Law* (Goodhart & Hanbury eds) (7th ed Methuen & Co Ltd London 1956) vol 1 p 3.
36 Holdsworth at 4.
37 *Ibid* at 32.
38 *Ibid* at 32-49.
39 *Ibid* at 397.
40 *Ibid* at 397.
41 *Snell's Principles of Equity* (Megarry & Baker eds) (27th ed Sweet & Maxwell London 1973) at 8.
42 Holdswoth at 399-400.
43 Snell at 8.
44 *Ibid.*

influenced his decisions.[45] During the 17th century the system became more rigid and predictable. More cases were reported, more precedents became available, similar cases began to be decided based on precedent, and the principles of the courts of Equity became as fixed as (though different from) those of the common law courts.[46] The tension between discretion and rigidity that was characteristic of the early common law arose in Equity as well.[47]

Equity accepted, as a starting point, that the common law was there. As a result, Equity never evolved into a complete system of law on its own. The Equity courts dealt with some types of disputes that the common law courts did not.[48] In other disputes their jurisdictions overlapped. In both types of cases the procedures employed and remedies provided were entirely different from those of the common law courts.[49] The inevitable result was that winners in the common law courts, armed with their common law orders, could become losers in the courts of Equity, and ordered not to act upon their common law rights on pain of contempt of (Equity) court. What amounted to an increasingly bitter territorial dispute among the judiciary was resolved by King James I in *Earl of Oxford's Case*[50]. The ruling was that when Equity and common law produce inconsistent results, equity prevails.[51]

In 1873-1875, the *Judicature Acts* amalgamated most of the courts into one Supreme Court of Judicature, and every judge in every division of that court was empowered to administer both common law and Equity.[52] This is often described as a fusion of common law and equity, but it was their administration that was fused, not the principles and rules themselves. Since the *merger of the administration of* common law and Equity, the two systems of rules have remained separate, although each can be pleaded and applied in any courtroom.

Basic notions of property in things evolved relatively early in the common law system. By the time the courts of Equity got into serious conflicts with the common law courts, the common law of property in things was more developed than most other areas of law. Equity courts accepted the common law basics as a starting point. Consequently, the Equity courts had little influence on the development of the rules governing property in things. We shall occasionally run across a peculiarly Equitable remedy, but property in things was mostly of common law development.

---

45 Snell at 8.

46 Story, *Commentaries on Equity Jurisprudence* MM Bigelow (13th ed Littleton Fred B Rothman & Co 1988) at 17.

47 Snell at 13.

48 Holdsworth at 407.

49 Story at 20-24.

50 (1615) 1 Rep Ch 1 & App; 1 W & TLC 615; Holdswoth at 459-465.

51 Holdsworth at 463.

52 Snell at 14. Most Commonwealth jurisdictions enacted similar statutes soon after, though some, notably New South Wales, kept a separate Equity bar until the latter half of the 20th century.

CHAPTER 2

TYPES OF PROPERTY IN THINGS

A   POSSESSION

Possession is a form of property in things. It has been recognized as such since time immemorial.[1] There is a good deal of wisdom in the folklore "possession is nine parts of the law". Indeed, the tenth part might as well have been "how to get and keep it", as possession was clearly the most important form of wealth until at least the 19th century.[2] It is, therefore, odd that there is no consensus on its exact meaning.[3]

Possession, like other forms of property, is a relationship.[4] To say that someone holds possession of a thing is to make a prediction that the state will intervene on the holder's side to restrict the liberty of others in dealing with the thing.[5] Judicial attention has been focused on the definition most often in cases where the defendant interfered while the plaintiff was in the act of acquiring possession.[6]

---

1 Technically, in the common law system, "time immemorial" means before 3 September 1189, the day that Richard the Lion Heart ascended the throne of England. The date was selected as a limitation on prescriptions of easements over land and enshrined in the *Statute of Westminster* of 3 Edw I C 39 (1275) in the following terms: "none shall presume to declare of the seisin of his ancestor further, or beyond the time of King Richard, uncle to King Henry, father to the king that now is". The term is much misused.

2 Apart from property in land, where the word "possession" is sometimes used, though unfortunately with a somewhat different meaning. It was probably only with the rise of capitalist investment, sometime after the expansion of overseas trading companies in the 17th century that, for more than a rare breed of financier, wealth became measured by investment through forms of property like debt and "joint stock", the forerunner of today's corporate shares. Interested readers might try WR Scott *The Constitution and Finance of English, Scottish and Irish Joint-Stock Companies* to 1720 (Cambridge University Press 1912).

3 Canadian law "does not recognize the existence of a single concept of possession applicable for all purposes": *Lifestyles Kitchens & Bath v Danbury Sales Inc* [1999] CarswellOnt 2594 (SCJ) at para 12 per Cullity J. For a survey of some of the views see Harris, "The Concept of Possession in English Law" in *Oxford Essays in Jurisprudence*, Guest ed 1961 pp 69-106. Contrast Tay, "Possession in the Common Law" (1964) 4 *Melbourne University Law Review* 284-320. She suggests that possession is not a form of property at all but a state of fact. However, it is the legal consequences flowing from the factual proof of possession that distinguishes it as a form of property.

4 See Chapter 1 "Property and Things Contrasted".

5 *Ibid.*

6 "In order to discover the facts which constitute it, it will be found best to study them at the moment possession is first gained. For then they must all be present in the same way that both consideration and promise must be present at the moment of making a contract." Holmes, *The Common Law* at 215-216.

Possession comprises a physical and a mental element.[7] Four cases involving fox hunting, fishing, and salvaging wrecked ships illustrate the judicial development of these two factors.

In *Pierson v Post*,[8] Mr Pierson shot a fox while Mr Post was chasing it. Mr Post claimed that was interference with his possession of the fox. He lost because he hadn't acquired possession before the fox was shot. His intent was clear, but mere pursuit was insufficient to prove the requisite degree of control to prove possession. Mr Pierson could deal with the fox as he liked so long as no one else had established a property relationship to inhibit his liberty.

Young v Hichens[9] again turned on the degree of control required to prove possession. The plaintiff was fishing and had nearly encompassed several fish in his net. The defendant, by rowing his boat near the opening of the net, disturbed the fish and prevented their capture. The plaintiff sued in trespass which required proof of possession. He lost. Lord Denman pointed out "it does appear almost certain that the plaintiff would have had possession of the fish but for the act of the defendant, but it is quite certain that he had not possession". Only "actual power over the fish" would suffice.

In *The Tubantia*[10] possession was proved. A Dutch ship, sunk in 1916, was found by the plaintiffs who initiated salvage operations in 1922 and continued sending divers down in the following spring and summer. By July of 1923 the plaintiffs had fixed buoys and tackle to the wreck to assist the divers in their salvage work. Then the defendants anchored a ship nearby, sent down some divers and got sounding lines entangled with the plaintiffs' lines. The plaintiffs sought damages and an injunction against interference with possession of the wreck.

The court suggested that the following questions must be answered in determining whether a person had taken possession of a thing.[11]

> [W]hat are the kinds of physical control and use of which the things in question were practically capable? Could physical control be applied to the res [thing] as a whole?

---

7 The two factors are variously stated. For example: "possession ... must imply, first some actual power over the object possessed, and secondly, some amount of will to avail oneself of that power" [*State v Strutt* 236 A 2d 357 at 360, 4 Conn Cr 501]; "possession is that condition of fact under which one can exercise his power over a corporeal thing to the exclusion of all others" [*Rice v Feyewe* 24 F 240 at 263]; and, restated in the form of three elements, (a) actual or potential physical control, (b) intent to exercise dominion and (c) external manifestation of intent and control [*Padke v State Cr App* 293 So 2d 312, 52 Ala App 397, affirmed 293 So 2d 314, 292 Ala 290.

8 *Pierson v Post* 3 Ca. 175, 2 Am Dec 264 (NY 1805).

9 *Young v Hichens* (1844) 6 QB 606, 115 ER 228 (Eng QB)

10 *Tubantia (The)* [1924] P 78 (Eng HC).

11 [1924] P 78 at 89.

Was there a complete taking? Had the plaintiffs occupation for practical purposes sufficient to exclude strangers from interfering with the property? Was there animus possidendi?

Particularly important were the buoys and salvage equipment that the plaintiffs had fixed to the wreck. Presumably these were the strongest evidence manifesting the existence of a claim in the circumstances.[12] The conclusion was that the plaintiffs had taken possession sometime before the defendants arrived.[13]

> There was animus possidendi in the plaintiffs. There was the use and occupation of which the subject matter was capable. There was power to exclude strangers from interfering if the plaintiffs did not use unlawful force. ... I hold that the plaintiffs had, in July 1923, the possession of the Tubantia and her cargo, which they allege.

Eads v *Brazelton*[14] also involved a dispute over the salvage of a wreck, this time in the Mississippi River. The plaintiff, having determined the wreck's location, marked it by putting blazes on lines of trees near the river bank so that the lines intersected at the wreck. When the defendant began salvaging the wreck the plaintiff sued but lost. One reason given was his lack of effective control.[15] More likely the critical factor was lack of display of his intentions. Property is a relationship between a property holder and others. How was anyone else to know of the relationship the plaintiff had in mind? No one stumbling upon the wreck would have noticed the slightest manifestation of the plaintiff's claim of possession. He may have found[16] the wreck, but he didn't take possession of it.

There is, of course, much more to be said about possession. For now we can summarize what the four cases tell us possession *is*.

> **Possession is a form of property in things. Possession of a thing is proved by the coexistence of (i) physical control and (ii) manifest intent to exclude others.**

The required degree of physical control will vary with the nature of the thing. Elusive

---

12 "The appliances I have mentioned, and the frequently interrupted access to the wreck which the plaintiffs had in the summer of 1923, are the evidences of possession at the dates in question in this case on which the plaintiffs rely." [1924] P 78 at 89.

13 [1924] P 78 at 90. An injunction was granted ordering the defendants to refrain from doing anything near the wreck and the question of damages was referred to the registrar.

14 *Eads v Brazelton* 22 Ark 499, 79 Am Dec 88 (Ark SC, 1861).

15 "His intention to possess was useless without detention of the property [sic]; ... to his desire to possess there was not joined a prehension of the thing". 79 Am Dec 88 at 97 per Fairchild J. The problem with this focus on "prehension" [meaning to take hold, grasp] is that the wreck, unlike a fox or a fish, is unlikely to go anywhere of its own volition. Control over a wreck must be measured in relation to other potential salvers. This concept, and this case, are further explored in Chapter 5 "Taking Possession of Things Found".

16 Finding something is insufficient to establish property. Possession may be taken of the thing, but that must be proved by the usual tests.

things like fish and game will require more extensive control than inanimate objects or slugs.[17] Control is, to some extent, measured by its appearance to others in the circumstances, although it is not necessary that a person be able to exclude all others without assistance. "A powerful ruffian may be within equal reach and sight when a child picks up a pocketbook, but if he does nothing, the child has manifested the needful power as well as if it had been backed by a hundred policemen."[18]

A simple way to characterize the intent required to prove possession is to focus on the general nature of property. Property is a relationship between people. Possession of a thing is a form of property and thus a form of relationship between people. The intent required to prove the relationship called possession is measured by assessing the claimant's attitude toward other people, not by speculating about his attitude toward the thing: did he or did he not manifest the intent to exclude others from interfering with the thing.[19]

B   RIGHT TO IMMEDIATE POSSESSION

Right to immediate possession is a form of property in things. Some analysts think it isn't. Consequently, I must explain why I say it is.

The label is somewhat inelegant. It means that the holder is at liberty to seize possession of the thing from its current possessor. Note the verb in that sentence - the holder *is* at liberty. The fact that someone will be entitled to take possession at some time in the future, no matter how certain, doesn't prove right to immediate possession *now*. That's why I include the word "immediate" in the name of the form of property.

The holder also has a common law action for possession of the thing. As we shall see later, actions for interference with property in things do not necessarily result in orders to transfer possession: the remedy may be damages.

---

17 For example:
  "timber which ... has been sawed into lumber, ... cannot be carried about on the person, and the question arises as to what kind of physical control, in order to amount to possession, was practical. ... From the evidence in the case at bar ... it could have been found that, for all practical purposes, the plaintiff was in possession of the lumber [which was lying on state land] at the time it was destroyed by fire."
New England Box Company v C & R Construction Company 150 ALR 152, 49 NE 2d 121 (Mass 1943) per Cox J at 150 ALR 162. This case is more fully analyzed in Chapter 7 "Dispossessed Prior Possessors".
  18 Holmes, *The Common Law* at 185. If the ruffian took possession from the child's grasp in those circumstances he would be liable for dispossession.
  19 "If what the law does is to exclude others from interfering with the object, it would seem that the intent which the law should require is an intent to exclude others." Holmes, *The Common Law* at 221-222.

My purpose here is simply to define right to immediate possession. It means the following when used in this book.

> *Right to immediate possession is a form of property in things. A holder of right to immediate possession is at liberty to seize possession of the thing and has standing to invoke state assistance in gaining possession.*

As we shall see later, right to immediate possession crops up in many familiar situations. It is held by a buyer of ownership of a specified thing after sale and before delivery, by a bailor upon termination (or breach of term of) bailment, and by a dispossessed former possessor. Some of the remedies available to these parties are difficult to understand unless right to immediate possession is accorded property status.

C   OWNERSHIP

"Ownership" and "own" are the most commonly used property words in the English language. Nobody knows what they mean. We have a general sense of what people are getting at when they use the term ownership, or when they say "title" which is usually a synonym. But the problem is precision. No one defines it. The common law never developed a theory of what constitutes ownership. Consider what that means in practice. Suppose a plaintiff who relies on a claim of ownership to prove his case encounters a defendant who denies the claim. That puts the plaintiff to the task of alleging facts sufficient to prove ownership. The usual response by a plaintiff in this situation would be to assert "I bought it from the previous owner" (meaning he acquired ownership by a transaction of sale from someone who held ownership prior to the transaction) and then proceed to prove the sale transaction.

However, what if the defendant denies that the seller held ownership? The fact that the plaintiff says his seller was an owner doesn't make it so. The plaintiff must prove the seller's ownership. Merely proving a long string of such transactions won't suffice. The issue will always be how to prove that the previous people in the transaction chain became owners, a point which is impossible to establish until we address the real questions: what *is*, or what *proves*, ownership of a thing?

The common law cases don't provide much assistance. Nevertheless, the term is used extensively by judges and legal analysts. Its use derives from a preoccupation of thought that, for things other than land, one owner can almost always be found whose claims will prevail over the claims of all others.[20] One merely has to ask "claims to what" and the

---

20 Consider the following statement, with which, in my experience, many property analysts today would profess agreement.

"The property in goods can only belong to, or be vested in, one person at one time: in this respect it resembles the seisin or feudal possession of lands. ... [T]he law knows no such thing as a remainder or reversion of a chattel. ... The action in Trover tries the right of

house of cards collapses. There are many circumstances in which a defendant can concede a plaintiff's ownership, yet prevail in a dispute over possession. For example, people who hire cars for the day have contractual defences against repossession. Whether an owner of a thing defeats a non-owner in litigation over what will happen to the thing depends as much on other relationships between the two litigants as it does on ownership.

The early common law didn't need a definition of ownership. Common law remedies were based on possession. Usually the person in possession of a cow or a sheep was the only one who held any property in it. Indeed, in the absence of documentary evidence, possession was often the only evidence of proprietary interest. Sometimes the person in possession would be brought to court as a defendant and accused of having interfered with the plaintiff's prior possession. The issues would be (i) did the plaintiff hold possession at some time in the past and (ii) did the defendant interfere with that possession? That, in most cases, disposed of the matter.[21]

"Ownership" and "own" had become firmly implanted in legal jargon by the 19th century. But the words were not used consistently to describe a form of property in things. I think that 19th (and late 18th) century analysts saw it as follows.

> Things were clearly identifiable. Property was a way of associating person and thing. People owned property.

> In land, one could "own" several types of property. A might "own" an estate while B "owned" the reversion and C "owned" a leasehold interest and lived on the land.

> In things other than land, one "owned *the* property".[22] This may be where property and things became confused, for if there was but one form of property in

---

possession, and may or may not determine the property." *Williams On Personal Property* 1st ed (Sweet London 1848) 21, 24.
From the surrounding text it is evident that the author meant to equate the word "property" with what lawyers today are in the habit of calling ownership. I am suspicious about the accuracy of everything except for the first part of the last sentence.

21 See Pollock and Wright, *Possession in the Common Law* (Oxford Clarendon Press 1888) 5: "The Common Law never had any adequate process in the case of land, or any process at all in the case of goods, for the vindication of ownership pure and simple". Similarly, at 118: "The ordinary conception of theft is that it is a violation of a person's ownership of a thing; but the proper conception of it is that it is a violation of the person's possession of the thing". Compare the following comment from *Williams On Personal Property* 1st ed (Sweet London 1848) 21: "strange as it may appear, there is no action in the law of England by which the property in goods is alone decided". It is clear from the surrounding text that Mr. Williams was using the word "property" to mean ownership.

22 See *Williams on Personal Property* (Sweet London 1848) 21: "personal property is essentially the subject of absolute ownership, and cannot be held for any estate. The property in goods can only belong to, or be vested in, one person at one time: in this respect it resembles the seisin or feudal possession of lands."

things then the two expressions "A 'owns' property in the thing" and "A 'owns' the thing" would be functionally identical. This became the prevailing wisdom.

Thus, by the 19th century, "own" was being used in its everyday conversational sense. "Own" had become the verb in the sentence rather than a noun denoting a particular form of property, as in the phrase "the form of property A holds is ownership".

But what did it mean? What was it that a person who "owned property" had, or could do? To interpret the phrase we must remember two facts: first, possession of a thing was effectively the only enforceable form of property in the early common law; second, property in a thing, then as now, was simply a label which indicated that state assistance was available to restrict others' access to the thing. It was when possession for a limited period of time became more common that the terminology became obscure.

> So feeble and precarious was property without possession, or rather without possessory remedies, in the eyes of medieval lawyers, that possession largely usurped not only the substance but the name of property, and when distinction became necessary in modern times, the clumsy term "special property" was employed to denote the rights of a possessor not being owner.[23]

The "clumsy term 'special property'", noted by Pollock and Wright in 1888, was popularized by Blackstone, who may simply have picked up an 18th century usage and spread it about. He and his disciples used "special property" and "qualified property" (or sometimes both adjectives together) throughout their many editions. The following is Blackstone's description of what happens in bailment, a common transaction of which hiring a car is a typical modern example.[24]

> In all these circumstances there is a special qualified property transferred from the bailor to the bailee, together with the possession. It is not an absolute property, because of his contract for restitution; the bailor having still left in him the right to a chose in action, grounded upon such contract. And on account of this qualified property of the bailee, he may (as well as the bailor) maintain an action against such as injure or take away these chattels.

As we shall see later, the same conclusions can be drawn without the mysterious terminology. The bailee holds *possession*, not some mumbo-jumbo "qualified property", and therefore has the same remedies as any other possessor. The bailor holds either

---

23 Pollock and Wright, *Possession in the Common Law* (Clarendon Press Oxford 1888) 5.

24 *Blackstone's Commentaries Vol II* (15th ed 1809) 452. The obscure terminology was copied by Chancellor Kent in his similar work on American law. "Absolute property denotes a full and complete title and dominion over it; but qualified property in chattels ... means a temporary or special interest, liable to be totally divested on the happening of some particular event. ... A qualified property in chattels may also subsist when goods are bailed, or pledged, or distrained. In those cases, the right of property and the possession are separated; and the possessor has only a property of a temporary or qualified nature ... ." Kent 2 *Commentaries on American Law* (Blackstone Publishing Co 1889) 348-350.

ownership or, upon termination of the bailment, will hold *right to immediate possession*, and if the bailor has any remedy against a third party it must be based one of those forms of property.

Whatever the cause, the terminology became confused after Blackstone's time and no definition of the word "ownership" emerged in the common law system. It might be possible to fully analyze property in things without using the word. However, retaining ownership as a concept can enable us to shorten otherwise prolix descriptions of certain relationships. In this book, the word "ownership" conveys the following messages.

> *Ownership is a form of property in things. A holder of ownership of a thing either (i) holds possession of the thing which no one is at liberty to interfere with, or (ii) holds, or will when a contract expires hold, right to immediate possession of the thing, while someone else holds possession or right to immediate possession after transfer.*

I acknowledge that is somewhat awkward for a definition, and I fear that we may come across situations in which it is not quite accurate. Fortunately, we can work out most of our theory of property in things with minimal use of the term ownership.

D   SECURITY INTERESTS

Security interests in things are statutory creations. There were none at common law.[25]

Because there were none, lawyers invented some complex transactions - pledges[26], hire-purchase agreements[27], conditional sales contracts[28], chattel mortgages[29] - to authorize

---

25 See "Other Claims Distinguished".

26 A pledge is a transfer of possession of a thing, intended to secure a debt, and including the prospect of a return of possession when the debt is paid. Contrast a pawn, which is a variation on the pledge transaction whereby the pledgee (pawnee) is authorized by the terms of his contract to transfer to a third party whatever property the pledger (pawnor) holds in the thing pawned. Thus, in a typical pawn transaction, the owner of a thing will transfer to the pawnee both possession of the thing and the power to transfer ownership to a third party. Possession of the thing pawned may be recovered from the pawnee, but not from someone who takes a transfer of possession (and ownership) from the pawnee: see *Franklin v Neate* (1844) 13 M & W 481, 153 ER 200 (Eng).

27 In a hire-purchase transaction the parties' intent is that ownership of a thing will eventually be transferred from seller to buyer, but only possession of the thing is transferred at first, the agreement specifying that the seller is to retain ownership until the agreed series of payments is completed.

28 In a conditional sales contract, both possession and ownership of a thing are transferred from seller to buyer in exchange for the buyer's promise to complete a series of payments to the seller. The contract specifies that ownership will revert to the seller upon default of payment.

29 In a chattel mortgage the owner of a thing transfers ownership to a lender, but usually retains possession of the thing. The mortgage agreement specifies that the lender will return ownership of the thing to the borrower upon repayment of the loan.

creditors to take possession of things from debtors upon default of payment. The problem with these inventions was their incapacity for striking socially acceptable balances, both between creditors and their debtors and between creditors and third party purchasers from the debtors.[30]

The 20th century brought major statutory reforms in the laws of most jurisdictions. One of the most successful was the *Uniform Commercial Code* (*UCC*) in America. The *UCC* started out as an ambitious attempt to codify American commercial law. It has been adopted with only minor variations by all American states (except Louisiana, whose French history and legal heritage require major adaptation of common law ideas). Each of nine "Articles" handles a major subdivision of commercial law, followed by two on transitional provisions. Article 9, dealing with security interests, has been adapted in several Canadian provinces that have passed legislation called the *Personal Property Security Act* (*PPSA*).[31] I shall refer to the *PPSA* style of legislation.

In jurisdictions that have enacted these statutes the first step is to sweep into the statutory framework all attempts to create forms of property for security purposes. The statutes apply to "consensual transactions in which the parties intend that personal property and fixtures will serve as security for repayment of monetary transactions".[32] The preliminary question to be addressed is, therefore, what purpose the parties to a transaction had in mind. It is not important that the parties did not use a particular statutory formula or used words not found in the statute.[33] If the objective was to secure debt, the *PPSA* applies. If not, or if the forum has no *PPSA*, the common law rules apply,[34] in the absence of some other, more particular local statute.

---

30 "In the development of our law, two principles have striven for mastery. The first is the protection of property: no one can give a better title than he himself possesses [holds]. The second is the protection of commercial transactions: the person who takes in good faith and for value without notice should get a good title." *Bishopsgate Motor Finance Corporation Ltd v Transport Brakes Ltd* [1949] 1 KB 336 (Eng KB) *per* Denning LJ. Note that these are described as principles not rules. They conflict when pushed to their limits. The issue in a difficult case is often which of the two principles is to prevail in the circumstances.

31 See Ontario *Personal Property Security Act* SO 1989 C16; Alberta *Personal Property Security Act* SA 1988 C P-4.05; British Columbia *Personal Property Security Act* SBC 1989 C 36; Manitoba *Personal Property Security Act* RSM 1987 C P-35; Saskatchewan *Personal Property Security Act* SS 1979-80 C P-6.1; Yukon *Personal Property Security Act* RSY 1986 C 130 P 3.2. Similar statutes have been enacted in other Commonwealth countries. The statutes also purport to create security interests "in intangibles", meaning security interests in property *other* than property in things. How one could hold a security interest, a form of property, in a form of property is beyond me; it smacks of "owning possession" or "possessing a bond" (the legal concept, not the bond certificate).

32 McLaren, *Secured Transactions in Personal Property in Canada* 2d ed (Carswell Company Limited Toronto 1989) Vol 1 p 1-5. This book by my colleague Richard H McLaren is the leading work in the field and should be consulted for details beyond the scope this summary.

33 See, for example, Ont *PPSA* s 2, noting that the Act applies to "every transaction without regard to its form".

34 *Century Credit Corp v Richard* (1962) 34 DLR 2d 291 (Ont CA) illustrates the pre - *PPSA* situation. The plaintiff was the assignee of a Quebec conditional sales contract from the vendor, which made the plaintiff owner of a car possessed by the conditional purchaser and located in Quebec. The conditional

The main function of the *PPSA* is to create a priority system to rank the claims of various secured creditors. Several different security interests may be created in the same thing. They can be ranked in priority, regardless of the fact that they may have been created under the laws of various jurisdictions. Each *PPSA* jurisdiction operates a local registration system. Earlier holders must register to formalize their security interests and give them priority over later ones.

The *PPSA* technique is based on the statutory creation of two new forms of property - called a "security interest" and a "perfected security interest" - that were unknown at common law. It is simply explained by assuming a mundane transaction involving three parties. Buyer (soon to be known as Debtor) is eager to buy, but short of cash. Seller is eager to sell, but wants payment in cash. Banker (soon to be known as Creditor) has cash to lend, but is insecure about most people's creditworthiness.

A security interest in a thing first comes into existence when it "attaches". This is a statutory code word indicating that three prerequisite steps - (i) the formation of intention by Debtor and Creditor to create the security interest, (ii) the transfer of "value" (for example, the advance of a sum of money from Creditor to Debtor), and (iii) acquisition by Debtor of some form of property in the thing - have been completed. At that stage Seller has been paid and is out of the game, Creditor holds a security interest in the thing and, in a typical transaction, Debtor holds possession and probably ownership.

The security interest held by Creditor does not, however, become particularly valuable property until it becomes fully enforceable against third parties. Its value is enhanced upon completion of a second step, called "perfection", a step that Creditor will be keen to take as soon as possible. Perfection is another code word in the statute. It means that (i) attachment has already occurred and (ii) certain other steps, usually involving filing documents in a public registry have been completed. The purpose of requiring the document filing is to provide access to information about the security interest to anyone who cares to search the registry for entries under either Debtor's name or the serial number or other identifying characteristics of the thing in which the security interest is held. Anyone dealing with Debtor now is able to assess his creditworthiness by checking the registry. Anyone who now lends money to Debtor, or any hapless buyer who seeks to acquire ownership of the thing from Debtor without doing such a check, is taking a serious risk. If Debtor defaults, the holder of the perfected security interest (Creditor) is

---

purchaser took the car to Ontario and purported to transfer ownership to a dealer. The conditional sales contract was not registered in Ontario. The dealer was able to sell ownership to the defendant, an innocent purchaser under Ontario sales law. This transaction created ownership for the defendant which superseded that of the plaintiff. That was a straightforward application of the common law choice of law rule that the transfer of property in a movable thing is governed by the law of the *situs* of the movable thing at the time of the transaction.

statutorily authorized to seize possession of the thing[35] and is then statutorily empowered to transfer ownership of the thing to another buyer.[36]

A perfected security interest under the *PPSA* clearly fits our definition of property in a thing. We can particularize the property definition as follows.

> *Property* **[perfected security interest]** *is a relationship. There are always three people in the relationship. The first person is the state.*

> *The second person is someone whom the state has concluded is the holder of a specified form of property* **[perfected security interest]**. *The third is any other person* **[eg, the hapless buyer]** *whom the state has not concluded is the holder of that specified form of property.*

> *The state will suppress the civil liberties of the third person* **[the hapless buyer gets dispossessed and disowned]** *to the extent they fall within the scope of the form of property held.*

Personal Property Security statutes enacted by various jurisdictions provide perfect examples of how legislatures can create new forms of property unknown to the common law. There may be other types of security interests in things created by statutes in various jurisdictions.

E   OTHER PROPERTY IN THINGS

There are no other types of property in things, except as created in some jurisdictions under particular statutes for particular purposes. All property claims *to things* can be expressed in terms of the four categories set out above.

There are many other, primarily statute-based creations answering to the description of property, though they are not forms of property in things.[37] The distinction turns on whether the property holder is able to restrict others' *access to a particular thing*, or can merely restrict the exercise of civil liberty by others only in ways not directly related to using or possessing a thing. The latter belongs in the category *property other than property in things*. For example, a patent might restrict the liberty of those who would copy or otherwise make use of a useful industrial design. The design itself is not a thing: it is merely a description of how to make a thing, and how to use it. The patent holder

---

35 Possession can be seized from anyone found holding possession. That will often be a hapless buyer who paid for a transfer of ownership and possession from Debtor without checking the PPSA registry.

36 The key to the system is the simple mechanism whereby after default on the debt Creditor is able to transfer ownership to a stranger without ever having held ownership. The new buyer's acquisition of ownership, commonly at an auction, extinguishes the previous ownership held by Debtor.

37 The word "thing" as used in this book, means "a material object, a body; a being or entity consisting of matter, or occupying space". See Chapter 1 "Property and Things Contrasted" for more details.

does not hold any form of property in any of the thousands of things made by using the design,[38] but will be able to restrict their production and distribution.

This is a critical, if somewhat awkward distinction.[39] Failure to adhere to it has confused common law property analysis. Separating the two major sub-categories enables much of what follows to be expressed in plain English.

F   OTHER CLAIMS DISTINGUISHED

The assertion that there are only four forms of property in things may prove controversial. However, many common terms that are used as if they described forms of property really describe either (i) things in which property is held, (ii) defences available to a property holder in particular circumstances, or (iii) transactions to effect the disposition or acquisition of property.

In each of the examples below, the property involved readily falls into one of the four categories listed above, once the terminology is clarified. These examples are not exhaustive, but the technique can be used to dispose of other, similar misnomers.

Negotiable instruments are sometimes misdescribed as forms of property. A negotiable instrument is a thing, usually a piece of paper, which has been "endorsed" (signed or otherwise marked to signify the creator's consent) with the intent that it be delivered (by transfer of possession) to another person. A familiar example is a cheque. The significant thing about a negotiable instrument - what makes it "negotiable" - is that ownership of the instrument (the thing) passes to whoever acquires possession of it unless he knows at the time of acquisition that the transferor's claim of ownership is defective. While a complex body of rules has developed governing the use of negotiable instruments, ownership, possession, and the right to immediate possession are sufficient property words to describe the relationships among the various players in the game.

---

38 The defendant in *Monsanto Canada Inc v Schmeiser* [2004] 1 SCR 902 discovered what turned out to be the plaintiff's patented canola growing on the periphery of his land. Once aware of the plants' properties (herbicide did not kill them), he decided to collect and cultivate the seeds. Finding that Schmeiser had infringed Monsanto's patent, McLachlin CJ stressed (at para 17): "Everyone agrees that Monsanto did not claim protection for the genetically modified plant itself, but rather for the genes and the modified cells that make up the plant". Did Monsanto "claim protection" for the genes and modified cells, or simply restrict Schmeiser's liberty use the genes and modified cells to produce the plant?

39 As important as the distinction between property in things and property in land, which itself is confused by common lawyers' dogged usage of the ancient labels "real property", which includes most forms of property in land, and "personal property", which includes leasehold (and a few other) interests in land, all property in things, and all property other than property in things. The irony in the ancient usage is that the adjectives "real" and "personal", which originally described the types of remedies available, ceased to distinguish the categories in practice centuries ago.

Pledges, pawns, and mortgages are often referred to as if they were forms of property. They are transactions.

— Collateral?

A pledge is a transfer of possession of a thing for the purpose of securing a debt, the transferor's intent being to retake possession of the thing when the debt is repaid. The transferee ("pledgee") may hold possession so long as the debt is outstanding, but is obliged by the terms of the transaction to retransfer possession upon payment.

A pawn is a variation on the pledge transaction whereby the pawnee is authorized by the terms of his agreement to transfer to a third party whatever property the pawner holds in the thing pawned. Thus, in a typical pawn transaction, the owner of a thing will transfer to the pawnee both possession of the thing and the power to transfer ownership to a third party. Possession of the thing pawned may be recovered from the pawnee, but not from someone who takes a transfer of possession (and ownership) from the pawnee.[40]

A mortgage is a contractual transfer of property in a thing held by the transferor (mortgagor), accompanied by a contractual obligation imposed on the transferee (mortgagee) to retransfer the same form of property in the thing upon payment of the debt. Thus, for example, the owner of a thing may secure a loan by signing documents to evidence a transfer of ownership to the lender. This allows the borrower to retain possession and use of the thing while periodic payments of the loan are made, but gives the lender all the remedies of an owner should default occur. A mortgage transaction is thus similar to a pledge transaction - each being a contractual transfer of property incorporating a contractual obligation to retransfer the same form of property upon repayment of a debt - differing primarily in the form of property traditionally transferred.[41]

The differences among these three types of transactions have more to do with what form of property the parties agree to transfer than with distinctions inherent to the transactions

---

40 See *Franklin v Neate* (1844) 13 M & W 481, 153 ER 200 (Eng): "the pawnor of a chattel still retains his property in it, though qualified by the right existing in the pawnee, [by] which he has a right to sell and by the sale to transfer that [the pawnor's] property to the buyer and if the pawnee on the buyer's tendering him the amount due refuses to deliver [possession of the thing], the buyer may maintain trover".

41 It seems always to be assumed by analysts that the transferor in each of these transactions held ownership of the thing before the transfer took place. See, for example, *Crossley Vaines Personal Property* 5th ed 448: "a pledge is a transfer of immediate possession by way of security, whereas under a mortgage the security is the transfer, contingently, of legal or equitable ownership". Similarly, see *Harold v Plenty* [1901] 2 Ch 314 (Eng). Yet both transactions could be completed by a transferor who held possession but not ownership. The possessor could transfer possession in exchange for a loan, but could by the same contract gain a right to immediate possession upon repayment: is that not a pledge transaction? The possessor could contract for a future creation in the lender of a right to immediate possession should default of payment occur: apart from the question who holds what property, is that any different from a mortgage transaction? Traditionalists may object, and could no doubt dredge up some musty judicial commentary pronouncing the suggested results impossible, but must we continue to complicate our theories of property with the mantras of long-dead judges and writers?

themselves. This is typical in the jargon created by commercial practice, and may be useful business shorthand. However, the careless adoption of commercial jargon has confused early 21st century property law. This confusion will become apparent as we progress through the material on acquisition and disposition of property.

A lien is sometimes misdescribed as a form of property. A lien is a defence.[42] Consider the common form of "mechanic's lien" which protects a mechanic who adds value by doing work on a thing. The owner of a car takes it for repairs. The mechanic takes possession of the car. So far, this is a classic bailment transaction. The parties intend that the work will be done, after which possession of the repaired car will be retransferred to the owner. However, until the mechanic is paid for the work the owner's usual claim for possession will be unenforceable because the mechanic has a "lien".[43] The lien is simply a defence which arises out of the circumstances and protects the mechanic against a judicial order for possession of the car. To see that this is all a lien is, one need only note the consequences of the mechanic's voluntarily giving up possession - the lien is lost.[44] Thus, while possession is held, the mechanic has a defence against interference with his possession. Once possession is given up there is nothing to defend against. The lien has disappeared.

---

42 "Like a right of action for damages [an artificer's lien] is a remedy for breach of contract which the common law confers upon an artificer to whom the possession of goods is lawfully given for the purpose of his doing work upon them in consideration of a money payment. ... The remedy can be excluded by the terms of the contract made with the artificer either expressly or by implication from other terms ... It is a remedy in rem exercisable upon the goods and its exercise requires no intervention by the court, for it is exercisable only by an artificer who has actual possession of the goods subject to the lien. ... A common law lien, although not enforceable by action, thus affords a defence to an action for recovery of the goods by a person who, but for the lien, would be entitled to immediate possession." *Tappenden v Artus* [1964] 2 QB 185 (Eng CA) at 194-195 per Diplock LJ. The case dismissed an owner's claim for possession of a van which had been repaired by the defendant mechanic following instructions given by a third party, who acquired possession from the owner by a non-contractual bailment transaction. The van had broken down. The third party had contracted with the mechanic for repairs, but had refused to pay after the repairs were done. A somewhat similar case, *Humber Shiprepairers Ltd v Norport Project Developments Limited* (unreported) Eng CA 1990, emphasized the self-help nature of the lien by refusing an injunction to a sub-contractor claiming a lien for repairs to a ship when the main contractor threatened to re-take possession. The reasoning was based on the distinction between a right and a remedy. A simpler solution would have been to deny the injunction on the traditional ground that the lien claimant hadn't proved the inadequacy of a damages award should the contractor seize possession.

43 The elements that give rise to a lien are set out in *Scarfe v Morgan* (1838) 4 Mees & W 270, 150 ER 1430 (trover for a mare). See also *Broadwood v Granara* (1854) 10 Exch 417 (Eng) and *Robbins v Gray* [1895] 2 QBD 501 (Eng CA): both cases deal with innkeepers' liens. For a critical summary of common law liens see Goldstein "Case Note" 17 Cornell LQ 279 (1932).

44 The lien is destroyed if possession is given up voluntarily, but not if the claimant is deprived of possession through the fraud of the debtor [*Re Turnstall & Case* (1847) De G 577 (Eng); *Wallace v Woodgate* (1824) 1 C & P 575, 171 E R 1323 Eng)] or through the wrongful act of a third party [*Re Carter* (1885) 55 LJ Ch 230 (Eng)].

These examples illustrate that most discussions of alternative forms of property can be reduced to the simple terminology of the four forms listed above. The following diagram charts property in the detail thus far exposed in this book.

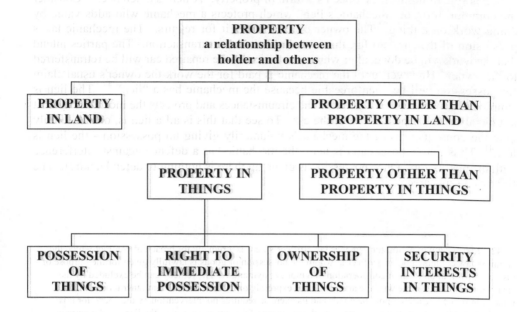

PART II

DISCOVERY AND CREATION;

ESCAPE AND DESTRUCTION

Part I described property as a legal relationship, identified four types of property in things, and noted that a holder of property in a particular thing can enlist the judicial branch of government to suppress the liberty of a non-holder to use or otherwise deal with the thing, usually by becoming the plaintiff in a legal proceeding (a trial) against the defendant non-holder.

A plaintiff loses at trial, absent proof (or defendant's concession) that plaintiff held property. Plaintiff must produce evidence to show acquisition of the form of property claimed. Absent proof of disposition, it will be assumed that plaintiff still holds that form of property. Plaintiff must also prove that defendant's interference with the particular form of property claimed occurred after acquisition and before disposition.

There are only a few techniques of acquiring and disposing of property in things. Some are peculiar to certain forms of property; some apply to all forms.

Some acquisitions and dispositions are accomplished by one person acting alone. Most of the rules about hunting and herding animals, prospecting for minerals and manufacturing artifacts have been recognized for centuries. However, the judicial decisions are often not clearly explained. Questions remain about what evidence is required to prove acquisition or disposition of what forms of property.

CHAPTER 3

FIRST POSSESSION OF THINGS

A   DISCOVERY: THE FIRST FINDER'S PROPERTY

The first possessor of a thing occurring in nature gets a property claim enforceable against anyone else in the world.[1]

Gold nuggets, diamonds, and dinosaur fossils are classic examples of this category. The discoverer of a gold nugget lying in the wilderness will ordinarily pocket it and hie himself to the nearest town to broadcast his claim under the watchful eye of the local constabulary. Having thus manifested his intent to exclude all others from messing with the gold nugget which he now has within his control, he has assembled all the evidence necessary to prove that he holds possession of it.[2] His possession of the gold nugget will be legally protected against everyone except (i) the state claiming under confiscatory rules, (ii) a prior possessor whom he has dispossessed, or (iii) an owner.

State claims of this kind are rare in common law countries.[3]

Prior possessors should not be a problem in this example. Our protagonist has *discovered* the gold nugget: it was not, in this case, previously possessed and lost.[4] This leaves open the possibility that it was possessed, but not lost, at the time the discoverer took possession. There is only one situation in which this could arise: the nugget may have been found on land in which someone else held an estate[5] and, by virtue of some rules we'll cover later,[6] the estate holder may have had possession of the nugget despite being ignorant of its existence. Let's assume that there was no estate holder in the wilderness area under consideration, and that the state has no claim.[7]

---

1 Except in the case of things of which the state has by legislation claimed ownership or precluded the holding of property. Examples are strategic minerals like uranium, objects appealing or abhorrent to religious prejudices, and even (surely most curious) intoxicating liquors. See *Rex v MacEwen* [1947] 2 DLR 62 (PEI SC), in which a thief was acquitted of stealing liquor on the ground that, under prohibition legislation, no one held property in it: he was convicted of stealing the bottle.

2 Possession of a thing is proved by the coexistence of (i) physical control and (ii) manifest intent to exclude others: see the analysis and definition set out in Chapter 2 "Possession".

3 See Chapter 5 "State Claims".

4 See Chapter 7 "Finders on Defence".

5 An estate is the most common form of property held in land at common law. Briefly, the English common law rule was that the King held *ownership* of all land in his kingdom. His subjects held *estates* in the land. These were, in theory, less valuable forms of property although the greatest of them, the estate in fee simple, is practically the equivalent of ownership under a benign or figurehead monarch.

6 See Chapter 7 "Finders on Defence". This was the result in *Goddard v Winchell* 86 Iowa 71, 52 NW 1124 (1892), in which a 66 lb meteorite imbedded 3 ft deep was held to be "the property of" the estate holder rather than the man who unearthed it.

7 This, as we'll see later, seems unlikely. The state (under a relatively pure version of the common law system) is the owner of all land within the state borders. Wouldn't the owner of land (whether a proper

Thus, only an owner could legally deprive our discoverer of possession of the nugget. The rule that the owner of a thing can successfully sue its possessor by finding is so well established that it is difficult to find a case for which it forms the *ratio*. Even in *Armory* v *Delamirie*, the most famous finding case of them all, this point was *obiter*:[8]

> the finder of a jewel, though he does not by such finding acquire an absolute property or ownership, yet he has such a property as will enable him to keep it against all but the rightful owner ... .

Here, there is no owner. The nugget was discovered. No prior claims exist. The discoverer in possession has the best claim in the world on these facts.

How do we describe the property held by someone who has not only possession that will prevail over most, but possession that will defeat all? I noted earlier that, while no definition of the word "ownership" of a thing can be found in common law cases, it is regularly used to describe the legal position of a person who *holds possession of a thing which no one is at liberty to interfere with.*[9]

Our discoverer holds ownership of the nugget. Discovery of natural things can generate ownership, as ownership is defined in this book. The first finder of a thing occurring in nature is, unless the state or a previous possessor has a claim, at liberty to take possession of it. If he does not take possession of it, his discovery will not serve as the basis for any legal claim.[10] It isn't discovery that makes the discoverer an owner. It is by taking possession, or permitting someone else to do so,[11] that the prospector acquires ownership

---

King or some republican conception of The State) have at least as good a claim to possession of things on or in the land as an estate holder who holds his estate of the owner (the King)?

8 In *Armory v Delamirie* (1722) 1 Str 505, 93 ER 664 (Eng) a chimney sweep found a jewel and took it to a jeweller for evaluation. The jeweller refused to return possession of the jewel. The owner, whose existence was presumed because the jewel was cut rather than natural, was not to be found. Thus, the action was brought by a prior possessor against his possessor by transfer (a bailment transaction). The prior possessor won, although no one doubts that the owner would have prevailed over both jeweller and chimney sweep had she appeared and claimed possession. Similarly, see *Clark v Maloney* 3 Del 68 (1840), in which the first finder of some pine logs prevailed over the second finder after they drifted away from the first finder's mooring.

9 See Chapter 2 "Ownership".

10 The finding cases clearly establish that it is not the happenstance of finding itself that generates possession, but the subsequent acts of exercising control over the found thing and manifesting intent to exclude others: see Chapter 5 AFinding and Taking Possession of Things".

11 This predicts an outcome which is, so far as I am aware, unsupported by precedent in the common law. What if X the discoveror merely notes the location and subsequently confides it to Y, whereupon Y rides out of town and takes possession of the nugget? According to the meaning of "ownership" set out in Chapter 2, it describes the position of someone who either (i) holds possession of the thing which no one is at liberty to interfere with, or (ii) holds, or will when a contract expires hold, right to immediate possession of the thing, while someone else holds possession or right to immediate possession after transfer. Is Y the

of the gold nugget.

This is not a surprising result. Gold nuggets, the Koh-I-Noor diamond, and dinosaur bones can be found in museums throughout the common law world, often displayed in the form in which they were discovered except for some cleaning, minor cutting and polishing, and rearrangement. Are they not owned, either by the museum corporation or by some philanthropist who claims ownership through a series of transactions from the discoverer? If so,[12] what is the root of that ownership? It cannot lie in transaction; the common law is clear that, apart from certain limited circumstances, a buyer can get no better property than the seller holds.[13] Nor is ownership established by the manual labour involved in the cleaning, cutting and polishing, or arranging. The root of ownership must lie in the first possession of the discoverer.

Things occurring in nature are classified for purposes of childhood games as animal, vegetable, or mineral. That elementary classification will suffice here. Vegetables[14] and minerals[15] become owned by first possession through discovery, except where the state has a confiscatory claim or an estate holder in land had prior possession.

Animals may be subject to different rules. Conventional wisdom says that wild animals are a special case and can not be owned, whereas domestic animals can. We'll see about that, after we investigate the acquisition of property through creation of things.

---

owner of the nugget by virtue of being first possessor [part (i) of the definition] or did X become the owner at the moment Y took possession *if and only if* permission to take possession was confided to Y [part (ii)]? I see no reason why these could not be the rules.

12 If not, is "ownership" a useful term in the common law system? I have defined it simply by contrast to the *relative* superiority of the possessor's claim, which defeats most, though not all others. If the term means something grander, and if possession through discovery is not a sufficient root, then a vast proportion of the things in which we claim property are not owned by anyone. This would not change the outcome, as the possessor of a natural thing could rely on his possession to defeat all other claimants, so long as the possession could be traced through a series of transactions back to the discoveror.

13 See Chapter 8 "Purchase and Sale".

14 To most common lawyers, growing things like garden crops and trees, are *profits a prendre*. They mean that "profit to take" is a form of property that someone holds in them which works something like this. Things attached to the land are (except for such flimsy connections as tying down a kite or temporarily nailing a picture to the wall) part of the land for property analysis. Trees and garden vegetables have no separate existence, and the holder of property in the land has a land law claim against anyone interfering with them, until their connection with the land is severed. Once the connection is severed, a plant begins a separate existence. It either becomes owned by a first possessor through discovery or is already possessed because of the estate holder's manifest intent to exclude all comers from objects lying within his controlled borders: see generally the cases collected in Chapter 7 "Finders on Defence".

15 Minerals may be construed as part of the land, particularly where they are lying below the surface of land rather than at ground level. As such, interference with them may generate a trespass to land action by the holder of an estate in the land.

B   CREATION OF THINGS

1   Manufacture of Artifacts

The maker of a new thing acquires ownership of the thing by being its first possessor. This rule applies except where (i) the state has precluded the holding of property in the thing created or (ii) property continues to be held in one or more constituent things from which the new thing was assembled.

Example The Ford Motor Company makes cars in a factory in Dearborn, Michigan. The cars are shipped to dealers all over the world. People pay large sums of money to the dealers in exchange for possession of the cars and, so they believe, ownership. Yet, in transactions like this the general rule is that a buyer gets no greater property than the seller held.[16] Either the dealer - and thus tracing back, the Ford Motor Company - previously held ownership or else millions of car owners aren't.

The rule of ownership through creation is derived in much the same way as the rule of ownership by discovery: if first possession of, say, a gold nugget, is not the root of ownership in the common law then it is difficult to imagine what is. Once it is determined that the creator of a new thing was its first possessor, the same arguments will apply. However, a preliminary issue arises in the case of creation of things.

"Thing", in this book, means a material object, a body, a being or entity consisting of matter, or occupying space.[17] We are concerned here exclusively with the acquisition of property in things.[18] Most so-called new things or manufactured things are nothing but reworked, combined, or otherwise transmuted old things. How do we distinguish between the creation of a new thing and the mere alteration in character of existing things in which property was already held?

The creation of new things can be characterized according to either the situation or the process. Common law analysts have classified by making lists. They describe the situations in which they see things created. By contrast, physical scientists observe creative events, speculate about the causes, then classify by describing what process they think occurred. The former tends toward long lists of categories, perpetuated by devotion to precedent. The latter simplifies classification and research by tending toward fewer major categories. It is the way of the future. When a controversial case comes to court,

---

16 See Chapter 8 "Purchase and Sale".

17 See Chapter 1 "Property and Things Contrasted".

18 Activities like sex do not qualify; drugs do; concepts like rock and roll don't. Property often is acquired by engaging in activities and through the formulation and articulation of concepts: contracting, composing rock operas (do *soi disant* musicians compose hip-hop eras these days?) or writing books create forms of property, but *not property in things*.

whether a new thing has been created is a question of fact, not a question of law.[19] Facts about the world around us are proved by the expert evidence of credible witnesses, and academic credentials in science are the passport to expert status.[20] Consequently, scientific methods of classification by process will tend to update and usurp the old common law categories.

What categories of creation can we look forward to? *Accession* and *mixing* are existing categories that will likely continue to be listed. They occur frequently and some fairly clear rules have been worked out. Accession describes the combination of things which remain separately identifiable, but operate or are seen as a new, recognizable unit: a new car can be precisely identified as by listing the engine, body parts, tires, etc which combine to form the whole, but it is hardly a useful or efficient way to describe what the Ford Motor Company makes. Mixing describes either of two processes. One is the combination of units of fungible items into larger units of mixed, separately unidentifiable fungibles. The other is the blending of previously identifiable things into a new mass not obviously recognizable as the parts combined. Turning grapes into wine is an example in the latter category. It is probably the projected expense of reversing the process and determining who held property in which of the constituent things that marks the borderline between accession or mixing and mere packaging, such as stapling together two photographs or putting dollar bills in a purse. Whether the creator of a new product becomes its first possessor and owner, and the related question whether a holder of property in one of the constituent things has lost his property through destruction of that thing, will probably continue to be determined by a set of existing rules. We'll cover those later.

Molecular rearrangement and genetic engineering are just accession and mixing in miniature. The latter tends to be of particular concern to us conservative carbon creatures, sceptical about scientific motivations and watchers of B-movies. These methods of creating new things will probably be treated by legislatures and judges as new categories requiring new rules. However, such rules do not fit under this heading. If thing B results from a transmutation of metal A, or if creature B is cloned from creature A, it will likely be the process by which this was achieved which will concern legal analysts, not the simple matter of who holds property in thing B. Inhibiting other people's liberty to replicate the process, thereby protecting the creator's capital and intellectual investment in

---

19 Essentially, questions of fact ask what happened between or to the litigants while questions of law ask what judicial orders are appropriate in the circumstances. Precedent - what other courts have done in comparable situations in the past - is irrelevant to the determination of questions of fact, but highly influential in solving questions of law. The precise distinction between the two is elusive, but is much discussed in the law of evidence.

20 There is a rule of evidence to the effect that a witness must by qualified as an expert before his opinions will be heard. Lesser mortals are directed to abjure opinion and confine their testimony to descriptions of what they observed. As any fool can see, there is no distinction between what I think I observed and what I opine that I observed, but the supposed distinction seems to work and is regarded as important. Consult a textbook on the law of evidence for further details.

the research, is the subject matter of patents, trademarks and copyright. These are sub-categories of property other than property in things and can be better understood once the analysis of property in things is completed.

We may soon see many new forms of artifacts, but property in the things created may continue to be analyzed according to the rules set out here. Propagation of vegetable and animal species has usually been treated as a separate concept in common law analysis. We shall see under the next two headings whether different approaches are warranted.

2   Crops

Cultivation of vegetable crops is another means of creating new things. Crops tend to originate as attachments to land and are regarded as part of that land until the connection is severed.[21] The planter claiming first possession might therefore be met by the perfectly rational defence from an estate holder in land that the thing has no separate existence and can not be the subject matter of a property claim.

The defence works. Crops planted on land are part of the land, the legal theory must be consistent, and the crops do not exist as such. The question of possession does not arise until the connection is severed. Upon severance, the first possessor could prove ownership, unless the planter could establish prior possession or ownership by arguing that the grown plants are merely the metamorphosed seeds in which he again holds property now that they are no longer disguised as land.

The analysis is different where plants are grown on land in which no one holds property,[22] or not on land at all. In the case of crops not grown on land, hydroponic and air-plants for example,[23] the rule of first possession after creation would seem to apply,

---

21 We'll revisit the concept of things affixed to land in Chapter 7, as part of the analysis of an estate holder's claim to possession of things lying on or under the surface of the land.

22 In the early common law of property in land, which still prevails in many common law jurisdictions (most Canadian provinces, for example) there is no such land, as all land is owned by the Queen. She owns all constituent parts of the land regardless whether one of her subjects holds an estate in the land. She rarely attempts to enforce her land claims, which may explain why the law of the land maintains the ancient legal theory that she has them.

23 This may not be a theoretical possibility, given the definition of land in most common law countries. Cases involving access to caves and trespass by low-flying aircraft have recognized that land in which an estate can be held is three dimensional and shaped like a truncated cone. The upper and lower limits are probably defined as the outermost reaches to which the estate holder has subjected the airspace and substratum to any use of his choice, while the sides of the cone are projections from the center of earth through the surface boundaries. Land, by this definition, would comprise all the solids, liquids and gasses within the truncated cone. Even plants grown hydroponically would, unless the tray is suspended remarkably high above or deep beneath the surface, be buried within the defined airspace and form part of the land even though not part of the dirt. I acknowledge that Lionel Smith is correct that, if this is the definition of land, cows don't exist. That is a problem for another day.

again unless the plants are identified with the seeds.

3   Birth of Livestock

Birth involves the creation of a new entity, separate from the parents that created it. The general rule giving ownership to the first possessor through discovery would seem applicable in the case of a newborn[24] domestic[25] animal[26] unless (i) the state has restricted the holding of property in the animal[27], or (ii) a prior ownership claim exists.

A prior ownership claim might exist in most cases, if it is a rule that the brood of domestic animals are owned by the owner of the mother.[28] This will turn out to be the first possessor of the offspring in most cases, given normal farming habits: where it is not, the claim by the owner of the mother (and thus of the offspring) would prevail.[29] Anyone able to prove a transfer of ownership of prospective offspring from the owner of the mother would then become the owner as of the time of birth.[30] This ordinary rule of acquisition by transfer, and not some special rule regarding domestic animals, accounts for the cases holding that a lessee of a stock of sheep becomes the owner of any lambs

---

24 Arguments could, I suppose, be made as to whether the animal existed as such between conception and birth. If so, anyone possessing the unborn's environment - the mother or the fertilized egg in normal gestation - would be able to prove the intent and control requirements and claim possession. I have arbitrarily opted for birth as the starting point for the existence of animals. The only practical alternative must surely be conception. Whether the starting point for domestic fowl is the chicken or the egg is anybody's guess.

25 "Domestic" animals include all varieties of animals that live in association with humans by habit or training. Domestic is contrasted with "wild". The two adjectives describe mutually exclusive and jointly exhaustive sub-categories of the animal kingdom. We'll explore the distinction, and whether different rules apply to wild animals, under the next heading, "Capture and Escape of Wild Animals".

26 "Animal" includes fish, birds and any other living creatures.

27 There are few such rules in common law countries, except for the anti-slavery laws which prohibit the holding of property in humans.

28 This was assumed to be an established rule as early as the *Case of Swans* (1592) 7 Co Rep156, 77 ER 435 (Eng), which ruled that swans were an exception owing to their lifelong fidelity and shared responsibility for their young. Cygnets are thus co-owned by the owners of the two parents. Whether co-ownership could be established for other species who behave like swans is uncertain. Anyhow, the general rule seems accepted as such: see eg, *Calhoun v Reid* [1927] 3 WWR 429 and *Tucker v Farm and General Investment Trust Ltd* [1966] 2 QB 421 (Eng CA).

29 See Chapter 2 where "ownership" is described as follows.

    Ownership is a form of property in things. A holder of ownership either (i) holds possession of the thing which no one is at liberty to interfere with, or (ii) holds, or will when a contract expires hold, right to immediate possession of the thing, while someone else holds possession or right to immediate possession after transfer.

An owner is generally assumed to have the best property claim in the common law system, subject to transactional defences and state confiscation: see Chapter 7 "Finders on Defence".

30 See Chapter 8 "Purchase and Sale". This might be a situation where it would be useful to prove that the offspring came into existence, and thus was owned, before the time of birth, as the possessor of the mother might otherwise find it difficult to prove damages should an injury to the mother-to-be prevent the birth of a healthy young animal.

born during the term of the lease. The judges in those cases found that the parties intended that the lessee would own the lambs. This leaves open the possibility that other transacting parties might conclude a different bargain. Two English cases illustrate the point.

Wood v *Ash and Foster*[31] involved 20 year leasehold interests in land and a stock of sheep. The lease[32] specified 1000 sheep. At the end of 20 years the flock had multiplied and no original sheep were alive. The lessor claimed ownership of all the sheep and demanded possession on the basis that the lease had expired. The ruling was that all the sheep were owned by the lessee who was now contractually obliged to transfer ownership and possession of 1000 of them to the lessor. The reasoning was that whereas repairs to leased "dead goods" resulted in a windfall to the lessor at the end of the lease:

> in the case of a stock of cattle the progeny do not follow the same principle - the lessor shall never have them because then the lessor shall have the rent, and the lessee shall have no profit.

Though this sounds in isolation like a property rule, I think it was meant to be an interpretation of the terms of the leasehold contract. First, repairs to an inanimate thing are hardly comparable to births in a flock of sheep, as the property is held in each individual sheep, not in some notional grouping (the flock) which is periodically repaired by replacement parts (the lambs). Second, for "dead goods" a contract could reverse the property rule.[33] It seems unlikely that common law judges would resist their normal inclination to hold contracting parties to whatever bargain they had struck, simply to protect foolish shepherds.

Tucker v *Farm and General Ltd*[34] was a similar case. P acquired possession of some ewes under a hire-purchase[35] contract. Lambs were born. P contracted to sell ownership of the ewes and the lambs to the plaintiff Mr. Tucker who, lacking adequate space for them, allowed P to retain possession. The defendant lender sought to protect its position under the hire purchase contract by seizing possession. The plaintiff made no claim regarding the ewes, but demanded possession of the lambs as owner. Who now owned the lambs became the only issue. Had P acquired ownership of them when they were born? The court ruled that he had. Again, the reasons for judgment could be read as

---

31 *Wood v Ash and Foster* (1586) 74 ER 139 (Eng QB).

32 The lease was a simple bailment contract whereby the owner of sheep transferred possession of the sheep to the lessee, retaining ownership and thus the right to immediate possession of *those* sheep (if those sheep still existed) when the bailment contract ended. We'll deal with concept of bailment in Chapter 10 "Bailment: A Separate Transaction?" A leasehold interest in land is another form of property.

33 See Chapter 4 "Accession, Mixing and Fixtures".

34 *Tucker v Farm and General Investment Trust Ltd* [1966] 2 QB 421 (Eng CA).

35 This is a sale transaction whereby possession is first transferred on the understanding that periodic payments will be made and, following a final, usually nominal extra payment, ownership will be transferred to the purchaser.

enforcing a property rule giving ownership to the possessor at birth,[36] but were more likely meant as interpreting the parties' contract to include an implied term transferring ownership of any lambs born during the term of the contract to P.[37]

The property rules concerning acquisition of property upon creation of domestic animals are relatively simple. It remains to be seen whether these rules can be applied to all animals and, if not, how to distinguish "domestic" animals, to whom the rules would apply, from "wild" animals, to whom they would not.

C CAPTURE AND ESCAPE OF WILD ANIMALS

On a pleasant rural vista in early 19th century New York, Squire Lodowic Post set his hounds after a fox and thundered down the road to immortality. His place in common law folklore was assured by the unsportsmanlike conduct of one Mr Pierson, who gunned down the fox and carried the body away. The court found Mr Pierson's manners deplorable, but upheld his liberty to do what he did.

Pierson v *Post*[38] was a liberty case. Mr Pierson maintained his liberty to shoot the fox. Mr Post claimed that he had held property in the fox at the time it was killed. Had he proved this, shooting the fox would have been an interference with the property relationship between him and everyone else, including Mr Pierson. But property does not just happen: it must be acquired. The issue was whether Mr Post had acquired a form of property in the fox. The conclusion was that he had not.[39]

> The question ... is whether Lodowick Post, by the pursuit with his hounds ... acquired such a right to or property in the fox, as will sustain an action against Pierson for killing and taking him away. ... It is admitted that a fox is an animal ferae naturae, and that property in such animals is acquired by occupancy only. These admissions narrow the decision to the simple question of what acts amount to occupancy, applied to acquiring right to wild animals.

---

36 Lord Justice Diplock seemed to decide the case on this basis. He said, at [1966] 2 QB 431, "where ... property (sic) and possession are divided, the English rule and the rule in the civil law is that the progeny and the produce of the livestock belong to the person entitled to the possession".

37 Lord Justice Harman, at [1966] 2 QB 429-430, surmised that (i) the lessee of an apple orchard could market the apples and keep the proceeds, and (ii) that lambs were to sheep as apples to trees. Where the first proposition came from is unclear: he did not explain that this would likely be understood by lessor and lessee to be a term of the lease. Lord Denning was somewhat clearer (at 428):

> if the progeny did not belong to the lessee, it would mean that the lessor would have the rent and the lessee would have no profit - which would be absurd. ... I see no distinction whatever between a lease and a hire-purchase agreement ... . I hold that on this hire-purchase agreement, nothing being said about progeny, any progeny that arose during the hiring belonged to the hirer. *The parties must have intended this in the very agreement* ... [so] the farmer, on selling the lambs, could pay the instalments which were ... due in June or August. [Emphasis added]

38 *Pierson v Post* 3 Cai 175, 2 Am Dec 264 (NY 1805).

39 *Ibid* at 267.

The writers [citing Brackton, Justinian's Institutes, Fleta, Puffendorf, and Bynkerschock] say pursuit alone vests no property or right in the huntsman and that even pursuit, accompanied with wounding, is equally ineffectual for that purpose. ... The case now under consideration is one of mere pursuit ... .

However uncourteous or unkind the conduct of Pierson toward Post in this instance may have been, yet his act was productive of no injury or damage for which a legal remedy can be applied.

Until Mr Post managed to complete the act of taking possession, Mr Pierson was equally at liberty to do so. Like competitive bidders at an auction, each was free to attempt to gain property in the thing so long as neither of them had yet established a property relationship to inhibit the liberty of the other.

Young v *Hichens*[40] was a remarkably similar case. Mr Young was net fishing and had almost encompassed a school of fish in his net when Mr Hichens rowed his boat near the opening. This disturbed the fish and prevented their capture, though it seems that the net was not touched. Mr Young sued in trespass. He lost because, like Mr Lodowick Post in pursuit of the fox, he had not yet acquired possession of the fish when the incident occurred.

It does appear almost certain that the plaintiff would have had possession of the fish but for the act of the defendant, but it is quite certain that he had not possession ... . [T]he question will be whether any custody or possession has been obtained here.[41]

The law seems clear from these cases: hunters and fishers can acquire possession of the wild animals they pursue by completing their intended acts of bringing them under control.[42]

---

40 *Young v Hichens* (1844) 6 QB 606, 115 ER 228 (Eng QB). See also *Pollexfen v Crispin* (1671) 1 Vent 122, 80 ER 84 (Eng), a fishing case for Latin buffs.

41 *Ibid, per* Lord Denman.

42 Possession of a thing is proved by the coexistence of (i) physical control and (ii) manifest intent to exclude: see Chapter 2. This seems consistent with what was said in *Pierson v Post* 2 Am Dec 264 (NY 1805) as to what would have been sufficient to prove possession by Mr. Post:

actual bodily seizure is not indispensable to acquire ... possession of wild beasts; ... on the contrary, the mortal wounding of such beasts, by one not abandoning his pursuit, may ... be deemed possession of him; since thereby the pursuer manifests an unequivocal intention of appropriating the animal to his individual use, has deprived him of his natural liberty, and brought him within his certain control. So also incompassing and securing such animals with nets and toils, or otherwise intercepting them in such a manner as to deprive them of their natural liberty, and render escape impossible, may justly be deemed to give possession of them to those persons who, by their industry and labor, have used such means of apprehending them.

Fish, game, and fowl[43] have thus long been recognized in the common law as objects of the acquisition of property by unilateral act. The form of property acquired seems clearly enough to be possession, and is referred to as such in the 1844 fishing case.[44]. But not everyone calls it possession. The terminology used in this area causes much confusion. Blackstone[45] used the obtuse term "qualified property". The term was needed because he confused property with things and used "own" as a verb meaning "to hold property", rather than to denote a specific form of property one might hold. Thus:[46]

> property in possession [by which Blackstone meant 'things'] is divided into two sorts, an *absolute* and a *qualified* property.

> First, then of property in *possession absolute*; which is where a man hath, solely and exclusively, the right, and also the occupation, of any moveable chattels ... Such may be all *inanimate* things ... : such also may be all *vegetable* productions, as the fruit or other parts, when severed from the plant, or the whole plant itself, when severed from the ground; none of which can be moved out of the owner's possession without his own act or consent, or at least without doing him an injury, which it is the business of the law to prevent or remedy.

> [A]nimals that are not of a tame or domestic nature are either not the objects of property at all, or else fall under our other division, namely that of *qualified, limited,* or *special*

---

43 From *Hannam v Mocket* (1824) 2 B & C 934, 107 ER 629 (Eng), one might conclude that it was possible to acquire property only in edible or otherwise useful species. The plaintiff held property in land where rooks were in the habit of nesting. The plaintiff hunted them. The defendant drove the rooks away by shooting guns nearby, on other land. An action by the plaintiff was dismissed, the reasons for judgment suggesting that that because the rooks were "destructive in their habits, not known as an article of food, or alleged to be so ... the plaintiff could not therefore have any property in them". This analysis cannot be relied upon. The issue for property analysis is *whether* the plaintiff wanted to hunt the rooks, not *why* he wished to do so. It was clear from the facts that he did hunt them. The result is supportable, as the plaintiff was unable to prove that he had yet acquired property in the rooks. However, any suggestion from these *obiter dicta* that he could not have done so must be rejected.

44 *Young v Hichins,* above.

45 *Blackstone's Commentaries on the Laws of England* was one of the most influential works in the common law system. The first edition was published by the Clarendon Press at Oxford in four volumes between 1765 and 1769. It influenced the development of American law. Stories of itinerant frontier judges carrying Blackstone in their saddlebags as their only written reference work may not be exaggerated. I have used the 15th edition (1809). Random checks have satisfied me that his terminology wasn't any clearer in the earlier editions.

46 *Blackstone's Commentaries Bk II* (Clarendon Press Oxford 1766) at 391. We can see that Blackstone meant possession of things in the following quote from the 15th ed (1809) Bk II at 395:

> property may also be of a qualified or special nature, on account of the peculiar circumstances of the owner, when the thing itself is very capable of absolute ownership. As in the case of bailment ... there is no absolute property in either the bailor or bailee ... for the bailor hath only the right, and not the immediate possession; the bailee hath the possession, and only a temporary right.

This can be simplified as follows. Ownership is not the only form of property one may hold in things: for example, in bailment transactions, the bailor continues to hold ownership while the bailee holds possession, though only during the term of the bailment agreement. We'll fully explore these concepts in Chapter 10 "Bailment: A Separate Transaction?".

property: which is such as is not in it's nature permanent, but may sometimes subsist, and at other times not subsist. First, then, a man may be invested with a qualified, but not an absolute, property in all creatures that are *ferae naturae*, either *per industriam, propter impotentiam*, or *propter piivilegium*.

Blackstone's vague expression has plagued property analysis for more than 200 years. His curious labels are reproduced in all the major secondary sources. Chancellor Kent, in his Americanized imitation *Commentaries on American Law*[47], got at the concept in the following way:[48]

> Absolute property denotes a full and complete title and dominion over it; but qualified property in chattels is an exception to the general right, and means a temporary or special interest, liable to be totally divested on the happening of some particular event. ... A qualified property in chattels may also subsist when goods are bailed, or pledged, or distrained. In those cases, the right of property and the possession are separated.

Chancellor Kent equated "absolute property" with ownership and "qualified property" with possession. Others have tended to reproduce Blackstone's labels without much analysis of what the various terms mean or how they relate to other known forms of property. Thus we find in *Halsbury's Laws of England* whole new categories of property on wild animals.[49]

> There is no *absolute property* in wild animals while living ... . There may, however, be what is known as a *qualified property* in them, either:
> (1) *ratione impotentiae et loci* (eg young animals while unable to fly or run);
> (2) *ratione soli* (on account of the soil);
> (3) *ratione privilegii*.

This unfortunate legacy of Blackstone has been copied by rote in virtually all works in the common law world.

The concept of "qualified property" was invented to account for a fairly common situation involving wild animals. Once captured, their nature is to escape captivity. Once escaped, they might be recaptured by another hunter. Could the first captor regain possession by legal action against the second? Everyone assumed that the answer was no. But it was a well known common law principle that the owner of a thing could defeat a possessor.[50] This meant that the first captor could not have been the owner and another term was required.

---

47 Blackstone Publishing Co 1889.

48 Kent 2 *Commentaries on American Law* (Blackstone Publishing Co 1889) at 348 and 350.

49 3rd ed Vol 1 at 655 para 1252.

50 Except where the possessor had a defence arising from a transaction with the owner: see the cases analyzed in Chapter 7 "Finders on Defence".

Possession would have been an adequate term. But people have not consistently regarded possession as a form of property at all,[51] it being a widespread misconception that there could be only one form of property (alternatively called "ownership" or "the property") in things. However, there is nothing to be gained by attempting to demonstrate the folly of this view. Let us instead see whether some sense can be made of the wild animal cases by using the concepts of possession and ownership as defined in this book.[52]

Four questions arise in the analysis. First, there is the definition: what is it that marks an animal as "wild"? Second, do the common law cases support the proposition that wild animals can be possessed but cannot be owned? Third, what are the details of the suggested property distinctions: are the rules about gaining, holding, and losing property in animals different if the animals are wild? Fourth, is there any rational basis for maintaining a separate category for wild animals or can the usual rules governing property in things be applied?

The distinction between "wild" and "domestic" animals has not been stated consistently. The most common definition describes domestic animals as "all such beasts and birds as by habit or training live in association with man"[53] and then consigns all others to the wild category. This definition will serve the purpose here. The prevailing view appears to be that animals are wild or domestic by species, not by individual behaviour.[54] Thus, a

---

51 We see this as early as the case of *Sutton v Moody* (1697) 1 Ld Raym 250, 91 ER 1063 (Eng), where property in conies (an odd animal that seems to have borne the same relationship to the development of English property law that drunkenness did to the constitutional law of Canada) was disputed. The reasons for judgment contain the following throw-away line: "generally there is no property in things which are ferae natura, ... and therefore if a man keep conies (as he may) he has a possessory property in them, so long as they abide there; but if they run into the land of his neighbour, he may kill them, for then he has the possessory property". The same point is made some 200 years earlier in *Anon* (1496) Kiel 30, 72 ER 186 (Eng). For an interesting development of the idea that possession is only a fact rather and not a form of property, see AES Tay, "Possession in the Common Law" (1964) 4 *Melbourne University Law Review* 284-320.

52 I defined each of these terms and explained how each fits into the common law system of analysis in Chapter 2 "Possession" and "Ownership".

53 *Halsbury's Laws of England* (3rd. Ed) Vol 1 at 655. Compare the *Canadian Encyclopedic Digest* (3rd Ed) 1A 6-13, where animals are classified as (i) ferocious, (ii) dangerous, (iii) mischievous, and (iv) harmless, the first three being assigned to the wild category.

54 This must be what is meant by expressions like "it is a question of law not of fact, whether an animal is domestic or wild" [*Halsbury's Laws of England* (3rd Ed) Vol 1 at 655.] and "it is the function of the judge and not of the jury to decide whether an animal belongs to the class of domestic animals or to the class of wild animals" [*McQuaker v Goddard* [1940] 1 KB 687, [1940] 1 All. ER 471 (Eng CA)]. In *McQuaker*, a camel bit a zoo visitor. The trial judge's job was to tell the jury what laws they were to apply to whatever they determined to be the facts of the case. He told them to refrain from speculating about the wildness of the particular camel on the ground that all camels were categorically domestic according to the law of England. His ruling was upheld. Some doubt is cast on this position by cases involving the concept of *animus revertendi* [basically the "homing" tendency of household pets], where judges sometimes seem to be deciding the wild versus tame issue on the basis of whether the animal was escaping or trying to return home. I think, however, that these cases are concerned with whether the animal was in or out of possession while running free: the point is explained near the end of this section on wild animals. For a

moose or kangaroo that exhibited all the characteristics usually associated with domestication would remain classified as wild, for wild is the way of their moose and kangaroo relatives. Thus, a cat that ran away from its ancestral home, cut a swath of terror across several towns, and was finally cut down in a blaze of FBI or RSPCA gunfire would be written up as a deviant *domestic* cat, there being no legal way to rid itself of the ignominy of its forebears' deigning to live with people. Other distinctive characteristics, such as whether an animal tends to stick around when not penned up or to return when allowed to roam, seem to be modifying factors for rules applying within the wild category. The rule determining whether a particular animal is domestic or wild seems rooted in the proclivity of that animal's kith and kin to live as a part of or separate from human communities.[55]

Do the common law cases support the proposition that wild animals can be possessed but cannot be owned? The unthinking response is yes. It is said to be so whenever a dispute arises concerning property in an animal not normally kept as a pet or herded on farms.[56] But *why*? Maybe a popular view is myth.

Property law, like the rest of the field of law, looks to what happened in the past in an attempt to predict the future. To resolve particular disputes, judges examine evidence created around the time of the dispute and listen to people's recollections about what they observed at that time: these are attempts to reconstruct a past event. In a quite different way, we look to the past to find rules that govern the dispute. This latter exercise tests the received wisdom about the rules of the game. Sometimes the facts being examined expose a critical flaw in the wording of the rules. The flaw in the supposed rule that would preclude ownership of wild animals lies in the elevation of a difficult evidentiary point to a rigid, but impractical rule.

We don't need different rules about gaining, holding, and losing property in wild animals.

Gaining possession of a wild animal is exactly the same as gaining possession of any other thing. We have seen that a hunter or fisher can take possession by rendering the

---

contrary view, holding that a particular tamed elephant was not a wild animal and that the "original owner" retained "property" in it despite the fact that the ungrateful beast escaped, see *Mahadar Mohanta v Balaram Gagoi* (1908) ILR 35 Calc 413.

55 There is some room for difference of opinion within a particular species. Two Canadian cases illustrate the point. In *Campbell v Hedley* (1917) 37 DLR 289, 39 OLR 528 (Ont CA) a fox that was born in captivity in at least the third generation of foxes bred in pens by the plaintiff was held to be wild. In *Ebers v MacEachern* [1932] 3 DLR 415 (PEI CA) a ranch bred fox was held to be a domestic animal. Either one case is wrong or else the latter case was decided on the ground that foxes were protected under a provincial statute called *The Domestic Animals Act*, a point mentioned but not noted as conclusive in the case. Compare *Falkland Islands Co v The Queen* (1864) 2 Moo PC (NS) 266 (Eng), holding that roving cattle were wild: what a proper citation!

56 That is, it is said that one can hold only "qualified property" in animals "*ferae naturae*", which I equate with the statement that only possession of wild animals is possible.

animal powerless to regain its independence. However, this focus on achieving mastery over the prey diverts analysis from the main point of property law. Property is a relationship between people.[57] Possession, a form of property, is defined in terms of the possessor's attitudes and aptitudes vis-à-vis other people, not as a struggle for mastery between man and beast. The sole reason for legal rules is to regulate potential disputes between competing people: this is why possession of a thing is defined by the conjunction of control over the thing and manifestation of intent to exclude others.[58] The required degree of control over the thing is measured in terms of whether the thing has been brought within the intended possessor's sphere of dominance. Anticipation that there may be a few remaining gold nuggets along the Yukon River is insufficient to give me possession of any that are there, even if I advertise my intent in the Cleveland Plain Dealer. Even if I spot one of those nuggets through my binoculars, I can not prove possession until I get rather closer; like Mr. Post and the fox, I must put myself in a position which *of itself* would suggest to anyone passing by that I have achieved control and that I intend to maintain it. Holding it in my hand or sifting it in my pan would suffice. The main difference with wild animals is that they exhibit more active resistance to the taking of possession than do gold nuggets, at least according to our perception. But the test for gaining possession is the same.

As we saw earlier, the original source of ownership for things occurring in nature is first possession at the time of discovery. It is traditionally cited as a rule that wild animals can not be owned. Whether a thing is owned will be moot during peaceful uncontested possession, regardless whether the thing possessed is a wild flower or a wildebeest. Consequently, to test this so called rule, we must look to situations involving maintaining and losing possession. In what circumstances does a former possessor hold right to immediate possession? What happens when things get lost, or animals run away?

If the thing was *owned* there is no problem. The essence of ownership is that an owner out of possession holds right to immediate possession except where someone holds possession through transaction with the owner.[59] The owner always wins against a possessor when things owned are missing, stolen or strayed.[60] But conventional wisdom has it that there is no such claim in the case of formerly possessed escaped wild animals. The question is - why?

---

57 See Chapter 1 "Property and Things Contrasted".

58 I defined possession and contrasted it with other forms of property in things in Chapter 2 "Possession". See also Chapter 5 "Finding and Taking Possession of Things", where the elements of possession are further developed.

59 Included in the protected group are those who acquired possession from a prior owner under terms which have not expired and those who acquired possession through a chain of transactions from the owner.

60 Only the anti-slavery laws and lack of an available defendant prevented such a claim by James Morrison Weatherby George Dupree! The owner might lose if new ownership has been created, for example through an auction following default under a personal property security statute or (rarely) by crown grant, or if possession was acquired by transaction in "market overt". The latter concept has limited application today: see Chapter 8 "Purchase and Sale".

One possibility is that it really is a rule that wild animals can not be the objects of ownership. But this flies in the face of the general rule that the first possessor of a thing found in nature becomes the owner unless there is a previous ownership claim. No one suggests that previous ownership is the reason for a special wild animal rule.[61] The most commonly cited reason is that wild animals will instinctively escape if left unguarded, but that hardly supports the suggested rule: moored logs and home-made boats will float away if not carefully tied up, freshly cut crops may blow away in a hurricane, and the law of gravity may dispossess a mountaineering prospector of his newly discovered gold nugget. In none but the wild animal cases is it suggested that possession cannot be regained from subsequent possessors, *so long as the thing can be identified.*

Is it anticipation that escaped wild animals can not be identified that prompts the supposed rule? If so, no such rule is needed, as failure to prove that the gold nugget (or fox) now possessed by the defendant is the same gold nugget (or fox) discovered (or first hunted down and captured) by the plaintiff will lead to dismissal of the plaintiff's claim. Nor can the reason be the difficulty of proving that the previous possession of a wild animal was a *first* possession, thus qualifying as the root of ownership. Whether the plaintiff was the first possessor need be proved only on the balance of probabilities, and whether this is more difficult with a wild animal than with other things will vary with the stocks of fish and game and the number of hunters and fishers in the area. Besides, what about branded animals? What about unbroken wild mustangs, and the cattle roaming the plains of the Wild West? Were all those rustlers we saw hanged in movies innocent victims of trumped-up property claims?

Many cases discuss the question of loss of property through escape of wild animals. Just about everyone seems committed to a rule holding that escape defeats the "special" or "qualified" property (ie, possession) acquired by capture and leaves the first captor with no remedy against other hunters.[62] Two cases, however, illustrate the difficulties with the "special property" rule.

---

61 Well, Blackstone advanced the following weak analysis:
> the law has therefore wisely cut up the root of dissention, by vesting the things themselves (sic) in the sovereign of the state: or else in his representatives appointed and authorized by him, being usually the lords of manors.

This was disavowed by his own editor [*Blackstone's Commentaries Book II* 15th ed 1809 at 419]. Others have tried to argue for governmental ownership of fish and game by pointing out that licences are required to hunt and fish. Drivers, stock brokers and veterinarians are also licensed: does the state hold ownership of all motor vehicles, share certificates and household pets?

62 This is recited as a rule in virtually every work on the common law of property in things. It is rarely discussed or examined, just recited. Is it yet another example of Blackstone's habit of inventing convenient rules rather than examining and explaining basic principles? Note that it was for the very reason that [so he said] wild animals could not be owned that he invented or borrowed from some unknown source the concept of "qualified property".

Kearry v *Pattison*[63] involved a swarm of bees. The plaintiff had kept bees for some time and was conceded to have held possession of them while they lived in their hive. Some of them swarmed and settled on land in which the defendant held property. The defendant at first refused to allow access and, by the time he relented, the bees had flown away. The plaintiff sued in conversion, alleging interference with his property in the bees and seeking compensation for the value of that property. The plaintiff lost. His property in the bees was held to have ceased when he lost the power or liberty to pursue them across the land boundary. The Judge seems to have thought that his property in the bees continued so long as they were in sight and he had the power to pursue them. Whence this rule?[64] What do the act of pursuit and visual contact have to do with maintaining possession? Was the plaintiff's ability to identify the bees the issue?[65] The reasons for judgment provide no insight on this point. Nor is there a satisfactory explanation of the importance of the ability to pursue. Lord Justice Goddard muddied the waters.[66]

> It is said: But a swarm which fly out from my hive are mine so long as I have power to pursue them. The whole of this argument comes down to what Blackstone means when he says 'and have power to pursue them'. In my view he is there saying no more than that the law with regard to bees is the same as it is with regard to any other wild creature which is reduced into possession and in which a man has a qualified property so long as he keeps it in possession. If a wild deer which lives in my park gets out, I am at liberty to pursue it and get it back. ... If, however, that animal gets on to another person's land, I have no right to follow it on to that land, but if I do follow it I can retake the animal; I shall be once more possessed of the animal, but I shall be liable in trespass to the owner [*sic*] of that land.

---

63 *Kearry v Pattison* [1939] 1 KB 471, [1939] 1 All ER 65 (Eng CA). See also *Goff v Kilts* 15 Wendell 550 (NY 1836) and *Brown v Eckes* 160 NY Supp 489 (1916), two old American bee cases which do little to clear up the difficulties explained here. There is nothing so peculiar and enigmatic about bees that yet another special rule is required.

64 Lord Justice Slesser cited Blackstone, Bracton and Justinian as sources of the following rule: "the bees when they swarmed, so long as they were in his sight and so long as he had power to pursue them, would remain his property [*sic*]" [1939] 1 KB 471 at 478.

65 This seems to have been the concern in an earlier (and functionally identical) case, *Quantrill v Spragge* (1907) 71 JP Jo 425. The only two distinctions in that case were: (i) after the bees had flown into the defendant neighbour's back yard the defendant's son disturbed the bees by shaking the bush on which they had alighted, causing them to fly away before the pursuing plaintiff could calm and re-hive them, and; (ii) the plaintiff won. Liability was based on the finding that when the defendant's son shook the bush "the property in the bees remained in the plaintiff when they alighted on defendant's trees, for the plaintiff *had not lost sight of them and could identify them*" (emphasis added). The English Court of Appeal intended to discredit this ruling in *Kearry v Pattison*, but the latter case provides no more cogent rationale for the supposed rule concerning hot pursuit and visual contact.

66 [1939] 1 KB at 481. Lord Justice Slesser was no more helpful. He assumed that pursuit and visual contact were sufficient to maintain possession on the basis that Blackstone said it was so. Thus, he reasoned, the plaintiff's property in the bees had ceased to exist when they crossed the land boundary because "the power to pursue them which constitutes them chattels referred to in the old books means and can only mean that they may still be so regarded when the swarm is in such a place that their owner [*sic*] has still the right to pursue them in order to capture them [whereas here] the bees ... had ceased to be in the disposition or power of the plaintiff altogether" [at 479].

Lord Justice Goddard concluded that the defendant neighbour was at liberty to take possession of the bees by hiving them for his own benefit, although he had not bothered to do so. Note, however, that he speaks of *retaking* possession in his example, not of possession continuing during pursuit. Why wouldn't the defendant have the same liberty as soon as the bees escaped captivity, if the plaintiff did not hold ownership? Wouldn't escaped bees be the same as never-possessed bees, if prior possession does not prevail over subsequent possession and if first possession is not a source of ownership? Where is the *property* distinction between a once possessed but recently escaped deer and the nearly, but not yet possessed fox that Mr. Pierson got away with killing.[67] Only an ownership through first possession rule would make sense of Goddard's LJ distinction. Then the outcome would be different, as the owner's right to immediate possession would have prevailed. There are problems with this case no matter which of the suggested rules we apply.

In *Bowlston* v *Hardy*[68] the defendant held property in land where he made two coneyburrows (I wonder how). He somehow acquired possession of some coneys and put them in the burrows where, after the fashion of coneys the world over, they became fruitful and multiplied. Some of the coneys escaped to neighbouring land where they destroyed a corn crop. The plaintiff, holder of an estate in the neighbouring land, sued for damages and lost. The ruling appears to be based on a finding that the defendant held no property in the coneys and was therefore not liable for the damage they caused. There are at least three flaws in that analysis. First, the defendant clearly took possession of the coneys at some time. His possession would have continued while they remained in or near their burrows, based on both the wild animal cases between estate holders and trespassing hunters[69] and the general trend in cases involving possession by trespassing

---

67 See *Pierson v Post* 3 Cai 175, 2 Am Dec 264 (NY 1805), set out above. Lord Justice Goddard may have thought that pursuit gave rise to some sort of property claim, even in the case of an escaped deer. The gap in the quote I set out above consisted of the following sentence. "I dare say that while I am pursuing it [the hypothetical escaped deer] another person has not a right to come between me and the animal, so as to prevent me retaking it". I dare say Goddard LJ is wrong.

68 *Bowlston v Hardy* (1597) Cro Eliz 548, 78 ER 794 (Eng CB).

69 There is a long line of mostly English cases establishing rules governing trespassing hunters and their quarry. Two examples give the flavour of these rules. *Churchward v Studdy* (1811) 14 East 49, 104 ER 596 (Eng) was a trespass action in which the defendant had killed and removed a hare which his dogs had started outside but pursued on to land in which the plaintiff held an estate. The court ruled "if A start a hare in the ground of B and hunt and kill it there, the property continues all the while in B, but if A start a hare in the ground of B and hunt it into the ground of C and kill it there, the property is in A the, hunter, but A is liable to an action of trespass" (quoting Holt J from an earlier case). In *Pamment v Thompson* (1921) 20 OWN 89 (Ont CA) the plaintiff held property in some marshland. He posted notices at the boundary forbidding hunting and trapping. The defendant defied the warning, set traps, and caught some muskrats. This resulted in a ruling to the effect that wild animals in a state of nature, when killed, belong to the estate holder of the land where they are taken. These cases tell us little about the general process of acquiring, holding, and losing property in wild animals. This is why the judges in *Pierson v Post* 3 Ca. 175, 2 Am Dec 264 (NY 1805) concluded that they were in an area of unsettled law despite the common circumstances of

finders.[70] Second, the outcome flies in the face of later decisions about using land in an unconventional manner which allows strange creatures or substances to escape and lower the value of property in neighbouring land.[71] In effect, the case suggests that while a keeper of ordinary domestic animals would be liable for damage to neighbouring crops, no liability is incurred for equally foreseeable crop damage by non-domesticated animals brought to the land. Third, the reasons for judgment occupy one page and give little indication of what the judge was thinking. The gist is:[72]

---

the case.

> Most of the cases which have occurred in England, relating to property in wild animals, have either been discussed and decided upon the principles of their positive statute regulations, or have arisen between the huntsman and the owner of the land upon which beasts *ferae naturae* have been apprehended; the former claiming them by title of occupancy, and the latter *ratione soli*. Little satisfactory can, therefore, be derived from the English reports. [2 Am Dec at 265-266].

There must be a more basic rule, applicable both to things like jewellery found on land and to animals killed by trespassers: see *Parker v British Airways Board* [1982] 2 WLR 503 (Eng CA), in which Donaldson LJ attempted, with some success, to simplify the rules emerging from the possession by finding cases. *The British Airways* case is commented on extensively later in Chapter 7 "Finders on Defence".

70 A trespasser who claims to have found something on land in which another holds an estate is likely to have his claim for possession defeated by the estate holder, who will usually be found to have held possession of the thing before the trespasser did, even though the estate holder was ignorant of its existence. The conclusion is based on the estate holder's intention to bar all others from the land. The estate holder's claim is even more likely to prevail where general warnings are posted against trespass or against removing anything from the land. It makes little sense to conclude that an estate holder has possession of inanimate objects he is unaware of, yet does not have possession of animals he deliberately brought to the land. We'll cover the cases upholding estate holders' claims to objects on the land in Chapter 7 "Finders on Defence".

71 See *Rylands v Fletcher* (1868) LR 3 HL 330 (Eng HL).

> The person whose grass or corn is eaten down by the escaping cattle of his neighbour, or whose mine is flooded by the water from his neighbour's reservoir, or whose cellar is invaded by the filth of his neighbour's privy, or whose habitation is made unhealthy the fumes and noisome vapours of his neighbour's alkali works, is damnified without any fault of his own; *and it seems but reasonable and just that the neighbour who has brought something on his own property (which was not naturally there), harmless to others so long as it is confined to his property, but which he knows will be mischievous if it gets on his neighbour's should be obliged to make good the damage which ensues if he does not succeed in confining it to his own property.* But for his act in bringing it there no mischief could have accrued, and it seems but just that he should at his peril keep it there. [Emphasis added]

This wording, coming from a higher court some 270 years later, would appear to dispose of the distinction proposed by Anderson J in *Bowlston v Hardy*, between the neighbourly annoyance of "a lime-kiln or dye-house" (which he surmised would be a ground of liability) and the coney invasion ("but it is not so here, for the conies of themselves went into the plaintiff's land").

72 *Bowlston v Hardy* (1597) Cro Eliz 548, 78 ER 794 (Eng CB) *per* Anderson, J. The quote continues: "he who hath the damage thereby may well kill them, and they may be said to be his conies when they are upon his lands". This is beside the point. Whether a neighbour is at liberty to kill animals damaging crops is measured by the tort test of reasonable response in protection of one's property. See *Hamps v Darby* [1948] 2 KB 311 (Eng CA), in which the defendant shot some of the plaintiff's racing pigeons which were eating his crop of peas while on their daily exercise from the plaintiff's loft 1.5 miles away. The plaintiff won tort damages, but only because (relying on *Cresswell v Sirl* [1948] 1 KB 241 (Eng KB) (a dog shooting case), the defendant bore the onus of proving (i) that damage to the crops was imminent and (ii) there was no other practical means to stop the pigeons: the defendant failed the second test.

although one hath conies in his land, he hath not any property in them, because they are *ferae naturae*. And to have an action against one for damage done by savage and wild creatures, wherein he hath not any interest, *and they cannot be known whether they come out of his land*, is unreasonable ..." [Emphasis added]

Did this judge think that the identity issue was behind the supposed rule inhibiting ownership of wild animals? Identifying the invading conies does not seem to have a problem on these facts. As well as being an unreliable precedent, the case tells us little about property in wild animals, except to recite and apply the same old precept: wild animals can not be owned.

What, then are we to make of the following statement from *Blackstone's Commentaries*:[73]

> if a wild swan is taken, and marked and turned loose in the river, the owner's property in him still continues, and it is not lawful for any one else to take him: but otherwise if ... the swan leaves the neighbourhood.

What is it about marking a swan that changes the form of property held? Surely the nature of the swan is unchanged. The marking, like the branding of a Texas longhorn or a Queensland crocodile, could only serve to advise other people that the swan (i) had been previously possessed (ii) by someone who now claims ownership by first possession. That claim is easy enough to make, but is of no consequence if wild animals cannot be owned. But I have praised Blackstone with enough faint damns. Here, he may have stumbled upon the missing piece in the wild animal puzzle.

Maybe there is no special rule for wild animals.[74]

Also relevant here is the concept of *animus revertendi*, the "homing" tendency exhibited by some captive or domesticated animals. Some hold that the exhibition or lack of

---

73 *Blackstone's Commentaries Bk II* (15th ed 1809) at 292. Blackstone may have made this one up, as he footnoted "Crompt. of courts, 167, 7 Rep. 16", but only after the colon.

74 The cases involving exotic wild animals taken far away from their natural habitats seem to go against this thesis. When such an animal escapes, the likelihood of easy identification and ready recognition by others as an import having a prior possessor argue in favour of ownership by first possession. See, however, *Mullet v Bradley* 53 NY Supp 781 (NYCA 1898). A sea lion, of a type peculiar to the west coast, was captured by a great white hunter off the coast of California and transported across America where it was held in a holding pen in Long Island Sound. It escaped and was captured by the defendant some 70 miles away. The prior possessor failed in his action for possession. Note, however, that the plaintiff's lawyer may have lost the case by conceding the critical point: "*it is conceded* that sea lions are *ferae naturae* and *that the law applies which holds that only a qualified right of property can be acquired in them, a right which is wholly lost when, escaping from their captor, without any intention of returning, they resume their former freedom*." [Beekman PJ at 782, emphasis added]. As usual, the authorities cited for this proposition were Blackstone, Kent, and a few cases which also faithfully recited and applied Blackstone's edict. Has no one ever argued that Blackstone had it wrong?

animus revertendi is what distinguishes a wild member of a species from a tamed one. This cannot be so if the distinction between wild and domestic animals is based on species. The question usually comes up when a not obviously domestic animal has strayed and been captured or killed by a stranger who is then sued for interference with the prior possession or for repossession. If ownership is proved, or if the prior possession can be proved to have continued to the time of interference, the plaintiff will win. Consequently, the defendant claims that the animal was wild, thus alleging that ownership was impossible, and that it had escaped, thus destroying the control requisite of the possession claim. I suggest that it is the second of these, the loss of control, to which the issue of *animus revertendi* is relevant. An animal which can be proved to have returned from excursions in the past, or to have been attempting to come home when stopped by the defendant, is simply a willing participant in its own control. Its behaviour proves the possession claim in much the same way as would a leash or the fence around a pasture, however long the rope or large the enclosure. The homing tendency may well prove a continuing possession, but it is irrelevant to both classification of the animal and to the ownership issue.

As to the acquisition of property by gunning down wild animals, the rules seem clear. The hunter gets *ownership* of the carcass unless someone else held property (ownership, possession, or a right to immediate possession I assume) when the killing occurred.[75] There is nothing anomalous about this rule, whatever the possibilities for ownership before death. A dead *former* wild animal is not a wild animal at all; its character is so changed by the act of killing that it makes no sense to treat it as the same entity. Damages, not possession of the carcass, would be the appropriate remedy when a domestic animal was killed and there is no reason for the rules to be different because the dead body used to be inhabited by a creature of the wild. The cases involving killing animals tell us nothing much about the acquisition and disposition of property in live ones.

The subject matter here has been acquisition and disposition of property in things. Wild animals, despite the lengthy analysis, are nothing but rather vivacious things. They are, admittedly, more elusive than most things, but is the call of the wild a sufficient reason to abandon general principles and invent special rules? Is a caged tiger any more likely to escape than a gold nugget found by a mountain climber with a hole in his backpack? If the finders can identify tiger and nugget in the subsequent possession of someone else, why not let the same rules of recovery apply to both?

I have attempted to demonstrate three things about property in wild animals. First, it is by no means clear from the common law cases why they could not be owned. Second, if there is no such rule, a few of the decided cases are wrong. Most wild animal ownership

---

75 This is, I think, uncontroversial. For want of a better case on point, see *Louis Denker Inc v The Polar Star* (1965) 51 MPR 152 (PEI CA).

claims would founder on the identity point, unless the animal had been branded or was otherwise easily identifiable. Finally, if there is no rule prohibiting the ownership of wild animals, the principle of ownership through first possession will prevail and the law of property in things is simplified.

CHAPTER 4

DESTRUCTION

Property in a thing ceases to exist when the thing itself is destroyed.[1]

Property is a relationship between people. Property in a thing is a relationship between people whereby the state assists the holder of the property in suppressing the liberties of other people in dealing with the thing - handling it, viewing it, using it in some way, or transferring property in it to someone else. Without the "it" the notion of property *in the thing* becomes meaningless.

Loss of property through destruction of a thing often gives rise to, or makes more valuable, property in another thing. I categorize common examples under the next three headings.

A   NATURAL DECOMPOSITION

Some things rot. If they decay and blend into the surface of land, they are part of the land for property analysis. If pieces blow away they may become lost to human awareness, or found (whereupon the finder, if still in a common law country, would be treated as a first finder and could become owner of the new thing), or drift onto and become part of land in which someone else holds property. In any case, there must come a stage in the decomposition when the rotting thing becomes the rotted thing - where the character of the original thing has so changed that it is viewed as a new thing or things.

Transmutation of elements is a more exotic form of rot. The old dream of changing base metals into gold may have died, but in the nuclear age elements break down into other elements in the lab and in the wild. So far this seems to have caused no major property litigation, perhaps because in the lab the possession of the resulting elements usually continues and is undisputed, whereas in nature there are no claimants. There is no reason why the rules would be different from the case of ordinary chemical decomposition.

---

1 A plaintiff who held property in a thing at the time it was destroyed may sue the destroyer for damages, but who then holds property in "it" will be moot. "If bricks or timber belonging to A be wrongfully taken by B and built by him into a house belonging to C, A cannot recover them against C, although their identity is clear: and the reason given is that the nature of the material is changed": *Gough* v *Wood & Co* [1894] 1 QB 713 (Eng CA). The reason offered in that case was "that it has become real property". That's another example of confusing property with things. What the judge probably meant to say was that what looked like another brick in the wall was, for purposes of legal analysis, now affixed to and part of the land. Whoever held an estate in the land would prevail over the former brick-owner whose claim would founder on the question "what brick?".

B ACCESSION, MIXING AND FIXTURES

1 Accession: Things Altered

Accession is the process whereby a thing becomes either worked into a clearly different type of thing or combined with one or more things to form a composite unit.[2] Someone loses property as a result. After accession, it is impossible[3] or impractical[4] to break down the composite into its constituent parts. Some reliable rules determine who gets property in what.

Common lawyers use "accession" to describe both processes listed above,[5] yet each warrants a different analysis. The two were distinct in Roman law, where "*specificatio* was the making of a new article out of the chattel of one person by the labour of another" whereas "*accessio* was the transfer of title which took place when two chattels belonging to different persons were combined into a single article".[6]

In the case of someone's labour changing the nature of a single thing - the Roman *specificatio* - the main issue is by what standard we determine that the thing has become so changed that property in it has passed. The traditional test held that property in the original thing ceased to exist when the reworked product was no longer identifiable as the

---

2 For example, "bricks built into a wall become part of the house, thread stitched into a coat or planks and nails and pitch worked into a ship under repair become part of the coat or ship": *Appleby* v *Myers* (1867) LR 2 CP 651 (Eng). The following definition will do, apart from its confusion of property and things.

> Accession [is] a principle ... by which the owner of property becomes entitled to all which it produces, and to all that is added or united to it ... and by which ... the possessor of property becomes entitled to it, as against the original owner, where the addition made to it by his skill and labor is of greater value than the property itself, or where the change effected in its form is so great as to render it impossible to restore it to its original shape: *Austrian Motors Ltd* v *Travelers Ins Co* 275 SE 2d 702 (Ga CA 1980) at 704 *per* Carley J.

3 "The doctrine of accession is carried no farther than necessity requires, and it is applied only to cases where the compound is such as to render it impossible to apportion the respective shares of the parties": *Rendell* v *Associated Finance Pty Ltd* [1957] VR 604 (Aust HC), dealing with a reconditioned engine installed in a truck. When judges talk of impossibility, they mean expense; it would always be possible to undo the accession if money were no object.

4 "[Accession] applies where something is added to, attached to, or mixed with something else so that it cannot again be separated without the destruction or serious injury of the whole so formed": *Bousquet* v *Mack Motor Truck Co* 168 NE 800 (Mass 1929), holding that attaching tires to a truck did not constitute accession.

5 See Sawyer, "Accession in English Law" (1935) 9 Australian LJ 50. He classified accessions as (i) cases on fixtures, (ii) cases of labour under contract, and (iii) cases dealing with things "which have been bound together and to which the doctrines adopted from the Roman law have been applied".

6 Slater "Accessio, Specificatio, and Confusio: Three Skeletons in the Closet" (1959) 37 Can Bar Rev 597 at 598. Mr Slater suggested grinding corn into flour and making grapes into wine as examples of *specificatio*, which he contrasted with using A's cloth to patch B's coat, *accessio* in Roman law.

same item[7]. This test is based solely on physical identity. The original thing no longer existed, any property formerly held in it had disappeared, and ownership of the new thing was held by its possessor. The test was applied in *Ochoa v Rogers*. Possession of a stolen car somehow came into the hands of a government agency. The defendant contracted for ownership of the car as "junk", paid $85.00, and spent about $800.00 converting it into a truck. The owner of the car sued for possession and lost.[8]

> When the appropriation of property is made in good faith under a mistake of facts, and the taker has by labor expended upon said property by converting it into a ting entirely different from the original and of greatly increased value, the title to the property will pass to the person by whose labor the change has been wrought and, the original owner can only recover the value of the article at the time it was taken.

This is often called "the doctrine of specification", no doubt from the Roman root.

The physical appearance or "specification" test has its limitations in a world where visual identity has diminished in importance as a forensic test.[9] It probably has been replaced by a "relative value" test, which determines a transfer of property by examining the extent to which the labourer has increased the original value of the property in the thing.[10]

---

7 "Such a change is said to be wrought when wheat is made into bread, olives into oil, or grapes into wine. ... It is ... regarded as a destruction or consumption of the original materials, and the true owner is not permitted to trace the identity into the manufactured article for the purpose of appropriating to his own use the labor and skill of the innocent occupant who wrought the change; but he is put to his action for damages as for a thing consumed, and may recover its value as it was when the conversion or consumption took place." *Silsbury* v *McCoon* 3 NY 378 at 385 per Ruggles, J.

8 *Ochoa v Rogers* 234 SW 693 (Texas 1921) at 695. Beware the *obiter dicta* regarding good faith, which has nothing to do with the common law test as to whether the nature of the thing has changed. The judge may have been thinking about a concept from the field of Equity, a separate system of rules administered in courts throughout the common law system. The view that a wrongdoer can not acquire property may have originated in the civil law. It was mentioned in three early New York cases – *Betts v Lee* 5 Johns 348, *Curtis v Grant* 6 Johns 168, and *Chandler v Eston* 9 Johns 362 – and was applied in *Silsbury v McCoon*, above, to give the owner of some corn ownership of whisky made by a non-innocent convertor. Compare *Gidney v Shank* [1996] 2 WWR 383 (Man CA). The facts were similar to *Ochoa v Rogers*, but the court reached the opposite result, perhaps because the case was argued on points of unjust enrichment, not possession.

9 See Brown *The Law of Personal Property* 2nd ed (Callaghan and Co Chicago 1955) at 57, noting the difficulty in determining whether a new species has been created by reworking an old one: "It is arbitrary and unjust to hold that he who makes wine from another's grapes acquires title to the resulting product, while he who carves a work of art from another's stone does not".

10 "It is a well recognized rule of law that where one, in reliance on a supposed right, without intending any wrong, expends labor and material on property of another which greatly enhance its value and the value of the original property is insignificant in comparison with the value of the finished product, title to the property in its converted form will pass to the person who has added his labor and materials, compensating the original owner for the value of the original property": *Walch* v Beck 296 NW 780 at 782 (Iowa 1941) at 782 *per* Garfield J. This case involved fixtures - the affixation of a thing to land - rather than accession, but Garfield J cited 1 *Corpus Juris Secundum* "Accession" as authority for the proposition. See also *Wetherbee v Green* 22 Mich 311, 7 Am Rep 653 (1871).

Like specification, the relative value test has its shortcomings, as value may be hard to establish[11] and it is difficult to predict by what proportion value must be increased to qualify. On the other hand, in an industrialized society, the relative value approach is simpler in most situations.[12]

When two or more things are joined together - the proper *accessio* of Roman law - two issues arise. The first is whether accession has occurred at all. If not, property in the things stays as it was before they were joined.[13] As noted above, whether accession or mere attachment has occurred is said to depend on the impossibility or impracticability of separation, but the issue is surely one of difficulty or (more likely) expense of undoing what was done.[14] The second issue, once accession is proved, is who gets property in the combined things. The rule most commonly applied is that the owner of the principal thing gains ownership of the combination and the accessory no longer exists.[15] Generally, this means that the less valuable is taken to accede to the more valuable,[16]

---

11 For example, a preliminary sketch of "The Nail in the Bannister" by R Stornaway may have been drawn on a sheet of paper that fell off the back of a lorry. The artist is likely to claim that the blank page was greatly improved, but what is the market value of an R Stornaway? Moving from the sublime to the pedestrian, the average Eskimo carving is a step down from the raw beauty of the unvarnished soapstone, yet I have no doubt that it would rate as an improvement on the basis of market value. The reason why there is a demand for Eskimo artlessness and not for petrified buffalo dung, notwithstanding the roughly comparable supply of each, is one of the great mysteries of economics. The Daily Telegraph of 8 Dec 88 reported at page 17 that "Californian socialites" have taken to wearing "fossilized dinosaur dung" (coprolite) - is it too late to be bullish on buffalo?

12 As Oscar Wilde pointed out, there is no shortage of people who "know the price of everything and the value of nothing".

13 In *Frank Dunn Trailer Sales Ltd v Paziuk* (1994) 127 Sask R 303, the appellant leased a vehicle to L. The lease stipulated that all alterations, additions and improvements to the vehicle would "become the property of" the appellant lessor. L replaced the factory stereo with stereo equipment loaned to him by the respondent and installed a radar detector belonging to the respondent. L failed to make his lease payments. The vehicle was repossessed by the appellant, who subsequently removed the equipment installed by L. The respondent sued for and won possession of the equipment. The decision was affirmed by the Saskatchewan Court of the Queen's Bench. It was difficult for the appellant to successfully argue that accession had occurred after he had separated the equipment from the car.

14 See *Lewis v Andrews and Rowley Pty Ltd* (1956) 73 WN (NSW) 670 at 677 *per* Manning J: "I am unable to agree that detachability is the test. Indeed the question as to whether one article can be detached from another may be merely a question of degree".

15 See *Twin City Motor Co v Rouzor Motor* Co 148 SE 461 (1924), citing *Pulcifer v Page* 32 Me 404: "It is a general rule of law that if the materials of one person are united to the materials of another by labor, forming a joint product, the owner of the principal materials will acquire the right of property in the whole by right of accession". See also Brown *The Law of Personal Property* 2nd ed (Callaghan and Co Chicago 1955) at 58: "When the goods of two different owners are incorporated together, the title to the resulting product goes to the owner of the principal goods". Compare *Jones v De Marchand* (1916) 10 WWR 841 in which beaver skins were made into a coat, but it was ruled that their identity was not destroyed and the owner of the skins prevailed.

16 Note the confusion of property and things in that statement. It is the form of property held in the thing which is valuable, not the thing itself. Would you pay more for possession of the Mona Lisa (for, say, 15 seconds) than for ownership of the Mona Gorilla? If you answered yes, go back five footnotes. Note also

although good arguments can be made against the accession of gigantic machines to tiny parts, no matter what the relative ownership costs of the two.[17] Judges are human after all, and humans are swayed by well presented arguments, not by formulas in books like this. Nevertheless, the principal *versus* accessory characterization seems to work and usually depends on market value.

Several cases involving adding parts to automobiles have proposed and refined a set of four rules to determine when accession has occurred.[18]

(1)   Can there be a separation of the original article without destroying or injuring the whole?[19]

(2)   Has the incorporated chattel ceased to exist as a separate thing?[20]

---

that other forms of property, not just ownership, can be acquired or lost by accession.

17 "Words such as [indistinguishable and inseparable] were relatively easy to apply to such cases as where a shipwright repaired a boat, or a seamstress embroidered cloth, but they may cause difficulty today if they must be applied, for example, to a case where a small screw has been replaced at the very heart of a complicated piece of mechanism": *Lewis* v *Andrews and Rowley Pty Ltd* (1956) 73 WN (NSW) 670 at 677 *per* Manning J.

18 This arrangement of the rules may be found in *Regina Chevrolet Sales Ltd* v *Riddell* [1942] 3 DLR 159 (Sask CA). The case involved a conditional sales contract for a truck, the plaintiff seller retaining ownership and a right of repossession upon default until payment in full. After delivery, the truck was equipped with 8 tires. The defendant seized possession of the tires under a chattel mortgage and the plaintiff repossessed the truck. The buyer was thus out of the picture and the only question was whether the defendant's claim to possession of the tires was defeated on the ground that they had ceased their separate existence and become part of the truck. Curiously, the plaintiff won.

19 *Lincoln Bank & Trust Co* v *Netter* 253 SW 2d (Ky CA 1952). In an action for possession of a truck or its ownership value by the seller under a conditional sales contract against a garageman who repaired the truck by installing a motor block assembly, generator, carburetor and radiator, the plaintiff lost. The repairs and parts were united to the machine so as to become an integral part thereof by accession and could not be removed by plaintiff. See also *Twin City Motor Co* v *Rouzer Motor Co* 148 SE 461 (1929) (accession of motor to car, even though readily detachable without damage); *Goodrich Silvertown Stores* v *McGuire Motor Ltd* [1936] 4 DLR 519 (Co Ct) (accession not applicable to tires on a car); *Dawson* v *Floyd Dunford Ltd* [1961] OWN 225 (Co Ct) (tires remain separate from truck: a conditional seller repossessed a truck and resold ownership of it, but it may have been relevant that the buyer on the resale had notice that there was a separate property claim to the tires); *Atlas Assurance Co* v *Gibbs* 183 A 690 (Conn) (engine readily detachable from car: no accession); *Bousquet* v *Mack Motor Truck Co* 168 NE 800 (Mass 1929) (no accession of tires to truck).

20 *Dawson* v *Floyd Dunford Ltd* [1961] OWN 225 (Co Ct) (tires remain separate from truck: a conditional seller repossessed a truck and resold ownership of it, but it may have been relevant that the buyer on the resale had notice that there was a separate property claim to the tires). *Lewis* v *Andrews and Rowley Property Ltd* (1956) 73 WN (NSW) 670 (property in those accessories which were readily identifiable and could be detached from the vehicle without damage thereto did not pass to the owner of the vehicle). In the *Lewis* case, Manning J (dissenting) thought that this was the only reliable test for accession. He criticized the four part test, saying (at 677) "[i]n my opinion, the test may be stated as follows: Has the chattel which has been attached to or incorporated in another chattel ceased to exist as a separate chattel". Similarly, see *Rendell* v *Associated Finance Pty Ltd* [1957] VR 604 (truck engine; decision possibly based on intent of owner of the engine rather than on identifiability).

(3)   Would a removal destroy the utility of the principal article?[21]

(4)   What was the degree and purpose of annexation?[22]

These rules have been criticized. It must be kept in mind that they are only guidelines. Asking and answering the four questions in any particular case is unlikely to determine the outcome, but it will help to organize the argument. In the end, doesn't it all come back to the original question whether (perhaps for one of the above four reasons) one of the things can be regarded as having ceased to exist?

Contracts may supersede the accession rules. For example, the owner of an engine may contract with the owner of a car to join the two into one working unit, but may stipulate that the property of each continues. Such a term prevails because of the general rules governing property transfers.[23] It is always advisable to check for transactions under which things became attached to one another before applying the accession rules.

When property is lost through accession, the loser may have an action for damages against the person who destroyed the thing in which the property was held. Putting it that way suggests that the usual remedies for interference with property apply and that the appropriate measure of damages is the value of whatever form of property was held in the thing immediately before accession. In most cases the plaintiff simply sues for damages and leaves the question of accession moot.[24] Finally, I suppose that a claim in

---

21 *Lincoln Bank & Trust Co* v *Netter* 253 SW 2d (Ky CA 1952) (motor block assembly, generator, carburetor and radiator held to have become part of a truck by accession). *Goodrich Silvertown Stores* v *McGuire Motor Ltd* [1936] 4 DLR 519 (Co Ct) (not applicable to tires on a car). *Bousquet* v *Mack Motor Truck Co* 168 NE 800 (Mass 1929) (not applicable to tires on a truck). *Regina Chevrolet Sales Ltd* v *Riddell* [1942] 3 DLR 159 (Sask CA) (tires are an integral part of a truck necessary to its proper working). *Lewis* v *Andrews and Rowley Pty Ltd* (1956) 73 WN (NSW) 670 (articles essential to the operation of the vehicle become, when affixed, incorporated with it so that ownership of them passes to the owner of the vehicle).

22 See *Goodrich Silvertown Stores* v *McGuire Motors Ltd* [1936] 4 DLR 519 (Co Ct) (tires can be detached without injury to the vehicle and the doctrine of accession is not applicable). The doctrine of title by accession does not apply to equipment of a car which a buyer and seller do not intend to be merged into its structure and which is clearly distinguishable, and as readily detachable from it as are tires and tubes. See also *Lewis* v *Andrews and Rowley Pty Ltd* (1956) 73 WN (NSW) 670, ruling that property in those accessories which were readily identifiable and could be detached from the vehicle without damage thereto did not pass to the owner of the vehicle.

23 It is well-known rule in common law systems that property is transferred from one person to another *by transaction* when so intended by the transferor: see generally Part III. This is not to say that property can not be transferred other than when intended by its holder, but that where parties are in the process of transacting rather than acting alone the transfer by transaction rules are likely to be applied if at all possible. This is probably what Professor Guest was getting at when he suggested "if A lets to B a motor car on hire-purchase, and B installs in it a reconditioned engine let to him on hire-purchase by C, it must not be supposed that the situation will necessarily be the same as if the engine were B's own property (sic)" in "Accession and Confusion in the Law of Hire-Purchase" (1964) 27 Mod L Rev 505 at 512.

24 The effect will then be the same, as satisfaction of the judgment for damages has the effect of

"restitution" is always a possibility where a holder of property in the principal thing is thought to be "unjustly enriched" by the accession. I recommend a specialist book on that rather undisciplined topic before any expensive conclusions are drawn.

2   Mixing: Things Confused

Mixing is the blending of fungibles into a common mass. It leads to the destruction of identity of the ingredients and a resulting loss of property in them. However, the blend can be treated as an identical but larger version of each portion. Anyone who held property in any of the ingredients becomes the holder of the same form of property in an unseparated portion of the blend[25] and, by seeking a court order if necessary, can use that property claim to have the blend apportioned. Typical examples of mixing are grains or oils in common storage and shipping containers.

Some say that the rule is not so simple.[26] They suggest a more complex rule designed to achieve "substantial justice between the parties".[27] They don't explain why the simple rule doesn't work.

Everyone seems to agree that when the mixing took place by accident the owners[28] of the fungible ingredients become common owners of the resulting mixture. Thus bales of

---

transferring the plaintiff's property to the defendant: *Harris* v *Christianson-Kerthlly Co* 303 SW 2d 422 (Texas 1957); *Shiavo* v *Cozzolino* (1942) 131 Conn 388 57 A 2d 723 (Conn 1942).

25 *Buckley* v *Gross* (1863) 3 B & S 566, 122 ER 213 (Eng) was a classic case of mixing. Quantities of tallow were stored by various owners in a Thames-side warehouse. Fire melted the tallow which flowed into the main sewers and the river. The plaintiff purchased possession of some of the tallow from a finder. The police seized possession and turned it over to the municipal corporation which, acting under an obscure statute, transferred ownership to the defendant. The plaintiff's conversion action failed. Justice Blackburn opined that "probably the legal effect of such a mixture would be to make the owners tenants in common in equal portions of the mass, but at all events they do not lose their property in it".

26 Blackstone (as usual) started a trend along these lines. "Where a man wilfully causes or allows property of another to be intermixed with his own without the other's knowledge or consent, the whole belongs to the latter, for the law to guard against fraud, allows no remedy on such a case": 2 *Blackstone's Commentaries* 405. Brown *The Law of Personal Property* 2nd ed (Callaghan and Co Chicago 1955) accepts this and says (at 63) that disputes involving intermixture are resolved by looking at 2 factors: (i) the kind and quality of the two or more lots of goods, and (ii) the circumstances through which the intermixing came about. Similarly, see Crossley Vaines *Personal Property* 4th ed (Butterworths London 1967) at 387.

27 See Slater "Accessio, Specificatio and Confusio: Three Skeletons in the Closet" (1959) 37 Can Bar. Rev 597 at 607: "the common law looked to the cause rather than the effect of the mixing, and this is the principle followed in the modern law. The question of title is subverted in favour of that of the taking and of the achievement of substantial justice between the parties". This sounds like law and Equity confused. Common law and Equity are not fungibles and can't be mixed in this way. Equity may be used to restrain judicially perceived abuses of the common law, and even to give alternative remedies, but the rules of common law property are clearer than all this Equityspeak makes it appear.

28 As usual, all the analysis is written in terms of ownership. There is no reason to think that the rules would be different for the holders of other forms of property in the things mixed, as the purpose of the rules is to identify the new thing - the mass resulting from the mixing - in which those who held some form of property in the ingredients now hold similar property.

cotton damaged and unidentifiable after a shipwreck[29], oil collected from leaking containers during shipment,[30] and missing chestnuts lost at sea[31] resulted in shared losses when it was not proved whose commodities were affected.

The major issue in these cases must be whether the ingredients were fungibles, for if they were not then either (i) the identity of each ingredient is only temporarily obscured and property in it remains unaffected,[32] or (ii) two or more unlike substances have been combined and the rules of accession apply. Whether two commodities are fungibles is a question of fact, which means in the practice of law it is a question of proof. It is simply not helpful to assert, as some analysts do, that the mixing rules are not applicable if it is possible to separate and identify the subject matter, no matter how difficult.[33] Possibility of separation is only a question of expense. All the tea in China could be separated and sourced to each producing hectare if anyone were foolish enough to fund the chemical analysis at the warehouse. The claim that the ingredients were fungibles will usually be made be a plaintiff who has something to gain by that conclusion.[34] The claim is more likely to succeed in cases where the ingredients are of the type that the common, unscientific experience of judges treats as indistinguishable and where the defendant is not willing to invest in some scientific research. Where the mixing was done by the plaintiff in circumstances that do not look accidental, it may be that a judge will be more sceptical than usual and require more direct proof that the ingredients were fungibles.[35]

---

29 *Spence* v *Union Insurance Co* (1868) LR 3 CP 427 (Eng). The bales of cotton were marked and 43 of them were owned by the plaintiff. The defendant was the plaintiff's insurer. The ship was wrecked, all the cotton on board was damaged to some extent, and the marks on some of the bales were obliterated. Justice Bovill concluded " when goods of different owners become by accident so mixed together as to be indistinguishable, the owners of the goods so mixed become tenants in common of the whole, in the proportions which they have severally contributed to it". The case involved interpretation of an insurance contract, not a dispute between claimants of property in the mixture.

30 *Jones* v *Moore* (1841) 4 Y& C 351, 160 ER 1041 (Eng). Oil leaked from labelled casks during shipment from Columbia to England. Some was lost, but some was collected and ownership of it was sold as one mass by the captain. The accounts were settled on the basis of tenancy in common. See also *Sandeman & Sons* v *Tyzack and Branfoot SS Co* [1913] AC 680 (Scot HL).

31 *Gill and Duffus (Liverpool) Ltd* v *Scruttons Ltd* [1953] 2 All ER 977 (Eng). Marked bags of chestnuts burst and some were lost. The plaintiff, short by some four tons, sued the shipping company for damages. Citing *Spencer* v *Union Marine Insurance Co Ltd* (1868) LR 3 CP 427 (Eng), the court held that a fair method of apportionment would have been to divide the mixed loose chestnuts among the consignees in proportion to the differences between the total weight of the chestnuts, whether in sound or damaged bags.

32 See, for example, *Smith* v *Torr* (1862) 7 F & F 505, 176 ER 227 (Eng) (the doctrine of "confusion" does not apply to distinct chattels like chairs and tables, but to commodities such as corn, wine, oil, etc, of which there could be a commingling of substance); *Colwill* v *Reeves* (1811) 2 Comp 575, 170 ER 1257 (Eng) (it is impossible that articles of furniture can be blended together); *Gilmour* v *Buck* (1874) 24 UCCP 187 (Ont) (logs, though similar, found to be identifiable).

33 See Crossley Vaines, *Personal Property* at 387.

34 See, for example, *Lupton* v *White* (1808) 13 Ves 432, 33 ER 817 (Eng), in which an agent claimed to have mixed his portion of the production of a lead mine with that of his principal. The agent lost it all.

35 In *Glencore International A.G et al* v *Metro Trading International Inc* [2000] EWHC 199 (Comm), the court had to determine who held property in a mix of different grades of oil. Justice Moore-Bick said at

Maybe this is why some analysts suggest that different rules apply in such cases. If so, they are forgetting the human aspects of the legal process and unnecessarily complicating the rules.

Contracts may supersede the mixing rules in exactly the same ways as noted in the analysis of accession set out above.[36] Similarly, an action for damages against the person who did the mixing will invoke the usual remedies for interference with property, and circumvent the mixing question.

3 Fixtures: Things Nailed Down

Imagine what used to be an identifiable thing that has become, by affixation, part of the land. That is what people mean to describe by the word "fixture". The word doesn't really describe any *thing* at all, in the present tense. The thing that used to exist is now simply part of the land and any property formerly held in it ceased to exist when it stopped being a thing separate from the land. The word "fixture" literally means a bump on the land that used to be a thing separate from the land (or several things, like building materials) before being attached to the land by some person at some past time.

The law relating to fixtures is simple, though its expression is too often complicated by sloppy language. Once a thing has become part of the land property in it is held by whoever holds property in the land simply because "it" no longer is.[37] The real issue is, by what tests do we determine whether the technique of affixation, which may range from tethering a horse to building a house, is sufficient to merge the thing with the land. The test is said to focus primarily on the intent of the person who, in the past, created the connection between the thing and the land.[38] However, the most reliable evidence of that intention is usually taken to be the degree or type of affixation.[39] Put another way: "[i]t is

---

para 185: "[a]s in other cases of mixing, any doubts about the quantity or value of the oil contributed by the innocent party should be resolved against the wrongdoer".

36 The issues and the complications are essentially the same as accession. For examples of contractual analysis in mixing situations, see *Jessel* v *Bath* (1867) LR 2 x. 267 (Eng) and *Cox* v *Bruce* (1886) 18 QBD 147 (Eng).

37 "If a piece of timber which was illegally taken ... have been used in building or repairing, this, although it is known to be the piece which was taken, cannot be retaken, the nature of the timber being changed, for by annexing it to the freehold it is become real property:" *Gough* v *Wood* [1894] 1 QB 713 (Eng). What the judge meant in the last line is that by annexing it to the *land* it is become *land*.

38 Compare two cases involving carpets. In *LaSalle Recreations Ltd v Canadian Camdex Inv Ltd* (1969) 68 WWR 339 (BCCA) at para 32, MacFarlane JA said, "the object of the annexation was the better and more effectual use of the building as a hotel and not the better use of the [carpet] as [a carpet]". In *Botham & Ors v TSB Bank Plc* [1996] EWCA Civ 549, Roch LJ said, "[c]arpets can easily be lifted off gripper rods and removed and can be used again elsewhere. In my judgment neither the degree of annexation nor the surrounding circumstances indicate an intention to effect a permanent improvement in the building."

39 "It is a question which must depend on the circumstances of each case, and mainly on two

abundantly clear that the degree and mode of annexation do not govern whether a chattel has become a fixture and cannot be separated from the object or purpose of annexation".[40] Details of the tests used in various common law cases can be found in any standard work on the topic of property in land.

Some cases suggest there are special rules for "tenant fixtures".[41] See, for example, *Frank Georges Island Investments Ltd v Ocean Farmers Ltd,*[42] where the Court held that a tenant would be entitled to remove structures from land provided that (i) they were erected for trade, ornament or domestic convenience, and (ii) they could be removed without serious damage to the land or losing their essential character or value.[43]

Does the first requirement exclude any thing? If not for trade, ornament or domestic convenience, why would anyone nail a thing to land? Does the second element add anything to the analysis? If the removal of a structure from land would cause serious damage to the land, it will no doubt be more difficult to convince a judge that the structure is not part of the land. Maybe the so-called "tenant fixtures" rules are all about credibility. A judge would probably believe a tenant who says, "I used *only* four nails so that I could remove my statue of Terrence Gene Bollea[44] easily at the end of my lease".

---

circumstances, as indicating the intention, viz., the degree of annexation and the object of the annexation. ... Perhaps the true rule is, that articles not otherwise attached to the land than by their own weight are not to be considered as part of the land, unless the circumstances are such as to shew that they were intended to be part of the land, the onus of shewing that they were so intended lying on those who assert that they have ceased to be chattels, and that, on the contrary, an article which is affixed to the land even slightly is to be considered as part of the land, unless circumstances are such as to shew that it was intended all along to continue as a chattel, the onus lying on those who contend that it is a chattel": *Reynolds v Ashby & Son* [1904] AC 466 (Eng HL) at 474 *per* Blackburn J. For examples of these tests being applied, see *Holland v Hodgson* (1872) LR 7 CP 328 (Eng) (looms attached to stone floor of mill held part of the land even though easily removable without serious damage to the floor) and *Wake v Hall* (1883) 8 App Cas 195 (Eng HL) (miners who erected buildings and machinery for mining purposes entitled to remove them, as nature of annexation showed intent was to annex them only temporarily).

40 Anger and Honsberger *Law of Real Property* Oosterhoff and Rayner ed (Canada Law Book Aurora 1985) at 1014.

41 "Tenant fixtures" were described in *Stack v T Eaton Co* (1902) CarswellOnt 399 as a rule which applied uniquely to fixtures attached by tenants to the leased land. Chief Justice Meredith described this category of fixtures as follows at 338: "in the case of tenants' fixtures put in for the purposes of trade, they form part of the freehold, with the right, however, to the tenant, as between him and his landlord, to bring them back to the state of chattels again by severing from the soil, and that they pass by a conveyance of the land as part of it, subject to this right of the tenant.

42 *Frank Georges Island Investments Ltd v Ocean Farmers Ltd* 2000 CarswellNS 74 (SC) (corporate tenant operated aquaculture business on an island and constructed a cottage, twine shed, outhouse and buoy shed; lease expired; tenant brought application to remove the structures; tenant conceded that the four buildings were fixtures, but argued that they were "tenant fixtures" and thus capable of being severed). The Court said (at para 37) "the sole issue is whether these four structures possess those particular characteristics which would then qualify them as tenant fixtures, capable of being removed by a tenant prior to the end of a lease term".

43 *Ibid* at para 45.

44 Ring name: Hulk Hogan.

The same judge might not believe someone with a more permanent proprietary interest who said the same thing.

A person who loses property in a thing that was affixed to land may be entitled to compensation. He would have a damages claim against the affixer. However, an estate holder may have become enriched innocently and be immune to a tort claim. In some jurisdictions it is regarded as a rule of common law that one who improves land mistakenly thinking he holds an estate can force a transfer of property in the land, compensating the holder only for the market value prior to improvement;[45] in some other jurisdictions a similar power has been statutorily given to judges.[46]

Property disputes after affixation may be complicated by security interests in the thing that was affixed, depending on when the security interest attached.[47]

In sum, property in a thing may be lost when the thing itself - through accession (labour caused change in its nature or merger with another thing), mixing (confusion of fungibles), or affixation (to land) - ceases to exist.

C   DEATH OF LIVESTOCK

Isn't death of an animal an example of transmutation or accession? A self-propelled carbon based thing stops behaving like its fellow creatures and begins imitating a rock or a vegetable. Why don't we conclude that it and any property held in it have ceased to be?

To some extent we do. We examined ownership and possession of the dead bodies of former wild animals in Chapter 3 "Capture and Escape of Wild Animals". I opined there

---

45 See *Walch* v *Beck* 296 NW 780 (Iowa 1941). This seems a rather awesome power, quite unlike the historical common law, and I am sceptical about its attraction to judges in places like Canada, Australia, and England.

46 See, for example, the Ontario *Conveyancing and Law of Property Act* RSO 1980 c 90 s.37(1):

> Where a person makes lasting improvements on land under the belief that it is his own, he or his assigns are entitled to a lien upon it to the extent of the amount by which its value is enhanced by the improvements, or are entitled or may be required to retain the land if the court is of opinion or requires that this should be done according as may under all circumstances of the case be most just, making compensation for the land, if retained, as the court directs.

The improver is likely to lose out if he makes the improvements under some transaction whose terms suggest that no such remedy is contemplated.

47 A security interest in a thing that attached, (a) before the thing became affixed, has priority over the claim of any person who has an interest in the land; or (b) after the thing became affixed, has priority over the claim of any person who subsequently acquired property in the land, but not over any person who had a registered interest in the land at the time the security interest in the goods attached and who has not consented in writing to the security interest or disclaimed an interest "in the fixture". *Personal Property Security Act* RSO 1990 c P10 s 34. Similar rules exist in other jurisdictions: AL s 36; BC s 36; MN s 36; NB s 36; NL s 37; NS s 37; PEI s 36; SK s 36; YK s 35; UCC s 9-313.

that the hunter gets ownership of the carcass unless someone else held property in the animal when the killing occurred.[48] Many English cases suggest that right to immediate possession may be held by an estate holder in the land where the animal was gunned down.[49] It is difficult to make much sense of them.[50] Maybe they can be rationalized as disputes between finders of things and estate holders in land where the things were found, for which we have some clear and simple rules.[51]

The rules are probably clearer on domestic animals. It is unlikely that anyone in western society cares to assert property in the dead bodies, unless they are conventional sources of food or the remains of household pets. In the former case ownership is likely retained by the owner of the animal by virtue of some notion that the live animal was "meat on the hoof". If the primary reason for owning such animals is to turn them into food, their slaughter does not really change society's perception of their nature and the accession rules are not invoked. Does the same argument apply when beef cattle die a natural death?[52] As to the bodies of household pets, should competing property claims be made, the pet owner is likely to win the sympathy of any normal judge and a favourable result is

---

48 *Louis Denker Inc* v *The Polar Star* (1965) 51 MPR 152 (PEI CA).

49 Some of them say that the "right of hunting and shooting" in an interest in the land - that is, part of the definition of the property held in the land: *Ewart* v *Graham* (1859) 7 HL Cas 331 (Eng); *Keble* v *Hickringill* (1706) 11 Mod Rep 74, 88 ER 898 (Eng) (duck decoys); *Lowe* v *Adams* [1901] 2 Ch 598 (Eng) (shooting pheasants); *The Earl of Lonsdale* v *Rigg* (1856) 11 Exch 654, 156 ER 992 (Eng) (cattlegates and grouse). That would also appear to be what was behind the reasoning in *Pamment* v *Thompson* (1921) 20 OWN 89 (Ont CA), although the estate holder was simply awarded damages against the defendant for trespass.

50 The cases tend to be inconsistent and loaded with strange sub-categories and "respect for property" rhetotic that gets in the way of sober analysis. See, for example, *Blades* v *Higgs* (1865) 20 CB (NS) 214, 144 ER 1087 (Eng) (killing rabbits) which notes "if creatures *ferae naturae* when shot are the property of the man on whose land they are shot, then the taking of them by a stranger would be larceny, but all the authorities show that is not so". Some of them suggest that there are two classes of wild animals, those viewed as "vermin ... unprofitable to man" in which no one holds property and "game ... profitable to man" to which a "general right" is held by the estate holder: see *Ewart* v *Graham* (1859) 7 HL Cas 331 (Eng), *Bowlston* v *Hardy* (1597) Cro Eliz 517, 78 ER 794 (Eng) (conies), and *Hadesden* v *Gryssel* (1608) Cro Jac 195 (Eng) (conies, yet again). The real reason is likely capsulized in a throwaway line by Lord Westbury in *Blades* v *Higgs* (1865) 20 CB (NS) 214, 144 ER 1087 (Eng) at 1090 (killing rabbits): "the property in game found and taken [*ie* killed] by a trespasser on the land of A must vest either in A or the trespasser [and] it would be unreasonable to hold that the property vests in the trespasser or wrongdoer". We'll encounter this bias again in the finding cases.

51 See Chapter 7 "Finders on Defence" where some rules based on the estate holder's intent to exclude others from all things within the controlled boundaries of the land are explored.

52 Or when they get hoof and mouth and are shot and buried: see the movie *Hud*, or better still, listen to Bill Cosby's magnificent version of the two cows discussing their imminent demise in *Hud*, concluding with one cow's advice (too late) to "wipe that foam from 'round your mouth". Compare *R* v *Edwards and Stacey* (1877) 36 LT 30 (Eng). Three (little?) pigs, bitten by a mad dog, were shot and buried at their owner's orders. The defendants dug up the bodies and took the meat to the local market. They were convicted of larceny (theft), which was impossible unless the owner retained property after they were killed (*and* after they were affixed to the land by burial) even though he did not perceive them as useful for food. I've criticized the case under "The Concept of Abandonment".

likely, although a careful analysis can not be anticipated. The more likely scenario for disputes about dead pets involves the expense of disposal; here, as with human bodies, responsibility for ridding the neighbourhood of a health hazard can be allocated without deciding who, if anyone, holds property in the remains.[53]

Consider the possibilities categorically.

(1)   Dead animals are food, clothing, trophies, or garbage.

(2)   Gourmands, the fashionable, and great white hunters want to hold property in the first three; no one is likely to want property in the fourth.

(3)   Death either changes the fundamental nature of the beast or it does not.

    (a)   If death is a form of transmutation, property held in an animal ceases to exist at the time of death.

    (b)   If death is not transmutation, property held in the live animal continues to be held in the dead body.

(4)   If no property continues through the moment of death - either because of transmutation or because no one held property before death - the first possessor acquires ownership of the body.

(5)   There are no other rules.

Finally, dead bodies eventually rot. We've covered that, under "Natural Decomposition".

D   DEATH OF A PROPERTY HOLDER

People die.[54] Property, being a relationship between people, cannot exist as a concept without some person to hold the property.[55] We thus know that a holder of property ceases to hold it upon death. The thing usually carries on, unaffected unless it was a pet, and almost always someone else acquires some form of property as a result of the death. I include the topic here only to illustrate that destruction of self is another way of unilaterally disposing of property.

---

53 Common law judges have traditionally resisted the notion that anyone can hold property in a human corpse. Why this is so is unclear, though it is probably just another example of the tyranny of a religious minority over the rational and the disinterested. The morbid may wish to consult *Haynes Case* (1614) 12 Co Rep 113, 77 ER 1387 (Eng), involving a grave robber's conviction for theft of "winding sheets", but not of the corpses around which they were wound.

54 They say it is a fundamental truth. I attribute it to Trish Callon.

55 I explained this in detail in Chapter 1. It is axiomatic to the theory of property set out in this book.

E   THE CONCEPT OF ABANDONMENT

Some common law analysts say that property in a thing can not be abandoned - that it continues in the holder until transferred to some other person. They must be wrong.

Haynes Case[56] is cited as the root authority for this proposition.

> William Haynes had digged up the several graves of three men and one woman in the night and had taken their winding sheets from their bodies, and buried them again: and it was resolved by the justices at Serjeants Inn, Fleet Street, that the property of the sheets remain in the owners, that is, in him who had property therein, when the dead body was wrapped therewith; ... Also a man cannot relinquish the property he hath in his goods, unless they be vested in another; and accordingly, at the said assizes he was severally indicted for taking each of these sheets: and the first indictment was of petty larceny, for which he was whipped; and at the same assizes he was also indicted for the felonious taking of the three other sheets, for which he had his clergy, and so escaped the sentence of death, which he well deserved, for this inhuman and barbarous felony.

Haynes would have been acquitted if the winding sheets were found to have become part of the land upon burial, or if no one held property in them at the time he took possession. The justices at Serjeants Inn, Fleet Street, must have been inclined to a guilty verdict. As they say, hard cases make bad law.

Another case widely cited on abandonment is *R v Edwards and Stacey*.[57] Three pigs bitten by a mad dog were shot and buried by their owner. The defendants dug them up and took the meat to the local market. They were convicted of larceny. The appeal court reviewed the way in which the Chairman of Magistrates put the case the jury, noting:

> in his opinion there had been no abandonment, as Sir William's [the owner's] intention was to prevent the pigs being made any use of; *but that if the jury were of opinion that he had abandoned the property they should acquit the prisoners.* [Emphasis added]

The conviction was affirmed, the only question considered being "[w]hether there was evidence on which the jury were justified in convicting the prisoners of larceny". Given the Chairmen's direction to the jury, the only point decided in this case was one of fact: the jury determined that the owner did not intend to abandon ownership of the dead pigs. The case is no authority against the possibility of abandonment. Indeed, it leans the other way.

---

56 *Haynes Case* (1614) 12 Co Rep 113, 77 ER 1389 (Eng).
57 *R v Edwards and Stacey* (1877) 36 LT 30 (Eng).

A 1928 Australian case[58] considered and clearly ruled against the possibility of abandonment in the common law. The analysis is curious. Justice Clark indicated that abandonment was possible in Roman law, impossible according to *Haynes Case*, and in some sort of half-way house according to three wreck cases,[59] which he was inclined to discount. Then, somewhat quixotically, he announced his preference.[60]

> Can the owner of a chattel divest himself of his rights as owner by abandoning the chattel? This appears to me to be a question which has never been settled, but I must answer it one way or another in order to determine this case. ... On the whole I think that I should adopt the rule that the intentional abandonment of a chattel by the owner of it does not divest him of his ownership ... .

The judge quoted Holdsworth, *History of English Law* Vol VII at 496 - an unusual choice of precedent. Holdsworth offered the following reason why abandonment was impossible.[61]

> This is a somewhat curious rule, but owing to the common law theory of ownership and possession, it causes no such inconvenience as it would have caused in Roman law. A person who takes possession under such circumstances has by virtue of his possession all the rights of an owner, except as against the former owner, and if the former owner has really abandoned his ownership the possessor is in substance the owner for he has the rights of an owner against all the world.

What can "if the former owner has really abandoned his ownership" possibly mean if abandonment is impossible? Why "former owner"? Would he not continue as owner if his attempt at abandonment failed? The inherent contradictions in the last sentence are sufficient to dispose of Holdsworth's point. As to Justice Clark - well, sometimes even easy cases make bad law.

There is a simple argument in favour of abandonment at common law. The acquisition of property is a voluntary act. No one can be forced to acquire it.[62] Property is a

---

58 *Johnstone and Wilmot Pty Ltd* v *Kaine* (1928) 23 Tasmanian Law Reports 43. The defendant contracted to sell ownership of a truck to the plaintiff by way of a conditional sales contract. The plaintiff became displeased with the performance of the truck and left it sitting by the roadside, apparently expecting the defendant to repossess it. The defendant did. Somehow, the plaintiff later recovered damages against the defendant for conversion. Something here does not make sense.

59 *Brown* v *Mallet* 5 CB 599 (Eng), *White* v *Crisp* 10 Ex 312 (Eng), and *The Crystal* [1894] AC 508 (Eng HL) all supported the concept of abandonment. According to Justice Clark "[t]hey may be explained on the ground that abandonment will exempt from liabilities which attach to the owner while in possession or on the ground that such abandonment is permitted, and indeed common in the case of wrecked ships, though not necessarily in the case of other chattels". So he says.

60 23 Tasmanian Law Reports at 56-57. He gives the impression of having flipped a coin in order to reach this conclusion.

61 As reproduced in 23 Tasmanian Law Reports 43 at 57.

62 Discoverers need not take possession. Finders, as we shall soon see, are at liberty to leave lost

relationship among people in the common law system. The relationship gives the property holder the advantage of state assistance in suppressing the liberties of other people. Is there anything to be gained by precluding the property holder from removing himself from that privileged position until some transferee volunteers to occupy it? Put another way, what state interests are served by a rule allowing a property holder to renounce his property one day and to change his mind the next day, or the next month, or six years later?[63] It has nothing to do with imposing liabilities on the property holder: regardless whether it is possible to abandon ownership or possession of a Bengal tiger, letting the tiger escape near a shopping mall would attract tort liability. Must a property holder blow the thing up, endangering others and wasting resources, before we conclude that his property in the thing is gone?[64]

The unilateral disposition of property is clearly possible in American law.[65]

A Canadian court assumed abandonment to be possible in *Canada (Attorney General) v Brock*.[66] A police officer stopped Mr Brock for speeding. Several bundles of American $100 bills in a plastic bag were under the car seat. Mr. Brock denied ownership at the scene, but showed up at the police station the next day and claimed ownership. The A-G Canada claimed that Mr Brock's denial of ownership at the scene proved he had abandoned the banknotes. The BC Supreme Court defined abandonment.[67]

> Abandonment is generally defined as the voluntary relinquishment by its owner or holder, with the intention of terminating his ownership, possession and control and without vesting ownership in any other person.

The court found that Mr Brock's behaviour disproved that intention, as he reclaimed

---

articles where they find them. Not even by gift or inheritance can property be foisted upon an unwilling transferee: see, generally, Chapter 9 "Gift".

63 Eventually, a limitations statute will intervene in most jurisdictions and either destroy the property if no claim is made within the limitation period or at least preclude any legal actions to enforce it after that time.

64 The relationship called property, once established, continues until terminated by some destructive event. Holmes, Jr. pointed out that, although we require an offer and consideration to create a contract, the contract is not ended merely because the promisor has second thoughts or the flow of consideration is postponed. "When certain facts have once been made manifest which confer a right there is no general ground on which the law need hold the right at an end except the manifestation of some fact inconsistent with its continuance": Holmes, Jr. *The Common Law* (Little Brown and Co Boston 1881) at 186. The question is, what constitutes a "the manifestation of some fact inconsistent with its continuance"? A mutual agreement terminating a contract parallels the mutuality that created it. Abandonment mirrors the unilateral acquisition of property.

65 *State v West* 235 SE 2d 150 (NC 1977) (owner may abandon, in which case finder becomes owner); *Katsaris v US* 499 F Supp 282 (Fla 1980) (abandonment can proved by intent plus action); *Anderson v Pettit*, 309 NYS 2d 974. Nor is this only a recent view. The American digests are full of listings under "Abandoned and Lost Property".

66 *Canada (Attorney General) v Brock* (1991) 59 BCLR (2d) 261 (BC SC).

possession of the banknotes on the following day.[68]

The plaintiff's mother in *Stewart v Gustafson*[69] sold an estate in farm land to the defendants. The parties agreed that the seller would have limited time to remove machinery and equipment and that any items remaining after the deadline would be considered abandoned and could be disposed of at the discretion of the purchaser. The defendants disposed of some things after the deadline and the plaintiff brought an action for wrongful detention and conversion of them. Justice Klebuc listed the following factors as supporting an inference of an intention to abandon: (1) passage of time; (2) nature of the transaction; (3) the owner's conduct; and (4) the nature and value of the property.[70] The judge held that Mr Gustafson was entitled to infer abandonment because of the nature of some of the things.[71]

> Although Mr. Stewart did not by word or deed relinquish his interest in the second group of chattels, I am satisfied that no liability attaches to Mr. Gustafson upon his disposal thereof for three reasons. First, an intention to abandon can be inferred from the very nature of a chattel. Here, the buildings were worth far less than the cost of moving the same intact. The lumber was worthless.

He drew the opposite conclusion about tools and equipment stored in the welding shop.[72]

Abandonment is possible throughout the common law system. This is a radical idea only if you believe those other people who said it couldn't be done.

---

68 At paras 31, 32. The decision was overruled by the Court of Appeal ((1991) 59 BCLR (2d) 261) and leave to appeal was denied by the Supreme Court of Canada ((1994) 85 CCC (3d) vi (note)). The BCCA decision was based on a finding of fact that Mr Brock never held possession of the banknotes, not on the abandonment issue.

69 *Stewart v Gustafson* [1999] 4 WWR 695 (Sask QB).

70 *Ibid* at para 17. Passage of time must be a key factor: see *Ontario v Mar-Dive Corp* (1996) 141 DLR 4th 577 (ship "Atlantic" sank after collision with ship "Ogdensburgh" in 1852; former owners of the *Atlantic* sued the *Ogdensburgh* for the "total loss", indicating that the owners had no salvage intentions; held, ownership abandoned). Compare, however, *Colombus-America Discovery Group v Atlantic Mut Ins Co* 974 F 2d 450 (USCA 4th Cir 1992) (ship carrying gold sank in 1857 hurricane; insurers paid millions in insurance claims; plaintiff began salvaging gold 131 years later; plaintiff claimed ownership; USCA concluded that insurers had not abandoned their interest in the gold).

71 *Ibid* at para 38. See also *Simpson v Gowers* 1981 CarswellOnt 721 (Ont SC) (estate in farm land sold; soya beans left in barn; abandoned).

72 *Stewart v Gustafson* at para 40.

PART III

THE LOST AND FOUND

DEPARTMENT

Finders keepers. Possession is nine parts of the law. Like most old husband's tales, these ones are usually true. A lawyer must know when they are false.

We have already seen the consequences of first (ever) possession. We now move on to prior possession. The finding cases occupy the heartland of the common law of property in things. A finder who takes possession of a lost thing usually commences two types of relationships. One, possession of the thing, protects the finder against strangers. The other, right to immediate possession, obliges the finder to some, though not all, prior possessors of the thing.

Who may do what to whom is easy to determine, once we identify the finder's relationship to any particular antagonist. Simply and accurately identifying the antagonist's position is the key.

In the next three chapters we examine the meaning of possession by finding, explain how such possessors are protected against strangers, and categorize plaintiffs who defeat possessors who claim to have found lost things.

CHAPTER 5

FINDING AND TAKING POSSESSION OF THINGS

A   LOSING AND FINDING THINGS

Things get lost all the time. Sometimes they get found. Finders may or may not take possession of things they find. The obligations of finders to losers and the legal position of a possessor by finding are fairly simple. There are four basic points:

    (i)   finding creates neither property in the thing found nor obligation to past or present property holders;

    (ii)   taking possession upon finding is not interference with property in the common law system;

    (iii)   a finder who takes possession is in the same position as any other possessor;

    (iv)   a possessor by finding will lose possession to the holder of right to immediate possession of the thing found.

These four points require some elaboration.

First, *finding creates neither property in the thing found nor obligation to past or present property holders*. To find a thing is to spot it in the bushes, to watch it floating down the river, or to note its position on the ground while flying over a vast and unmapped landscape. The state will not intervene on the side of such a finder and subsequent finders are uninhibited by claims he makes.[1] The finder may be thought a swell chap if he reports what he saw, particularly if his report assists a property holder in recovering possession of the inherited antique watch in the bushes, the rented boat that floated away, or the *PPSA*[2] listed cattle that stampeded mysteriously in the night. But the property holder has no action for the simple failure to report the finding.[3]

---

1 *Eads* v *Brazelton* 22 Ark 499, 79 Am Dec 88 (1861) illustrates the point. The plaintiff located a wreck in the Mississippi River and marked its location by putting blazes on lines of trees near the river bank so that the lines intersected at the wreck. When the defendant began salvaging the wreck the plaintiff sued but lost. The conclusion was that he may have found the wreck, but he failed to take possession and thus held no property in it.

2 The *Personal Property Security Act*, which is a Canadian label for statutes derivative of Article 9 of America's *Uniform Commercial Code* (*UCC*): see Chapter 2 "Security Interests". Such Acts provide a statutory framework for creating, registering, and enforcing security interests in things while abolishing or rendering uninteresting various common law techniques like reservation of title under conditional sales contracts, chattel mortgage transactions, and hire-purchase agreements. They have ravaged property literacy: can anyone explain the difference between cattle trespass and chattel mortgages these days?

3 Chief Justice Coke said "when a man doth find goods ... at the first it is in his election whether he will take them or not into his custody ... but when he hath them ... he ought to keep them safely": *Isaack* v *Clark* (1615) 2 Bulstr 306, 80 ER 1143 (Eng).

Second, *taking possession upon finding is not interference with property in the common law system.*[4]

The accuracy of this statement depends upon some subtle, yet critical distinctions. Finders find lost things; pickpockets aren't finders. But on to the less obvious.

I bet you couldn't draw a detailed floor plan of your house just now to accurately describe the location of every single thing there that you own or possess. Despite that, they are not lost and therefore they can not be found. Anyone who takes possession of one of them without your permission is interfering with your property in the thing.[5]

By contrast, I lost that foreign banknote[6] that fell out of my pocket on the meadow last week. It has probably been picked up by someone by now. That someone would be quite willing to restore possession of it to me should I advertise or if I found out about his gain and convinced him of my loss. Nevertheless, I expect that he will in good conscience spend it on a treat during his next trip abroad on the assumption that I have abandoned hope. Whether spending it constitutes interference with my property is, of course, a separate question, and depends upon the accuracy of his expectation of abandonment. This is partly a function of the denomination of the banknote. No judge would believe that the average meadow walker would shrug off the loss of a 10,000 pound note. Any judge in the pre-Euro era would have expected precisely that in the case of a 10,000 lira note when the exchange rate was several thousand lira to the pound. But in neither case has the finder interfered with my property in the foreign banknote by the simple act of taking possession: of this there is no probable doubt, no possible doubt whatever.[7]

---

4 That is, no damages can be collected by the loser against the finder for the simple act of taking possession rather than leaving the thing where it lies. "It is the law of charity to lay up the goods which do thus come to his hands by trover [ie, by finding, from the French *trouver*], and no trespass shall lie for this": Coke CJ again in *Isaack* v *Clark* (1615) 2 Bulstr 306, 80 ER 1143 (Eng KB), in which a finder who took possession of a bag of coins was found not liable for damages to the loser. Old cases on the writ of replevin confirm this. Replevin was not maintainable "unless in a case in which there has first been a taking out of the possession of the owner": *Mennie* v *Blake* (1856) 6 E & B 842, 119 ER 1078 (Eng) *per* Coleridge J. Whether the loser can recover possession from the possessor by finding is a separate question: we'll deal with it later.

5 The advanced reader will have noted that my possession can be based on the rule giving estate holders possession of things on the land where an intent to exclude outsiders from such things can be inferred from the nature of the premises or the circumstances under which the outsider is there. We examine his rule in Chapter 7.

6 If it were not a foreign banknote the analysis might be complicated by a statute making the local currency "negotiable". A person who comes into possession of a "negotiable instrument" by transaction becomes, in most circumstances, the owner: this protects innocent receivers of stolen local banknotes (grocers, for example) from having the money they take in seized by others (the butcher next door, for example) who were robbed; the innocent receiver of possession of a stolen car (neither being a negotiable instrument) would not be so fortunate.

7 Gilbert O'Sullivan, the Irish singer, may also have said this.

Some say there is a distinction between lost things and mislaid things. This only clouds the issue. There is a distinction is between lost and not lost. But isn't that irrelevant unless the issue is whether, as in the pickpocket example, the so-called finding was achieved by dispossessing the alleged loser? Consider another example.

> A passenger on an underground railway saw a package left on the seat by another passenger who had alighted. There were no marks on it. He got off at the next stop, taking the package with him. He told a station guard that he proposed to advertise for the owner. The owner was not involved in the subsequent action for possession and the railway corporation won.

This case[8] is much cited for its ruling that the defendant had not found the package because it was not lost but "mislaid" by the unidentified passenger.[9] But did that matter? The dispute was not about interference with the owner; the railway corporation was not the owner and could not plead the owner's case. The question was whether the defendant could retain possession against the owner of the vehicle in which he took possession of the package. The answer was no. Maybe this was because the railway corporation already had possession of the package and all other unattended baggage in the vehicle.[10] Maybe the defendant lost because he dispossessed the railway corporation.[11] If so, whether the other passenger "lost" or "mislaid" the package was a red herring.

Thomas v Canada (Attorney General)[12] rejected the "it was mislaid, not lost". Mr Thomas received a parcel in his post office box. The parcel contained $18,000 in

---

8 *Foulke v NY Consolidated Railway Co* 127 NE 237 (NYCA 1920).

9 "Lost property is not mislaid property or property voluntarily put in the place intended and forgotten, but property the possession of which is parted from casually and involuntarily": 127 NE 237. The "mislaid" concept is critically analyzed and (for my money) exposed as nonsense in Cohen "The Finders Cases Revisited" 48 Texas L Rev 1001 at 1004-1012 (1970). As Cohen points out (at 1006) "there is no fundamental difference between deliberately placing an object on a surface and unintentionally ... leaving it there and deliberately placing an object in your pocket and unintentionally having it leave ... through a hole. In both cases the subjective state of the actor is the same [and his control is gone]". For an extreme example of the fine distinctions invited by the "mislaid" concept, see *Durfee v Jones* 11 RI 588 (1877), in which bank notes clearly placed in a safe by someone were ruled lost only because they appeared to have slipped by accident into a crack between the outer casing and the lining.

10 This was the basis of the decision in the *NY Consolidated Railway* case, despite the much quoted lost *versus* mislaid distinction. "It [the package] had then become in the custody and the potential actual possession of the defendant. ... The right of the defendant to the custody and actual possession of the package was superior and paramount to the taking of the plaintiff." The railway corporation was said to have taken possession as a "gratuitous bailee". I have some difficulty with this classification: see Chapter 10 "Bailment: a Separate Transaction?" I suggest possession was attained by virtue of control over the vehicle and intent to exclude others from interfering with objects in it, much as an estate holder may hold possession of things within the boundaries of the land. This point is covered in Chapter 7 "Finders on Defence".

11 See Chapter 7 "Finders on Defence", particularly *Parker v British Airways Board* [1982] 2 WLR 503 (Eng CA) which is set out at length there.

12 *Thomas v Canada (Attorney General)* 2006 ABQB 730.

banknotes and was addressed to another post office box. Mr Thomas photocopied the banknotes, then transferred possession to the police. The owner of the banknotes was never found, but the police refused to return possession to Mr Thomas. The A-G Canada argued that Mr Thomas could not be a finder in law because the envelope was not lost but misplaced. Justice Trussler pointed out the irrelevance of the distinction.[13]

> Nothing turns on this. What is important is that Thomas took possession of the money when he opened the envelope. He took the money out of the envelope, counted at least some of it and photocopied the bags to preserve a record of it. When Thomas released the money to the police it was not his intention to convey a gift or to abandon the money. [...] [T]herefore his possessory rights to the money continued even after the money was turned over to the police.

Justice Trussler saw that the issue was about possession. Between the Attorney General of Canada and Mr Thomas, who had acquired possession first? Mr Thomas had.

The distinction between "lost" and "mislaid" has often been raised in cases involving pocketbooks left in retail premises.

Some have led to convictions for theft and have thus turned on the intentions of the defendant shopkeeper. Was he zealously guarding the article until its owner returned or sneaking a chance to enrich himself before the owner came looking? This examination of the defendant's state of mind has nothing to do with whether the pocketbook was better described as lost or mislaid; do the judges routinely discuss the distinction merely because it was raised in a vain defence?[14]

In others, disputes have arisen between the keeper of the retail premises and a customer or employee claiming to have found the pocketbook left behind by someone else.[15] The issue then is not whether the article was lost, and thus found, as opposed to being mislaid, and thus misappropriated. Rather, the issue is whether the shopkeeper had possession and was dispossessed. Looked at in this way, the issue is the same as it would be if the dispute were between the person who spotted the unattended pocketbook and the person

---

13 *Ibid* at paras 58-59.

14 See, for example, *R v West* (1854) 6 Cox CC 415 (Eng) in which a customer left a purse at the defendant's market stall. The defendant took possession, but she denied having seen it when the customer returned. Not surprisingly, the defendant was convicted of larceny. The judge commented that the defendant had not found the purse because it was not lost.

15 See *Bridges v Hawkesworth* (1851) 21 LJQB 75 (Eng) (plaintiff customer finds banknotes on floor of retail shop; owner not involved; defendant shopkeeper does not get possession), *McAvoy v Medina* 11 Allen 548, 93-94 Mass 548 (1866) (plaintiff customer picks up pocketbook left by someone on table in defendant's barbershop; owner not involved; barber gets possession), and *Jackson v Steinberg*,200 P 2d. 376 (Ore 1948) (chambermaid takes possession of eight $100 bills in hotel guest room; owner not involved; defendant employer gets possession). We'll review those cases in more detail in Chapter 7.

who left it unattended.[16] The issue in each case is whether the thing was *out of possession* when the person who took possession claims to have found it.

Maybe that's all lost means. Maybe a thing is lost if, once having been possessed, it no longer is, due to the previous possessor's unilaterally forfeiting control while retaining the intent to exclude others. It must be unilateral, for if someone dispossessed him or a voluntary transfer took place the thing is not lost.[17] The intent to exclude others must remain, for otherwise abandonment, not loss, has occurred. The loser may well be able to recover possession from the finder who takes possession, but that is a quite different matter. To repeat the point: taking possession upon finding is not interference with property in the common law system.

Third, *a finder who takes possession is in the same position as any other possessor.* The finder's possession is a form of property. The state will assist a possessor in precluding or redressing interference by anyone who does not hold property in the thing found. Against other property holders - of ownership, of right to immediate possession, or of a security interest in the thing found - the possessor by finding may or may not prevail, depending upon a few simple rules.[18] The key point is that these rules are not unique to finding. They are the same property rules that affect possession attained by other means. The *transaction* rules between the parties to a particular dispute may differ: for example, a person who acquired possession by contract may be contractually obliged (and lose possession) to someone whom a possessor by finding would defeat.[19] But the purpose here is to establish the property rules. Other rules affecting property holders are more easily understood once the property basics are set. In property law, once it is established that a finder has taken possession, disputes are resolved on the basis of his possession of

---

16 That is, the question is whether the latter held possession at the time the former took possession. If not, the finder is not liable for damages because he has not dispossessed the prior possessor. Whether the prior possessor can recover possession from such a finder is quite another question, as we soon shall see. Edward R Cohen, in his article "The Finders Cases Revisited" 48 Texas L Rev 1001, suggests (at 1014) that common law courts outside America have generally ignored the "lost" *versus* "mislaid" distinction. He is quite correct. He suggests that this is "because they have found *place of finding* infinitely more desirable and flexible". I doubt that it is flexibility which attracted British Commonwealth courts. Rather, the control of estate holders over the boundaries of land and manifestations of their intent to preclude others from interfering with things within the boundaries lead directly to the conclusion that all things there are already possessed: this theory is developed fully in Chapter 7.

17 Waif [a thing which was stolen and discarded by the thief during flight] may prove an exception. The rule still applies if the thief, a possessor after all, lost the thing. However, if the thief abandoned it, what I said may not be strictly accurate. Waif is not a big problem in our law anymore.

18 There really are only a few such property rules, although they have not been stated consistently or universally applied in common law cases. We'll analyze conflicts between a possessor by finding and other holders of property in the thing found in Chapter 7.

19 For example, A may have transferred possession of a rental car to B under a contract that specifies that B must transfer possession to C upon C's arrival from abroad. A can invoke the rules of contract to obtain a judicial order that B complete the transfer to C. It would not, however, be accurate to state that B or C holds right to immediate possession of the car. A contractual right to cause a future transfer of property in a thing is not a form of property in the thing: see *Lister* v *Stubbs* (1890) 45 Ch D 1 (Eng CA).

the thing found, not upon the act of finding.

Fourth, *a possessor by finding will lose possession to the holder of right to immediate possession of the thing found.* This is a simple priority rule. The key to using it is the preliminary step of determining whether a claimant holds right to immediate possession. The most likely such claimants are owners out of possession and prior possessors, but whether they are what they claim to be, how they got into that position, and precisely why their claims succeed have not always been explained clearly in common law cases. As we shall soon see, the arguments in cases involving finding have little to do with finding as such and are mostly concerned with whether the thing was lost, whether the finder took possession, and whether some other person holds right to immediate possession.

The common law finding cases illustrate and develop these basic points.

B   TAKING POSSESSION OF THINGS FOUND

A finder is at liberty to take possession of things he finds. Possession, like any other form of property, is a relationship.[20] To say that someone holds possession of a thing is to predict that the state will intervene on the holder's side to restrict the liberty of others in dealing with the thing.[21]

Possession comprises a physical and a mental element. Possession of a thing is proved by the coexistence of physical control and manifest intent to exclude other people. Because possession of lost things can be of great value, and because most things are lost and found where people assemble, disputes have often arisen as to who first found a thing and took possession of it. Such disputes help to clarify the two elements of possession.

Keron v *Cashman*[22] is the classic dispute among finders. Five boys were walking along railway tracks in New Jersey in 1896. The youngest, a nine year old named Crawford, picked up an old stocking that was stuffed and tied at both ends. Cashman, the oldest boy, snatched it from him or fetched it after it was thrown away (the evidence being unclear) and the boys began hitting one another with it. The stocking broke open during this play and some rags, ribbons and $775 in banknotes spilled out. An equal division was initially proposed and apparently was in progress when the boys were interrupted. The father of one of the boys turned the banknotes in to the police chief the next day. No owner appeared. Crawford claimed possession by finding; the other boys sought equal division. The matter was thus referred to the courts.

---

20 See Chapter I "Property and Things Contrasted".
21 *Ibid.*
22 *Keron* v Cashman, 33 A 1055 (NJ 1896).

It is useful to note the narrow issue in dispute, particularly because the judge seems to have forgotten it while expressing his reasoning. The only issue in the case was whether Crawford who first picked up the stocking thereby got possession of the banknotes inside. If yes, then the others could get possession only by dispossessing Crawford. If no, then no further judicial decision was required as the others conceded Crawford an equal share.

Did Crawford take possession of the money when he first picked up the stocking? Vice-Chancellor Emery dealt with the issue as follows:[23]

> the lost money which is the subject of the present controversy must be treated as legally found while in the common possession of all the defendants [because] the old stocking which contained the money and the other articles was, at the time the stocking burst open, in actual use by all the defendants as a plaything and for the purpose of play only.

The answer, I take it, is no. The phrase "legally found" only mystifies the analysis, and how "common possession" was achieved before the money was "legally found" is unexplained. However, what I think the judge meant is that *no one found and took possession of the banknotes before the stocking burst open.*[24]

> The stocking itself ... was not ... treated either by the boy who first picked it up or by any of the others as an article over which any ownership or possession was intended to be asserted for the purpose of examining or appropriating its contents. ... [A]s to this money, the first intention or 'state of mind' as it is called in some of the authorities, arose [when the stocking burst]. ... [Had Crawford] the boy who first picked up the stocking, retained it, or tried to retain it for the purpose of examining its contents ... the original possession or retention of the stocking by Crawford, its original finder, for such purpose of examination, might perhaps be considered as the legal 'finding' of the money enclosed ...

This quotation covers the two elements of possession. It notes the lack of control by Crawford. It also refers to the missing intention. The case is unusual in that the actual intentions of the boys at various times seem to have been in evidence. Usually only outward signs of intent perceived by others, manifestation of intention, are relied on, as most witnesses are unlikely to recall disadvantageous intentions. The judge went on to find that a finder has no property claim unless he takes possession and that one cannot take possession upon finding without forming some intention in relation to the thing found.[25]

---

23 33 A 1055 at 1056.
24 33 A 1055 at 1056.
25 33 A 1055 at 1057. Vice-Chancellor Emery can be made to say almost exactly this by replacing his terms "legal finder" with possessor and "lost property" with lost thing. Contrast *Perry* v *Gregory* 2003 CarswellPEI 97. Plaintiff and Defendant went on metal detecting expeditions. On one such expedition, Plaintiff received a signal from his machine. He asked Defendant to verify the reading, and stepped away so his machine would not interfere. Defendant got a positive reading, dug up an 18th century PEI Regiment belt plate, and handed it to Plaintiff. Plaintiff kept possession, but loaned it to Defendant on at least two

All of the cases agree that some intention or state of mind with reference to the lost property is an essential element to constitute a legal 'finder' of such property, and the peculiarity of the present case is that the intention or state of mind necessary to constitute the finder must relate to the lost money enclosed within a lost stocking, and not to the lost stocking itself, in the condition when first found; and under the circumstances established by the evidence in this case, the finder of the lost stocking was not, by reason of such finding, the legal finder of the lost money within the stocking. A decree will therefore be advised dividing the money equally between the defendants.

More recently, an Ontario court considered the same issue. In *Stonkus v The Queen*,[26] the plaintiff, a VIA Rail employee, came upon an unattended duffel bag at Union Station while on a break. In accordance with VIA Rail's policy, he deposited the bag with the baggage room senior and filled out a claim tag. Another VIA Rail employee opened the bag; it contained some $90,000 in American banknotes. The issue before the Ontario Court of Justice was whether the applicant was "a "true finder" at common law".[27] What the judge probably meant was whether the Mr Stonkus ever acquired possession of the bag. The answer was no.[28]

> In the present case it cannot be said that the Applicant purported to control the money nor did he in any way indicate an intention to possess the money. The Applicant was not aware of the contents of the bag when he found it and turned it in to lost and found. He only became aware of the contents of the bag some 43 days later. He lost the claim tag at some time subsequent to finding the bag and turning it in. [...] In the circumstances, it cannot be said that the Applicant was a true finder.

Again, the applicant, found the bag but he failed to take possession of it.[29]

Keron v Cashman, and *Stonkus* must not be extrapolated too far. It was not either plaintiff's failure to appreciate the value, or specific nature of the container's contents that cost him the ruling he sought. In each case, it was his failure to prove any proprietary attitude.

Another case, *Grafstein v Holme and Freeman*,[30] invites useful speculation on this point.

---

occasions. The judge held (at para 23) that the belt-plate "belonged" to Plaintiff. Defendant failed to show intention to exclude Plaintiff from it when he dug it up.

26 *Stonkus v The Queen* [2001] OJ No 1771.

27 *Ibid* at para 14.

28 *Ibid* at para 29.

29 Compare *Millas v British Colombia* [1999] BCJ No 3007 (BC), a case involving a bag finder who was able to prove that he held possession of the bag and the banknotes in it. In ordering that possession be returned to the plaintiff, Provincial Court Judge Baird Ellan held at page 5: "It is clear that while Mr. Millas retained only fleeting possession and conveyed the money directly to the police, he exercised control of it with a view to possessing it as against all but the true owner".

30 *Grafstein v Holme and Freeman* (1957) 12 DLR 2d 727 (Ont CA).

Holme was employed by Grafstein to keep his cellar clean. In the course of his duties Holme found a locked metal box. He showed it to Grafstein, who told him to put it on a shelf. Some time later Freeman, who was working as a handyman for Grafstein, became curious and cut the lock with a hacksaw. In the box was $37,910 in banknotes.

Grafstein won the ensuing fight for possession of the banknotes, possibly because he held an estate in the land where the box and money were stumbled upon by Holme.[31] But what if this had not been the case? Could we conclude that either Holme or Grafstein had taken possession of both box and contents before Freeman discovered the nature of the contents?

I suggest that Grafstein did exactly that. The nature of the container, a locked box without a key, made examination of the contents difficult without damaging the container itself. Grafstein clearly exercised control over the container, thereby restricting access to whatever was inside. The fact that he kept the locked box on a shelf in his basement surely manifested his intention to exclude others - particularly other persons invited there for a limited purpose as Holme and Freeman were. Even if the container had been an old stocking, Grafstein's actions would probably have been interpreted as the taking of possession of the contents. The fact that it was a locked box merely enhanced the degree of control and made it easier to conclude that he intended to monopolize whatever turned out to be inside.[32]

Eads v *Brazelton*[33] was a dispute over the salvage of a wreck in the Mississippi River. The plaintiff, having determined the wreck's location, marked it by putting blazes on lines of trees near the river bank so that the lines intersected at the wreck. When the defendant began salvaging the wreck the plaintiff sued but lost. The plaintiff's degree of control over the wreck was ruled insufficient.[34]

> The occupation or possession of property lost, abandoned, or without an owner must depend upon an actual taking of the property. ... Brazelton never attained to the possession of the wreck; ... he therefore had no title to it by occupancy; had no right upon

---

31 Whether Holme took possession of the box or its contents is complicated by the fact that he was an employee who found the box in the course of his duties. It could be argued that any possession he took was as agent for his employer or that he was contractually bound to relinquish to his employer possession of any objects found on the premises.

32 This conclusion was previewed in *Keron* v *Cashman* 33 A 1055 (NJ 1896) at 1056. Vice-Chancellor Emery, in explaining that no possession had been taken of the money hidden in the stocking, said: "[h]ad the stocking been like a pocketbook, an article generally used for containing money ... I think the original possession or retention of the stocking by Crawford ... might perhaps be considered as the legal 'finding' of the money enclosed, with other articles, in the stocking". Contrast *French* v *Sorano* 247 NW 2d 182 (Wis 1976) (banknotes found in car not possessed).

33 *Eads* v *Brazelton* 22 Ark 499, 79 Am Dec 88 (Ark 1861).

34 79 Am Dec 88 at 96-97 *per* Fairchild J. Had the plaintiff succeeded in proving possession of the wreck he would have thereby proved possession of the contents without yet knowing their description or the value of possessing them.

which judicial protection could operate. He had considered the wreck as his as its finder, but had not actually appropriated it to himself; his intention to possess was useless without detention of the property; ... he had not moved the wrecked property or secured it.

More control over the thing to be possessed was required. What degree of control would suffice was left to be decided in subsequent cases.

The plaintiff in *Eads* v *Brazelton* also foundered on the manifestation of intent requirement. Referring to the evidence before him, Fairchild J noted: "[i]t is not established that the defendants knew that Brazelton was about to work on the America".[35] The judge believed that Brazelton intended to salvage the wreck, but the important question was whether he had manifested that intent so that others might perceive it. Famous American fox hunting and bee-keeping cases were cited as pertinent contrasts. "[Post's] intention against the fox was unmistakable, but his act of possession was incomplete".[36] "Marking a bee-tree was a more emphatic claim against the bees than Brazelton's marks were upon the wreck, but was not sufficient to vest a right in the finder."[37] In short, the plaintiff found the wreck, but he failed to take possession of it. He therefore had no claim.

Eads, *Stonkus* and *Keron* v *Cashman* all show that there is a dividing line between finding and taking possession of a thing. Each described in fairly specific terms what was required to prove possession and then explained what particular facts in that case led to the conclusion that the line had not been crossed.

The Tubantia[38] fell on the other side of the line. The court applied the same tests and this time found sufficient facts to prove possession by the finder. A Dutch ship, sunk in 1916, was found by the plaintiffs, who initiated salvage operations in 1922 and continued sending divers down in the following spring and summer. By July of 1923 the plaintiffs had fixed buoys and tackle to the wreck to assist the divers in their salvage work.[39] Then the defendants anchored a ship nearby, sent down some divers and got sounding lines entangled with the plaintiffs' lines. The plaintiffs sought damages and an injunction against interference with possession of the wreck.

---

35 79 Am Dec 88 at 94. He said in a footnote that the plaintiff attempted, but failed, to prove that the defendant had used the marks on the trees to locate the wreck.

36 79 Am Dec 88 at 98, referring to *Pierson* v *Post* 3 Cai 175, 2 Am Dec 264 (NY 1805).

37 79 Am Dec 88 at 98, referring to *Gillet* v *Mason* 7 Johns 17.

38 *Tubantia (The)* [1924] P 78 (Eng HC). The wreck appears to have been in international waters, some 50 miles offshore and within 20 miles of France and Belgium. I have never understood how the law of England became applicable.

39 This was characterized in the case as "in the nature of fixed plant on and around the Tubantia, such that when the weather and the state of the tide permitted, divers could by its use work in and upon the wreck and among the cargo". The plaintiffs had extracted a small amount of cargo and spent about _40,000 by the time the defendants arrived.

The court ventured the following proposition: "a thing taken by a person of his own motion and for himself, and subject in his hands or under his control, to the uses of which it is capable, is in that person's possession".[40] Particularly important were the buoys and salvage equipment which the plaintiffs had fixed to the wreck, presumably as these were the strongest way of manifesting the existence of a claim in the circumstances.[41] The plaintiffs had taken possession sometime before the defendants arrived.[42]

> There was animus possidendi in the plaintiffs. There was the use and occupation of which the subject matter was capable. There was power to exclude strangers from interfering if the plaintiffs did not use unlawful force. ... I hold that the plaintiffs had, in July 1923, the possession of the Tubantia and her cargo, which they allege.

Both prerequisites of possession had been clearly satisfied in this case. Comparison with *Eads* v *Brazelton*[43] is informative. The degree of control over the Tubantia was greater, possibly because the salvage work was more advanced by the time the defendant came on the scene. What about intent? It seems to have been accepted in *Eads* that the plaintiff intended to exclude others from the wreck, yet the judge ruled that the intent requirement was not satisfied. The key distinction is that this intent would not have been apparent to passersby in *Eads*, but was made perfectly obvious – *ie*, manifested - in *The Tubantia*.

There are thousands of finders cases in the common law system. Almost all of them are resolved in part by a conclusion that either the finder or someone else had possession. However, the elements of possession are rarely discussed. Sometimes this is because someone's possession is conceded and the case is fought on some other issue.[44] In too many cases, however, the eventual loser in the case is ill-advised as to the importance of proving possession. That often happens as a result of careless terminology, which deflects attention from the details of what must be proved,[45] both in the reported cases

---

40 [1924] P 78 at 89. The court also suggested (at 89) that the following questions must be answered in determining whether a person had taken possession of a thing. "[W]hat are the kinds of physical control and use of which the things in question were practically capable? Could physical control be applied to the res [thing] as a whole? Was there a complete taking? Had the plaintiffs occupation for practical purposes sufficient to exclude strangers from interfering with the property? Was there animus possidendi?"

41 "The appliances I have mentioned, and the frequently interrupted access to the wreck which the plaintiffs had in the summer of 1923, are the evidences of possession at the dates in question in this case on which the plaintiffs rely." [1924] P 78 at 89.

42 [1924] P 78 at 90. An injunction was granted ordering the defendants to refrain from acting near the wreck and the question of damages was referred to the registrar.

43 *Eads* v *Brazelton* 22 Ark 499, 79 Am Dec 88 (Ark SC 1861), set out above.

44 This is usually the situation in cases involving estate holders and things found on land or disputes over possession of things found by employees in the course of their duties. Both these topics are covered in Chapter 7.

45 See, for example, *Lawrence* v *Buck* 62 Me 275 (Maine 1874), in which the plaintiffs spotted a chain cable lying part in a river and part coiled up on the bank. Having hauled about 60 ft out of the river, the plaintiffs left for the night. By morning the defendants had removed the cable. It was proved that the defendants had found the cable several days earlier, had pulled it part way out of the water and, being

and in current practice.

Popov v Hayashi[46] is an example. On 7 Oct 2001 at PacBell Park in San Francisco, Barry Bonds hit his 73rd homerun of the season, setting a new record. The ball reached the softball glove of Mr Popov in the stands, just as a crowd of people descended on him and forced him to the ground. Mr Hayashi was standing near Mr Popov. He too was forced to the ground. While on the ground he saw the loose ball. He picked it up, rose to his feet and put it in his pocket. Justice McCarthy defined the most critical factual finding to be whether Mr Popov retained control of the ball as he descended into the crowd. There was no reliable answer to this question so Justice McCarthy made up a new rule, under the pretence of equity.[47]

> Where an actor undertakes significant but incomplete steps to achieve possession of a piece of abandoned personal property and the effort is interrupted by the unlawful acts of others, the actor has a legally cognizable pre-possessory interest in the property.

Thus, he determined that Mr Popov and Mr Hayashi had an equal and undivided property interest in the ball.[48]

> Mr. Hayashi's claim is compromised by Mr. Popov's pre-possessory interest. Mr. Popov cannot demonstrate full control. Albeit for different reasons, they stand before the court in exactly the same legal position as did the five boys [from *Keron v Cashman*]. Their legal claims are of equal quality and they are equally entitled to the ball.

There was no need for the judge to discuss any "pre-possessory interest" in the homerun ball. If Mr Popov could not demonstrate control of the ball then he never held possession of it and could have no claim to possession of it.

In summary, a finder has no property in the thing found unless he assembles the evidence to prove possession. To take possession he must achieve some degree of control over the thing and must manifest his intent to exclude others. The degree of control required will vary, depending on the characteristics of the thing and the circumstances in which it was found. The manifestation of intent must be broadcast; it must be sufficiently clear to advise any remotely curious observer that the finder is making a proprietary claim.

---

called away by work, had left it as the plaintiffs later saw it. Justice Danforth said (at 276): "the defendants were the first finders, and (if it were necessary) ... before the finding of the plaintiffs, they had taken possession by such acts of ownership as the nature and condition of the property under the circumstances allowed ...". It isn't obvious why the plaintiffs' control and manifestation of intent were closer to *The Tubantia* facts than to *Eads v Brazelton*. Some clarification of these requirements would have been helpful.

46 *Popov v Hayashi* 2002 WL 31833731 (Cal).

47 *Ibid* at 7.

48 *Ibid* at 8.

Next we investigate potential property claims by and against a possessor by finding.

CHAPTER 6

FINDERS ON OFFENCE

The traditional starting point for finders on offence is *Armory* v *Delamirie.*[1] A chimney sweep had found and taken possession of a jewel. He took it to the defendant jeweller for appraisal. When the defendant refused to return possession of the jewel, the boy sued in trover.[2] No questions were asked about where the jewel was found and no other claimants appeared. The case is thus a pure possessor by finding against stranger dispute and the ruling was uncomplicated:

> the finder of a jewel, though he does not by such finding acquire an absolute property or ownership, yet he has such a property as will enable him to keep it against all but the rightful owner ...

Whether this is strictly accurate remains to be seen, but it leads to an impeccable conclusion on the facts. The jeweller in *Armory* v *Delamirie* was given possession by the plaintiff for the limited purpose of appraisal.[3] That transfer of possession would have been a perfect defence had he been accused of dispossessing the boy. But the plaintiff's complaint was that the jeweller was *withholding* possession after the expiry of the agreed term for which possession had been transferred. The jeweller held no other property in the jewel. The jeweller was ordered to return possession or pay damages. Despite the fact that the boy was not in possession at the time the dispute arose, having transferred possession to the jeweller by a bailment transaction, the case has traditionally been cited for the proposition that *possessors by finding prevail against defendants who hold no property in the thing found.*

This analysis is uncontroversial so far. Now let's take it toward its logical conclusion. *Possessors by finding prevail against defendants who hold no property in the thing found irrespective of the circumstances of finding.* Indeed, the fact that the thing was found is a red herring: it is possession that the courts protect against strangers, not the way possession was acquired.

> One who has acquired the possession of property, whether by finding, bailment, or by mere tort, has a right to retain that possession as against a mere wrongdoer who is a stranger to the property. Any other rule would lead to an endless series of seizures and reprisals in every case where property had once passed out of the possession of the rightful owner.[4]

---

1 *Armory* v *Delamirie* (1722) 1 Str 505, 93 ER 664 (Eng).

2 Trover was one of the common law actions for interference with property in things. It is explained in detail in a note to *Wilbraham* v *Snow* 2 Wms Saunders 87 at 89 (omitted from the English Reports version).

3 He thus held possession as a bailee: see Chapter 10 "Bailment: a Separate Transaction?". A bailee is obliged to return possession to the bailor, or to someone he designated, upon expiry of *or refusal to carry out* the terms of the bailment transaction.

4 *Anderson* v *Gouldberg* 53 NW 636 (Minn 1892) (action to recover possession of logs cut by plaintiff).

Many have resisted this proposition; few have explained their objections. The perceived problem seems to be that a "wrongdoer" must not profit by his actions. This is a misguided sentiment. Consider the position of a trespassing boy who finds a gold watch, puts it in his pocket and leaves the premises. Either he has possession or he does not: he certainly has control and manifest intent to exclude others. Assume the owner has disappeared.[5] The boy, a trusting sort, shows the watch to a Rogue whom he meets on the street. Rogue examines the watch and pockets it. I say the boy had possession and can sue for return of possession. I should draw the same conclusion, on the same basis, if Rogue had picked the boy's pocket, or beaten him up and stolen[6] the watch. How would the "boy had no possession" school analyze Rogue's actions?[7]

Bird v *The Town of Fort Frances*[8] is one of the few cases in which a court was forced to address this point.[9] A 12 year old boy, surely a trespasser and possibly a thief, crawled

---

Compare *Parker* v *British Airways Board* [1982] 2 WLR 503 (Eng CA) at 506 *per* Donaldson LJ: "[the rule in *Armory*] must be right as a general proposition, for otherwise lost property would be subject to a free-for-all in which the physically weakest would go to the wall".

5 If the owner shows up he will be awarded possession against the boy. An owner holds right to immediate possession in lost things: see "Owners' Claims" in Chapter 7. Note that this will not change the conclusion that the finder held possession between the time he took possession and the time he returned possession to the owner.

6 I use the word advisedly. If the boy did not have possession of the watch it could not be stolen from him. This "would lead to an endless series of unlawful seizures and reprisals" as pointed out in the quotation from *Anderson* v *Gouldberg* set out above, *except that only the reprisals would be unlawful*, as neither criminal nor civil consequences would follow the seizures.

7 They might refer you to *Cartwright* v *Green* (1802) 8 Ves 405, 32 ER 412 (Eng). Ann Cartwright hid 900 guineas in a secret bureau drawer and died. Ownership of the bureau was inherited, or possession of it was acquired (the facts are ambiguous) by her brother, and later transferred to Dick, who sent it to Green for repairs. Green opened the drawer during repairs. The usual fight for possession of the coins followed. Lord Chancellor Eldon, in the course of reaching the unremarkable conclusion that Green could not keep possession, advanced a remarkably complex theory of property.

> If I send a bureau to a cabinet maker for repair, he possesses the bureau as against me; but I possess the contents of a secret drawer in the bureau as against him if he finds and takes them with intent permanently to deprive me of them; yet he would surely possess the same contents as against a third person who steals or takes them tortuously while the cabinet-maker possesses the bureau.

Not so. Either the cabinet maker holds possession of the coins or he does not. If he does, he may be forced to relinquish possession to someone holds right to immediate possession (the plaintiff for example). The Lord Chancellor has confused the simple issue of who *holds* a form of property in a thing with the quite separate (and equally simple if kept separate) issue of who can force a transfer of that form of property by invoking judicial action.

8 *Bird* v *The Town of Fort Frances* [1949] OR 292, [1949] 2 DLR 791 (Ont).

9 *Anderson* v *Gouldberg* 53 NW 636 (Minn. 1892) was another. The plaintiff sued for and won possession of some logs he had cut, the defendant having dispossessed him. Before ruling the plaintiff's prior possession sufficient in the quote set out above, the judge noted that,

> the plaintiff's obtained possession of the logs in the first instance by trespassing upon the land of some third party. Therefore the only question is whether bare possession of property, though wrongfully obtained, is sufficient title to enable the party enjoying it to maintain replevin against a

under a pool room and emerged in possession of a tin which obviously had been placed on a ledge forming part of the understructure. Inside the tin was about $1500 in banknotes. The boy took the banknotes home and handed them to his mother. A policeman eventually found out what had happened, inquired, and was handed the banknotes by the mother. When no one claimed ownership, possession of the banknotes was transferred to the town treasurer. The mother brought an action for possession on behalf of the boy.[10]

The boy won. Chief Justice McRuer clearly saw that the boy was a trespassing finder, but ruled that this made no difference to the dispute before him, which was between a possessor by finding and a stranger. Whether the estate holder in the land where it was found could have defeated the boy's claim was moot.[11] The judge stopped short of finding "felonious intent" – *ie*, he declined to draw the conclusion that the boy was a thief – but he said *obiter* that such a finding would not have affected his conclusion. The boy had taken possession of the bank notes and was entitled to the same judicial protection against strangers as any other possessor.[12]

Another wrong-doer recovered possession in *Webb v Chief Constable of Merseyside*.[13] A police officer had seized possession of some banknotes from suspect Roy Webb. The Liverpool County Court decided that, on the balance of probabilities, the money was

---

mere stranger who takes it from him.
For further analysis of this type of claim, see the later heading "Dispossessed Prior Possessors".

10 This is probably not strictly accurate. Before the action was commenced the town treasurer had "deposited the money in a bank account". The legal effect of this was to create a debt contract requiring the bank to pay on demand a sum equal to the deposited capital plus accumulated interest. The particular bank notes had re-entered circulation upon deposit and no previous possessor or owner retained right to immediate possession even if the notes could be traced. The boy was suing for the bank account, that is, for the depositor's contractual right of withdrawal, or its value.

11 Interestingly, the estate holder turned up during the trial, but was scared off by McRuer's, CJ ruling that he could either hold his peace or be joined as a party to make his claim at the risk of incurring costs should he lose. How his claim might have fared is covered in Chapter 7.

12 Compare *Buckley* v *Gross* (1863) 3 B & S 566, 122 ER 213 (Eng), which might have upheld the broad proposition in favour of possessors but for an obscure statute. Quantities of tallow were stored by various owners in a Thames-side warehouse. Fire melted the tallow and it flowed into the main sewers and the river. The plaintiff purchased possession of some of the tallow from a finder. The police seized possession from the plaintiff and, when the owners could not be traced, sold ownership to the defendant. The plaintiff sued the defendant to regain possession. He lost, but only because of the *Police Act* 2 & 3 Vict c 71 s 29. Chief Justice Cockburn described the impact of the statute as follows:

the magistrate ... may make an order for the delivery of the article ... to the real owner, if he can be found; if he cannot, then the magistrate may make an order for the detention of the article; and, it would appear, by implication, ... to sell, after the lapse of twelve months. ... The possession of the plaintiff was lawfully taken out of him by the order of the magistrate, and after that the defendants acquired possession; and therefore the possessory right of the plaintiff could not be enforced.

Similarly, see *Irving* v *National Provincial Bank Ltd* [1962] 2 QB 73 (Eng CA) (police seizure under statutory power from suspected thief).

13 *Webb v Chief Constable of Merseyside* [2000] 1 All ER 209 (Eng CA).

proceeds of drug trafficking. Mr Webb appealed against the refusal to return possession to him. The Court of Appeal ruled in his favour.[14]

> [The Chief Constable] has no continuing right to retain the money in the face of a better claim by Roy Webb to possess it, notwithstanding the finding ... that, on the balance of probabilities, the money was the proceeds of dealing in drugs.

Some judges have complicated the analysis by enforcing what they call "public policy" to the detriment of the wrongful possessor.[15] Justice Lightman, put paid to that theory in *Costello v Chief Constable of Derbyshire*.[16]

> There are authorities (e.g. Bird) which reveal a natural moral disinclination (on occasion expressed in terms of public policy) to recognise the entitlement of a thief, receiver or other wrong-doer to the protection by the law of his possession, and one decision (namely Solomon) refusing such protection. But it is clear from Webb that such a disinclination and public policy do not afford a sufficient ground to deprive a possessor of such recognition and protection. This conclusion is in accord with that long ago reached by the courts that even a thief is entitled to the protection of the criminal law against the theft from him of that which he has himself stolen ... .

The general proposition - possessors by finding prevail against defendants who hold no property in the thing found irrespective of the circumstances of finding - is supportable.[17] However, readers familiar with the common law cases will not be persuaded without some clarification. One of the more controversial of those cases, *Bridges* v *Hawkesworth*,[18] illustrates the problem.

> Plaintiff, a traveller for a firm with whom the defendant shopkeeper had dealings, called on business. While leaving, the plaintiff picked up a parcel from the floor. He showed it to the defendant's "shopman" and then opened it. Inside were banknotes worth _55. The plaintiff asked the defendant to hold possession and advertise for the owner. Three years later, there having been no response to the ad, the plaintiff asked for possession, offering to pay for the ad and to indemnify the shopkeeper against any future claims. Refused, he

---

14 *Ibid* at 227 (*per* Pill LJ).

15 See *Solomon v Metropolitan Police Commissioner* [1982] Crim LR 606, in which public policy was said to preclude a thief from recovery. See also *Baird v British Colombia* [1992] BCWLD 2435 (BC CA) at para 24: "I am satisfied that ... the conduct of Mr Baird giving rise to his claim is so tainted with criminality or culpable immorality that as a matter of public policy the Court should not assist him to recover". Isn't public policy a matter for politicians, not judges?

16 [2001] 3 All ER 150, citing Smith & Hogan *Criminal Law* 9th ed p 522.

17 It makes no difference whether the person who holds no property in the thing found is a defendant or a plaintiff: the rule resolves disputes between possessors by finding and strangers. I have used this formulation to illustrate that a finder's possession (indeed, any possession) is an offensive weapon which the holder wields against the rest of the world. Non-stangers - eg owners, dispossessed prior possessors, estate holders in land where things are found, the state in treasure trove cases - may hold right to immediate possession, a superior offensive weapon: more about that later.

18 *Bridges* v *Hawkesworth* (1851) 21 LJQB (ns) 75 (Eng).

sued "to recover the notes". He lost in the County Court, but won on appeal.

The appeal, according to Patteson J, "resolves itself into the single point ... whether the circumstances of the notes being found *inside* the defendant's shop, gives him, the defendant, the right to have them as against the plaintiff who found them".[19] In other words, the issue was whether the defendant had held possession of the notes on the floor before the plaintiff picked them up.[20] If yes, that possession was protected against strangers like the plaintiff. If no, the plaintiff was a possessor by finding and the defendant shopkeeper was just like the jeweller in *Armory v Delamirie*. The judges' answer was no.[21]

> The notes never were in the custody of the defendant, nor within the protection of his house, before they were found, as they would have been had they been intentionally deposited there. ... We find ... no circumstances in this case to take it out of the general rule of law that the finder of a lost article is entitled to it against all parties except the real owner; and we think that rule must prevail, and that the learned Judge was mistaken in holding that the place in which they were found makes any legal difference.

Note the logical progression. Step 1: the defendant did not hold possession of the notes before the plaintiff picked them up. Step 2: *consequently*, the plaintiff defeated the defendant because *possessors by finding prevail against defendants who hold no property in the thing found irrespective of the circumstances of finding.*

Bridges v *Hawkesworth* is wrong.[22] It is wrong in its conclusion at step 1, that the shopkeeper did not have possession of the banknotes on the floor. Step 2 is not the problem. If the plaintiff was the possessor by finding of a lost – ie, out of possession - thing, then the plaintiff's possession prevails against the shopkeeper, a stranger. The circumstances of finding[23] may determine whether someone other than the finder holds property in the thing found. However, the circumstances of finding can have no effect on

---

19 The defendant's lawyer argued that his client had possession and recited a Latin maxim, a formerly fashionable courtroom practice. "That [the latin maxim] assumes that they are deposited there for custody of the owner of the house intentionally. The facts of this case negative that the defendant knew anything about the notes being in his shop." 21 LJQB (ns) 75 at 78 *per* Patteson J]. Might the defendant have won if his lawyer spoke English?

20 "It was well asked on the argument, if the defendant has the right, *when* did it accrue to him? If at all, it must have been antecedent to the finding by the plaintiff, for that finding could not give the defendant any right": 21 LJQB (ns) 75 at 78 *per* Patteson J.

21 21 LJQB (ns) 75 at 78 *per* Patteson J.

22 See Chapter 7.

23 I am being a bit careless with this term. See Chapter 5, "Losing Things and Finding Things" where I suggested that the issue is not whether the article was lost and thus found (as opposed to being mislaid and thus misappropriated) but whether the shopkeeper had possession and was dispossessed. The issue between the parties in *Bridges v Hawkesworth* was whether the thing was *out of possession* when the plaintiff claimed to have found it. As I said earlier, this may be all that "lost" means. It doesn't matter: the common law protects possessors, not finders.

the relationship between a possessor by finding and a stranger who holds no property at all.

Why? Because that relationship is possession!

This brings us to the question of what a possessor by finding can do to protect his possession against strangers. The answer, not surprisingly, is that he can do what any other possessor can.

Self help is the most common remedy. Threats of violence tend to be frowned on, but manifestation of the intent to exclude others *within the law* is the possessor's primary offensive weapon and is sufficient to deter most strangers. Whether armed response is within the law, and whether polite reminders deter, vary widely among the common law jurisdictions. However, a possessor by finding faced with violence is usually well advised to surrender possession and resort to legal action to recover possession or damages later, to avoid both personal injury and potential legal liability for over-reaction. Similarly, when a possessor by finding has been dispossessed by a stranger, retaking possession by peaceful means is permissible. Resort to trespass or violence is likely to prove costly. A civil action for repossession is the approved method.

An action to regain possession of a thing sounds more straightforward than it is. There is the possibility of an alternate remedy, damages. It is by no means clear when damages, rather than an order for possession, will be awarded. Also, the calculation of damages in possession cases is almost always wrong, due to a serious property *versus* thing confusion in most of the precedent cases. Our previous example helps to illustrate the problem.

> A trespassing boy finds a gold watch, takes possession and leaves the premises. The boy shows the watch to a Rogue whom he meets on the street. Rogue examines the watch and pockets it. Rogue previously held no property in the watch.

The boy has been dispossessed by Rogue. He brings a legal action against Rogue. Consider the possibilities. The boy may seek repossession or damages; his lawyer probably advises alternative claims for both. Rogue may have disposed of possession of the watch to someone who has disappeared. The watch may have become damaged in the interim, or may have been destroyed. Rogue may place a higher value on possession than the boy does and may be happy to pay damages. Who gets to decide what the remedy will be?

Can the boy get an order for repossession? He can not if the watch no longer exists, or has disappeared: judges are not in the habit of issuing futile orders.[24] But what if Rogue

---

24 It is useful to keep in mind that all judges can do is give a defendant a choice of doing what the judge recommends or going to jail for contempt of court. It is fanciful to pretend that a judicial order means more than that; a determined Rogue, told to transfer possession to the boy, could easily destroy the watch and

still holds possession? Can a defendant use the judicial system to force a transfer of possession by insisting on damages as the transfer price? Whether possession or damages was the remedy, and what was the appropriate time for assessing damages, used to be dictated by the form of the plaintiff's claim.[25] Many jurisdictions now have rather less rigid rules of practice. They allow an action to be brought without using one of the old technical labels, invite the plaintiff to specify alternative remedies, and leave the selection of remedies to judicial discretion.[26] Under such a system, it is likely that a plaintiff can force an order for repossession against a defendant in possession who would rather pay damages, but local practices may vary.

Can the boy get an order for damages? The answer is unclear in a situation where the defendant is willing and able to restore possession of the undamaged watch. Interim damages may be the only way to compensate the plaintiff for the time since dispossession, but if the purpose of the action is to restore the plaintiff's loss, isn't repossession preferable to a judicial estimate of damages? Where the watch has disappeared, or has been damaged, damages may be the appropriate remedy.

The focus then shifts to a simple question: what is the measure of damages for loss of possession of a watch?

The obvious answer - an amount of money equal to the proven value of the plaintiff's possession of the watch - is generally regarded as wrong. The conclusion of most analysts is that the plaintiff collects damages equal to the *ownership* value of the watch.

---

take the consequences. The whole system works only if we assume that most defendants will be persuaded to comply with the order. It would make no sense for a judge, in such a system, to issue an order which could not possibly be obeyed.

25 The common law causes of action are a fascinating, but much misunderstood topic. There is an admirable explanation in R Sutton, *Personal Actions at Common Law* (Butterworths London 1929) at 46-71. In *trover* the plaintiff alleged that the defendant had been found in possession and sought damages on the ground that the defendant was depriving the plaintiff of the value of holding possession (at 49). In *detinue*, which evolved before trover, the plaintiff alleged wrongful detention and sought possession of the thing, although the defendant "could wage his law" and "was at liberty to satisfy the judgment by paying the value of the property and keeping it" (at 50). *Conversion*, in which the plaintiff sought damages and alleged that the defendant had "converted [the thing] to his own use", developed later and usurped the roles of trover and detinue. *Trespass* "was the appropriate remedy [for] direct invasion of a right by force ... while case lay [if] one of those elements was lacking" (at 57). *Replevin* tested whether a distraint had been warranted and was therefore only available against defendants like landlords and sheriffs who had levied distress [seized possession as security]: the remedy was damages, but this was because the plaintiff would have already applied to the sheriff, promised to sue upon the illegality of the original distress and to retransfer possession should he lose, and had the thing *replevied* before commencing the action; thus, the plaintiff held possession and sought damages for temporary dispossession (at 66).

26 In my own jurisdiction, Ontario, this is the general approach of the *Courts of Justice Act* SO 1984 C 11 s 117 and of Rule 44.01 of the *Rules of Practice*, subordinate rules relating to the conduct of legal actions and of interest chiefly to the Ontario bar. This is not the place to go into detail concerning these unhappily worded rules or similar ones in other jurisdictions.

Their analysis goes something like this: (i) "against a wrongdoer possession is title",[27] (ii) "one who takes [possession from a possessor] is a wrong-doer and cannot defend himself by showing that there was title in some third person",[28] and (iii) therefore the plaintiff gets "the full value of the article wrongfully taken".[29] That can't be right.

Boy and Rogue help illustrate the point. What if, seconds after Rogue dispossessed boy, Owner saw Rogue consulting the watch and grabbed it? Neither boy nor Rogue has any claim against Owner.[30] To award the boy the ownership value of the watch is to overcompensate him for his loss. He lost possession. The value of ownership is the market price of possession forever. We now know that the owner was about and that the boy's possession would not have lasted long. *Or do we?* Owner might or might not have found the boy in possession - why did we not consider that possibility before? Why does Rogue's dispossession by Owner cause us to speculate? All Owner's appearance has done is change the odds on how long the boy's possession would have lasted, but for Rogue's intervention.[31]

The amount of the boy's loss is the value of the property he held. The property he held was possession and we value possession by assessing a *rental* value. The marketplace sets the cost of possession of a rental car, or a rented tuxedo, by fixing a daily rate; the rental value is worked out by multiplying that rate by the length of time of possession.[32]

---

27 *Winkfield (The)* [1902] P 42 (Eng CA) (an action by a possessor through bailment for damages against a tortfeasor who held no property. See also *Jeffries* v *Great Western Railway Co* (1856) 5 El & Bl 802, 119 ER 680 (Eng).

28 *Jeffries* v *Great Western Railway Co* (1856) 5 El& Bl 802, 119 ER 680 (Eng); *Halsbury's Laws of England* 3rd ed vol 38 p 758 para 1247 (f), (g).

29 *Wilson* v *Lombank Ltd* [1963] 1 WLR 1294 (Eng), in which the innocent possessor of a stolen car won damages against the defendant trespasser. The assessed damages were equal to the amount the plaintiff had paid to a previous possessor when he thought, wrongly, that he was purchasing ownership. The plaintiff would have lost less if he had not been tricked by the previous transferee, which is hardly attributable to the defendant. The case is criticized in more detail in Chapter 10 "Bailment: a Separate Transaction?". See also *Winkfield (The)* [1902] 2 WLR 503 (Eng CA) at 55 *per* Collins MR: "[i]t cannot be denied that since the case of *Armory* v *Delamirie*, not to mention earlier cases from the Year Books onward, a mere finder may recover against a wrongdoer the full value of the thing converted". So he says: I deny it.

30 Everyone agrees, I think, that an owner can recover possession against a possessor by finding and against a thief (or possessor by tort): see "Owners' Claims" in Chapter 7. Owner here has resorted to self help.

31 Note also that it makes no substantial difference whether Owner repossesses the watch before or after the hearing, or whether he ever shows up at all. Those who say that there is a rule against raising the fact that the plaintiff was only a possessor and putting him to the proof of his damages also claim that there is an "exception" to the rule when the defendant has restored possession to the owner: see *Salmond on Torts* (13th ed) at 280. Real rules don't have exceptions (with one exception: consider the rule, "there's an exception to every rule").

32 Ignoring special deals like "weekend" rates and volume discounts. If the thing is damaged it is the possessor's rental value, not the ownership value, that is lowered. Incidentally, the conventional theory seems to be that the possessor of a rented car collects the ownership value from a car thief! I don't think so! Such rental transactions are dealt with in Chapter 10.

The boy lost the rental value of the watch for the length of time he would have retained possession, but for Rogue's act of dispossession. It may be difficult to estimate that length of time, just as with another type of tort damages it is difficult to project the lifetime earnings loss of a disabled accident victim. But we do not pretend that every accident victim would have become a prominent brain surgeon. Avoiding difficult calculations is a poor excuse for pretending that possessors are owners.

Let's examine the three step charade noted above. First, "against a wrongdoer possession is title [*ie*, ownership]". This notion may have grown out of the 19th century transition from the old forms of action, which were all based on possession of things, to new causes of action developed to protect property other than property in things - property like patents, copyright, and corporate shares. During that transition, there evolved the rather foggy notion that for things other than land, ownership was *the* property and only owners had legal claims. I described the problem with that terminology in Chapters 1 and 2. It caused many analysts to forget that possession has always been a form of property in the common law system, and interference with possession has always been sufficient cause for legal action. It makes no sense to pretend that the possessor of a thing is its owner when he clearly is not.

How do we know the plaintiff is not the owner? Look at the second supposed rule: "one who takes [possession from a possessor] is a wrong-doer and cannot defend himself by showing that there was title in some third person". This is worded as if it were a rule of evidence, directed at preventing the defendant from proving certain facts. If so, its proponents are confused about what the defendant is trying to say. The defendant admits dispossessing the plaintiff and is prepared to compensate the plaintiff for his loss. The only remaining issue is the amount of loss the plaintiff suffered. Evidence that someone else held property in the thing is relevant *if it tells us something about that issue*. The issue is the value of the plaintiff's possession, and that is a function of how long his possession would have lasted. Evidence that someone else owned the thing is probative of that issue. It also suggests that the defendant is clearly not the owner. The supposed rule would suppress evidence that the plaintiff, who claims the ownership value, is lying about the nature of his claim.

The third step - the plaintiff gets "the full value of the article wrongfully taken" is just another example of confusing property and things. Can you value a painting, or a car? Would you pay more for possession of the Mona Lisa say for 15 seconds) than for ownership of the Mona Gorilla; more to rent (ie, acquire possession of) a new Lincoln for a day than to buy (ie, acquire ownership of) a new Diet Chevy? Things don't have value; property does. If the third proposition was meant to follow from the first two, it falls with them.33 If it was meant to be independent, it simply makes no sense unless translated to "plaintiff gets the full value of the *property* wrongfully taken". Rogue in our example

---

33 As falls Wichita, so falls Wichita Falls (as a Texican would say).

deprived the boy of his probably temporary possession of the watch. The full value (judicially determined from the admissible evidence) of that temporary possession is the amount of damages Rogue must pay.

That brings us back to our starting point. In *Armory* v *Delamirie*:[34]

> the Chief Justice directed the jury, that unless the defendant did produce the jewel, and shew it not to be of the finest water, they should presume the strongest against him, and make the value of the best jewels the measure of their damages: which they accordingly did.

Consider what that means in terms of evidence and facts. As to quality, the chimney sweep was in no position to classify the jewel. The jeweller was, and the jury, having no evidence on the point, estimated the high-quality end of the spectrum of possibilities. Similarly, the jeweller seems not to have brought up such key questions as where the jewel was found, which might have helped the jury determine whether the owner was likely to appear. Having no evidence on the point, there was no reason to predict the chimney sweep's early dispossession. The jury could properly have valued his possession at or near the ownership value.[35]

The position of a possessor by finding who becomes a plaintiff is easily summarized. There are legal rules protecting possession. A possessor by finding is, like any other possessor, able to take advantage of them. The proper remedy for interference with possession is a return of possession, or damages. In the case of damages for dispossession, 20th century analysts wrongly equated the value of possession with the value of ownership.

---

34 *Armory v Delamirie* (1722) 1 Str 505, 93 ER 664 (Eng)

35 I don't say that that is what the jury did. The jury relied on the law given to them by the judge and the judge relied on the law argued by the parties' lawyers, who are unlikely to have dwelt on the distinction between ownership value and possession value. Common law analysts sometimes make too much of reasons for judgment, forgetting that they tend to be a product of the arguments presented by two barristers, rather than a thoughtful overview of the area in dispute. The academic's most useful task is to devise theories that account for the facts of a broad range of cases, rather than just reproduce and compare judicial summaries of the law.

CHAPTER 7

FINDERS ON DEFENCE

We saw, under the previous heading, how a finder's possession is legally protected against those who hold no form of property in the thing found. Some people, however, can win possession from the finder as plaintiffs in legal actions.

Neither finding a lost thing nor taking possession of it is actionable.[1] Traditionally, it has been considered a service to holders of property in the thing found to remove it to a safe place.[2] No payment is due for this service[3] and no liability is incurred.[4] However, a finder may find himself legally dispossessed if the right person happens along.

Plaintiffs who win possession from finders fall into four major categories. First, the *owner* of the thing found almost always wins. Second, a *prior possessor* has almost as good a claim as the owner: there are sub-categories of prior possessors and, particularly in the case of estate holders and things found on land, there is no consensus that prior possession is sufficient or necessary. Third, an *employer of the finder*, or certain others with whom the finder had dealings, may be able to get an order to transfer possession without proving any property in the thing found. Finally, *the state* may have a claim.

A   OWNERS' CLAIMS

Owners defeat possessors by finding in actions for possession. This proposition has been accepted for so long that, apparently, there are no cases trying the issue. We generally find the point made *obiter* in related cases.[5]

---

1 See "Losing Things and Finding Things" in Chapter 5.

2 "It is the law of charity to lay up the goods which do thus come to his hands by trover [*ie*, by finding, from the French *trouver*], and no trespass shall lie for this": *Isaack* v *Clark* (1615) 2 Bulstr 306, 80 ER 1143 (Eng KB) *per* Coke CJ (finder who took possession of a bag of coins was found not liable for damages to the loser).

3 There is no shortage of suggestions to the contrary among the "ought-istic" school of law. See, for example, *Nicholson* v *Chapman* (1793) 126 ER 536 (Eng). Advertisements offering rewards may generate contractual obligations: see the next heading "Owners' Claims".

4 See *Isaack* v *Clark* (1615) 2 Bulstr 306, 80 ER 1143 (Eng KB) (finder who took possession of bag of coins not liable for damages to loser). Similarly, no "felonious intent" is imputed from the simple act of taking possession upon finding: *R* v *Christopher* (1849) 8 Cox 91 (Eng) (purse found in meadow); *R* v *Matthews* (1873) 12 Cox 489 (Eng) (when defendant took possession of two stray heifers, "the presumption is that he took them for safe custody"). A conviction is possible if the finder intended to deprive the holder of property in the thing: see *R* v *David Thurborn* (1849) 2 C& K 831 (Eng) (defendant spending bank note after hearing that X had lost it) and *Rex* v *Wynne* (1786) 1 Leach 412, 168 ER 308 (Eng) (coachman opening and removing contents of box left in coach by passenger).

5 Chief Justice Coke in *Isaack* v *Clark* (1615) 2 Bulst 306, 80 ER 1143 (Eng KB): "when a man doth finde goods ... it is in his election whether he will take them or not into his custody, but when he hath them, one only hath then right unto them, and therefore ... if he be wise, he will then search out the right owner of them and so deliver them unto him" (plaintiff alleged previous possession; defendant found to be bailee). Justice Patteson in *Bridges* v *Hawksworth* (1851) 21 LJQB(ns) 75 (Eng) at 78: "the general rule of law [is] that the finder of a lost article is entitled to it against all parties except the real owner" (finder defeats

A plaintiff's ownership claim is too rarely disputed. Most people these days claim ownership of things through sale or gift transactions, but a sale or a gift can transfer only what property the seller or giver held.[6] Most plaintiffs will find it difficult to prove a chain of transactions from some indisputable source of ownership. The sure ones are (i) discovery[7], (ii) creation[8], (iii) purchase in "market overt"[9] (where applicable), (iv) purchase from a statute-based purveyor such as the holder of a "perfected security interest" in a thing who seized possession and sold ownership[10] and (v) state grant (which is rare in the case of things other than land, and which is analyzed later). Apart from relatively new cars, how many of the things we claim to own could be proved by reliable documentation or witnesses to have come into our possession through or after one of those events? The recommended response to an ownership claim is "so you say".[11]

Once the plaintiff's ownership is either conceded or proved the case is virtually over. The owner will get an order for possession or damages.[12] The amount of damages would be the ownership value of the thing.[13]

---

keeper of shop where bank notes found). Similarly, see *Hamaker* v *Blanchard* 90 Penn St 377 (1879) (servant in hotel finds bank notes and wins possession against employer).

6 This is one of the most important basic points in the common law of property. By tradition or pretension, it is usually expressed by mouthing a Latin phrase, *nemo dat quod non habet*. Many people seem to think that an effective response is the Equity-mongers' refrain – "a bona fide purchaser for value without notice [of a defect in the putative seller's title]" gets ownership. Anyone who believes that will have difficulty explaining why an innocent dupe who thinks he bought ownership of a stolen car gets dispossessed when the police find the car and contact the owner.

7 See Chapter 3 "Discovery: the First Finder's Property".

8 See Chapter 3 "Creation of Things".

9 Certain areas of the City of London in England were designated "market overt" and purchasers from sellers there bought ownership even if the things "fell of the back of a lorry" and were thus precariously possessed by the sellers. See *Market Overt Case* (1596) 5 Co Rep 83b, *Anon* (1701) 12 Mod Rep 521. The concept was not generally adopted in other common law countries.

10 Well known examples are Article 9 "Secured Transactions" of the *Uniform Commercial Code*, adopted in most American states, and the *Personal Property Security Act* in various Canadian provinces. For a basic analysis, see Chapter 2 "Security Interests".

11 In *Moffatt* v *Kazana* [1969] 2 QB 152 (Eng) the transferee of an estate in land moved into the house and eventually found banknotes hidden in a biscuit tin. The previous estate holder, now dead, had been seen several years earlier removing some banknotes from where the tin was hidden. The judge concluded:

> the evidence ... is susceptible of only one reasonable inference, namely that there was _1987 in the biscuit tin belonging to Mr Russell ... . If one starts from that point, it is argued on behalf of the plaintiffs [inheritors from Russell] that Mr Russel was the true owner of the money.

Well, the plaintiffs would say that, wouldn't they? What about the equally reasonable inference that Mr Russell stole the money long ago? Why did he keep it secret? Could the plaintiffs *prove* ownership?

12 As to which of damages or possession can be ordered at whose whim, see "Finders on Offence" in Chapter 6. The answer may depend on local rules of civil procedure peculiar to each jurisdiction.

13 This can be less precise than it sounds: see Waddams *The Law of Damages* (Canada Law Book Toronto 1983) at 6 ff. "The Meaning of Value".

A finder who takes possession is not obliged to seek the owner,[14] although it is easy to find offhand judicial statements suggesting otherwise. If the finder simply keeps the thing safe, makes no use of it, and returns possession when the owner shows up and asks for it, no damages are payable at all. The reason becomes clear when we look at the gist of the plaintiff's claim. In detinue, the old cause of action for regaining possession, the plaintiff lost unless a demand for possession had been made before the action was commenced.[15] The finder's possession before the demand was not regarded as "wrongful detention", which was the key to the action: keeping the thing safe and refraining from seeking the owner are too passive to be described by the word detention.[16] Consequently, the owner does not get damages for the time from loss until request for repossession from a finder who simply kept possession. This must be the result even where the owner retraced his steps and would have found the lost thing had the finder not moved it. Many finders take possession and try to find the owner without thinking about potential legal consequences or financial gain. Expanding the scope of liability for possessors by finding might discourage finders from taking lost things into safekeeping, wouldn't enhance the owners' repossession prospects, and might keep lost things out of circulation: none of these is in the economic interests of society.

By contrast, hiding or "converting" the thing found may increase damages. A finder who conceals his find might owe damages for prolonging the time out of possession, though this might be hard to prove. A finder who "converts to his own use"[17] the thing found would, in the old days, have been liable for damages from the time of the conversion. It isn't always clear why. The finder of a pretty thing does not increase the loss to the plaintiff by enjoying looking at it rather than keeping it in a closet.[18]

---

14 In *Ramsay* v *Bell* (1872) 1 PEI 417 the defendant driver was hired by a third party to drive the plaintiff to a reception. The plaintiff left a "plaid" with no identification marks on it in the carriage. The defendant, who was not a common carrier, took it to the person who had hired him, for delivery to the owner. It disappeared. The plaintiff sued in trover and lost. The defendant was said to be "only a bailee by finding [and] I consider he was not guilty of any culpable negligence, and did quite as much to restore it to and find out the owner as the law in such a position required him to do". Obviously, the law does not require much in terms of seeking the loser.

15 For a wonderful example of this rule in action, see *Clayton* v *LeRoy* [1911] 2 KB 1031 (Eng CA): a detinue writ was issued approximately two hours before the demand and refusal took place; the action was dismissed.

16 Admittedly, this may vary with the nature of the thing. Keeping gold coins or an icon in a closet might be regarded as passive storage; would the same be said of a closeted dog? What about a homing pigeon?

17 Though this phrase trips nicely off the tongue, what exactly does it mean? Reference books don't clearly explain it. Maybe it describes any act that a bystander would think inconsistent with someone else's property claim (which includes most things that most of us do most of the time).

18 "An action in conversion ... looks primarily to the date of the wrong, apparently giving the plaintiff a substantially inferior remedy on a rising market": Waddams, *The Law of Damages* (Canada Law Book Toronto 1983) at 105. Justice Estey put it this way when commenting on the valuation of corporate shares in *Baud Corp NV* v *Brook* [1979] 1 SCR 633, 23 NR 181 (Alta SCC) at NR 200-201:

> In conversion, the measure of damages has been said to be the value of the shares at the date of conversion, and in addition, consequential damages represented by the loss of opportunity to

No reward is owed to the finder for his services.[19] There is some confusion about this among analysts, but it follows from basic principles. The common law does not impose a general obligation to rescue: passersby are at liberty to ignore the pleas of drowning victims - they may incure the wrath of the community, but not the sanctions of the state. A finder has an opportunity to rescue the owner from further enduring his loss. He is at liberty to take or forgo the opportunity. Non-rescuers and indifferent finders incur no damages; rescuers and helpful finders are entitled to no rewards. The system is balanced. Not every social obligation is backed by legal sanction. Of course, a finder who acts in response to an offer of reward may have a *contractual* claim. Such claims require the usual proof of offer, acceptance, and all the others elements of contractual formation, following which damages for breach of contract will be awarded.[20] However, without a contract a finder has no claim for a reward.

Nor does a finder in possession have a defence of lien.[21] Two quite different such defences might be tried. First, the finder can not retain possession until a reward is paid. Even if a contractual reward is due, the finder has a counter-claim, not a defence, and must give up possession while he sues for damages in contract.[22] Second, the fact that the finder has incurred expenses in keeping the thing safe for the owner may or may not

---

dispose of the shares at the highest price attained prior to the end of the trial. ... In detinue, the measure of damages has been said to be the value of the shares at the end of the trial, and in addition, damages for the detention.
But, practical as ever, Estey, J. added a cautionary note (N.R. p.213): "[o]ne must not become so lost in the technicalities of damages ... as to lose sight of the practical consideration of the cost of money ...".

19 Judges sometimes speak as if rewards were owed, but they don't mean it. See, for example, *Nicholson* v *Chapman* (1793) 126 ER 536 (Eng), referred to later on the question of finders' expenses. Chief Justice Eyre said: "[the defendant's actions] certainly entitles the party to some reasonable recompense from the *bounty* if not from the justice of the owner". Charity, generosity, and munificence are adequate renditions of what the good judge advised; legal entitlement is not. Compare *Watts* v *Ward* 62 Am Dec 299 (Ore 1854) (no reward without a promise).

20 Details can be found in any book on contracts. For examples, see *Symmes* v *Frazer* 6 Mass 344 (1810) and *Kincaid* v *Eaton* 98 Mass 139 (1867), where the ads were strictly construed against the finders. Note, however, that there is no consideration, and no contract, when a promise of reward is extracted by refusing to return possession until the promise is made: *De la O* v *The Pueblo of Acoma* 1 New Mex 226 (1857).

21 "A lien is a right in one man to retain that which is in his possession belonging to another, til certain demands of him, the person in possession, are satisfied": *Hammonds* v *Barclay* (1802) 2 East227, 102 ER 356 *per* Grose J. A lien is simply a defence which arises in certain limited circumstances and protects the possessor of a thing against someone who ordinarily would have a better claim. A classic example is a car mechanic who performs contract work on a car. The mechanic will not be ordered to give up possession before the debt is paid. See Chapter 2 "Other Claims Distinguished".

22 A lien arises either by the terms of a contract or, possibly, by implication from the circumstances and, in the latter case, the circumstances have been limited by the common law and don't include a lien for a contractual reward. Notwithstanding this general rule, some American judges have suggested that a finder has a lien for a contractual reward: see *Wentworth* v *Day* 44-45 Mass 352 (1841) (lost watch, $20 reward offered, lien upheld), *Wood* v *Pierson* 7 NW 888 (Mich 1881) (lost diamond pin, $25 reward offered, lien upheld); and *MacFarlane* v *Bloch* 115 P 1056 (Ore 1911).

create a claim for reimbursement, but it clearly does not authorize the finder to retain possession until he is paid.[23] The action for expenses, if it exists at all,[24] is not a defence to the owner's action for possession.

An owner's action for possession against a possessor by finding is straightforward, unless the plaintiff is put to the proof of his ownership claim.

B   PRIOR POSSESSORS' CLAIMS

This topic could prove pivotal, depending on the answer to a deceptively simple question. Is prior possession that was neither transferred[25] nor abandoned[26] sufficient to defeat a possessor by finding? The answer is unclear from the common law cases.

If proof of such prior possession does not defeat possession by finding, some new complexities emerge in the law of property in things. If it does, the law of property is simplified and ownership drops out of the analysis.[27]

Prior possessors making claims can be classified as (i) first possessors, (ii) dispossessed prior possessors, (iii) other prior possessors, and (iv) estate holders in land. It will be obvious by the end of this survey that there is substantial overlap among these categories

---

23 In *Binstead* v *Buck* (1777) 2 Black W 1117, 96 ER 660 (Eng), the plaintiff owner sued for possession of a pointing dog. The defendant finder refused to transfer possession until he was paid 20 shillings for 20 weeks' keep. The plaintiff won. In *Meekins* v *Simpson* 96 SE 894 (NC 1918), the plaintiff owner sued for possession of a bird dog. The defendant finder sought to introduce evidence of the cost of keeping the dog. The evidence was ruled not relevant to the possession claim on the ground that there was no lien.

24 In *Meekins* v *Simpson* 96 SE 894 (NC 1918), the bird dog case in the previous footnote, the judge suggested, *obiter*, that the finder might have a separate claim for the expense of keeping the dog. Contrast *Mosgrave* v *Agden* (1591) Owen 141, 74 ER 960 (Eng), in which a possessor by finding was not obliged to preserve six barrels of butter which decayed, but would have been liable had he used it and made things worse. Why could a finder, who has no obligation to spend money on upkeep, claim expenses voluntarily incurred? Is the distinction between bird dogs and butter, 20th and 16th centuries, or America and England? *Reeder* v *Anderson's Administrator* 34 Ky 193 (1836) and *Chase* v *Corcoran* 106 Mass 286 (1871) also suggest that expenses are payable to finders. For further analysis of this issue, I recommend a book on the topic of "restitution", perhaps under the heading "Compulsory Discharge of Another's Liability".

25 A prior possessor may have sold all property held in a thing to someone else in the past. For example, a watch may have left the manufacturer's possession years ago and passed through the usual wholesale - retail - second hand markets, and then been lost and found. I see no reason for supporting claims by the manufacturer, the retailer, or any other prior possessors who sold their property.

26 A previously abandoned possession or right to immediate possession is surely no basis for a future claim. Lost and abandoned are quite different concepts: see Chapter 2 'The Concept of Abandonment". I add the qualification in the text only to acknowledge that abandonment does not change the historical fact that property used to be held.

27 Maybe that is what Justice Auld was getting at in *Waverly Borough Council v Fletcher* [1996] QB 334 (CA) at 345 when he said, "[t]he English law of ownership and possession, unlike that of Roman law, is not a system of identifying absolute entitlement but of priority entitlement".

and that there are but a few simple rules hiding in the complexity of the common law cases. However, studying the cases in this way is instructive because it forces contemplation of the fundamentals of property law.

1   First Possessors

Common law cases are not argued and decided on the basis of first possession.

That is not surprising. There are some common law cases on *prior* possessors' claims, but a first possessor is both a prior possessor and an owner.[28] We already know that a possessor by finding is defeated by the owner of the thing found. Sensible first possessors sue as owners rather than speculating on first possession.

Wild animal cases might be an exception. As explained earlier, the conventional view is that wild animals cannot be owned.[29] If this were so, even a first possessor of a wild animal would not own it.

Campbell v *Hedley*[30] illustrates the point. The plaintiff bred foxes. One escaped, the defendant shot it, and the plaintiff sued for damages. The dead former fox was a third generation captive and had been born on the plaintiff's ranch. The plaintiff was thus the first possessor and did not hold possession when the fox was shot. The plaintiff was held not to be the owner on the ground that foxes were wild animals and wild animals could not be owned. The plaintiff lost because he proved no property in the escaped fox. The fact that the defendant killed the fox rather than taking possession of it makes no difference to the point being made here. Most owners win possession from finders because they hold *right to immediate possession*.[31] Killing the fox would have been interference with right to immediate possession if the plaintiff had held such property: he didn't, according to this court, so no damages were payable. The case may be wrong,[32]

---

28 See Chapter 3 "Discovery: the First Finder's Property".

29 I don't think this is a rule at all: see Chapter 3 "Capture and Escape of Wild Animals".

30 *Campbell* v *Hedley* (1917) 37 DLR 289, 39 OLR 528 (Ont CA).

31 Ownership and right to immediate possession are two of the four forms of property in things known to the common law system. They were defined as follows in Chapter 1.

    Ownership is a form of property in things. A holder of ownership of a thing either (i) holds possession of the thing which no one is at liberty to interfere with, or (ii) holds, or will when a contract expires hold, right to immediate possession of the thing, while someone else holds possession or right to immediate possession after transfer.

    Right to immediate possession is a form of property in things. A holder of right to immediate possession is at liberty to seize possession of the thing and has standing to invoke state assistance in gaining possession.

32 Either because common law tradition has mistakenly treated wild animals as a special case (as to which, see ACapture and Escape of Wild Animals" in Chapter 3) or because foxes born and living in captivity are classified as domestic animals, which was the conclusion in *Ebers* v *MacEachern* [1932] 3

but it is certainly inconsistent with any general rule that either prior possessors or first possessors defeat finders, as the fox was lost and the defendant found it.

There are other cases supporting prior possessors' claims against finders.[33] Yet first possession is just an example of prior possession and a first possessor can be in no worse position. Maybe *Campbell* v *Hedley* is wrong; I think it is. Maybe there is something special about wild animals; I don't think so. At any rate, this case is one of the few that invited argument on the basis of non-owning first possession. Unfortunately, that is not the way it was argued.

The common law cases tell us nothing about first possessors' claims as such.

2   Dispossessed Prior Possessors

A *dispossessed prior possessor* is a person whose possession was terminated by someone acting without lawful excuse. The term is a bit awkward. However, it emphasizes that the topic involves claims based on possession, not on ownership, and that possession ceased through someone's interference. Not included are those who transferred possession,[34] those dispossessed by someone who would have won an action for possession, and those who simply lost or abandoned the thing possessed.

I realize that this may seem off topic. This is a sub-category in the analysis of claims made against the general category of *finders* as defendants. Dispossessors are not finders.[35] Recall, however, that it is possession by finding, and not the phenomenon of finding itself, that is the focal point of the common law "finders' cases". Possession is the key to the analysis. There are more similarities than differences between the legal treatment of a finder's possession and that of possession acquired by other means. Some clarification of the nature of a dispossessed prior possessor's claim may be useful before asking whether it will defeat a possessor by finding.

A possessor who is dispossessed of a thing has *right to immediate possession*. That is a form of property in the thing, not merely a personal claim against the dispossessor. The essence of right to immediate possession is the holder's standing to invoke a judicial order for possession.[36] It follows that a dispossessed prior possessor defeats a finder in an

---

DLR 415 (PEI SC).

33 See below, "Dispossessed Prior Possessors" and "Other Prior Possessors: the Missing Link".

34 For example, by contract or by gift. A voluntary transfer can serve as a defence against a claim by the transferor for return of property, except as specified otherwise by the terms of the transfer.

35 We do not describe pickpockets as finders of things in other people's pockets. Finding a lost thing is not regarded as dispossessing the loser: see Chapter 5 "Losing Things and Finding Things".

36 Right to immediate possession is a form of property in things. A holder of right to immediate possession is at liberty to seize possession of the thing and has standing to invoke state assistance in gaining possession: see Chapter 1.

action for possession.

The problem with that syllogism is that it is rigged. The cases cited support the proposition that a dispossessed possessor holds right to immediate possession, but there is no guarantee that the judges who said so were using those words as I have defined them. However, other arguments establish the superior claim of a dispossessed prior possessor.

A prior possessor clearly has a claim for repossession against the dispossessor. This is often attributed to *Armory* v *Delamirie*, though it was said *obiter* there.[37] A later American case, *Anderson* v *Gouldberg*,[38] put the point more clearly.

> One who has acquired the possession of property (*sic*), whether by finding, bailment, or by mere tort, has a right to retain that possession as against a mere wrongdoer who is a stranger to the property. Any other rule would lead to an endless series of seizures and reprisals in every case where property had once passed out of the possession of the rightful owner.

The plaintiff's action was to recover possession of logs he had cut. He clearly was not an owner by first possession, having trespassed to cut down the trees.[39] His best claim was as a dispossessed possessor. The dispossessed prior possessor rule was also invoked in *New England Box Company* v *C & R Construction Company*.[40] The defendant was sued in tort for starting a fire that destroyed some cut timber. The plaintiff was not the owner of the timber. The state was. This came about as follows. The state had contracted with one H. that H. could cut and remove timber from described land, but the contract stipulated that any cut wood remaining on site after 15 Jul 1938 "shall be deemed abandoned and become the property of the Commonwealth". The plaintiff then contracted with H. for the transfer of ownership of some of the cut timber. When 15 Jul 1938 passed and the timber had not been removed, the state became the owner, the plaintiff's claim to ownership being limited to what property H. had to sell. The plaintiff

---

37 In *Armory* v *Delamirie* (1722) 1 Str 505, 93 ER 664 (Eng) the plaintiff had voluntarily given up possession by a bailment transaction and his claim was unauthorized detention, not dispossession. The case is analyzed in Chapter 6. *Anderson* v *Gouldberg* 53 NW 636 (Minn 1892), in which the plaintiff sued to recover possession of logs he had cut, is more directly on point. The judge said "[o]ne who has acquired the possession of property, whether by finding, by bailment, or by mere tort, has a right to retain that possession as against a mere wrongdoer who is a stranger to the property".

38 *Anderson* v *Gouldberg* 53 NW 636 (Minn 1892).

39 Trees growing on land are part of the land. The question of possession of the trees, as such, simply does not arise until the connection is severed. Upon severance (cutting down the trees) the first possessor would become the owner. The first possessor would be either the lumberjack or an estate holder in the land: see Chapter 3 "Crops". In *Anderson* v *Gouldberg*, "the plaintiffs obtained possession of the logs in the first instance by trespassing upon the land of some third party. Therefore the only question is whether bare possession of property, though wrongfully obtained, is sufficient title to enable the party enjoying it to maintain replevin against a mere stranger who takes it from him." [53 NW 636 (Minn 1892)].

40 *New England Box Company* v *C & R Construction Company* 150 ALR 152, 49 NE 2d 121 (Mass 1943).

continued to deal with the timber, leading to a judicial conclusion that the plaintiff held possession at the time the fire destroyed the timber.[41] The plaintiff sued in tort, alleging that the fire had been caused by the defendant's carelessness. A civil jury was directed by the trial judge to return a verdict for the defendant on the ground that the plaintiff did not hold "title" to the timber. On appeal, the plaintiff's possession was ruled a sufficient basis upon which to sue:[42]

> possession is prima facie evidence of title and ... against all persons not having a better right it constitutes, or rather answers for a right of property. An action alleging property may be maintained upon it; because a mere stranger who derives no title, right or authority from the previous owner cannot set up his title against the right thus obtained by possession. This is true, not only against one who disturbs that possession, but if the possession is not parted with voluntarily, it is equally so against anyone who afterwards meddles with the property without right.

The plaintiff's claim was for damages, not for possession (the timber having been destroyed). The case does not establish the proposition that a dispossessed prior possessor can sue his dispossessor for possession. However, it is difficult to see how the plaintiff could have a claim for damages for the loss of possession unless alternative claims for possession and damages could have been brought against a defendant who simply carried the timber away.

More directly on point is an obscure New Hampshire case, *Harrington v Tremblay*.[43] A "pocketbook" containing promissory notes and bank bills was owned by T. Shortly after T's death the defendant saw the plaintiff, T's business associate, in possession of the pocketbook. The defendant seized possession from her. The plaintiff made no ownership claim, but sued in trover: her claim was thus as a dispossessed prior possessor. She won. Unfortunately, the reasons for judgment ramble on about "presumptions", rather than simply treating possession as a form of property protected against dispossessors.[44]

> The presumption of law is that the person who has the possession of personalty has the property also; against a wrongdoer possession is title; and it is therefore immaterial

---

41 Justice Cox ruled (150 ALR 152 at 162) that,
    timber which ... has been sawed into lumber ,.... cannot be carried about on the person, and the question arises as to what kind of physical control, in order to amount to possession, was practical. ... From the evidence in the case at bar ... it could have been found that, for all practical purposes, the plaintiff was in possession of the lumber at the time it was destroyed by fire, see *The Tubantia* [1924] P 78.

42 150 ALR 152 at 160-161 *per* Cox J.

43 *Harrington v Tremblay* 61 NH 413 (1881).

44 *Harrington v Tremblay* 61 NH 413 (1881) per Blodgett J at 415-416. Another noteworthy point about this case is that the defendant, subsequent to the dispossession but before the trial, was appointed T's administrator. As such, the defendant became entitled to take possession of things owned by T immediately before his death. The judge quite correctly ruled that this subsequent appointment provided no defence to the plaintiff's action, as the defendant had no right to immediate possession at the time he dispossessed the plaintiff.

whether the plaintiff's possession was rightful or wrongful as against the defendant who apparently had no title whatever, and was a mere naked trespasser at the time he seized, carried away and converted the pocketbook and its contents. The further contention that {T] was the true owner does not aid the defendant. Upon the recorded facts the presumption is otherwise; and if it were not, it is no defence to the maintenance of the plaintiff's action, because a defendant in trover cannot set up property in a third person without showing some right, title, or interest in himself derived from such person.

The defendant was ordered to pay the face value of the promissory notes and of the bank bills, plus interest from the time the action was commenced. I have already criticized this way of evaluating a dispossessed possessor's damages,[45] but the case is correct in its ruling on the plaintiff's claim for repossession or *some* damages (however calculated).

In *R v Roberts,*[46] a deer and a car collided on a highway. The deer died. H, a friend of the driver, loaded the carcass on his truck. Before he could drive away, a police officer (Roberts) arrived and requested that the carcass be transferred to his cruiser, saying that it was required for tests at the Ministry of Natural Resources and that the meat would be given to an old folks' home. H fell for the story, and PO Roberts acquired possession of the carcass. He transferred possession to his girlfriend's father. PO Roberts was convicted of theft. Appealing the trial decision, he argued that "title" to the carcass of an animal *ferae naturae* would be "vested in the owner of the land upon which the animal was killed" (in this case, the Crown). If so, he argued, H never held possession of the carcass and could not have been dispossessed. Justice Lacourcière agreed with the trial judge and said, "at the relevant time, [H] had taken actual possession of the deer carcass. His possession was therefore protected, regardless of title, against anyone who could not prove a superior title."[47]

Not everyone agrees. There is a lengthy annotation to the report of the *New England Box* case[48] in which the ruling is criticized as wrong and dangerously misleading. The author presents a comprehensive survey of the common law cases, but his objections seem to be based on two major points. First, he suggests that possession is only evidence of "title", and is not to be treated as if it actually were title. That ignores the basic fact that possession, in the form of first possession through discovery or creation, is the root of nearly all property in things;[49] it does no good to pretend that ownership of (title to) things just falls out of the sky. Second, he assumes, or concludes by relying on common law cases, that if a dispossessed possessor wins damages it must follow that the amount of damages equals the ownership value of the thing. That is irrational, as already

---

45 See Chapter 6 "Finders on Offence".
46 *R v Roberts* (1991) 49 OAC 23 (Ont CA), leave to appeal to SCC refused [1992] WL 1330091.
47 *Ibid* at para 6.
48 150 ALR 152 (Mass 1943). The annotation, by JE Macy, begins at 150 ALR 163 and runs for some 90 pages.
49 See Chapter 3 "Discovery: the First Finder's Property" and "Creation of Things".

explained.[50] If these objections are discounted, the world of property in things is simple. Possession is a form of property; property is protected by the state; interference with property is actionable; dispossession is interference with possession; dispossessors pay; they pay the value of the plaintiff's possession.

There are not many reported cases in which dispossessors are sued on the basis of prior possession. Maybe this is because defendants typically fail to put plaintiffs to the strict proof of the usual allegation that the plaintiff also held ownership. Alternatively, it may be because the rule is so uncontroversial that such claims are easily settled once the facts are established. Interference with possession is actionable and, where the dispossessor retains possession, an order for repossession is simply one of the available remedies. How the plaintiff got possession is immaterial.[51] The sole issue is whether the defendant had any lawful excuse for the interference.

Dispossessors found in possession are thus easily defeated in litigation. Consequently, they are disinclined to keep possession for long and often purport to transfer ownership to unwitting buyers, skipping to Rio on the proceeds. The buyer in possession will lose if found and sued by the dispossessed prior possessor.

The reason is not because the plaintiff is treated as owner of the thing. By assumption in the category under discussion, the dispossessed prior possessor was not the owner.[52] Rational analysis is not advanced by reciting maxims like "against a wrongdoer possession is title" [ie. ownership].[53] Such expressions disguise the underlying reasoning process. The defendant has done no wrong: he is an unwitting victim of the dispossessor's chicanery. The dispossessed prior possessor's claim must be based either on his prior possession or on the event by which he was dispossessed. Allowing the plaintiff to pass himself off as if he owned the thing - which means lying about the facts of the case - hardly seems the best way to run a legal system.

Nor is the reason that the defendant is the transferee of some defective form of possession. It is true that the defendant did not succeed in acquiring ownership from the now departed rogue. The rogue who dispossessed the plaintiff did not have ownership to sell. The rogue held possession. The rogue's possession would have been protected

---

50 See Chapter 6 "Finders on Offence".

51 "Since the case of *Armory* v *Delamirie* it has been well established that mere possession is enough to entitle a person to sue in trover and that he need not show the manner in which possession was obtained": *Daniel* v *Rogers* [1918] 2 KB 228 (Eng CA) at 234 *per* Scrutton LJ.

52 That is, he was not a *first* possessor of the thing and was not someone who came into possession through a transfer of ownership from a previous owner. Claims by such plaintiffs have been dealt with above.

53 That was the position taken by the English courts in *Winkfield (The)* [1902] P 42 (Eng CA), an action by a possessor through bailment for damages against a tortfeasor who held no property. See also *Jeffries* v *Great Western Railway Co* (1856) 5 El & Bl 802, 119 ER 680 (Eng). We'll cover both cases in detail in Chapter 10 "Bailment: a Separate Transaction?".

against interference by other rogues.[54] A claim made by the prior possessor against other rogues could only have been based on right to immediate possession, as he lacked the physical control required to prove possession.

Some suggest that the rogue would hold possession vis-à-vis third parties while between the dispossessed prior possessor and the rogue who dispossessed him, the former's possession is "deemed" to continue. That is plain mystification. The rogue held possession from the time he dispossessed the prior possessor until the time he transferred possession (claiming to transfer ownership) to the unwitting buyer. The probable length of time the rogue would have retained possession, and thus the value of his possession, were lessened by the prospect of a repossession claim by the dispossessed prior possessor. That doesn't change the essence of possession itself. The form of property is the same, irrespective of its duration or marketability.[55]

To summarize the facts:

> DPP (a dispossessed prior possessor) has been dispossessed of a thing by Rogue; UB (an unwitting buyer) has paid money to Rogue and has taken possession of the thing, believing Rogue's lie that he was selling ownership as well as possession; Rogue has skipped to Rio; DPP now sues UB for possession.

As they say after the facts on a law school exam, discuss.

The possibilities are that the plaintiff loses or the plaintiff wins. I don't think the plaintiff will lose on these facts.[56] My objective is to propose a simple, workable theory that

---

54 See *Bird* v *The Town of Fort Frances* [1949] OR 292, [1949] 2 DLR 791 (Ont), in which the plaintiff was certainly a trespasser and possibly a thief, yet his possession was judicially protected. Note also *Harrington* v *Tremblay* 61 NH 413 (1881), set out above, in which the plaintiff won even though she seems to have had no lawful excuse for having taken possession of the pocketbook previously owned by her dead former business associate.

55 I reject any suggestion that the rogue held only "a precarious possession", which was thus all the unwitting buyer acquired. Possession as a form of property is simple, clear and understandable. Adding adjectives paints pretty pictures, but doesn't clarify ideas. Nor is it helpful to suggest that our unwitting buyer acquired the rogues liabilities along with his "rights" [*ie.* possession]. The rogue was liable for damages for dispossessing the prior possessor; any damages payable by the unwitting buyer will be for his own interference *after* he acquired possession, not for anything the rogue did before that time.

56 Unless the unwitting buyer was witting enough to make his purchase in market overt (where applicable), in which case he will have acquired ownership. Market overt is explained above under "Owners' Claims". Curiously, an early case, *Anon* (1609) Godb 160, 78 ER 98 (Eng), suggests that this might not be so. The full report reads as follows.

>> Note, that it was adjudged to be law by the whole Court, that if a man bail goods to another at such a day to rebail, and before the day the bailee doth sell the goods in market overt: yet at the day the baylor may seise the goods, for that the property of the goods was alwaies in him; and was not altered by the sale in market overt.

That is, of course, distinguishable on the bailment issue. However, the ruling makes a mockery of the concept of market overt and must be wrong.

generates a win for DPP (as that is the practical outcome) without being inconsistent with other, more general propositions in this book, or with the general run of results in the common law cases. I suggest that DPP acquired, at the time he was dispossessed, *right to immediate possession* of the thing, not merely a personal claim for damages against the Rogue who dispossessed him. The holder of right to immediate possession of a thing wins possession from a possessor of the thing. That is a general rule of property law. The *New England Box* case is consistent with that rule, despite the judge's complex approach:[57]

> possession is prima facie evidence of title and ... against all persons not having a better right it constitutes, or rather answers for a right of property. ... *This is true, not only against one who disturbs that possession, but if the possession is not parted with voluntarily, it is equally so against anyone who afterwards meddles with the property without right.* (Emphasis added)

Similarly, the plaintiff in *Harrington* v *Tremblay*[58] would have regained possession from anyone holding possession as a buyer from the defendant if the purported sale took place before the defendant's appointment as administrator of the estate: wouldn't she? Thus, in our simple example, DPP defeats UB in a classic test of which of two innocents pays for a Rogue's trip to Rio.

The alternative is that the dispossessed prior possessor loses.

As noted above, any claim by the dispossessed prior possessor must be based either on his prior possession or on the event by which he was dispossessed. The latter gives him a claim against the dispossessor, but not against the unwitting buyer, who acquired possession by transaction from the dispossessor. The unwitting buyer can be defeated only if prior possession is a sufficient ground for recovery.

What about third parties who acquire possession other than by transaction? There are, I think, two such situations. One occurs when the dispossessor is himself dispossessed. In the other situation the dispossessor either loses or abandons the thing, whereupon it is found by someone else. Can the new dispossessor or the finder defeat the dispossessed prior possessor?

The new dispossessor (Rogue 2) surely has no defence. The original rogue could recover possession from him on the basis of his own prior possession and dispossession.[59] If the

---

57 *New England Box Company* v *C & R Construction Company* 150 ALR152, 49 NE 2d 121 (Mass 1943), set out above.

58 *Harrington v Tremblay*, 61 N.H. 413 (1881) set out above.

59 This is suggested by the conclusion in *Bird* v *The Town of Fort Frances* [1949] OR 292, [1949] 2 DLR 791 (Ont) (in which the plaintiff was certainly a trespasser and possibly a thief), is implicit in *Harrington v Tremblay* 61 NH 413 (NH 1881) (in which the plaintiff won even though she seems to have had no lawful excuse for having taken possession of the pocketbook previously owned by her dead former

dispossessed prior possessor could defeat Rogue 1, who could in turn defeat Rogue 2, can't the dispossessed prior possessor claim possession directly from Rogue 2? Note that the answer again depends on whether the claim is based on prior possession or on the act of dispossession. Rogue 2 did not dispossess the plaintiff (DPP). Nor can the plaintiff's claim be based on the act of dispossession by Rogue 1, as Rogue 2 is not responsible for another's misdeeds. Yet, if the plaintiff does not prevail, Rogue 2 is in a better defensive position than the unwitting buyer in our earlier example.[60] That, while always a possibility, seems unlikely. The simplest solution is the one already proposed: the dispossessed prior possessor holds right to immediate possession - a form of property in the thing - against which the possession that Rogue 2 acquired by dispossessing Rogue 1 serves as no defence.[61]

What of the finder who finds and takes possession of a thing of which someone else was previously dispossessed? This, finally, brings us back to the main topic. As a finder his possession is protected against most people in the world.[62] Can a finder maintain possession against all but the owner, or does he lose to our dispossessed prior possessor?

Consider the simplest example.

> The rogue who dispossessed the prior possessor either loses or abandons the thing. It is found by a finder, who takes possession. The dispossessed prior possessor discovers the finder and sues for possession.

Whether the rogue lost or abandoned the thing makes no difference. He can only abandon his own claim, not someone else's.[63] Is there any theoretical basis for concluding that the finder is in a better position than the unwitting buyer?

---

business associate), and is specifically stated, *obiter*, in the quote from the *New England Box* case set out above.

60 The conclusion there was that if a rogue transferred possession to a buyer, after having dispossessed a prior possessor, the dispossessed prior possessor could recover possession from the buyer.

61 Adding any number of similar characters to the chain of events will make no difference to the outcome. Subsequent dispossessors are equally isolated from the first act of dispossession and are equally liable to their immediate predecessors in the chain: their positions are identical to that of Rogue 2. Similarly, if Rogue 2 (or Rogue n!) finds and dispossesses an unwitting buyer from Rogue 1 (or from any other previous rogue or earlier unwitting buyer!), his defence can be no better *unless an unwitting buyer has a defence and thus breaks the chain*, a conclusion I have already rejected.

62 See Chapter 6 "Finders on Offence".

63 Unless the law of waif still applies

> [W]aif is where the felon in pursuit waives the goods, or when the felon for fear of being apprehended, thinking that pursuit was made, having them with him in his possession flies, and waives the goods, in those cases they shall be said waived in law; ... and the reason that waif is given to the king, and that the party shall lose his property in such case is for default in the owner that he doth not make fresh suit to apprehend the felon ... and therefore the law has imposed this penalty on the owner ... .

Foxley's Case (1600) 5 Co Rep 109a, 77 ER 224 (Eng). Waif is seldom claimed these days.

The finder might be in a better position if what prejudiced the unwitting buyer's claim was the tainted transaction by which possession was acquired from the rogue. However, as concluded previously, it was the *fact* that possession was all he acquired on which the unwitting buyer's claim foundered; it was mere coincidence that the defendant's possession derived from the person who dispossessed the plaintiff. The unwitting buyer lost because the dispossessed prior possessor held right to immediate possession from the moment he was dispossessed, not because the defendant tried to purchase ownership and failed. The dispossessed prior possessor's right to immediate possession was sufficient to defeat the unwitting buyer's possession; it will also defeat the finder's possession, as possession of a thing (not ownership; not some mystical and exalted, adjective-laced form of modified possession) is what the finder acquired.

What do the common law cases tell us about that conclusion? Not much, probably because most such cases are settled on the basis of a spurious ownership claim by one of the two disputants. One case, however, is difficult to explain on any other basis. In *Dunwich Corp v Sterry*[64] the plaintiff was a "grantee of wreck". This meant that the state had granted the plaintiff corporation a proprietary claim to all things washed ashore from shipwrecks in the area. The plaintiff was authorized to take possession of any such wreck, but could be dispossessed should the owner show up and make a claim. In short, the plaintiff, though neither an owner nor a prior possessor, had *right to immediate possession* of all wreck. A cask of whiskey floated ashore; the defendant found and took possession of it. The plaintiff sued for possession and won. This confirms that the holder of right to immediate possession of a thing prevails over a possessor by finding. The result would be the same where right to immediate possession arises through prior possession and dispossession, rather than by state grant.

3   Other Prior Possessors: the Missing Link

Let's see, where are we? The subject is possession by finding. More particularly, the topic is defending an action for possession. The issue is the extent to which prior possessors defeat finders on defence.

The first possessor of a thing will win an action for possession against a subsequent possessor by finding. This may be because first possession proves ownership and owners defeat finders. Alternatively, what if proof of *prior* possession is sufficient to reclaim possession from a finder? / If it is, the traditional rule - owners win possession from finders - is nothing more than a particular example of the general proposition. I argued under the previous heading that *dispossessed prior possessors* win possession from finders. It remains to be seen whether prior possessors who were not dispossessed by someone also win.

---

64 *Dunwich Corp v Sterry* (1831) 1 B & Ad 831, 109 ER 995 (Eng)

As a general principle, prior possession defeats subsequent possession. Like any principle, this one is too general to be operational. It needs refinement. First we weed out the obvious categories. Abandoned prior possession doesn't count. Nor does transferred prior possession, unless the transfer was for a limited time and the time has expired.[65] Nor does legally extinguished prior possession.[66] Possessors by finding are defeated by prior possessors who ceased to hold possession in circumstances that do not mitigate against right to immediate possession.

A long-standing tradition of categorizing plaintiffs' claims in other ways prevented this proposition from being generally recognized. However, when various traditional categories are compared, when claims by bailees, previous finders of twice lost things, and losers of possession held under mistaken impression of ownership are examined for some common thread, it becomes evident that the common law cases generally support the proposition based on prior possession.

A clear example of a prior possessor defeating a finder occurred in *Sutton v Buck*.[67] The owner of a ship tried to transfer ownership and possession to the plaintiff. The ownership transfer failed, despite payment by the plaintiff, due to non-compliance with a ships' registry statute. The plaintiff therefore held possession of the ship under the mistaken impression that he was the owner. The ship broke up and some pieces of it drifted to the defendant's farm. The defendant, surely a finder, took possession. The plaintiff sued for possession and won. The plaintiff was nothing more than a prior possessor; the defendant behaved like any other finder, and was unaware of the mistake about the ownership transfer. There is no reason why the facts that the plaintiff thought he was the owner and had paid money to someone else would have any effect on the relationship between him and the defendant, a stranger. That relationship was a property relationship. The property was right to immediate possession, and it could only have been created by the plaintiff's prior possession and loss of the pieces of the ship.[68]

---

65 See Chapter 10 "Bailment: a Separate Transaction?"

66 See, for example, Chapter 4 "Accession, Mixing and Fixtures". If prior possession of a brick was destroyed because the brick became part of a house (*ie* part of the land), the prior possessor would have no claim against a new possessor of the phoenix-like brick after the house was demolished.

67 *Sutton v Buck* (1810) 2 Taunt 302, 127 ER 1094 (Eng).

68 *Sutton v Buck* was cited, with apparent approval, in three later English cases. In *Burton v Hughes* (1824) 2 Bing 173, 130 ER 272 (Eng), the plaintiff's possession as a bailee of hired furniture was (unsurprisingly) held sufficient to support an action for repossession against a stranger who dispossessed him. In *Dunwich Corp v Sterry* (1831) 1 B & Ad 831, 109 ER 995 (Eng), detailed under the previous heading, the plaintiff corporation's royal grant of right to immediate possession of all wreck washed ashore in the vicinity was sufficient to claim possession from the defendant finder. Finally, in *Daniel v Rogers* [1918] 2 KB 228 (Eng CA) at 234, Scrutton LJ referred to *Sutton v Buck* and noted: "[s]ince the case of *Armory v Delamirie* it has been well established that mere possession is enough to entitle a person to sue in trover and that he need not show the manner in which possession was obtained".

This brings us to the interesting problem of finders against finders. Sometimes a lost thing is found, taken into possession, lost again, then found and possessed by someone else. What happens in the unlikely event that the previous finder (F1) locates the subsequent finder (F2) and sues for possession? By hypothesis, neither owns the thing.[69] The plaintiff, F1, will probably recite the following well-known quotation:[70]

> the finder of a jewel, though he does not by such finding acquire an absolute property or ownership, yet he has such a property as will enable him to keep it against all but the rightful owner ... .

The defendant's response will be to say precisely the same thing! Yet only one of the two finders can win.

That was the issue in *Clark* v *Maloney*.[71] The plaintiff found 10 white pine logs in Delaware Bay. He moored them in a creek, but they broke loose and the defendant found them floating in the creek and took possession. The plaintiff sued in trover. Chief Justice Bayard directed the jury.[72]

> Possession ... in the absence of better title ... is as effective a support of title as the most conclusive evidence could be. ... The defence consists, not in showing that the defendants are the rightful owners, or claim under the rightful owner; but that the logs were found by them adrift ... and they insist that their title is as good as that of the plaintiff. *But it is a well settled rule of law that the loss of a chattel does not change the right of property; and for the same reason that the original loss of these logs by the rightful owner did not change his absolute property in them, but he might have maintained trover against the plaintiff upon refusal to deliver them, so the subsequent loss did not divest the special property of the plaintiff.* It follows, therefore, that as the plaintiff has shown a special property in these logs, which he never abandoned, and which enabled him to keep them against all the world but the rightful owner, he is entitled to a verdict. [Emphasis added]

So the subsequent loss did not divest the "special property" of the plaintiff. It is simply not true that possession by finding prevails against *all* but the owner. "Special property", that unfortunate term adopted from Blackstone,[73] meant some vague relationship that was

---

69 F1 was the finder of a *lost* thing, not the first finder (and thus the owner) of a previously undiscovered natural object. Ownership through first possession is explained in Chapter 3 "Discovery: the First Finder's Property". Lost means that someone had possessed it before, was no longer in possession, and had not abandoned it: see Chapter 5 "Losing Things and Finding Things".

70 From *Armory* v *Delamirie* (1722) 1 Str 505, 93 ER 664 (Eng).

71 *Clark* v *Maloney* 3 Har 68 (Del 1840).

72 *Ibid.* Chief Justice Bayard referred to possession as "prima facie evidence of property" and told the jury "[it] is for this reason that the finder of a chattel, though he does not acquire an absolute property in it, yet has such a property as will enable him to keep it against all but the rightful owner". As usual, the traditional terminology obstructed the clarity of his message. However, the result can easily be explained, once possession is defined as just another form of property in things and one accepts the possibility that prior possession prevails.

73 The derivation and spread of this term, and of the corresponding term "absolute property" (*ie*

112

somewhat less extensive than ownership but still a form of property in things. Nineteenth century judges usually meant what we now call possession when they used it. As we can see from the above quote, it was also used to describe right to immediate possession held by a person in a thing. The losing and finding of a thing did not alter the fact that the owner, though he was out of possession, continued to hold ownership of the lost thing. Similarly, if the finder in turn lost the thing, the fact that he was out of possession did not mean that he no longer held property in it. That finder's prior possession, which he no longer held because he could no longer prove the necessary control over the thing, was converted by the inadvertent loss of control into right to immediate possession, a different form of property in the thing. A subsequent finder could be dispossessed in litigation by any plaintiff holding right to immediate possession in the thing found - which any prior possessor or owner out of possession held.

Clark v *Maloney* is the kind of case that Casey Stengel would have called "rare but not unusual". The circumstances of twice losing and finding plus apprehension of the subsequent finder in possession, followed by resort to the courts, don't occur every day. But the conclusion is hardly surprising; after all, one of the finders had to win. Nor is the case unique. *Deadrick* v *Oulds*[74] was almost identical, with a finder's prior possession of a walnut log being held "a sufficient title" to regain possession from a subsequent finder. Note how once again "title", like its synonym ownership, is misused[75] because the judges seem unwilling to adopt the simple proposition that prior possession is a sufficient basis for the claim. Could it be that they simply haven't thought of it?

---

ownership), are explained in Ch 3 "Capture and Escape of Wild Animals".

74 *Deadrick* v *Oulds* 5 SW 487 (Tenn 1887). A walnut log, found washed up on the shore by the plaintiff, was proved to have been previously found, then lost, by the defendant. Justice Lurton reviewed the facts and summarized the defendant's claim.

> This log was lost, and had been lost in all probability for two or more years, when found entangled among the rocks and drifts in the gorge by the servants of defendant. It was then claimed for defendant and possession taken. This right of possession was not lost by the log subsequently drifting upon the land of plaintiff, and the defendant had a right to take and hold this log against all but the true owner, or one having a superior right of possession to that of the finder of lost property. ... The prior finding and possession of the defendant is sufficient not only to defeat the contention of the plaintiff, but was a sufficient title to have supported an action of replevin to recover the possession from any but the true owner." (5 SW 487 at 488)

Contrast *Lawrence* v *Buck* 62 Me 275 (Maine 1874), which belongs under the previous heading (defendants who found a chain cable in a river, removed part of it and left that portion coiled on the bank for a few days while working elsewhere; plaintiff took possession, mistakenly thinking it lost; defendants, *dispossessed* prior possessors, won).

75 Judicial misuse of this term was the subject of comment in *Roberts* v *Wentworth* 59 Mass R 192 (Mass 1849). The defendant in a trespass action had protested that the plaintiff was not an owner, due to bankruptcy. This led to a technical ruling on the trial judge's use of the term "title" during his jury direction. The view on appeal was that it did not mean only ownership as defined in law. "A party may have a title to property although he is not the absolute owner. If he has the actual or constructive possession of property or the right of possession, he has a title thereto, although another party may be the owner": 59 Mass R 192 at 193.

Prior possession by finding defeats a subsequent finder's possession: that is supported by the foregoing common law cases.

The only authorities I am aware of against this proposition are wild animal cases. One of them, *Mullett* v *Bradley*,[76] is directly contrary. Others, *Kearry* v *Pattinson*[77] and *Campbell* v *Hedley* [78] being the clearest examples, are indirectly opposed. They denied damages to a prior possessor for a defendant's interference with escaped wild animals. In each of these cases the plaintiff would have won, but for the traditional view that wild animals can not be owned, as in each case the plaintiff was the first (*ie,* original) possessor. I have already set out my views that these cases are wrong, that wild animals can be owned, and that the plaintiffs had claims based on ownership through first possession.[79] The wild animal cases really tell us nothing about prior possessors suing subsequent finders. They may or may not be followed in the future. If first possession of wild animals is an exception to the rule that first possessors can sue as owners, and if the exception is based on the nature of the beasts, it follows that *prior* possession of wild animals is an insufficient claim even if prior possession of other things prevails.[80] Alternatively, if the wild animal cases are overruled - if in the future plaintiffs like Mr Mullett recover possession of lost sea lions from later finders' transferees like Mr Bradley - either ownership through first possession or simple prior possession will do as the basis of a repossession claim.

This heading was sub-titled "The Missing Link". The reason is that the situation of *Prior Possessor* v *Finder* tells us something fundamental about the relationships among holders of ownership, possession, and right to immediate possession - the three key forms of common law property in things. Those relationships can now be summarized.

Everyone agrees that finders lose possession to owners of the things found. First

---

76 *Mullett* v *Bradley* 53 NYS 781 (NY 1898). A sea lion of a type found only in the Pacific was captured, taken across the country, and kept in captivity by the plaintiff on Long Island. It escaped, was recaptured by a stranger some 70 miles away, and possession was sold to the defendant. The plaintiff failed in his action for repossession.

77 *Kearry* v *Pattinson* [1939] 1 KB 471 (Eng). Bees kept by the plaintiff swarmed and settled on land in which the defendant held an estate. The plaintiff was not permitted by the defendant to pursue them and lost an action to recover damages, it being held that his property in the bees ceased when they escaped.

78 *Campbell* v *Hedley* [1917] 37 DLR 289 (Ont CA). Plaintiff, a breeder of foxes, was held to have lost his property in a third generation captive fox when it escaped. The reason given was that foxes were wild animals and could not be owned. The defendant, who shot the fox, was not liable in damages.

79 See Chapter 3 "Capture and Escape of Wild Animals". Note also the anomalous view of wild swans in *Blackstone's Commentaries* 15th ed (1809) at 292: "if a wild swan is taken, and marked and turned loose in the river, the owner's property in him still continues, and it is not lawful for any one else to take him: but otherwise if ... the swan leaves the neighbourhood". Is this because a marked swan is identifiable within a neighbourhood that can recognize the mark, because swans are unlike other wild animals, or because Blackstone (or the wild animal rule) is wrong?

80 Otherwise, prior possession would be superior to first possession. But first possession is just a special case of prior possession and is usually more advantageous. If prior possessors defeat subsequent finders, but first possessors don't, we have an unexplained contradiction.

possession of a thing, whether through discovery in nature or by manufacture, has always been the root of ownership. Consequently, a prior possessor of a lost thing who proved he was a first possessor, or traced his acquisition of possession through a series of transactions to the first possessor, proved ownership and defeated a finder. Put another way, first possession is sufficient in the common law to dispossess the finder of a lost thing; so is prior possession derived from the first possessor.

Prior possession that was terminated by theft is also sufficient to defeat a finder - or so it appeared under the previous heading. Cases and hypothetical situations analyzed there involved finders of things that had been stolen, then lost or discarded by rogues. The finders were not implicated in the acts of dispossession, yet they lost to the dispossessed prior possessors. A pattern began to emerge. Could it be that prior possession is of itself a sufficient claim to regain possession from a finder at common law?

If previous finders defeat subsequent finders, and the cases say they do, prior possession must be the basis of the claim. Prior possession is all that a previous finder who was not a first finder held. Possession is all the subsequent finder holds. Prior possession defeats possession!

Does the concept of ownership have any remaining use in the common law system?

Consider an owner in possession of a thing. When we say he holds ownership, we are predicting (i) that the state will order repossession against anyone who dispossesses him, (ii) that he can recover possession from a finder should he lose the thing, (iii) that he will get damages equal to the estimated value of undisturbed possession for the useful life of the thing if he is permanently dispossessed, and (iv) that transferees from him will be treated in the same way. Now consider any other person in possession of a similar thing. Without knowing whether he owns the thing, we can make exactly the same prediction on points (i) and (ii). On point (iii), we may anticipate that someone could possibly win possession from him, estimate that possibility as best we can on the available facts, and lower the value of his possession accordingly. Then, on point (iv), we can safely predict that transferees from the possessor will be treated in the same way. In short, the only difference between possession by an owner and mere possession is the value of the possession each holds.

Consider an owner out of possession. Against a finder the owner wins either possession or damages. So does a prior possessor. Again, the only difference is the amount of damages awarded if the plaintiff can't regain possession from the finder. We assess the amount of damages by estimating the value of the property each plaintiff holds. In the former case it is said that we are valuing the owner's *ownership*. Note that we get the same result if we say that the plaintiff holds *right to immediate possession* of the thing. We then value that property (right to immediate possession) by predicting that upon repossession he could have retained possession forever. This focuses attention on the basis of the finder's liability, as a finder pays damages for inhibiting the plaintiff in regaining possession of the thing and not for the original loss of possession. By contrast, a rogue who dispossessed the plaintiff would be required to pay two types of damages, one for dispossessing the plaintiff (interference with possession) and a second for his not restoring possession (interference with right to immediate possession) at the trial.

Compare a prior possessor's claim for damages. The reason why the prior possessor could have won possession from the finder was because he held right to immediate possession of the lost thing. No other explanation makes sense. The defendant did not dispossess the prior possessor, owed him no contractual obligations, and holds possession as a finder, which is legally protected against strangers who do not hold property in the thing found.

Where repossession is impossible, damages are assessed. Against a finder, the damages are for interference with the prior possessor's right to immediate possession; against a rogue who dispossessed him, there would also be damages for the interference with possession. The amount of damages might be less than the owner's damages, but that has to do only with the estimated value in the hands of that plaintiff of restored possession of that missing thing.[81] In sum, the only difference between an owner out of possession and other prior possessors is in the *value* of right to immediate possession each holds.

If so, ownership is not a separate form of property in the common law system. The term now looks like ambiguous shorthand, sometimes meaning "possession projected to last for the useful life of the thing possessed" while at other times describing "right to immediate possession equal in value to possession projected to last for the useful life of the thing possessed". Like most shorthand, it does no harm so long as those using it and those reading or hearing it are both clear as to which meaning is intended, but does substantial damage to effective communication when used as jargon. Ownership is used as jargon in most common law dialogue.

We now turn to everyone's favourite area - cases involving estate holders in land and possessors claiming to have found things on the land. They provide further evidence that prior possession is the key.

4   Estate Holders and Things Found on Land

Most things are lost on land. People hold property in land. Legal precedent and history

---

81 Just as right to immediate possession of a car (which is what you hold between the time you sign the form at the car rental agency and the time you take possession of the car) varies in value depending on (i) the length of the rental term, and (ii) the type of car rented. I dare say that six months' possession of a Lincoln (and possible even a Cadillac) has a higher market value than projected possession forever (*ie*, ownership) of a battered Diet Chevy.

tell us that the most common forms of property in land are called "estates".[82] Anyone claiming to have found something on land is likely to be met with a claim for possession by someone holding an estate in the land.[83]

Sometimes estate holders win. Twentieth century analysts disagreed about why. There is little purpose in canvassing the various views. If property in things is structured as described in this book, one would expect estate holders' claims to be supportable by one of two theories. One would be some as yet unexplored theory peculiar to estate holders and related to the nature of land or property in land. The other would be that estate holders win when they prove prior possession. The former theory is superfluous, and the latter theory works.

Proving this requires some detailed analysis of common law cases. Various judicial and academic theories can be organized around six cases, spanning 131 years.[84] The six cases illustrate the common law method, whereby particular facts condition judicial thinking, but theories are developed through judicial re-thinking. It is remarkable how short the reports of the early cases are.

The six cases involved claims by estate holders concerning the following things.

1	banknotes on the floor of a retail shop	(1851)
2	a pocketbook on a table in a barbershop	(1866)

---

82 The system began with 1066 and all that. William I claimed to *own* all the land in England: survivors agreed. William allowed other people to use the land upon terms agreed between him and powerful "Land Lords". They held "estates" *in* the land. The various types of estates were just another form of property. Thus, to say that X held an estate in a specific area of land was simply to predict that the power of the state (ie. the king) would be thrown behind the person described as the holder of the property when he was threatened by intruders. The estates were held *of* the king: this meant that the king continued to hold ownership of the land and that the king's support could be anticipated only so long as the holder of the estate had not defaulted on his obligations to the king. That is the genesis of today's land law terminology. It is also, much to the chagrin of each generation of law students, a lot closer to today's theoretical basis of property in land than one would suspect. In common law Canada for example, the Queen still owns all the land. Others hold various estates in land of the Queen. Thus, a suburbanite does not "own" his own house: *She* does; the suburbanite probably holds "an estate in fee simple". Thus an apartment dweller who "rents" is more accurately described as holding a leasehold estate in the land", even though he lives in mid-air, on the 14th floor. In other common law countries some of the basics of land law have been altered - as in America, where the Revolution abolished the concept of Crown ownership of all land - but the terminology and much of the analytical superstructure lingers on. See a book on land law, traditionally called "Real Property", for details.

83 That person could be the state, particularly in jurisdictions which maintain the original theory that the Crown owns all land. See "State Claims", later in this Chapter.

84 Buried treasure, within a category of things called "treasure trove" is eliminated from this survey. It is covered later under the heading "State Claims". "Treasure-trove is a name given by the early common law to any gold or silver in coin, plate or bullion found concealed in the earth, or in a house, or other private place, but not lying on the ground, the owner of the discovered treasure being unknown": *Weeks v Hackett* 71 A 858 (Me 1908) *per* Whitehouse J.

3	a pre-historic boat two meters underground	(1886)
4	two gold rings at the bottom of a pool	(1896)
5	a brooch in a house requisitioned by the army	(1945)
6	a bracelet in an airport departure lounge	(1982)

Our story begins in 1851 with *Bridges* v *Hawkesworth*.[85] The plaintiff was a traveller representing suppliers with whom the defendant shopkeeper had dealings. The plaintiff called on business. While leaving, the plaintiff saw a parcel on the shop floor. He showed the parcel to the defendant's "shopman" and they opened it. Inside was _55 in banknotes. The plaintiff asked the defendant to keep the parcel at the shop and advertise for the owner. The defendant did, and three years passed without response. The plaintiff then asked for possession of the banknotes, offering to pay for the advertisement and to indemnify the defendant against any claims by the owner. The defendant refused; the plaintiff brought an action "to recover the notes". On appeal from a County Court decision in favour of the defendant, the sole issue was "whether the circumstances of the notes being found *inside* the defendant's shop, gives him, the defendant, the right to have them as against the plaintiff who found them".[86]

The plaintiff won. The reasons for judgment are two pages long. After canvassing the arguments, Patteson J ruled that the shopkeeper simply had no claim to possession.[87]

> We find, therefore, no circumstances in this case to take it out of the general rule of law that the finder of a lost article is entitled to it against all parties except the real owner; and we think that rule must prevail, and that the learned judge was mistaken in holding that the place in which they were found makes any legal difference.

Note the ratio. *In these circumstances*, the fact that the parcel was inside the defendant's shop made no difference. The interesting question is why. Why *might* it make a difference in other circumstances? Why didn't it here?

There are three obvious possibilities: deposit by the owner; a rule that estate holders defeat finders; the estate holder already held possession.

Possibility No 1. A package seen lying in a shop might have been deposited there for safekeeping. In such a case possession would have been transferred directly from the missing owner to the shopkeeper. The shopkeeper would be a bailee, a possessor by

---

85 *Bridges* v *Hawkesworth* (1851) 21 LJQB 75 (Eng).

86 It was assumed, or agreed by the litigants, that the wrapped banknotes had been dropped accidentally in the shop by the owner. Starting from that assumption, Patteson, J concluded: "[t]he plaintiff found them on the floor, they having been manifestly lost by someone. This right [possession by finding, quoting from *Armory* v *Delamirie*] would clearly have accrued to the plaintiff had the notes been picked up by him outside the shop ...". (21 LJQB (ns) at 77-78).

87 *Ibid* at 78. Of course, the defendant held possession at the time of the trial, by virtue of having been asked three years earlier to take steps in search of the owner. According to Patteson J "[t]hese steps were really taken by the defendant as the agent of the plaintiff".

transfer.[88] If lost means previously possessed but currently out of possession, then the package could not have been found in those circumstances because it was not lost.[89] That was not the situation in *Bridges* v *Hawkesworth*. There, the package had been dropped accidentally on the floor, the shopkeeper knew nothing about it, and the plaintiff found it.[90]

Possibility No 2. It might be a rule that an estate holder in land where a thing is found always defeats the finder. That is unlikely. We shall see from later cases that there is little support for such a rule among judges and academics. If it is a rule, *Bridges* v *Hawkesworth* is wrong.[91]

Possibility No 3. A package seen lying in a shop might have been lost by the owner, but possession may be held already by the shopkeeper. Loss by the owner negatives the possibility that a *transfer* of possession took place.[92] Yet possession by the shopkeeper need not depend on acquisition by transaction. *Nor need it depend on proof that the shopkeeper found the package.* A review of some basics may clarify the point. To say that a shopkeeper holds possession of a package is simply to predict that the state will intervene on the shopkeeper's side to restrict the liberty of others in dealing with the

---

88 See Chapter 10 "Bailment: A Separate Transaction?". Note that either an owner or a prior possessor could have transferred possession to the shopkeeper.

89 See Chapter 5 "Losing Things and Finding Things".

90 Justice Patteson (at 77) rejected a Latin maxim recited by the shopkeeper's lawyer, saying that it,
assumes that they are deposited there for custody ... The facts of this case negative that the defendant knew anything about the notes being in his shop ... [and] do not warrant the supposition that they had been deposited there intentionally. ... The notes never were in the custody of the defendant, nor within the protection of his house, before they were found, as they would have been had they been intentionally deposited there.
Similarly, see *Hamaker* v *Blanchard* 90 Penn St 377 (Penn 1879) (domestic servant in hotel finds bank bills in public parlor; owner not found; servant defeats hotel keeper for possession).

91 This would hardly be the judge's fault. Neither lawyer suggested that the general rule from *Armory* v *Delamirie* was that "the finder of a lost article is entitled to it against all parties except the real owner [*and the estate holder in the land where the thing was found*]". If *Bridges* v *Hawkesworth* is wrong, I think it must be wrong on some other, narrower point. By the way, it is not noted in the facts that the shopkeeper was an estate holder. However, the case has always been dealt with on the basis that he was and a shopkeeper without a freehold or leasehold estate in the land would be keeping a precarious shop.

92 A transfer of property is a conscious, bilateral exchange transaction between two persons. Transfers create obligations between the parties which are based on and vary with the details of the transaction. The coincidental acts of losing and finding may add up to a disposition of possession by the loser and an acquisition of possession by the finder, but they no more constitute a transfer than 3 apples + 3 oranges constitute 6 appleoranges. Judges are aware of this distinction. In *Gilchrist Watt and Sanderson Pty Ltd* v *York Products Pty Ltd* [1970] 1 WLR 1262 (NSW JCPC) Lord Pearson said (at 1268) that calling a finder a bailee "is not etymologically accurate, because the word 'bailee' is derived from the French 'bailler' meaning to deliver or hand over, and there is no delivering or handing over to a finder". This point is further developed in Chapter 10 "Bailment: a Separate Transaction?". Unfortunately, later in the same case (at 1270) Lord Pearson consciously misused the word bailment, excusing himself on the ground that it was common practice to do so in the English courts. That's the whole problem. The solution is to define and use words precisely and generate fewer rules that don't contradict one another.

package.[93] To prove that this shopkeeper held possession of that package lying on that floor is quite another matter: that requires evidence. Evidence of an earlier acquisition of possession would do. Transfer from a previous holder or taking possession upon finding would suffice, absent evidence of an intervening disposition, because property acquired is held until disposed of in some way. The only purpose of proving such an acquisition would be to prove that the shopkeeper held possession when the traveller picked up the package. Direct evidence that the shopkeeper held possession - which would involve listing the elements of possession and proving that each of them was then present - would do just as well. The latter method of proof was not attempted in *Bridges* v *Hawkesworth*.[94] As to the former, the plaintiff tried, but failed.[95]

We leave *Bridges v Hawkesworth* with three possible theories about when an estate holder prevails, and with a fairly clear notion of why the shopkeeper there didn't. The first possibility, that a deposit for safekeeping occurred between owner and shopkeeper, was unsupported by the facts. The second possibility, that estate holders always defeat finders, was not argued. The third possibility, that the shopkeeper held possession of the package while it was lying on the floor, was argued and rejected as not proved by the facts. In the third possible theory, the critical question is whether the shopkeeper held possession of the package when the traveller says he found it: how that possession came about is an incidental point. Each of these theories had its moments in subsequent cases.

McAvoy v *Medina*[96] came 15 years later and started an American trend. The defendant was a barber. The plaintiff was a customer in his shop. The plaintiff saw a pocket-book lying on a table and picked it up. He told the barber to keep it to give to the owner and suggested advertising. No owner appeared and the plaintiff sued for possession. The reasons for judgment took less than a page. It was an agreed fact at the trial that the

---

93 See the development of the definition in Chapter 2 "Possession". The underlying analysis of the nature of property is covered in Chapter 1"Property and Things Contrasted".

94 Except to the extent of alleging a transfer of possession for safekeeping, which was already rejected under possibility number 1.

95 The plaintiff's lawyer pointed out that, by extension of the defendant's argument, "if the plaintiff, after picking up the notes, had said, I will keep them and endeavour to find the true owner, the defendant might have brought trover for the notes..." (at 77). Only proof of prior possession would support a claim in trover. Justice Patteson picked up this point in his reasons for judgment (at 77).

> The case resolves itself into the single point ... whether the circumstances of the notes being found *inside* the defendant's shop, gives him, the defendant, the right to have them as against the plaintiff who found them. ... [I]f the defendant has that right, *when* did it accrue to him? If at all, it must have been antecedent to the finding by the plaintiff, for that finding could not give the defendant any right. If the notes had been accidentally kicked into the street, and then found by someone passing by, could it be that the defendant was entitled to them, from the mere fact of their having been originally dropped in his shop? If the discovery had not been communicated to the defendant, could the real owner have had any cause of action against him, because they were found in his house? Certainly not. The notes never were in the custody of the defendant, nor within the protection of his house, before they were found ... .

96 *McAvoy* v *Medina* 11 Allen 548, 93 Mass 548 (1866). It was not noted in the facts that the barber held an estate the land, though he probably did.

120

pocket-book had been placed on the table by a customer and accidentally left there. Justice Dewey regarded that fact as a critical distinction from *Bridges* v *Hawkesworth*.[97] He ruled that the plaintiff had not found the pocket-book because it was not lost.[98]

> [T]o place a pocket-book upon a table and to forget to take it away is not to lose it, in the sense in which the authorities referred to speak of lost property. We accept this as the better rule, and especially as one better adapted to secure the rights of the true owner. In view of the facts of this case, the plaintiff acquired no original right to the property ... .

Note the reasoning. The pocket-book was not lost, so it could not be found: therefore the plaintiff lost ("acquired no original right").

Did Justice Dewey mean that the plaintiff didn't acquire possession when he picked it up? That can't be so, as the definition of possession has nothing to do with finding things. Possession of a thing is proved by the coexistence of physical control and manifest intent to exclude other people.[99] Both of these were negatived when the plaintiff left the barber in possession to seek the owner,[100] but I think the judge was focussing on what occurred before that, when the plaintiff first picked up the pocket-book. That was when the question of possession arose. What would have happened if the plaintiff had then said "I will keep it and endeavour to find the owner"? Might the defendant then have had an action for possession of the pocket-book? That was the hypothetical question put by the finder's lawyer in *Bridges* v *Hawkesworth*.[101] The answer there was no, on the ground that the defendant shopkeeper did not hold possession of the parcel on the floor. Isn't the answer here yes? Isn't the critical distinction in *McAvoy* v *Medina* that the barber held possession of the pocket-book on the table before the customer picked it up?

---

97 He said it was distinguishable, because the parcel of banknotes in *Bridges* v *Hawkesworth* was "found on the floor, and had not been placed there voluntarily by the owner".

98 93 Mass 548 at 549, quoting the first sentence from a Tennessee case, *Lawrence* v *The State* 1 Humph (Tenn) 228.

99 See Chapter 2 "Possession". The fact that a thing was lost means only that no one was dispossessed by the act of taking possession. I can take possession of a wine glass at dinner in my friend's house. If he is not my friend, or if I have not been invited to dinner, or especially if he's out of town and I broke in, I may by sued (and prosecuted) for dispossessing him. But I have taken possession, mad my possession would be protected by the state against other intruders in each of those circumstances. The detailed requirements for taking possession are explained in Chapter 3 "Discovery: the First Finder's Property" and Chapter 5 "Taking Possession of Things Found".

100 The barber clearly held possession at least from that time. The real issue in the case was whether he would continue to hold possession after the trial. That depended on whether he had been holding possession as bailee (*ie.* consensual transferee of possession) of the plaintiff or by virtue of his own possession arising before the plaintiff picked up the pocket-book. Maybe that is how Justice Dewey saw the case: his earlier quote continued "... the plaintiff acquired no original right to the property, *and the defendant's subsequent acts in receiving and holding the property in the manner he did does not create any*". [Emphasis added] Did he mean that the defendant *acquired* no property in the pocketbook when the plaintiff left him in possession because he already held possession before that time?

101 *Bridges* v *Hawkesworth* (1851) 21 LJQB 75 (Eng) at 77.

That has been the view in subsequent American cases. However, they came to that view by a curious process. The distinction was explained as follows one year later. "To discover an article voluntarily laid down by the owner within a banking house ... is not the finding of a lost article. The occupants of the banking house ... were the proper depositories of an article so left."[102] By 1920, some 54 years later, this characterization of estate holders as "the proper depositories" of things left behind by customers had become substantially less vague. *Foulke* v *NY Consolidated Railway Co*[103] was a battle for possession between the corporate operator of a subway railway system and a passenger who had picked up a package apparently left by another passenger on a seat in one of the railway cars. The conclusion was that the package was not lost, but "mislaid",[104] and that the railway corporation had become "a gratuitous bailee for the safekeeping of the package" before the second passenger picked it up.[105] How could this be, given that a bailee acquires possession by transaction? That question was answered in 1968: the rule "is based on the legal fiction that mislaid property is presumed to have been left in the custody of the owner or occupier of the premises upon which it is found".[106] In other words, let's pretend that the estate holder acquired possession by mythical transfer from the person who "mislaid" the thing; never mind that the parties presented no evidence of any such transaction, or that the estate holder admits that he didn't know the thing was there. It wasn't found at all. That rascal says he found it, but he really (pretend really) took it out of the estate holder's possession. The estate holder retains possession if he held possession at the time of trial. If not, he wins as a

---

102 *Kincaid* v *Eaton* 98 Mass 139 (Mass 1867). The defendant had left his pocket-book on a desk in the lobby of a bank. The plaintiff picked it up while at the bank. He took the pocket-book to the defendant's address in response to the following newspaper ad: "One hundred and ten dollars reward. Lost, a pocket-book containing papers valuable only to the owner. The finder can have the above reward by returning book and contents to [the newspaper office]." The defendant offered only $10. The plaintiff made it clear that he was not satisfied, though he took the money and returned possession to the defendant. The plaintiff's contract action for the rest of the reward failed on the ground that as the pocketbook was "mislaid", not lost, he had not found it and therefore had "not established a legal right to the reward according to the terms by which it was offered". Rather strictly construed, don't you think? I shouldn't like to try collecting on King John's notice for the return of James James Morrison Morrison's mother from that judge.

103 *Foulke* v *NY Consolidated Railway Co* 127 NE 237 (NYCA 1920).

104 "Lost property is not mislaid property or property voluntarily put in the place intended and forgotten, but property the possession of which is parted from casually and involuntarily": 127 NE 237

105 "It [the package] then had become in the custody and the potential actual possession of the defendant. It was the right of the defendant and its duty to become ... a gratuitous bailee for the safekeeping of the package until the owner should call for it. ... The right of the defendant to the custody and actual possession of the package was superior to the taking of the plaintiff": 127 NE at 238-239.

106 *Hurley* v *City of Niagara Falls* 289 NYS 2d 889 (NY 1968) *per* Bastow J at 891, affirmed without reported reasons 255 NE 2d 917 (NYCA 1969). The plaintiff was an independent contractor hired to renovate the defendant's basement. He found $4990 in banknotes hidden by someone other than the defendant behind a block on the floor of the cabinet enclosing the sink. It was held that a New York statute requiring that found things be turned over to the police had abolished the distinction between lost and mislaid things. The finder won.

dispossessed prior possessor.[107]

That is silly. Edward R Cohen pointed out that to apply this so-called rule[108]

> requires no fewer than eight specific assumptions of fact, none of which is capable of proof [by the parties to the action] and none of which is subjected to the requirements of proof at trial. ... [As the loser has disappeared] virtually all *mislaid* cases are decided on the unknown subjective state of an unknown individual.

The legal process involves the application of general principles of law to particular facts proved by evidence presented by the parties in particular cases. The process doesn't work when judges and lawyers are distracted from this straightforward, though difficult exercise. To speculate about whether an ostensibly found thing was lost or mislaid is to meander down a garden path.

The parties got on to the garden path in *McAvoy* v *Medina*[109] by agreeing to a critical fact - that the pocket-book had been placed on the barber's table by a customer and accidentally left it there. The subsequent customer who picked it up need not have conceded that fact. All we know is that he claimed as a possessor by finding, he conceded the fact, and he lost. Would he have won if, when asked how it got there, he had simply said "I don't know"? Let's review our three possible theories.

Possibility No 1. A pocket-book seen lying on a table in a shop might have been deposited there for safekeeping. There was no evidence of any such purpose. Leaving it there without asking whether the barber was willing to accept the deposit - to participate in the bailment transaction - seems an odd way to go about negotiating transfer of possession. It is not clear that the judge decided the case on this theory. All he said was that it wasn't lost, that the plaintiff therefore wasn't a possessor by finding, and that for some unarticulated reason awarding possession to the barber struck him as a result "better adapted to secure the rights of the true owner". Maybe the judge in *McAvoy* v *Medina* just thought he had legislative power to give away possession as he saw fit. Anyway, this case seems to be the root of a tenuous distinction between "mislaid" things and "lost" things.[110] It is assumed that the pocket-book was deposited for safekeeping.

---

107 See "Dispossessed Prior Possessors" *supra*. It's amazing how intelligent people can be tricked by codewords. Judges appear quite comfortable applying "legal fictions" like this. Compare their reactions to plain speech like "let's pretend". Compare your reaction. Is there any meaningful distinction between the two labels?

108 Cohen "The Finders Cases Revisited" 48 Texas L Rev 1001 at 1004 and 1010. Professor Cohen was, I think, of the view that the so-called "mislaid" rule is nonsense. For an extreme example of the fine distinctions invited by the "mislaid" concept, see *Durfee* v *Jones* 11 RI 588 (1877) in which bank notes clearly placed in a safe by someone were ruled lost only because they appeared to have slipped by accident into a crack between the outer casing and the lining.

109 *McAvoy* v *Medina* 11 Allen 548, 93 Mass 548 (1866).

110 The distinction never caught on outside America, although it was the basis of the decision in an

Possibility No 2. It might be a rule that an estate holder in land where a thing is found always defeats the finder. This possibility was not raised in *McAvoy* v *Medina*.

Possibility No 3. The pocket-book might have been lost, yet the barber might have proved possession other than by virtue of a transaction with the loser. This possibility was apparently not raised.

In the next case, *Elwes* v *Brigg Gas Co*,[111] both parties held estates in the land. The plaintiff held a life estate.[112] The defendant corporation was in occupation of the land under the terms of a 99 year lease, and thus held a leasehold estate.[113] The defendant dug up a prehistoric boat while excavating about six feet below the surface. Excavation was permitted by the lease, which authorized the erection of certain structures while reserving mineral rights to the plaintiff. Justice Chitty explained that a buried boat could be characterized in any of three ways - as a mineral, as "part of the soil in which it was imbedded" or as "retaining the character of a chattel". He concluded that he need not select one characterization over the others as the plaintiff won on all three. In the judgment of Chitty J, the boat was not found at all because the plaintiff held property in it before the defendant dug it up and took possession.[114]

> The first question ... is whether the boat belonged to the Plaintiff at the time of the granting of the lease. I hold that it did ... [and if] regarded as a chattel, I hold the property in the chattel was vested in the Plaintiff [who was] in possession of the ground ... down to

obscure Canadian case, *Heddle* v *Bank of Hamilton* (1912) 17 BCLR 306 (BCCA) (wallet left on desk used by customers in public part of bank; "involuntarily mislaid, and not lost"; "anyone seeing it there ... ought to regard it as under the protection of the house"). It was ignored, for example, in *Hannah* v *Peel* [1945] 2 All ER 288 (Eng) (dealt with later), on facts that clearly invited the "mislaid" argument. The cases in American law are utterly irreconcilable. Sometimes the thing is assumed to have been lost: see *Cleveland Railway Co* v *Durschuk* 166 NE 909 (Ohio 1928) ("no one would put a $20 bill beside him upon the floor of a street car, as he would a package"). Sometimes the thing is assumed to have been mislaid, as in the case of a bearer bond certificate on the floor of a safety deposit room in a bank: *Silcott* v *Louisville Trust Company* 265 SW 612 (Ky 1924). Sometimes the party denying that the thing was lost is required to prove that it was mislaid, which is of course impossible as the person who is alleged to have mislaid the thing has disappeared and would defeat both claimants if he showed up: see *McDonald* v *Railway Express Agency* 81 SE2d 525 (Ga 1954) (wallet containing money on floor of defendant's business premises held found by plaintiff; defendant did not prove that the wallet was "on the premises by virtue of the contractual duty of the [estate holder, who was also plaintiff's employer] to care for it"). A review of the digests reveals many other examples. The root of the problem is, as pointed out by Edward R Cohen, "The Finders Cases Revisited" 48 Texas L Rev 1001 at 1006, that there is no useful distinction between forgetting that you left something on a horizontal surface when you leave a building and forgetting that there is a hole in your pocket when you put something there. The intention to exclude others remains, but control is lost by inadvertence in both situations.

111 *Elwes* v *Brigg Gas Co* (1886) 33 Ch D 562 (Eng).

112 A form of property in land that terminates upon the death of some specified person, usually the holder of the estate.

113 A form of property in land predetermined to last either a specified time (usually months or years) or terminable at the whim of the person who created it.

114 33 Ch D at 568.

the centre of the earth, and consequently in possession of the boat. The plaintiff then, being thus in possession of the chattel, it follows that the property in the chattel was vested in him. Obviously, the right of the original owner ... had for centuries been lost or barred, even supposing that the property had not been abandoned. ... [I]t makes no difference, in these circumstances, that the Plaintiff was not aware of the existence of the boat.

Note the structure of this analysis. Assume the buried boat to be identifiable as such rather than merged as part of the land. Assume a rule that gives an estate holder occupying land "possession" of everything in the space enclosed by a truncated cone whose projected point is at the centre of earth and whose sides pierce the surface at the horizontal boundaries of the land.[115] The buried boat was in that cone, so the plaintiff held possession of it. No one else owned it, through either abandonment or death of all likely inheritors, so the plaintiff owned it. Unless ownership or possession of the boat had been transferred by the lease, which Chitty J concluded was silent on the point, the plaintiff won as a dispossessed prior possessor and owner.

Ten years later this notion of possession of things within three dimensional land boundaries was further explored.

In *South Staffordshire Water Co v Sharman*[116] a workman was hired by an estate holder to clean out a pool. The workman picked up two gold rings from the mud at the bottom. The estate holder sued for possession and won. Lord Russell of Killowen offered a lengthy and much criticized analysis of why the estate holder had lost in *Bridges* v *Hawkesworth*.[117] He was, however, brief and unequivocal as to why the South Staffordshire Water Company won.[118]

---

115 Unless the Flat Earth Society people have it right. Judges used to say "*cuius est solum eius est usque ad coelum et ad inferos*" or words to that effect. I think they were expressing an old-fashioned view that the holder of an estate in land held property in a mass of earth, air, (fire?) and water extending from the centre of earth to the sky. That the sky part was a bit excessive became evident in the early days of the airplane and a vaguely defined upper boundary became recognized. These days, the major airlines of the world are not trespassing when they fly across country 10,000 meters up. However, a neighbour who lays a horizontal line of tracer bullets across my lawn at a height of 1 meter *is* trespassing in my airspace. How the dividing line is drawn has yet to be conclusively decided, but it certainly has something to do with the height to which the particular estate holder is making use of the airspace. Eventually, the courts will come to grips with the underground question as well and, in my view, must surely set a lower limit by using the same test as for airspace. If this is correct, then the shape of land in which property is held is *a truncated* cone.

116 *South Staffordshire Water Co v Sharman* [1896] 2 QB 44 (Eng).

117 Subsequent cases and articles have roundly criticized his over-statement of the facts of *Bridges* v *Hawkesworth*. The best analysis, and an interesting commentary on how the passage of time enhances the precedent value of what judges did *not* say in previous cases, is found in Goodhart, "Three Cases on Possession" (1929) 3 Cambridge LJ 195. For the record, Lord Russell of Killowen asserted that the package in *Bridges* v *Hawkesworth* was dropped "in the public part of the shop" and was picked up by "a customer". The finder was a commercial traveller and there is no indication whatever that he was in a part of the shop open to the public.

118 [1896] 2 QB 44 at 46.

[T]he plaintiffs must show that they had actual control over the locus in quo and the things in it; but under the circumstances can it be said that the Minster Pool and whatever might be in that pool were not under the control of the plaintiffs" In my opinion they were.

He was not talking about the rings as if they were part of the mud in which they were buried. He was talking about estate holder's control over the rings as such. The *circumstances* proved that control. What were the circumstances? Generally, "the freeholders ... have the right to forbid anybody coming on their land".[119] More particularly, as to things not lying loose on the surface:[120]

> possession of land carries with it generally, by our law, possession of everything which is attached to or under the land ... and it makes no difference that the possessor is not aware of the thing's existence... [T]he legal possession rests on a real de facto possession *constituted by the occupier's general power and intent to exclude unauthorized interference.* That is the ground on which I prefer to base my judgment. [Emphasis added]

On the following page he pointed out that possession is held by an occupier of land who has "a manifest intention to exercise control over it and the things which may be upon it". This seems to have been intended both to distinguish *Bridges* v *Hawkesworth* and to clarify what was said about the occupier's intent in the quote set out above. The context is the key.

Looking at the comment about "manifest intention" in the context of the earlier statements clarifies the reasoning in this case. The estate holder had to prove prior possession of the rings. Possession of things is ordinarily proved by evidence of physical control and manifest intent to exclude others from interfering with them. An estate holder is conceded a substantial degree of control over the boundaries of the land: he need not post armed guards about the perimeter to enforce this control.

Most estate holders also intend to exclude uninvited callers from the grounds. The particular estate holder's pattern of behaviour may indicate otherwise. The social relationship between a particular visitor and the estate holder could diminish the ordinary expectation that the visitor was unwelcome. However, most people approaching most land boundaries are unlikely to assume that they are at liberty to browse about. They are far more likely to interpret any boundary marker as an indication, a *manifestation*, of the

---

119 [1896] 2 QB at 46.

120 [1896] 2 QB at 46-47. I have difficulty with the concept of "possession of land", as the word possession is defined in terms of control of and manifest intent to exclude others from *things* and I am not sure that the same mental and physical tests are appropriate in the case of land. I advocate the word "occupation" if the objective is to describe mere physical presence on the land. Otherwise, the long form "holding an estate in the land" seems less likely to cause confusion.

estate holder's intent to exclude most people and to admit some others on terms.

How far this can be translated into a manifestation of intent to preclude interference with things lying about the land might depend on several factors. Judges in particular cases are unlikely to list and explain all these factors: their task is to resolve the disputes before them.

The dispute before Lord Russell of Killowen was not unusual. An estate holder invited workmen on the land for a specific purpose: they were to clean out the pool. They must have been aware of having crossed a land boundary, of being where they were not usually welcomed. Given the terms upon which they were there, and considering that the usual boundary control had been relaxed on those terms, did they perceive a manifestation of intent concerning anything that might be hidden in the bottom of the pool? Who knows? They are unlikely to say that they did.

However, isn't the test more objective than that? Would most observers - would the traditional "reasonable man" - think that the estate holder generally manifested an intent to exclude others from getting at and taking possession of things that might be hidden in the pool? I think Lord Russell of Killowen thought so. Was this notice to all reasonable men varied by the particular terms of entry in this case? Lord Russell of Killowen thought not.

Elwes v *Brigg Gas Co.*[121] involved a buried prehistoric boat. *South Staffordshire Water Co* v *Sharman*[122] dealt with rings in the mud of a pool. In both cases the holder of an estate in the land defeated the person claiming to have found the things. Consider our three theories as to why.

Possibility No 1. The boat and the rings might have been deposited there by the owners for safekeeping by the estate holder. This theory was not considered, probably because it was incredible in the circumstances.[123]

Possibility No 2. It might be a rule that an estate holder in land where a thing is found always defeats a finder, at least so far as buried things are concerned. Justice Chitty in *Elwes* could be interpreted as having said this when he suggested that an estate holder held possession of all things within the cone shaped boundaries of the land. But he didn't explain *how* he reached that conclusion. Lord Russell of Killowen in *South Staffordshire*

---

121 *Elwes* v *Brigg Gas Co* (1886) 33 Ch D 562 (Eng)

122 *South Staffordshire Water Co* v *Sharman* [1896] 2 QB 44 (Eng).

123 It is more difficult to figure out why *Danielson* v *Roberts* 74 P 913 (Ore 1904) was not decided on the "mislaid" theory. Two boys, hired to clean out an old chicken coop, found a rusty can containing $7000 in gold coins. Strangely, they won possession as finders. "The fact that the money was found on the premises of the defendants, or that the plaintiff's were in their service at the time, can in no way affect the plaintiffs' right to possession."

clearly resiled from such a rule. He thought most estate holders could be proved to hold possession of most things buried inside the boundaries of the land. However, he left open the possibility of disproving this, in which case possession could be taken by a finder and the estate holder would have no claim. The theory that the estate holder always prevails begins to weaken as our survey approaches the 20th century.

Possibility No 3. The estate holder might be able to prove possession of things inside the boundaries of the land without having found them and without even knowing they were there. Salvors who take possession of wrecked ships acquire possession of any cargo inside even though they haven't seen it, can't identify it and aren't sure it survived intact.[124] The reason is that access is restricted by control over the wreck and the intention to appropriate what is there would be obvious to the normal observer who might happen by. Possessors of locked boxes hold possession of banknotes not known to be inside.[125] The reason is that the control and intent to exclude others manifested by the possessor of the box is not artificially restricted to the outside shell of the box, but extends to the space enclosed by the box and whatever is in that space. Compare Chitty's J description of the land as a three dimensional cone. This is a useful concept, provided we truncate the cone to take account of modern developments. Most estate holders provide boundary markers, commonly at surface level locations where others are most likely to enter. What exactly does posting such markers accomplish? Provided they convey at least two concepts - that control is being exercised and that the estate holder intends to restrict access to all things inside the perimeter - the markers could be sufficient evidence that the estate holder holds possession of anything contained in the truncated cone. Whether that information has been conveyed involves no philosophical questions about the nature of estates in land; it is simply a matter of interpretation of boundary markers in any particular case.[126] We don't know whether there really were

---

124 See *Tubantia (The)* [1924] P 78 (Eng) at 90, holding that the plaintiffs' early salvage operations on a wreck had established "the possession of the Tubantia and her cargo, which they allege". This case is dealt with in detail in Chapter 5 "Taking Possession of Things Found".

125 See *Grafstein v Holme and Freeman* (1957) 12 DLR 2d 727 (Ont CA), dealt with in detail in Chapter 5 "Taking Possession of Things Found". Commenting on this decision, an English judge endorsed this distinction between finding something and taking possession of it. "The Court treated the moment of finding the money as that at which the box was opened, rather than when the box was found [but] Mr. Grafstein had a superior claim because he took possession and control of the box *and of its unknown contents* when its existence was first brought to his attention:" Donaldson LJ in *Parker v British Airways Board* [1982] 2 WLR 503 (Eng CA) at 512. [Emphasis added] Lord Justice Donaldson made a list of rules about estate holders possessing things on land, noting (at 514) that an "occupier of a chattel, eg. a ship, motor car, caravan, or aircraft, is to be treated as if he were the occupier of a building for the purposes of the foregoing rules." Another case often cited on this point is *Cartwright v Green* (1802) 8 Ves 405, 32 ER 412 (Eng). Ann Cartwright died "possessed of" a bureau. She had hidden 900 guineas in a secret drawer. Possession of the bureau was sold to a Mr Dick, who sent it to the defendant carpenter for repairs. The carpenter found and took possession of the coins in the drawer. A motion was brought to determine whether the carpenter could be compelled to give evidence on discovery. A procedural rule excused him if the claim *alleged* facts amounting to a felony: he was excused. The mere allegation obviously proved nothing and nothing was really decided about the prior possessor's claim.

126 That, by the way, strikes me as the reason why estate holders traditionally held possession of dead

boundary markers with explicit messages in *Elwes* v *Brigg Gas Co.* but the leaseholder and life estate holder had negotiated terms of entry which Chitty J interpreted as a limited relaxation of the life estate holder's control and intent to exclude vis-à-vis such things as the buried boat. Similarly, there was no evidence of posted notices in *South Staffordshire Water Co* v *Sharman*, but the workers had entered the grounds on terms that made them aware of the general nature of the estate holder's control and intent to exclude. Lord Russell of Killowen was of the view that the estate holder's control over and manifest intent to exclude others from the gold rings in the pool had been proved.

We move to 1945 and our fifth case, *Hannah* v *Peel*.[127] The defendant held a freehold estate in a house which had been requisitioned by the army and was used as a sick-bay.[128] The plaintiff was a soldier occupying a room in the house. One night, while adjusting the blackout curtains, he knocked something loose from the plaster or woodwork around the window. In the morning light he saw that it was a brooch, covered with dirt and cobwebs. The judicial conclusion was that the plaintiff was a possessor by finding.[129]

Justice Birkett explained why, reviewing all the precedent cases in the process.[130] He summarized his view of the law as follows.[131]

---

former wild animals killed on the land. "So long as the grouse is upon a man's land he has a possessory property in it, but as soon as it flies or goes off his land his property is gone": *Earl of Lonsdale* v *Rigg* (1856) 11 Exch 654, 156 ER 992 (Eng), *per* Martin B. In *Pamment* v *Thompson* (1921) 20 OWN 89 (Ont CA) an estate holder held possession of muskrats trapped by the defendants, probably because of the warnings he had posted against hunting or fishing. The reasoning traditionally recited by judges - that "it would be unreasonable to hold that the property vests in the trespasser or wrongdoer [so] it must of necessity be vested in [the estate holder]": *Blades* v *Higgs* (1865) 20 CBNS 214, 144 ER 1087 (Eng HL) *per* Lord Westbury at 1090) - smacks of judicial moralizing: by what authority do judges give away property to supposedly deserving recipients?

127 *Hannah* v *Peel* [1945] 2 All ER 288 (Eng).

128 The defendant had, I think, inherited either a life estate or an estate in fee simple. Of course, the estate was held in the land, and the house was simply part of that land. Much has been made by other commentators of the fact that the defendant had never occupied the land: I am not convinced that matters at all, but the point is addressed later. As to what it means to say that the Army "requisitioned" the house, I am not sure. Probably "the Army" means the Crown. At common law, the Crown *owned* all land and the best anyone else could do was hold an estate *of the Crown*. The Crown thus had an owner's power to terminate or suspend such estates at will at common law. I am informed that this system may have changed somewhat in England in 1925, but I doubt that the details matter much for our purpose here. The defendant was paid _250 *per* year "as compensation for the requisitioning"; the defendant was, at best, a landlord and, at worst, a temporarily suspended estate holder.

129 The plaintiff had apparently contacted his superior officer and then the police. Some correspondence with the estate holder ensued. Somehow the estate holder got possession and purported to sell ownership to a retailer, who then sold possession of the brooch through his shop, thinking he was selling ownership. The plaintiff sued for possession or damages.

130 He was most critical of Lord Russell of Killowen's mis-statement of the *Bridges* v *Hawkesworth* analysis, calling his summary of the facts "a little remarkable": [1945] 2 All E.R. 288 at 291.

131 [1945] 2 All ER 288 at 294.

I think it is fairly clear from the authorities ... that a man possesses everything which is attached to or under his land. Secondly, it would appear to be the law ... that a man does not necessarily possess a thing which is lying unattached on the surface of his land ... But the [reason] has never been very clearly formulated in our law. He may possess everything upon the land from which he intends to exclude others ... or he may possess those things over which he has a de facto control ... That is all that I think I can usefully say about the authorities.

There are two odd points here. First, Birkett J set out a rule that all buried things are possessed, ignoring the qualifications from *South Staffordshire* v *Sharman*.[132] Second, he cited "de facto control" and "intent to exclude others" as alternative explanations of why an estate holder might hold possession of things on the surface.[133] It doesn't seem to have occurred to him that, because these are the constituent elements of possession, proof of both is required.

Moving from this confused statement of the law, Birkett J proceeded to decide the case before him.[134]

It is clear that the defendant ... was never physically in possession of the premises at any time. It is clear that the brooch was never his in the ordinary acception of that term, in that he had the prior possession. He had no knowledge of it until it was brought to his knowledge by the finder. ... [T]he brooch was lost in the ordinary meaning of words, ... was found in the ordinary meaning of words, and ... the true owner has never been found. ... The conclusion to which I have come is that I propose to follow the decision in *Bridges* v *Hawkesworth* and I propose to give judgment in this case for the plaintiff.

That doesn't make a lot of sense. If a house is part of the land, the brooch was buried in the land before the soldier accidentally dug it out. It may be clear to the judge that that the estate holder never had prior possession of the brooch, but it is not obvious from his summary of the law. What the fact that the estate holder was "never physically in possession of these premises" has to do with the issue of possession of the brooch is unclear and unexplained.

The brooch may well have been lost and found "in the ordinary meaning of words": so was the buried boat in *Elwes* and so were the gold rings in *South Staffordshire*, yet the estate holders held possession. Have the ordinary meanings of lost and found anything to

---

132 Ironically, having criticized Lord Russel of Killowen for mis-stating the facts of *Bridges*, he left out the key points in *Elwes* and suggested that the *South Staffordshire* case turned on the employment relationship, which is nonsense.

133 He quoted Holmes and Pollock. An editorial note at [1945] 2 All ER at 288 suggests that those who say that such things might not always be possessed by the estate holder are split "between those who regard the possession of an occupier as synonymous with intention to exclude others, and those who regard it as equivalent to de facto control".

134 [1945] 2 All ER 288 at 294.

do with the issue?[135]

All that really is clear here is that Birkett J *decided* that the estate holder never possessed the brooch, *concluded* that the plaintiff was a possessor by finding, and *thought* that he was following *Bridges* v *Hawkesworth*. His earlier summary of that case seems to have been that the place of finding was not relevant to the outcome.[136] That, of course, contradicts his summary of the law set out above.

The facts of *Hannah* v *Peel* presented a golden opportunity to update and clarify the law. The reasons for judgment merely added to the confusion. The field lay fallow 37 years.[137]

Then, in 1982, *Parker* v *British Airways Board*[138] came to the English Court of Appeal. The defendant held a leasehold estate in an area at Heathrow Airport. It was used as a lounge for first class and "executive club" passengers on international flights. The plaintiff, a passenger, found a gold bracelet on the floor of the lounge. He gave possession of it to an employee of the defendant, leaving his address and instructions to return possession unless the owner claimed it. No owner showed up, and possession was

---

135 Whatever the ordinary meanings of these words are, a judge sitting with a jury in a finding case would surely not have instructed the jury adequately if he simply said "go away, review the evidence, and if you think that you would say in everyday speech that the thing was lost and was found, then you may award possession to the finder".

136 "It is to be observed that neither counsel [in *Bridges* v *Hawkesworth*] put any argument upon the fact that the notes were found in a shop. ... The second thing to be observed is that there was no suggestion that the place where the notes were found was at all material; indeed, the judge in giving the judgment of the court expressly repudiated it and said: ... 'the learned judge was mistaken in holding that the place in which they were found makes any legal difference' ": [1945] 2 All ER 288 *per* Birkett J at 290. Is it true that the judge in *Bridges* v *Hawkesworth* expressly *repudiated* the notion that the location was material? Compare the view of Eveleigh LJ in *Parker* v *British Airways Board* [1982] 2 WLR 503 (Eng CA) at 517: "Patteson, J. ... was not saying that the place is an irrelevant consideration. He was saying that [in that case] there was nothing special about it".

137 Of course, the law was updated in books and many useful articles were written throughout the common law world. Edward R Cohen, writing in 48 Texas L Rev 1001 at 1013 (footnote 21) noted that *Hannah* v *Peel* showed "utter contempt" for the American "mislaid" doctrine. "How could a brooch get behind the top of a window frame unless it was placed there deliberately?" Judicial contributions during this period did little to clarify estate holders' claims. The Americans beavered away at the lost *versus* mislaid distinction. In Canada, *Grafstein* v *Holme and Freeman* (1958) 12 DLR 2d 727 (Ont CA) ruled in favour of an estate holder whose employee came across a locked box while cleaning the basement. The dispute was over possession of banknotes that turned out to be in the box when another employee broke the lock some time later, and the estate holder's position as employer plus his interim possession of the box influenced the decision. In England, *Corporation of London* v *Appleyard* [1963] 2 All ER 834 (Eng) ruled in favour of an estate holder when employees of an independent contractor hired to demolish a building uncovered a safe built into the basement wall. It contained banknotes. The safe "formed part of the demised premises [*ie*. the land]. The notes having been found in the safe, [the estate holders] had ... a better title thereto than the finders": McNair J at 838.

138 *Parker* v *British Airways Board* [1982] 2 WLR 503 (Eng CA).

not returned. The plaintiff won damages for conversion.

The sole issue was whether the defendant estate holder held possession of the bracelet before the plaintiff picked it up.[139] Lord Justice Donaldson surveyed the authorities and proposed his own complicated set of rules. Lord Justice Eveleigh was more succinct.[140]

> Whatever the difficulties which surround the concept of possession in English law, the two elements of control and animus possidendi must co-exist. ... Against all but the true owner a person in possession has the right to possess. It should follow therefore that an innocent handler of property who intends to take it for the purpose of discovering the owner and returning it to him should not be in danger of infringing any right in a third party. This makes it essential that the elements of possession should be apparent.

Here, Eveleigh LJ quoted Lord Russell of Killowen on the requirement that an estate holder's intention to control things on the land be manifest. He then continued.

> I regard Lord Russell of Killowen, CJ as saying that it is necessary for the occupier to prove that his intention was obvious. A person permitted upon the property of another must respect the lawful claims of the occupier as the terms upon which he is allowed to enter, but it is only right that those claims or terms should be made clear. What is necessary to do this must depend on the circumstances. Take the householder. He has the key to the front door. People do not enter at will. They come by very special invitation. They are not members of a large public group, even a restricted group of the public, as users of the executive lounge may be. I would be inclined to say that the occupier of a house will almost invariably possess any lost article on the premises. He may not have taken any positive steps to demonstrate his animus possidendi, but so firm is his control that the animus can be seen to attach to it. ... The firmer the control, the less will be the need to demonstrate independently the animus possidendi.

That is helpful. The issue is whether an estate holder held possession of a thing at a time in the past. He did if he proves it. Possession is proved by control and manifest intent. Control is measured by other people's lack of access:[141] this is easy for most estate

---

139 Lord Justice Eveleigh [1982] 2 W.L.R. 503 at 516: "for the defendants to succeed it must be shown that they had possession of the bracelet at the time when the plaintiff found it and took it into his possession". Lord Justice Donaldson (at 506) was less clear, describing the estate holder's claim as "based upon the proposition that at common law an occupier of land has ... rights over all lost chattels, which are on the land, whether or not the occupier knows of their existence." I assume he meant possession as it is difficult to imagine what other "rights over all lost chattels" estate holders would have. The third judge, Sir David Cairns, said that he agreed with the analysis of both and added only a few words (at 518) on manifestation of intent.

140 [1982] 2 WLR 503 at 516-517.

141 That is, control is a relative thing among people. It is not a contest between person and thing, as it is sometimes made to appear in the wild animal cases. Compare *Eads v Brazelton* 22 Ark 499, 79 Am Dec 88 (Ark 1861) (no control over Mississippi River wreck) with *Tubantia (The)* [1924] P 78 (Eng) (control over North Sea wreck). Compare *Keron v Cashman* 33 A 1055 (NJ 1896) (no control over banknotes in a found stocking) with *Grafstein v Holme and Freeman* (1958) 12 DLR 2d 727 (Ont CA) (control over banknotes

holders to prove. The intent required is intent to exclude. Proving that it was manifest is easier for some estate holders than for others. A man's home is his castle,[142] and no explicit manifestation is required at the front door or the back gate. A shopping mall is at the other end of the spectrum. More evidence of intent *to regulate interference with things lying about* is required as more people are let in. That explains *Bridges* v *Hawkesworth*: "Patteson, J. ... was not saying that the place is an irrelevant consideration. He was saying that [in that case] there was nothing special about it".[143]

Was there anything special about the British Airways executive lounge? Two points were argued. British Airways restricted access to the lounge, but that control was "exercised upon the basis of classes or category of user [and had] no real relevance to a manifest intention to assert custody and control over lost articles".[144] Potentially more helpful to the defendants' case was evidence of staff instructions about handling found things. "*But these instructions were not published to users of the lounge ... .*" [Emphasis added][145] From the point of view of the ordinary type of person invited to use the lounge, the estate holder had said nothing at all about things that might be lying on the floor.

Summing up, all three judges in *Parker* v *British Airways Board* approached the case by asking whether the estate holder had prior possession of the bracelet lying on the floor. All three said no. Each focussed on the lack of manifestation of intent to restrict access to or take charge of seemingly lost things. At least two thought that they were simply applying what Lord Russell of Killowen had said in the *South Staffordshire* case about the requirement for manifest intent. None of the judges indicated that he was overruling any of the previous cases,[146] or saying anything that hadn't been known for years.

---

in a found locked box). These cases are analyzed in detail in Chapter 5 "Taking Possession of Things Found". In none of them was the thing itself much affected by the degree of control being exercised. Contrast the greater degree of control proved by the estate holder in *South Staffordshire Water Co* v *Sharman* [1896] 2 QB 44 (Eng) with the lesser control in *Parker* v *British Airways Board* [1982] 2 WLR 503 (Eng CA). Control was not proved by assessing the effect of the estate holder's actions on the rings in the pool or the bracelet on the floor.

142 Though opening a stately house to the public would diminish the exclusivity, thus proving that a man's castle is not his home. It is one of the joys of life that paradoxes can be found outside the fields of mathematics and philosophy.

143 [1982] 2 WLR 503 *per* Eveleigh LJ at 517. Lord Justice Donaldson's view was similar. He said (at 510): "[t]he ratio of [*Bridges* v *Hawkesworth*] seems to me to be solely that the unknown presence of the notes on the premises occupied by Mr. Hawkesworth could not without more give him any rights or impose any duty upon him in relation to the notes" (at 510) and (at 506)"Mr. Hawkesworth undoubtedly had a right to exercise such control, but his defence failed".

144 [1982] 2 WLR 503 *per* Donaldson LJ at 515.

145 [1982] 2 WLR 503 *per* Donaldson LJ at 515.

146 Although Donaldson LJ was clearly a bit sceptical about how theory met practice in *South Staffordshire Water Co* v *Sharman*. Having recited Lord Russell of Killowen's theory that manifestation of intent was the key, he then noted at 510:

> Sharman's case itself is readily distinguishable, either upon the ground that the rings were in the mud and thus part of the realty [surely he meant part of the land] or upon the ground that the

Subsequent cases have told us nothing new.[147] A final review of our possible theories reveals the following.

Possibility No 1. Things apparently lost on land might be possessed by the estate holder because they were deposited there for safekeeping. Evidence of a consensual bailment transaction will prove this. Absent evidence, American lawyers continue to argue the dubious distinction between "mislaid" things, which are assumed deposited, and "lost" things, which are not. The argument was not even attempted, despite the ideal facts, in *Hannah* v *Peel*. The lost *versus* mislaid distinction is dead outside America.

Possibility No 2. It might be a rule that an estate holder in land always defeats a finder. We still see hints of such a rule for buried things[148] or trespassing finders. As to buried things, the gold rings in *South Staffordshire Water Co* v *Sharman* were buried, yet control and manifest intent were the proof of the estate holder's possession.[149] That suggests that some buried things might not be possessed.[150] As to trespassers, such hints sound like punishments or compensation for trespassing:[151] tort damages, not artificial property

---

finders were employed by the plaintiff to remove the mud and had a clear right to direct how the mud and anything in it should be disposed of ... .

147 See, for example, *Waverley Borough Council* v *Fletcher* [1995] 3 WLR 772 (Eng CA). The holder of an estate in land sued for and won possession of a gold brooch that was buried in the land until dug up by a non-trespasser using a metal detector. The judges seemed fixated on the distinction between buried and surface things. Compare *Webb* v *Ireland and the Attorney General* [1988] Irl M 565 (Irl SC), in which a trespasser using a metal detector dug up buried treasure worth millions. The judges didn't like the fact that he was a trespasser and relied on the analysis of Donaldson LJ in the *British Airways* case.

148 See, for example, Sir David Cairns in *Parker* v *British Airways Board* [1982] 2 WLR 503 (Eng CA) at 518: "the occupier has a better claim than the finder only if he had possession immediately before it was found and this is only so (in the case of an article not *in* or *attached to* the land, but only *on* it) when the occupier's intention to exercise control is manifest".

149 [1896] 2 QB 44 at 46-47 *per* Lord Russell of Killowen. His analysis of this point, set out earlier, was adopted by the English Court of Appeal as the principle underlying Theory No 3. If this is correct, there are but two possibilities. Some buried things might not be possessed and Theory No 2 is wrong. Alternatively, *the fact that they are buried is sufficient proof of control and manifest intent*, in which case they are possessed by Theory No 3 and Theory No 2 is superfluous.

150 If they are, why don't judges dispose of cases on this basis? In *Corporation of London* v *Appleyard* [1963] 2 All ER 834 (Eng) the safe was built into the wall of the cellar of a building, well buried by any standard, yet the estate holder's possession was determined by a more complex analysis. In *Hannah* v *Peel* [1945] 2 All ER 288 (Eng) the brooch was buried in the structure of the house which was part of the land, yet the estate holder could not prove possession. What does buried mean anyway? Are things lying on the floor of a cave buried? If so, why is there a distinction between underground airspace and aboveground airspace? If not, why is there a distinction between burial in solids, liquids and gasses: can a thing be buried in a transparent solid (ice), a translucent liquid (muddy water), or an opaque gas (thick fog)?

151 See, for example, Donaldson, LJ in *Parker* v *British Airways Board* [1982] 2 WLR 503 (Eng CA) at 506-507, suggesting that a trespasser can not take possession as a finder because "[w]rongdoers should not benefit from their wrongdoing". If the trespasser does not acquire possession, then any rogue who meets him carrying the thing on the street is at liberty to take possession. This would contradict Donaldson's, LJ earlier point (at 506) that the rule in *Armory* v *Delamirie* "must be right as a general proposition, for otherwise lost property would be subject to a free-for-all in which the physically weakest would go to the

rules, are the appropriate remedy. There is no longer any support for Possibility No 2.

Possibility No 3 survives and has evolved to a straightforward theory of possession. A thing was not found if it was not lost. A thing on land was not lost if the estate holder possessed it. Whether the estate holder possessed it depends on whether he can prove possession by the usual tests of control and manifest intent to exclude others from the thing.[152] The nature of the thing may tend toward proving either element of possession.[153] So may the type of premises: private premises with restricted access prove control and are often sufficient proof of manifest intent.[154] Does this mean that things dropped on the floor at a house party are possessed by the householder? Maybe, but do we know the answer before we find out what type of house it was (suburban bungalow or fraternity house), what type of party it was (intimate dinner or end of exams beer bash), how many people were there, and how many of those were gate-crashers? As premises are opened to larger categories of the public,[155] more particular proof of control over the thing may be required and some specific manifestation of intent, such as posted directions about turning in lost items, must be demonstrated. It is worth noting that *Bridges* v *Hawkesworth*[156] was probably wrongly decided, according to this theory. This need not

---

wall". The issue is whether, when the trespasser took possession, he did so by dispossessing the estate holder. This depends on whether the estate holder held possession, which has nothing to do with the act of trespass.

152 This can be applied even to things that were a part of the land, rather than separate things as such, before they were dug up. Suppose the prehistoric boat in *Elwes* v *Brigg Gas Co* (1886) 33 Ch D 562 (Eng) was part of the land. Digging it up changed its nature: from land it was reincarnated as a boat. Whatever property may have been held in its previous existence as a boat was terminated when it became land: see Chapter 4 "Accession, Mixing and Fixtures". The property the estate holder held in it *because* it was land ceased to exist when it became a boat once again. Either the estate holder or the finder is now owner by first possession, *but that possession must be proved*.

153 For example, a tin of beans on the floor of a grocery store is probably possessed by the storekeeper even if later proved to have been imported from another store and lost by a customer. I doubt that the shopkeeper has a claim against me if I take possession of a wallet left by a customer on a shelf among the tins of beans.

154 "If a bank manager saw fit to show me round a vault containing safe deposits and I found a gold bracelet on the floor, I should have no doubt that the bank had a better title than I, and the reason is the manifest intention to exercise a very high degree of control": *Parker* v *British Airways Board* [1982] 2 WLR 503 (Eng CA) per Donaldson LJ at 515. The results in American bank vault cases tend to support this view. See, for example, *Silcot* v *Louisville Trust Company* 265 SW 612 (Ky 1924) (bearer bond certificate on floor of safety deposit box room; bank wins possession; location described as "in a private room where only a limited class of people have a right to be ... and that class is composed of the customers of the trust company"). Compare *Dennis* v *Northwestern National Bank* 81 NW 2d 254 (Minn 1955) (bank awarded possession of currency found in safety deposit box area). Contra, see *Paset* v *Old Orchard Bank & Trust Co.* 378 NE 2d 1264 (Ill 1978).

155 "At the other extreme is the park to which the public has unrestricted access during daylight hours. During those hours, there is no manifest intention to exercise any such control": Donaldson LJ at 515 of the *British Airways* case.

156 *Bridges* v *Hawkesworth* (1851) 21 LJQB 75 (Eng). Goodhart thought that the case was wrong. "A shopkeeper only admits the public for the purpose of shopping. He intends to exclude them from whatever is not necessary to accomplish this end." Goodhart, "Three Cases on Possession" (1929) 3 Cambridge LJ

trouble us. The lawyers didn't argue the case that way. They likely would today.[157]

In short, the theory now is that the estate holder wins if he proves prior possession; otherwise, he loses to the finder. The holding of an estate in land and the way in which land is occupied are only relevant if they assist in proving the elements of possession.

C   EMPLOYERS' AND OTHER TRANSACTIONS BASED CLAIMS

Employees claiming as finders often lose possession to their employers. If the situation is in one of the previous categories, the fact of the employment relationship will not matter. However, an employer sometimes wins possession *because of* the employment relationship. Judges and academics have never been particularly clear about why.

Early theories were based on status. There was a time when many black people, however they may have been characterized for other purposes, were not accorded legal status as persons. It followed that slaves could not take possession of things they found: "a slave ... has no civil rights and can hold no property, except at the will and pleasure of his master [and] whatever he lawfully acquires and gains possession of, by finding or otherwise, is the acquirement and possession of his master".[158] This reasoning ceased to make sense after the abolition of slavery. Yet pre-20th century cases continued to regard the master as possessing things in the hands of his domestic servants.[159] A status based

---

195 at 199.

157 In *Trachuk v Olinek* [1996] 4 WWR 137 (Alta), an oil company leased ranch land and granted easements to other companies for the use and service of pipelines. The plaintiff estate holder fenced in a well site to prevent his cattle from entering. An easement holder hired the defendants to disconnect a pipeline. The defendants uncovered a plastic bag containing bundles of banknotes while digging in the well site. Plaintiff claimed that he was in control of the area. The evidence did not support his contention, and he lost.

> Trachuk erected the fence ... with the intention of excluding his livestock from that enclosure. He ... seldom entered the fenced enclosure. His purpose in any such entry was to remove his calves which had entered there. There is no evidence that Trachuk intended to exclude workmen such as the four defendants or any other representatives of the petroleum companies ... from entering ... and from effecting any installations or changes there. ... Olinek said that before arriving at the well site he had had no discussion whatsoever with Trachuk ... about going to the well site, that he himself decided how and where to work on site, and that there had been no direction from Trachuk as to how Olinek was to do his work at the well site. [At para 49]

158 *Brandon v Planters and Merchants Bank of Huntsville* 1 Stew 320 (Ala 1828). A slave found banknotes in the public square, and turned them over to the bank manager. The owner of the slave was held a possessor by finding. This makes sense. A dog could find something and could impede other people's access by threatening to bite anyone who approached the thing found. This might be sufficient to prove possession by the owner of the dog. It would be utter nonsense to say the dog held possession. In a legal system that denies slaves are people, slaves can't possess things, though their acts can prove possession.

159 See Pollock and Wright *Possession in the Common Law* (Clarendon Press Oxford 1888) at 60: "the rule is settled in our modern law that a servant does not possess by virtue of his custody"; and at 138 "a servant's custody is [not] in general sufficient to support an action or prosecution as for a taking of the thing

carry-over from the days of slavery is a likely rationalization.[160]

The status argument broke down as the "master-servant" relationship moved into commerce and industry. In 1879 a domestic servant in an hotel found bank bills in the public parlour, the owner was not found, and the servant won an action for possession against the hotel keeper.[161] In 1889 a bank porter, while sweeping the floor after hours, found a parcel containing £25 in banknotes; the owner was not found and the bank won possession "on the ground of the relation of master and servant", but there was no suggestion that the porter lacked capacity because of that relationship.[162] Instead, the reason was that he had found the banknotes in the course of his duties. This involved an interpretation of the terms of the employment contract.

We are not concerned here with contract interpretation but with property in things. The question is *the nature of the employer's claim*. The employer's claim has nothing to do with property in the thing found. It is the finder, not the employer, who exercises the control and manifests the intent which prove possession of the thing found. If the contract requires that possession be transferred to the employer, the employee is in breach of contract if he does not do so. The employer may then get damages or specific performance. But one who has contracted for a transfer of property in a thing does not yet hold property in it.[163] The employer does not own the thing found, he does not

---

from his possession". Why? Well, cases held that a servant could not sue in trespass when a stranger interfered, although the master could. Trespass to things is a remedy for interference with possession. If the remedy was not available to servants, it must be because servants aren't possessors. Were the cases wrong?

160 See Holmes *The Common Law* (Harvard U Press 1881 [Reprint] 1963) at 179. "A servant is denied possession ... simply as one of the incidents of his status. It is familiar that the status of a servant maintains many of the marks of the time when he was a slave."

161 *Hamaker* v *Blanchard* 90 Penn St 377 (Pa 1879). Compare *Danielson* v *Roberts* 74 P 913 (Ore 1904), in which two boys, hired to clean out an old chicken coop, found a rusty can containing $7000 in gold coins. They won possession as finders against the estate holder who hired them. It is unlikely that the boys would win on those facts today.

162 *M'Dowell* v *Ulster Bank* (1889) 33 Irish Law Times 225. Other early cases included *Haynen* v *Mundle* (1902) 22 CLT152 (Ont) and *Heddle* v *Bank of Hamilton* (1912) 17 BCLR 306 (BCCA). In the former the defendant shopkeeper's salesman picked up roll of banknotes from floor of the shop. The issue was "whether, owing to the plaintiff having been in the employment of the defendant, he is deprived of his rights as a finder". He was not. *M'Dowell* v *Ulster Bank* was distinguished on the ground that the bank porter's duties included turning in lost articles. In the latter, the Bank of Hamilton got possession of a wallet containing $800 in banknotes picked up by one of its employees from a desk used by customers in the public area of the bank. The case seems to have been decided on the American lost *versus* mislaid distinction (see previous heading). However, the judge also noted that "the plaintiff, a servant of the bank, should consider it to be within [the bank's] protection, and I think it was his duty to hand it over".

163 Remember, this is common law, not Equity. To say that someone holds property in a thing is to predict that the state will assist the holder of the property in restricting others' access to the thing. Suppose the bank porter in *M'Dowell* v *Ulster Bank* (1889) 33 Irish Law Times 225 had taken the package out of the bank, had accepted _5 from a stranger in exchange for a promise to sell ownership of the package, and had placed the package in the stranger's hands. He did not have ownership to sell, but surely the stranger now holds possession. The stranger has a contractual defence against the porter. Despite the fact that the judge

possess it, and he does not hold right to immediate possession of it. He gets possession, if at all, by performance of the contract before or after judgment.

Lister v *Stubbs*[164] shows why. The defendant was employed by the plaintiff as a foreman and purchasing agent. He purchased ownership of some dye-stuffs in bulk from a single supplier; thus far he was doing his duty as agent and ownership passed directly from the supplier to the employer. However, the defendant accepted a cash bribe from the supplier instead of negotiating a discounted price for the bulk sale. The plaintiff employer brought an action for an accounting of his agent's secret profits. This was not a problem. But the defendant had invested the profits and the employer sought to secure payment of his claim by tracing the bribe into the investment. He failed. The additional remedy of tracing would be available only if, before the investment was made, the plaintiff held property in the banknotes received as a bribe. Lord Justice Lindley, who had a clear view of what property meant, explained at some length.[165]

> If we were to accede to this application, I do not think that Stubbs could complain; but the question is, whether, having regard to the rules by which we are governed, we can properly make the order. I am clearly of opinion that we cannot. The real state of the case as between Lister & Co. and Messrs. Varley [the supplier] and Stubbs is this: Lister & Co., through their agent Stubbs, buy goods of Messrs. Varley at certain prices, and pay for them. The ownership of the goods of course is in Lister & Co.; the ownership of the money is in Messrs. Varley. Then Messrs. Varley have entered into an arrangement with Stubbs, who ordered the goods of them, to give Stubbs a commission. That is what it comes to. What is the legal position between Messrs. Varley and Stubbs? They owe him the money. He can recover it from them by an action, unless the illegality of the transaction afford them a defence; but the Appellants have asked us to go further, and to say that Messrs. Varley were Stubbs' agents in getting his commission from Lister & Co. That appears to be an entire mistake. The relation between Messrs. Varley and Stubbs is that of debtor and creditor - they pay him. Then comes the question, as between Lister & Co. and Stubbs, whether Stubbs can keep the money he has received without accounting for it. Obviously not. I apprehend that he is liable to account for it the moment that he gets it. It is an obligation to pay and account to Messrs. Lister & Co., with or without interest, as the case may be. I say nothing at all about that. But the relation between them

---

said *obiter* "the possession of the servant of the bank was the possession of the bank itself", the employer has no claim at all against the stranger and has only an action for damages against the porter. The employer is not the owner and is not a prior possessor. If he held right to immediate possession of the thing he could dispossess the stranger. He doesn't, and he can't.

164 *Lister* v *Stubbs* (1890) 45 Ch D 1 (Eng CA).

165 *Ibid* at 14-16. When Lindley LJ said "the relation between them is ... not that of trustee and *cestui que trust*" he was referring to one of the best known situations in the field of Equity. Sometimes a person holds property according to the rules of common law while another person holds the same property according to the rules of Equity. A typical example is inherited property in land held by a trustworthy adult on behalf of a child. The adult is called a "trustee" and people may deal with him as they would any other property holder so long as they do not become aware that he is doing something contrary to the child's interests or otherwise outside his mandate. The child, now more commonly called the beneficiary, is the *cestui que trust*; such a person had no standing at all before the common law courts.

is that of debtor and creditor; it is not that of trustee and *cestui que trust*. We are asked to hold that it is - which would involve consequences which, I confess, startle me. One consequence, of course, would be that if, Stubbs were to become bankrupt, the property acquired by him with the money paid to him by Messrs. Varley would be withdrawn from the mass of his creditors and be handed over bodily to Lister & Co. Can that be right? Another consequence would be that, if the Appellants are right, Lister & Co. could compel Stubbs to account to them, not only for the money with interest, but for all the profits which he might have made by embarking in trade with it. Can that be right? It appears to me that those consequences shew that there is some flaw in the argument. If by logical reasoning from the premises conclusions are arrived at which are opposed to good sense, it is necessary to go back and look again at the premises and see if they are sound. I am satisfied that they are not sound - the unsoundness consisting in confusing ownership with obligation.

It seems inappropriate that an employer has right to immediate possession of things found by employees, but not to things possessed through fraudulent dealings.[166]

When an employee's claim that he acquired possession by finding is disputed by his employer, three quite separate issues might arise. One is whether the thing was already possessed by someone, perhaps an estate holder in the land where the employee says he found it. Employers are often estate holders: their claims as such are analyzed under the previous heading and the employment relationship is irrelevant.[167] A second issue, whether the employer can take possession from a stranger who has somehow acquired possession from the employee, appears to be settled by *Lister* v *Stubbs*. The answer is no.[168] Finally, there is the question whether the courts will order the employee to transfer possession to his employer because of the employment relationship. Twentieth century cases say that the answer is yes if the employment contract created a contractual obligation to do so, but otherwise no.

---

166 In *Attorney-General of Hong Kong* v *Reid* [1994] 1 NZLR 1 the Judicial Committee of the Privy Council opined that *Lister* v *Stubbs* was wrong. I don't agree. The case involved a Crown Prosecutor in Hong Kong who accepted bribes in the course of his duties and invested the funds in estates in land in New Zealand. After he was convicted in Hong Kong his former employer succeeded in convincing the Judicial Committee that he held the estates in equity as a trustee, rather than as a debtor, thereby providing a nice windfall as the estates had risen in value. The English judges seemed utterly unconcerned about the prospect that future judges might adopt their analysis to the prejudice of the former fiduciary's innocent unsecured creditors. Canadian courts have gone down a different garden path, following *Soulos v Korkontzilas* [1997] 2 SCR 217, 32 OR 3d 716, 146 DLR 4th 214 (Ont SCC). They think that judges have the power to *impose* trusts in certain circumstances, which strikes me as claiming legislative power.

167 Except to the extent that the employment contract reveals the terms upon which the employee was on the land. That was the situation in *South Staffordshire Water Co* v *Sharman* [1896] 2 QB 44 (Eng CA), in which the defendants claimed, but lost, possession two gold rings in the bottom of a pool they were hired to clean.

168 The employee's contractual obligation to transfer possession to the employer isn't enforceable against a stranger. Of course, if the employer's claim is based on prior possession the stranger will lose, but the prior possession must be proved.

An employment contract traditionally describes, among other details, the scope of the employee's duties. This is where judges look when things are found by employees. Thus, in *Jackson* v *Steinberg*[169] a chambermaid took possession of eight $100 bills in an hotel guest room. No owner turned up and Hay J ruled in favour of her employer on contractual grounds.

> The decisive factor ... is the fact that the plaintiff was an employee or servant of the owner or occupant of the premises, and that, in discovering the bills and turning them over to her employer, she was simply performing the duties of her employment . ... [T]he search for mislaid or forgotten property was expressly within the scope of the plaintiff's employment, and the delivery thereof to her employer was a part of her admitted duty.

Most employment contracts probably do not mention searching for or turning in lost articles. Few cases tell us much about what other types of details to look for. An employer prevailed in *Grafstein* v *Holme and Freeman*,[170] probably because he held an estate in the land and already held possession of the locked box in the basement before his employee first saw it. A shopkeeper got possession of a jewel picked up from the floor of the shop by his sales clerk in *White* v *Alton-Lewis Ltd.*[171] A policeman patrolling at a drive-in theatre found a gold ingot on the ground and successfully resisted his employer's demand for possession in *Byrne* v *Hoare*.[172] Though his duty as a policeman brought him to the place, his police work was not viewed as the "effective cause" of finding it.

Finally, the claim of an employer was referred to in *Corporation of London* v *Appleyard*.[173] Two workmen employed by building contractors excavating an old cellar uncovered a wall safe containing _5728 in bank notes. The estate holder won on the basis of prior possession, but employees' liability was argued and McNair J noted *obiter* that "a servant who receives property or money, whether honestly or corruptly, by reason

---

169 *Jackson* v *Steinberg* 200 P 2d. 376 (Ore 1948) at 378-379. As usual, there was no need to decide when the employer acquired possession, so the judge did not particularly comment on it.

170 *Grafstein* v *Holme and Freeman* (1957) 12 DLR 2d 727 (Ont CA) (locked box in plaintiff's basement; 1st defendant hired to clean basement, sees box while cleaning; shows it to plaintiff, who tells him to put it on shelf; 2nd defendant later cuts off lock, revealing banknotes inside). See Chapter 5 "Taking Possession of Things Found".

171 *White* v *Alton-Lewis Ltd* (1974) 4 OR 2d 740 (Ont). The sales clerk was working at the time. "There was a duty on the plaintiff to act honestly and in good faith to her employer. There was in my opinion a duty, in the circumstances, to communicate to the employer the finding of the jewel on the premises ..." [Grossberg J at 747]. The report tells us nothing about what evidence convinced him of the duty. The judge went on to say, *obiter*, "the employer is deemed in law to be the finder". Did he have in mind the point on corporate employees, below?

172 *Byrne* v *Hoare* [1965] Qd R 135. "He was not conducting a search when he found it, and he had not been allowed access to a private place for the purpose of performing his duties, but was walking where any member of the public coming from the theatre might have walked. The fact that he was on duty when he happened to see the gold was merely coincidental": [Gibbs J at 149].

173 *Corporation of London* v *Appleyard* [1963] 2 All ER 834 (Eng).

of his employment, is accountable therefore to his master as principal".[174] Note again that it is the employee, not the employer, who acquires possession by finding: an obligation to account is not a form of property in the thing found.

Some employees, notably officers of corporations, are held accountable for property acquired in the course of or by reason of their positions on the ground that they owe fiduciary obligations to their employers. Such obligations evolved in the field of Equity, not common law, and are only imposed on employees in positions which give them extensive powers to control the employer's affairs. Cases based on fiduciary obligation tell us little about found things, though they help explain the important distinction between holding property and being obliged to account for it.[175]

Also in the field of corporate law, certain acts that appear to normal people to be performed by employees are interpreted by lawyers and judges as acts *of* the corporate person who employs them, rather than as individual acts done as agents *on behalf of* the corporation. Such an interpretation could lead to a conclusion that the corporate employer acquired possession by finding even though, had the employer been an individual, the employee would hold possession.[176] Both fiduciary obligations and the concept of individual employees acting as the corporation are best left to books on corporate law.

Other mundane or exotic contractual arrangements - a grubstake contract financing a prospector; a business venture under a partnership agreement; a joint venture between a multinational corporation and a foreign government - may give rise to similar claims for possession of things found. The most important step in the analysis is to determine who held or acquired possession. Other interpersonal obligations, such as a liability to account, can then be analyzed rationally.

---

174 [1963] 2 All ER 834 at 839. The workmen were employed by an independent contractor and would be accountable to their employer, not to the estate holder. An independent contractor retained possession of $4990 in banknotes found while remodelling the defendant's basement in *Hurley v City of Niagara Falls* 289 NYS 2d 889 (NY 1968), affm'd 254 NE 917 (1969).

175 The importance of this distinction is emphasized, and the cases on the accountability of fiduciaries are analyzed, in Welling *Corporate Law in Canada: the Governing Principles* 3rd ed (Scribblers Queensland 2006) at 374-412. The distinction was blurred in *Attorney-General of Hong Kong v Reid* [1994] 1 NZLR 1 (JCPC), but the case is surely wrong. Compare *Reading v Attorney-General* [1951] AC 507 (Eng HL), confiscating the proceeds of extortion by an Army NCO.

176 That may have been the reasoning in *Morrison v US* 492 F2d 1219 (1974). A sergeant in charge of an infantry squad claimed possession of $150,000 in American banknotes picked up in a cave while on patrol in South Vietnam in 1968. It was held that he was an agent of the US government, that the "finders" cases were not applicable, and that the money went the US Treasury, primarily because of certain provisions of the Uniform Code of Military Justice. Could the principle of employees acting *as* a corporate entity also apply to things found on a ship, a person in Admiralty Law? See the suggestion, by Dixon J in *Willey v Synan* (1937) 57 CLR 200 (Vict) at 216-217, that coins found by a sailor were really found by his employer.

D   STATE CLAIMS

States have legislative power to seize what they like and to make political hay by describing such seizures in popular ways. Even constitutional limitations can be changed by constitutional amendment. That is how the American income tax system - a common form of state seizure - got round the constitutional protection of property. Tax and other forms of seizure vary too much among states to be covered here. At common law, certain types of *things* could be seized by the King: these were *bona vacantia*,[177] wreck (flotsam, jetsam and lagan),[178] waif,[179] estrays,[180] royal fish and swans,[181] and treasure trove.

The state property claims at common law were royal prerogatives, personal to the king.[182] Whether they survive depends on the extent to which each common law country adapted the position of the Crown as an arm of government in its constitution or by statutes limiting governmental powers.

One - the law of treasure trove - has survived in many jurisdictions.[183] Special rules apply when certain types of gold and silver buried things are found. "Treasure-trove is a name given by the early common law to any gold or silver in coin, plate or bullion found

---

177 Things previously owned by someone who died without heirs became owned by the king. This must mean that a possessor by finding of *bona vacantia* could be dispossessed by the king as owner, though others say otherwise.

178 The king held right to immediate possession of parts of a ship or ship's cargo cast ashore by the tide following a shipwreck, or of an aircraft or cargo downed over tidal waters. The king's claim was subject to the owner's, and was often franchised to individuals living in the area. Flotsam floated ashore, jetsam washed ashore from below the surface, and lagan was wreck that had been marked by a buoy but broke free. See *Sir Henry Constable's Case* (1601) 5 Co Rep 106a (Eng).

179 Waif: the king might seize possession of things stolen, thrown away by the thief in flight, and not retrieved by the victim in hot pursuit or hue and cry. According to *Foxley's Case* (1600) 5 Co Rep 109a, 77 ER 224 (Eng), "the reason that waif is given to the king, and that the party shall lose his property in such case is for default in the owner that he doth not make fresh suit to apprehend the felon ... and therefore the law has imposed this penalty on the owner ...". I suspect that waif has disappeared from our law of property.

180 Cattle (*ie*, domestic animals excluding cats and dogs) found wandering in the king's manor were subject to seizure if the owner was unknown. Possession could be reclaimed by the owner until a year and a day after seizure, when ownership expired.

181 Whales and sturgeon were owned by the king, or at least the king held right to immediate possession of any that were caught in coastal waters. Wild and unmarked swans a'swimming in rivers were said to be owned by the king. It is difficult to see how markings could make a difference: someone had to do the marking, which would be theft, wouldn't it?

182 The royal prerogatives were "the residue of discretionary or arbitrary authority which at any given time is legally left in the hands of the Crown": *ATTORNEY-GENERAL v De Keyser's Royal Hotel Ltd* [1920] AC 508 (Eng HL) at 526, citing Dicey. In England, the royal prerogatives were cut down over the centuries by four major constitutional amendments, *Magna Carta* (1215 or 1225, as modified to 1297), *The Petition of Right* (1627), *The Bill of Rights* (1688), and *The Act of Settlement* (1700).

183 In Ontario, the crown has prerogative to unclaimed shipwrecks despite federal salvage legislation. See *Ontario v Mar-Dive Corp* (1996) 141 DLR (4th) 577 (Ont Gen Div).

concealed in the earth, or in a house, or other private place, but not lying on the ground, the owner of the discovered treasure being unknown."[184] The common law position was simple: treasure trove was owned by the king. Anyone digging up something meeting the description,[185] or diving for sunken treasure in coastal waters is likely to have it confiscated, though rewards are usually paid.

In America the concept of royal prerogative died with the revolution. No state has a claim to treasure trove unless created by local legislation.[186] Where no state claim exists, some cases have suggested that the holder of an estate in land where the treasure trove was found can have no claim.[187] This makes no sense. The constitutional abolition of a state claim would make treasure trove the same as other things for purposes of property analysis. Whether an estate holder has a claim depends on whether he can prove prior possession.[188]

Why the state does not make claims to other things found on land remains a mystery. In jurisdictions adhering to the original common law of property in land, people hold estates *of* the crown and the crown holds ownership of the land. The crown must therefore own thing look-alikes that form part of the land, like the prehistoric boat in *Elwes* v *Brigg Gas Co.*[189] As to things not attached, could not the crown claim prior possession on the same basis as an estate holder, particularly in places like state parks and game reserves where public access is controlled? It may be that states simply do not bother to pursue them, but the theoretical basis for such claims seems obvious.

Other state claims, such as forfeiture of property for unpaid taxes or something exotic like

---

184 *Weeks* v *Hackett* 71 A 858 (Me 1908) *per* Whitehouse J. Similarly, see *ATTORNEY-GENERAL* v *British Museum Trustees* [1903] 2 Ch 598 (Eng). Things hidden above ground level are included: *Hurley* v *City of Niagara Falls*, 254 NE 2d 917 (NY 1969). The definition is analyzed by Emden "The Law of Treasure Trove, Past and Present" (1926) 42 LQR 369.

185 See *Lord Advocate* v *University of Aberdeen* 1963 SC 533 (Scot).

186 *Weeks* v *Hackett* 71 A 858 (Me 1908), citing "a substantially uniform line of decisions in the American states", re-affirmed in *Campbell* v *Cochran* 416 A 2d 211 (Del 1980).

187 *Weeks* v *Hackett* 71 A 858 (Me 1908); *Vickery* v *Hardin* 133 NE 922 (Ind 1922); *Groover* v *Tippens* 179 SE 634 (Ga 1935); *Zornes* v *Bowen* 274 NW 877 (Iowa 1937); *Niederlehner* v *Weatherly* 69 NE 2d 787 (Ohio 1946).

188 *Schley* v *Couch* 284 SW2d 333 (Texas 1955) per Calvert J:
> Assuming ... that we are justified in departing from the common law doctrine of treasure trove because that doctrine is "inconsistent with the conditions and circumstances of our people' ... we should depart from it only to the extent necessary to nullify that doctrine. ... The rule as stated in American Jurisprudence is as follows: 'Where property, not treasure trove, is found imbedded in the soil under circumstances repelling the idea that it has been lost, the finder acquires no title thereto, for the presumption is that the possession of the article found is in the owner of the locus in quo.'

All we need to do in order to achieve our objective is to eliminate from the foregoing rule the words "not treasure trove".

189 *Elwes* v *Brigg Gas Co* (1886) 33 Ch D 562 (Eng), set out earlier.

treason, are less likely to involve lost and found things.

E SUMMARY OF THE LOST AND FOUND DEPARTMENT

Lost things are things which used to be possessed, but no longer are. Things that appear to have been lost on land may have passed into the possession of the holder of an estate in the land. If so, they are not lost. The estate holder need not know about the things in order to possess them. Whether he holds possession has nothing to do with whether the thing was "mislaid" by someone on the premises, as some cases suggest. Possession is proved by the usual tests of control and manifest intent to exclude others. These can be proved by controlling access to the land and manifesting an intent to prevent removal of anything inside the boundaries. The same tests apply to things in vehicles, or hidden inside containers. Things cannot be found unless they are lost.

A finder of a lost thing incurs no civil liability for taking possession of it. Generally, possessors by finding win disputes over possession against those who hold no property in the thing found. They lose to holders of right to immediate possession, which is a form of property in the thing. The key to defending a finder's possession is to determine which plaintiffs hold right to immediate possession. The only people who do are (i) owners, (ii) prior possessors who did not transfer or abandon possession or forfeit it through legal seizure, (iii) transferees of right to immediate possession, and (iv) holders of statutory property in the thing (such as a "perfected security interest" under a personal property security statute). In exceptional circumstances, treasure trove being the most common example, the state may take possession. Other claimants, such as the finder's employer, may be able to obtain a judicial order for a transfer of possession by invoking a contractual obligation, but such claimants hold no property in the thing found until the transfer occurs.

A finder who took possession, but is unable to return it when sued by the holder of right to immediate possession, will be ordered to pay damages. The amount of damages is limited to the value of the form of property held by the claimant, which may be substantially less than the ownership value of the thing found.

PART IV

ACQUISITION AND DISPOSITION

BY

TRANSACTION

Property in things is commonly acquired and disposed of by transaction. At least two people are always involved

Many transactions have nothing to do with the transfer of property in things. A contract of employment is one example: the transaction is a legally enforceable agreement whereby one person puts labour at the discretion of another in exchange for periodic payment; whether property in banknotes is transferred on payday or sums are credited to the employee's bank account is rarely the contentious issue if a dispute arises.

Three transactions, however, deal primarily with the transfer of property in things. Purchase and sale, gift, and bailment traditionally are treated as separate categories and governed by quite different rules. But suppose we focus on the property questions that arise in each category. The main property issues are (i) what forms of property are the parties dealing with and (ii) when does an acquisition or disposition take place. The common law cases hold that what evidence is relevant to these issues varies with the type of transaction used. Consequently, the simple property questions have become confused with the details of the transactions. I propose to work through each of these three transactions by focusing on the property issues involved. As we shall see, there is considerable overlap among the three. Their continued existence as separate categories is not warranted.

CHAPTER 8

PURCHASE AND SALE

A   BACKGROUND: THE CODIFICATION OF SALES LAW

Sale is a familiar way of acquiring and disposing of property in things. A seller and a buyer contract to transfer property. The sales contract is a transaction. For our purposes, a transaction can be defined as "an act or agreement ... in which more than one person is concerned, and by which the legal relations of such persons between themselves are altered".[1]

A sales transaction begins with one person (the buyer) desiring a form of property which he perceives that another person (the seller) holds in a thing. The seller and buyer agree upon terms in sufficient detail and with sufficient formality to constitute a contract. The purpose of the contract is to define the terms upon which each party's objective will be achieved. The buyer's objective is to acquire whatever form of property he thinks the seller holds in the thing. The seller's objective is to become enriched in some way. The rules of contract determine what future legal obligations they have managed to commit one another to: these rules do not concern us. Property rules determine whether and when the buyer's objective is achieved.

Precisely when a buyer acquires property in a thing is a crucial question in the common law system. It determines when his ability to exclude third parties from the thing begins. A holder of property in a thing has remedies against strangers; a contractual obligation to transfer property gives remedies against the other contracting party, but not against most other people. The rules governing the contractual transfer of property in things evolved through centuries of analysis of "bargain and sale". This was a precise term in the old forms of pleading. It described a past transaction by which property had already been transferred. The term would be used, for example, by a plaintiff who had acquired ownership by transaction from the previous owner, if faced by a defendant who held possession, admitted the existence of the contract to transfer, but denied that ownership had yet passed.

The best account of how the common law worked is in *Blackburn on Sale*, written in 1845.[2] Whether a contract amounted to a bargain and sale depended [3]

---

1 *Baker* v *SA Healy Co.* 24 NE 2d 228 (Ill 1939) per Hebel J at 234. Similarly, see *R* v *Canavan and Busby* [1970] 3 OR 353 (Ont CA) *per* Schroeder JA. "Transaction is a word of quite comprehensive import, which, so far as I am aware, has never been the subject of any exact legal definition. ... In its ordinary sense it is understood to mean the doing or performing of some matter of business between two or more persons." Our focus being on property in things, we are interested in transactions which alter the legal relationship (*ie*, property) not only between the transacting parties but also between each of them and any other person interfering with or claiming property in a thing.

2 Blackburn *A Treatise on the effect of the Contract of Sale on the Legal Rights of Property and Possession in Goods, Wares, and Merchandise* (William Benning & Co London 1845). The purpose noted in the introduction was "to discuss how far the property in goods is, by the law of England, affected by an

upon the construction of the agreement, for the law professes to carry into effect the intention of the parties as appearing from the agreement, and to transfer the property when such is the intention of the agreement ... The effect of a bargain and sale is to transfer the property in the goods without any delivery; in this respect English law differs from the civil law.

Our concern is with what property is transferred when. The rules are quite clear for a sale or barter[4] of ownership from a transferor proved or conceded to be the owner. The rules are less clear when the transferor does not hold ownership, when the proposed transfer is not by contract, or when a transfer of property other than ownership is proposed. The difference in clarity is due to *An Act for codifying the law relating to the Sale of Goods*, generally known as the *Sale of Goods Act (1893)*.[5] This statute was designed to codify the existing law rather than to effect law reform. The design was so successful that the property transfer provisions are enacted today across the Commonwealth in substantially unaltered form. To understand the purchase and sale of property in things, we begin with the 1893 codification. I shall make comparative reference to three other, more up to date enactments, these being the *Sale of Goods Act (UK 1979)*,[6] the *Ontario Sale of Goods Act*,[7] and the *Uniform Commercial Code* (UCC):[8] similar statutes can be consulted in most other common law jurisdictions.

B   SALE OF GOODS STATUTES

1   Transfer Upon Sale by Owner

Commonwealth sale of goods statutes apply only to transactions in which the buyer pays or promises the payment of money.[9] Both cash and credit transactions are covered, but

---

agreement concerning the sale of them". A larger second edition appeared in 1885. A third edition was published by Stevens & Sons Ltd in 1910, after the *Sale of Goods Act 1893* 56 &57 Vict C 71, and is, consequently, less useful on the common law background.

3 *Ibid* at 120 and 170.

4 Barter - the contractual transfer of ownership of a thing in exchange for a non-monetary consideration - is outside the scope of the sale of goods statutes, though covered by the *UCC*. For the results of a barter transaction, see later "The Common Law Residue".

5 *Sale of Goods Act (1893)* 56 & 57 Vict C 71.

6 *Sale of Goods Act (UK 1979)* 1979 C 54.

7 Ontario *Sale of Goods Act* RSO 1990 c S 1.

8 Article 3 of the *UCC* deals with "sales". The *Uniform Commercial Code* started out as an ambitious attempt to codify American commercial law. It has been adopted with only minor variations by all American states (except Louisiana, whose French history and legal heritage require major adaptation of common law ideas). Each of nine "Articles" handles a major subdivision of commercial law, followed by two on transitional provisions.

9 "A contract of sale of goods is a contract whereby the seller transfers or agrees to transfer the property in goods to the buyer for a money consideration, called the price": *Sale of Goods Act (1893)* s 1(1). The

property exchanges are not.[10] It is odd that statutory rules should apply when the seller runs the buyer's plastic card through a machine, but not when the seller accepts possession of a horse, a hawk, or a robe in payment, but that is a legacy of the 1893 codification.

The statutes apply primarily to contractual[11] transfers of ownership[12] of things.[13] We begin our analysis with two assumptions. First, assume that the seller either holds ownership of a thing or proposes to acquire ownership and pass it on to the buyer. Complications can be accounted for later. Second, assume the existence of a contract to transfer ownership from seller to buyer. The important question is not whether the transfer will occur in the future or when it occurs in the present tense, although these are what a lawyer tries to achieve by the documentation. Instead, just as a judge always does in a dispute in the common law courts, *we look back at what has already occurred to determine whether and when a transfer of ownership took place in the past.*

The intention of the parties is determinative if it can be established.[14] This is subject to

---

Sale of Goods Act (UK 1979) s 2(1) and the *Ontario Sale of Goods Act* s 2(1) are functionally identical. Note also s 57(3) of the Ontario statute which excludes transactions "intended to operate by way of mortgage, pledge, charge, or other security". Security transactions fall within the more up to date *Personal Property Security Act*: see Chapter 2 "Security Interests".

10 No sale has taken place, and the statutes do not apply, unless at least part of the consideration is money. See *Benjamin's Sale of Goods* 3rd ed (Sweet & Maxwell London 1987) at 31 [para 24] and the authorities cited there. A purchase by credit card involves a triangular payment scheme whereby the seller acquires a claim for money against the card-issuing institution, which later collects from the buyer under the card-issue contract: there is no requirement that the money payment come from the purchaser.

11 The property transfer rules (set out later) typically start off with the words "where there is a contract for the sale of ...", thus limiting their scope to contractual transfers.

12 "'Property' means the general property in goods, and not merely a special property": *Sale of Goods Act (1893)* s 62(1). The *Sale of Goods Act (UK 1979)* s 61(1) and the Ontario *Sale of Goods Act* s 1(1) are identical. "General [or absolute] property" were the arcane terms used in the 18th and 19th centuries for ownership, while "special [or qualified] property" meant possession: see Chapter 3 "Capture and Escape of Wild Animals". That sale of ownership is the primary focus of the statutes is also indicated by sections like s 22(1) (UK 1893 and 1979), concerning "where goods are sold by a person who is not their owner" (see later).

13 "'Goods' include *all chattels personal other than* things in action and *money,* and in Scotland all corporeal movables other than money. The term includes emblements, industrial growing crops, and things attached to or forming part of the land which are agreed to be severed before sale or under the contract of sale" [Emphasis added]: *Sale of Goods Act* (1893) s 62(1). The UK statute of 1979, s 61(1) is functionally identical, as is the Ontario *Sale of Goods Act* s 1(1) (but for the reference to Scotland). Coin of the realm and banknotes are excluded by the term "money", though foreign coins and banknotes are goods. The definition specifically excludes "things in action" (also known as "choses in action"), in order not to confuse 19th century lawyers, who traditionally used the term to describe either (i) an imaginary thing in which property other than property in things was conceived to be held, or (ii) the sub-category of property which is not property in things: see Chapter 1 "Property and Things Contrasted". Obviously, in a statute dealing with ownership of things, it wouldn't make a lot of sense to include in the definition of things concepts to which the term ownership could not be meaningfully applied. As to the second sentence in the definition, see the later analysis of "future goods".

14 "Where there is a contract for the sale of specific or ascertained goods the property in them is

148

the obvious qualifications that a seller could not have transferred ownership before he acquired it and before the thing was "ascertained".[15] The rule was the same at common law, as noted above. Thus, the easiest way to prove when a transfer of ownership of a specific thing owned by the seller occurred is by clear evidence of the parties' intent.

Clear evidence of intent is not always available. To assist in proving a time of transfer the statutes provide five rules that cover most situations. They are rules of interpretation and apply if the intention of the parties cannot be otherwise determined.[16] Dozens of books on commercial law analyze the five rules in depth. There is little purpose in replicating that analysis here. I am merely surveying transactions by which people acquire and dispose of property. The objective is to develop a simple analysis of *what property is transferred when*. We can paraphrase the rules as follows.

1   For most things owned by the seller, ownership is transferred at the time of contract.[17]

2   For things the seller must alter, transfer is postponed until the buyer has notice it is done.[18]

---

transferred to the buyer at such time as the parties to the contract intend it to be transferred": *Sale of Goods Act* (1893) s 17(1). The section goes on to make the terms, parties' conduct, and "the circumstances" relevant evidence. The *Sale of Goods Act* (UK 1979) s 17 and the Ontario *Sale of Goods Act* s 18 are functionally identical. See also Everett, "Romalpa Clauses: The Fundamental Flaw (1994) 68 ALJ 404.

15 Anyone denying that the first is not obvious is invited to (i) check any other book under the entry *nemo dat quod non habet* or (ii) pay me now for a transfer of ownership of all the used cars I might eventually acquire in the next 20 years. Of course, the seller can arrange to have someone else discharge his contractual obligation. "A contract of sale can perfectly well be performed by a seller who never has title at any time, by causing a third party to transfer it directly to the buyer": *Karlshamns Oljefabriker* v *Eastport Navigation Corp* [1982] 1 All ER 208 (Eng) *per* Mustill J at 215. As to the second qualification, where the thing is "unascertained goods, no property in the goods is transferred to the buyer unless and until the goods are ascertained": s 16 of the UK statutes of 1893 and 1979; the Ontario *Sale of Goods Act* s 17 merely deletes the words "unless and". "Unascertained" is not defined, but is generally thought to mean all goods except "specific goods", defined as "goods identified and agreed upon at the time a contract of sale is made": UK 1893 s 62(1); UK 1979 s 61(1); Ont s 1(1).

16 Section 18 of the *Sale of Goods Act (1893)*: "Unless a different intention appears, the following are rules for ascertaining the intention of the parties as to the time at which the property in the goods is to pass to the buyer." The preambles in the *Sale of Goods Act (UK 1979)* s 18 and the Ontario *Sale of Goods Act* s 19 are identical.

17 "*Rule 1*. Where there is an unconditional contract for the sale of specific goods in a deliverable state the property in the goods passes to the buyer when the contract is made, and it is immaterial whether the time of payment or the time of delivery, or both be postponed": *Sale of Goods Act (1893)* s 18. The *Sale of Goods Act (UK 1979)* s 18 and the Ontario *Sale of Goods Act* s 19 are functionally identical.

18 "*Rule 2*. Where there is a contract for the sale of specific goods and the seller is bound to do something to the goods for the purpose of putting them in into a deliverable state, the property does not pass until such thing be done and the buyer has notice thereof": *Sale of Goods Act (1893)* s 18. The *Sale of Goods Act (UK 1979)* s 18 and the Ontario *Sale of Goods Act* s 19 are functionally identical. Note that this postpones, but does not specify the time of transfer.

3   For things the seller must appraise to calculate the price, transfer is postponed until the buyer has notice it is done.[19]

4   If the buyer's approval is a term, ownership is transferred by acceptance or retention of possession beyond a reasonable time.[20]

5   For sales by description, ownership is transferred when things described are "unconditionally appropriated to the contract".[21]

These five statutory rules are good examples of a point made in the introductory comments. Where acquisition and disposition is by transaction the simple property issues tend to become confused with the transactional details. The five rules are not property transfer rules; they are rules for interpreting contracts. The sole objective of the rules is to find out what the parties intended - what they bargained for as the time or circumstances that would trigger a transfer of ownership. There is only one property rule here.

---

19 *"Rule 3.* Where there is a contract for the sale of specific goods in a deliverable state but the seller is bound to weigh, measure, test, or do some other act or thing with reference to the goods for the purpose of ascertaining the price, the property does not pass until such act or thing be done, and the buyer has notice thereof": *Sale of Goods Act (1893)* s 18. The *Sale of Goods Act (UK 1979)* s 18 and the Ontario *Sale of Goods Act* s 19 are functionally identical.

20 *"Rule 4.* When goods are delivered to the buyer on approval or on ʻsale or return' or other similar terms the property therein passes to the buyer: -

(a)   when he signifies his approval or acceptance to the seller or does any other act adopting the transaction.

(b)   If he does not signify his approval or acceptance to the seller but retains the goods without giving notice of rejection, then, if a time has been fixed for the return of the goods, on the expiration of such time, and, if no time has been fixed, on the expiration of a reasonable time. What is a reasonable time is a question of fact."

Sale of Goods Act (1893) s 18. The *Sale of Goods Act (UK 1979)* s 18 and the Ontario *Sale of Goods Act* s 19 are functionally identical. "Delivery" means "voluntary transfer of possession from one person to another": s 62(1)(1893); s 61(1)(1979); s 1(1)(Ont.).

21 *"Rule 5.*

(1)Where there is a contract for the sale of unascertained or future goods by description, and goods of that description and in a deliverable state are unconditionally appropriated to the contract, either by the seller with the assent of the buyer, or by the buyer with the assent of the seller, the property in the goods thereupon passes to the buyer. Such assent may be express or implied, and may be given either before or after the appropriation is made.

(2) Where, in pursuance of the contract, the seller delivers the goods to the buyer or to a carrier or other bailee or custodier (whether named by the buyer or not) for the purpose of transmission to the buyer, and does not reserve the right of disposal, he is deemed to have unconditionally appropriated the goods to the contract."

Sale of Goods Act (1893) s 18. The *Sale of Goods Act (UK 1979)* s 18 and the Ontario *Sale of Goods Act* s 19 are functionally identical. "Future goods" are "goods to be manufactured or acquired by the seller after the making of the contract of sale": s 62(1) (1893); s 61(1)(UK 1979); s 6(1) (Ont). Of course all sales are by description, but when a buyer says "I want that pink one, over there" the seller's acceptance appropriates it to the contract and Rule 1 applies.

Remember our assumptions. Looking back at events that already occurred we find that there was a contract to sell ownership and that the seller held ownership at the time of or after contracting. So far, the only property rule is:

> *ownership of a thing was transferred from an owner by contract of sale when the terms of transfer fixed by the contract were met.*

As we pick away at those assumptions, and as we move outside the statutes' scope, we can expect to find more rules. This we shall do, step by step. However, in this category - transfer upon sale by owner under the codified sale of goods statutes - that is the rule.

2   Transfer by Non-Owner

Sale of goods statutes enable buyers to acquire ownership of things not owned by sellers in three circumstances. The owner is disowned and the buyer becomes owner by a transaction the owner didn't participate in. The three transactions involve (i) a seller with voidable ownership, (ii) a "seller in possession" and (iii) a "buyer in possession". The quoted phrases are statutorily defined.

Voidable ownership is a precise term, unlike "void ownership" which is self-contradictory duckspeak. Voidable describes a state of affairs that exists in the present tense, but when viewed in retrospect may have become undone ("avoided") by intervening events. Once avoided, it is subsequently treated as if it never existed.[22] The statutes speak thus of voidable ownership.[23]

> When the seller of goods has a voidable title thereto, but his title has not been avoided at the time of sale, the buyer acquires a good title to the goods, provided he buys them in good faith and without notice of the seller's defect of title.

To make sense of this, one must read through the lamentable confusion between property and things that plagues common law dialogue. The seller[24] holds voidable ownership of a thing. He purports to sell ownership. The property held by the seller is transferred to the buyer at a time fixed by the usual interpretation rules: make that time T(transfer). The

---

22 Papal annulment of a contract of marriage is a perfect example. Unlike divorce, annulment retroactively changes that which people correctly used to think was so to what they subsequently see never was. Retroactive changes in foreign laws provide us with the most interesting legal examples: see *Starkowski (orse Urbanski, orse Juszcziewicz) v ATTORNEY-GENERAL* [1954] AC 150 (Eng HL), a bastard case that has nothing to do with property in things but is worth reading and thinking about.

23 *Sale of Goods Act (1893)* s 23. The *Sale of Goods Act (UK 1979)* s 23 and the Ontario *Sale of Goods Act* s 24 are functionally identical.

24 There is no contradiction here, as seller is defined as "a person who sells or agrees to sell goods": *Sale of Goods Act* (1893) s 62(1).

seller's voidable ownership is avoided at T(avoidance).[25] As we look back on what happened, the legal position is that the seller never held ownership at all, his supposed voidable ownership having been retroactively wiped out. However, the *Sale of Goods Act* says the following about the buyer. If T(avoidance) was before T(transfer) the seller held no property at T(transfer) and the buyer acquired none. If T(avoidance) was after T(transfer), the above section might have made the buyer the owner: the buyer acquired ownership if he was ignorant of the voidability flaw.[26]

A "seller in possession" is defined by the statutes as someone who previously held ownership, sold it, but is allowed to retain possession of the thing by the buyer. By doing so, the buyer creates the impression that the seller still holds ownership. The *Sale of Goods Act* enables a subsequent buyer from the seller in possession to obtain ownership of the thing.[27]

> where a person having sold goods continues or is in possession ... transfer by that person ... to any person receiving the same in good faith and without notice of the previous sale, has the same effect as if ... authorized by the owner...

A "buyer in possession" is statutorily defined as a buyer in a sale of goods transaction to whom the seller has transferred possession before transferring ownership. By doing so, the seller creates the impression that the buyer is already the owner. The *Sale of Goods Act* enables a subsequent buyer to acquire ownership by contracting with the buyer in possession.28

> Where a person having ... agreed to buy goods obtains, with the consent of the seller, possession of the goods ... transfer by that person ... to a person receiving the goods ... in good faith and without notice of any ... right of the original seller ... has the same effect as if ... with the consent of the owner.

If a possessor falsely claiming to be owner does not fit one of those two descriptions, a buyer acquires only what the possessor has to sell and is liable to be dispossessed by the owner.[29]

---

25 I am not concerned with the details of why property might be avoidable or what must be done to avoid it. *Benjamin's Sale of Goods* 3rd ed at 291 [para 476] suggests "the seller's title might be voidable on the grounds of fraud (including "equitable fraud"), misrepresentation, non-disclosure, mistake, duress, or "undue influence". The curious are invited to check elsewhere for what all that means.

26 What does "good faith" mean? I have yet to see a useful explanation of the term. I suspect it is meaningless.

27 *Sale of Goods Act (1893)* s 25(1). The *Sale of Goods Act (UK 1979)* s 24 and the Ontario *Sale of Goods Act* s 25(1) are functionally identical. The section also applies to a seller who is in possession of "title documents" in similar circumstances.

28 Ontario *Sale of Goods Act* s 25(2). The *Sale of Goods Act (1893)* s 25(2) and the *Sale of Goods Act (UK 1979)* are functionally identical. The buyer in possession rule does not apply to possession acquired by conditional sales agreement (UK s 25) or, in Ontario, if the seller retains a *PPSA* security interest (s 25(3)).

29 See *Barberree v Bilo* (1991) 84 Alta LR (2d) 216, where the plaintiff's husband took possession of

Sales in "market overt" were traditionally an exception to the general rule that non-owners cannot transfer ownership. This is recognized in the UK statute.[30] The term "market overt" had limited application, describing particular market areas in the City of London where things frequently fell off the backs of lorries. Neither lorries nor markets overt are found in most other jurisdictions.

Traditional British Commonwealth sale of goods statutes have no application to other transfers by non-owners. This is because the statutes restrict the term "sale" to contractual transfers of ownership for money.[31]

3   The Uniform Commercial Code

The American *Uniform Commercial Code* has wider implications. Sales of property in things[32] are covered in Article 2, comprising over 100 sections. Article 2 replaced the *Uniform Sales Act* of 1907, which was similar to the *Sale of Goods Act (1893)*. The UCC is quite different in design and effect. A major objective of the UCC was to de-emphasize the role of "title" in the resolution of commercial disputes.[33] Instead, specific problems that might arise are identified and particular solutions are legislated. This approach extends even to claims against third parties,[34] though it is unlikely that all third party issues can be solved without resort to the common law of property. The UCC is the place to begin looking for solutions when problems arise out of contractual transfers of property in things in the USA.

---

her motorcycle during their separation and transferred possession through sale to the defendant. The court held that the plaintiff was entitled to an order of replevin for transfer of possession of the motorcycle.

30 *Sale of Goods Act (UK 1979)* s 22(1). Neither the Ontario statute nor the UCC mentions the concept of market overt.

31 See above, "Transfer Upon Sale by Owner" and the *Sale of Goods Act (1893)* s 1(1), *Sale of Goods Act (UK 1979)* s 2(1), Ontario *Sale of Goods Act* s 2(1).

32 "*Sale* consists in the passing of title from the seller to the buyer for a price": Art 2-106. "*Seller* means a person who sells or agrees to sell goods": Art 2-103. "*Goods* means all things (including specially manufactured goods) which are movable at the time of identification to the contract for sale other than the money in which the price is to be paid, investment securities and things in action": Art 2-105.

33 A good overview of the UCC and an introduction to its detailed provisions can be found in 44 N Carolina L Rev 525-812 (1966). Article 2 - Sales is covered by DF Clifford (539-597) who notes (at 542) "the resolution of sales disputes starts not with the search for some fictional intention pertaining to who has title, but with the specific question posed by the facts at hand: who bore the risk of loss, can seller sue buyer for the price, etc".

34 Art 2-722 "Where a third party so deals with goods which have been identified to a contract of sale as to cause actionable injury to a party to that contract (a) a right of action against the third party is in *either* party to the contract of sale who has *title to or a security interest or a special property* or an insurable interest in the goods; ... ." [Emphasis added]. It isn't clear what "special property" means in the UCC.

Only (i) what forms of property are the parties dealing with and (ii) when does an acquisition or disposition take place, concern us here.

The *UCC* is not restricted to exchanges of ownership for money. Barter is included;[35] so are transfers of property other than ownership.[36] Contractual dispositions of possession and rights to immediate possession also come under the *UCC*.

As to when a transfer took place, the first place to look is the terms of the contract. The parties are free to stipulate terms and "title to goods passes from the seller to the buyer in any manner and on any conditions explicitly agreed by the parties".[37] This is subject to the prerequisite that property can not be transferred before "identification to the contract" of the goods, and to restrictions on security interests.[38] There seems room for debate as to the meaning of "explicitly agreed".

Absent explicit agreement by the parties, the *UCC* doesn't require that intent be inferred. Instead, it sets out simple transfer rules. "Delivery"[39] is a key consideration. Most sales involve transfers of ownership and most complications arose in the past when one party held ownership but the other held possession. Hence, the most basic transfer rule:[40]

> where delivery is to be made without moving goods ... already identified and no documents are to be delivered, title passes at the time and place of contracting.

This covers the vast bulk of everyday sales, for example ordinary grocery shopping. Two other rules identify situations in which transfer is delayed until delivery of documents or

---

35 A sale "consists in the passing of title from the seller to the buyer for a price" [*UCC* Art 2-106] and the price "can be made payable in money or otherwise" [*UCC* Art 2-304(1)].

36 Although "title" (undefined) is used in the definition of sale [Art 2-106], Art 2-403 says:

> a purchaser of goods acquires all title which his transferor had or had power to transfer *except that a purchaser of a limited interest acquires rights only to the extent of the interest purchased.* [Emphasis added]

Note the positive statement that the buyer acquires property. Contrast the approach in the *Sale of Goods Act (UK 1979)* s 21(1), which simply negatives the possibility that the buyer could acquire "better title than the seller had" except in specified situations. This must mean that a sale of possession or a right to immediate possession is within the contemplation of the *UCC*.

37 Art 2-401(1). In addition, each section in the *UCC* is deemed to contain the words "unless otherwise agreed": Art 1-102(3), (4).

38 Art.2-401(1). The concept of "identification" is expanded in Arts 2-501 and 2-105(2). Compare the prerequisite in the *Sale of Goods* statutes that goods be "ascertained". Attempts to reserve security interests are referred to *UCC* Article 9: "Secured Transactions; Sales of Accounts and Chattel Paper".

39 Delivery is defined, though in a curiously limited way, in Art 1-201: "delivery with respect to instruments, documents of title, chattel paper or certified securities means voluntary transfer of possession". Perhaps "instruments" is intended to include the thing in which the property being sold is held. At any rate, the common law definition of delivery is probably the same: see the analysis of delivery in Chapter 9 "Gift".

40 Art 2-401(3)(b).

154

goods is effected. Thus:[41]

> where delivery is to be made without moving the goods [but] the seller is to deliver a document of title, title passes ... when ... he delivers such documents.

Where a contract to transfer property in a thing requires delivery to the buyer:[42]

> title passes to the buyer at the time at which the seller completes his performance with reference to the physical delivery of the goods.

That is effectively all there is to the transfer rules. Requiring the seller to measure a quantity from bulk does not necessarily delay the property transfer;[43] nor does giving the buyer an opportunity to inspect the goods after delivery.[44] A buyer's rejection "revests title" in the seller.[45]

Two sections deal with the possibility that a buyer might acquire property held by someone other than the seller, in addition to the obvious situation of sale through an agent. Both are simpler than the provisions of the *Sale of Goods* statutes canvassed above. Article 2-403 says that the holder of a "voidable title has power to transfer a good title [*ie*, non-voidable] to a good faith purchaser for value". Finally, a merchant left in possession of things similar to his stock in trade has power to dispose of property held by the person who left them.[46] This is consistent with the overall scheme of the *UCC* whereby merchants are treated differently from casual sellers.

These rules, and other details of the *UCC*, are analyzed in detail in commercial law books. The objective here is to develop a simple analysis of what property was transferred when by a contract of purchase and sale. The *UCC* says that a seller transferred a form of property he held to a buyer according to the terms of the contract, either by explicitly setting out their intention or by creating (perhaps accidentally)

---

41 Art 2-401(3)(a). Note that this rule creates a "buyer in possession" situation.

42 Art 2-401(2), particularized as follows: "(a) if the contract requires or authorizes the seller to send the goods to the buyer but does not require him to deliver them at destination, title passes to the buyer at the time and place of shipment; but ... (b) if the contract requires delivery at destination, title passes on tender there".

43 Art 2-105(4) "An undivided share in an identified bulk of fungible goods is sufficiently identified to be sold although the quantity of the bulk is not determined. Any agreed proportion of such a bulk or any quantity thereof agreed upon by number, weight or other measure may to the extent of the seller's interest in the bulk be sold to the buyer who then becomes an owner in common."

44 See Art 2-513.

45 Art 2-401(4) "A rejection or other refusal by the buyer to receive or retain the goods, whether or not justified, or a justified revocation of acceptance revests title in the goods in the seller. Such revesting occurs by operation of law and is not a sale."

46 Art 2-403(2) "Any entrusting of possession of goods to a merchant who deals in goods of that kind gives him power to transfer all rights of the entrusted to a buyer in ordinary course of business." Subsection (3) defines "entrusting". A merchant is essentially a person in the business of selling property in things.

delivery details that trigger *UCC* transfer provisions. Note how (apart from including forms of property other than ownership and apart from not imputing an intent to the parties) this is functionally identical to the rule in the *Sale of Goods* statutes, which was

> ownership of a thing was transferred from an owner by contract of sale when the terms of transfer fixed by the contract were met.

The *UCC* also recognizes limited situations in which buyers acquire property not held by sellers. So far as the transfer of property by contract is concerned, the rest is left to the common law.[47]

C   THE COMMON LAW RESIDUE

The common law on contractual transfers of ownership for money was substantially identical to what was set out in the *Sale of Goods Act (1893)*.[48] Thus, where a seller owned a thing, ownership of it was transferred to a buyer according to the intent implied by the parties' contract. Where the seller was not the owner, a voidable title could only be passed on as such: the "seller (and buyer) in possession" rules enacted by the *Sale of Goods Acts* did not exist.[49] A buyer at common law could not buy ownership unless the seller had ownership to sell, except in market overt.

---

47 And to other statutory provisions. See, for example, *UCC* Art 9 and Chapter 2 "Security Interests", which deal with the acquisition and disposition of property in things for the purpose of securing debts.

48 The basic rule, that the transfer proceeds according to the parties' intent [1893 s 17(1)], "correctly represents the state of the authorities when the Act was passed": *Varley* v *Whipp* [1900] 1 QB 513 (Eng) *per* Channell J at 517. The five rules for interpreting the parties' intent are similar to the common law rules. Rule 1 and Rule 5 *codify* the common law: see *Benjamin's Sale of Goods* 3rd ed (Sweet & Maxwell London 1987) at 197 [para 280], at 205 [para 359], and at 220 [para 359] and cases cited there,. Rules 2 and Rule 3 reproduce the common law, *but add a delay of transfer until the buyer is notified*: ibid at185 [para 292] and at 187 [para 297]. Rule 4 codifies the common law except for a minor variation: ibid at 190 [para 302]. Other features of the statute, such as the implied warranty provisions, amended the common law but have little to do with the transfer of property.

49 The common law position was summarized in *Pacific Motor Auctions Ltd* v *Motor Credits (Hire Finance) Ltd* [1965] AC 867 (NSW JCPC). The case involved s 28(1) of the New South Wales statute, equivalent to s 25(1) ("seller in possession") of the 1893 Act.

> The English statutory provision ... was introduced in 1877 [in the *Factors Act*] with the object of mitigating the asperity of the common law towards an innocent party purchasing goods from a person who has all the trappings of ownership but in truth has no proper title to the goods. *Nemo dat quod non habet*. The purchaser has no defence at common law against the true owner, subject to certain exceptions which are set out by Willes J. in *Fuentis* v *Montis* (1868) LR 3 CP 268, 276-177. ... There is thus no doubt about the general intention of the original provision and the general mischief at which it was aimed. It was intended as a protection to innocent purchasers in cases where estoppel gave insufficient protection [*per* Lord Pearce at 882-883].

Johnson v *Credit Lyonais Co* (1877) 2 CPD 224 (Eng) is an example of the operation of the common law rule.

But ownership is only one form of property in things. What about the others?[50] When does a buyer acquire right to immediate possession under a contract of sale? When is possession transferred? The statutes say nothing directly about those issues, but much is written between the lines.

No statutory change of possession rules were enacted because of the nature of possession. Ownership can be transferred by the parties' intent; possession can't. A litigant can prove a past acquisition of ownership by documentation, but an acquisition of possession is proved by actions, not words. Delivery, defined as "voluntary transfer of possession from one person to another", is the key.[51] Possession is acquired under a contract of sale when the buyer, with the seller's cooperation, attains control over the thing and manifests intent to exclude others. Until delivery, a buyer had none of the common law remedies that depended on possession, even though he might have owned the thing.[52]

There is, however, an intermediate stage in many sale of goods transactions. Consider Rule 1, which covers the most common type.[53]

> Where there is an unconditional contract for the sale of specific goods in a deliverable state the property in the goods passes to the buyer when the contract is made, and it is immaterial whether the time of payment or the time of delivery, or both be postponed.

"*The property*" in the goods, as explained earlier, means ownership. The latter phrase about postponing delivery or payment is included for greater clarity. Postponing delivery will delay the transfer of possession, but not of ownership. What happens if payment is postponed? The unpaid seller has a lien for the purchase price, unless the contract included a term whereby the seller extended credit to the buyer.[54] The lien is a defence.[55]

---

50 Chapter 2 "Types of Property in Things" defines ownership, possession, right to immediate possession, and security interests as the only forms of property in things. Security interests are generally covered under specialty statutes and are outside the scope of sales contracts.

51 *Sale of Goods Act (1893)* s 62(1), *Sale of Goods Act (UK 1979)* s 61(1), Ontario *Sale of Goods Act* s 1(1). The *Uniform Commercial Code* defines delivery in the same way in Art 1-201, though only "with respect to instruments, documents of title, chattel paper or certified securities". Presumably, the common law definition is the same.

52 Trespass was probably such a remedy. Trespass is defined as "an act of direct physical interference with goods in the possession of another person": see *R* v *IRC ex p Rossminster* [1980] AC 952 (Eng HL) at 1000-1011. In *Johnson* v *Diprose* [1893] 1 QB 512 (Eng CA) at 516, Bowen LJ opined that the holder of right to immediate possession could also sue in trespass, but the opposite view was expressed in Pollock and Wright *Possession in the Common Law* at 145 on the ground that "it is difficult to see how there can be a forcible and immediate injury *vi et armis* to a mere legal right; and there are some parts of the law of trespass and theft which are inexplicable on such a view". As to when ownership passes to a buyer, see the five rules for ascertaining the parties' intent set out above "Transfer Upon Sale by Owner".

53 *Sale of Goods Act (1893)* s 18. The *Sale of Goods Act (UK 1979)* s 18 and the Ontario *Sale of Goods Act* s 19 are functionally identical.

54 A seller in possession has a *lien* - a defence against the buyer's claim to possession - until payment of the price, unless a term of the contract provides for credit: *Sale of Goods Act (1893)* s 41(1); *Sale of Goods*

It prevents the buyer from getting a judicial order for possession of the thing until the price is paid.[56] Between the time ownership passes to the buyer under Rule 1 and the time the purchase price is paid, the buyer has no claim to possession of the thing. Because of the seller's lien, he has not yet acquired right to immediate possession.

That was the situation in *Lord* v *Price*.[57] The plaintiff, having contracted to buy ownership of some cotton, left the seller in possession and the purchase price unpaid. The defendant took possession of the cotton, perhaps by mistake. The plaintiff sued him for conversion and lost. Baron Bramwell explained.[58]

> Here, there is no evidence that the plaintiff had any right of possession; that right was in the vendor, who was entitled to retain possession of the goods until the balance of the purchase money was paid ... Therefore, if the goods were tortiously removed ... it is manifest that the vendor could ... and that the plaintiff cannot, maintain this action.

We now can list the full range of property transfers in a typical transaction covered by Commonwealth sale of goods statutes. Where there is an unconditional contract for the sale of specific goods in a deliverable state, the buyer acquires *ownership* at the time of contracting, acquires *right to immediate possession* upon payment of the purchase price, and acquires *possession* upon delivery.

The transfer of right to immediate possession, like the ownership transfer, may be delayed in transactions where the seller must alter or appraise the goods, where the buyer must approve them, or where the sale is by description of "unascertained" goods. A review of the five rules set out earlier makes it easy to fix the time of transfer in any particular sale of goods transaction.[59]

Where alteration (Rule 2) or appraisal (Rule 3) is called for, the ownership transfer is delayed until the process is completed and the buyer is notified. Right to immediate

---

Act (UK 1979) s 39)1); Ontario *Sale of Goods Act* s 39(1).

55 A lien is often misconstrued as a form of property in things. In fact, a lien is just a defence which a possessor uses to retain possession against someone who, like the owner (buyer) here who, but for the lien, would have right to immediate possession. See Chapter 2 "Other Claims Distinguished".

56 The lien is lost if the seller voluntarily gives up possession, whether to the buyer of someone else.

57 *Lord* v *Price* (1874) LR 9 Ex 54 (Eng).

58 *Ibid* at 55. See also *Bloxam* v *Sanders* (1825) 4 B & C 941, 107 ER 1309 (Eng) and *Milgate* v *Kebble* (1841) 3 M & G 100, 133 ER 1073 (Eng). Either possession or right to immediate possession was sufficient to ground an action in detinue or trover (later conversion), but ownership was not. Contrast *Langton* v *Higgins* (1859) 4 H & N 402, 157 ER 896 (Eng), in which a supplier had contracted to supply oil of peppermint to both plaintiff and defendant. The supplier put oil in some bottles provided by the plaintiff, but transferred possession of the full bottles to the defendant. The plaintiff sued the defendant in detinue and won. Putting the oil in the bottles was an appropriation to the plaintiff's contract, ownership had passed to the plaintiff, and there was no unpaid seller's lien because the supplier had voluntarily given up possession. *Denny* v *Skelton* (1916) 115 LT 305 (Eng) (possession of oats transferred to the wrong buyer) was similar.

59 The rules are explained above, under the heading "Transfer Upon Sale by Owner".

possession is likely transferred as soon as the alteration or appraisal is done (subject to the unpaid seller's lien). That was the common law rule for ownership transfers, delay until notification being a statutory addition.

For sales on approval (Rule 4), right to immediate possession is probably transferred immediately. There is no unpaid seller's lien, as the intent is clearly to put the buyer in possession so he can make a decision.

For sales by description (Rule 5), the ownership transfer is delayed until goods are "unconditionally appropriated to the contract". This is due to the conceptual difficulty of holding ownership of unspecified things. A similar delay seems appropriate for right to immediate possession, for the same reason.

The statutory rules do not refer directly to transfers of right to immediate possession. They are rules for ascertaining the parties' intent. Ownership is transferred according to that intent. We can see now that the same transfer rule applies to right to immediate possession. If the parties intended a sale on credit, right to immediate possession is transferred at the same time as ownership; if not, the transfer is delayed until the unpaid seller's lien is discharged. Thus, in transactions covered by the *Sale of Goods* statutes - where there was a contract to sell ownership - there are three property transfer rules:[60]

> *ownership* of a thing was transferred by contract of sale when the terms of transfer fixed by the contract were met;

> *right to immediate possession* of a thing was transferred by contract of sale when the terms of transfer fixed by the contract were met;

> *possession* of a thing was transferred by contract of sale upon delivery.

The analysis thus far has been restricted to the types of transactions covered by legislation adapted from the *Sale of Goods Act (1893)*. Such legislation applies only to contractual transfers of ownership of things in exchange for money.[61]

Barter - the contractual transfer of ownership of a thing in exchange for a non-monetary consideration - is outside the scope of the sale of goods statutes, though covered by the

---

60 I have expressed the rules in the past tense because that is the way they are applied. The rules determine what property was transferred by a transaction that has already occurred. They are worded to account for the possibility that ownership, possession, or the right to immediate possession may have been acquired by the buyer without having passed through the seller. "A contract of sale can perfectly well be performed by a seller who never has title at any time, by causing a third party to transfer it directly to the buyer": *Karlshamns Oljiefabriker* v *Eastport Navigation Corp* [1982] 1 All ER 208 (Eng) *per* Mustill J at 215.

61 See above "Sale of Goods Statutes".

UCC.[62] When A swaps B "my car for your motorcycle" in a sale of goods jurisdiction, the statutory rules don't apply. Common law rules do. A plaintiff who bartered ownership of a watch for ownership of candlesticks sought to regain possession of the watch in *Emanual* v *Dane*. His action was summarily dismissed by Lord Ellenborough, who said[63]

> unless the contract be rescinded, this action cannot be maintained. The watch remains the property of the defendant, though the plaintiff be entitled to a compensation in damages for a breach of the warranty that the candlesticks were of silver. I cannot try a question of warranty in an action of trover.

Lord Ellenborough concluded that ownership of the watch had passed to the defendant. He didn't say when. However, there is no reason to think that contractual transfer was different at common law just because no money changed hands. Each party to the contract was bound to carry out the intent implied in its terms. Changing the consideration wouldn't change the intent as to time of transfer. A court would look to that intent to determine when ownership changed hands *unless there were some special transfer rules for barter*. The cases don't reveal any and there is no reason to think there are any.[64]

In sum, the transfer rules in barter of ownership are the same as in sale of ownership. Transfer of both ownership and right to immediate possession occurred according to the intent implied in the barter contract. Possession was transferred upon delivery. Whether each party had a lien until he gave up possession of one thing (the equivalent of paying the price in a sales transaction) or acquired possession of the other likely depends on whether the contract promised advance possession by one of the parties (the equivalent of credit).[65] The contractual intent is discerned by the same five interpretation rules as for

---

62 The definition of "sale" in the sale of goods statutes is restricted to money consideration. The *UCC* definition isn't.

63 *Emanual* v *Dane* (1812) 3 Camp 299, 170 ER 1389 (Eng). Lord Ellenborough thought an action to rescind the contract for fraud might achieve the plaintiff's purpose. Similarly, see *Power* v *Wells* (1778) 2 Cowp 818, 98 ER 1379 (Eng) (horse trade, with money on one side; no trover because property had passed) and *La Neuville* v *Nourse* (1813) 3 Camp 351, 170 ER 1407 (Eng) (burgundy for champagne; burgundy sour; *caveat emptor* applied).

64 *Blackburn on Sale* 1845 at 3 said simply "[i]f the consideration to be given for the goods is not money, it might, perhaps in popular language, rather be called barter than sale, but the legal effect is the same in both cases". As the purpose of his book was "to discuss how far the property in goods is, by the law of England, affected by an agreement concerning the sale of them", and as there were then no statutory rules on sale of goods, it hardly seems likely that he meant to exclude barter from the rest of the book. There are few barter cases and the time of transfer does not seem to have been controversial. *Halsbury's Laws of England* 4th ed vol 41 para 601 suggests: "[t]he law relating to contracts of exchange or barter is undeveloped but the courts seem inclined to deal with such contracts as analogous to contracts of sale".

65 I am speculating here. I base my conclusion on two factors. First, the unpaid seller's lien in sales transactions was a common law rule, not a statutory invention: see *Bloxam* v *Sanders* (1825) 4 B & C 941, 107 ER 1309 (Eng) and *Milgate* v *Kebble* (1841) 3 M & G 100, 133 ER 1073 (Eng) and *Lord* v *Price* (1874) LR 9 Ex 54 (Eng). Second, barter contracts and sales contracts were probably seen as functionally

sales, subject to the minor variations already noted which were inserted in the 1893 codification of sales law. The results thus far are unsurprising.

That brings us to the controversial stuff, sale or barter transactions not involving ownership. Consider a simple example.

> Fred finds an uncut diamond. He offers "to sell the diamond" to Bart for money. Bart accepts. Has a property transfer taken place?

This looks like a contract of sale. Let's call it *contract # 1*. The intent of the parties seems to be to transfer ownership and possession of the diamond from Fred to Bart. If Fred held ownership of the diamond at the time of contracting it was "an unconditional contract for the sale of specific goods in a deliverable state" and Rule 1 applies. Ownership was transferred when the contract was made. Bart acquired right to immediate possession if he paid the price and discharged Fred's lien. Possession must be transferred by delivery. But look at the facts again. Fred owned the diamond if he discovered it and took possession as the first finder.[66] Maybe he discovered the diamond; maybe he didn't.

Now we add a few facts. What if the diamond was mined in South Africa by O (clearly the owner), stolen by T (a common thief) who brought it to Fred's country and hid or lost it.[67] There can be no question about the form of property held by Fred - it is possession. Fred may or may not realize that he is not the owner by discovery. Does it matter what Fred thinks? Consider the possibilities.

Suppose Fred thinks he owns the diamond. Bart and Fred still have a contract of sale, Fred having contracted to transfer ownership of the diamond for a price.[68] Call it *contract # 2*. Fred can't transfer ownership and he may owe Bart damages for breach of contract if O or T makes a property claim. If Bart's objectives are thwarted the resolution depends on just what bargain was struck between Bart and Fred.[69] But T might never

---

identical at common law: see the previous footnote.

[66] See Ch 3 "Discovery: the First Finder's Property". Discovery is a root of ownership in the common law system. Alternatively, though unlikely in the case of a diamond, another first finder might have abandoned it.

67 My position is that it makes no difference which, and that both O and T can recover possession from Fred: see Chapter 7 "Finders on Defence".

68 A sale of goods contract is a contract "whereby the seller transfers or *agrees to transfer*" ownership: see the statutory definitions in "Sale of Goods Statutes" above.

[69] One possibility is that the contract could be undone for "total failure of consideration". That happened in *Rowland* v *Divall* [1923] 2 KB 500 (Eng CA). The defendant contracted to sell ownership of a car to the plaintiff and possession was transferred. It was discovered some months later that the defendant never held ownership, having been duped by a rogue. The owner seized possession of the car. The plaintiff settled with the person to whom he had tried to resell ownership and collected the entire price from the defendant. Rescission, rather than damages, was the remedy because the plaintiff "has not received any part of that

show up (fearing theft charges or deportation) and O might announce his claim but not pursue it (being a rich diamond miner with better ways to spend his time). What property does Bart hold? How did he acquire it? When?

On the other hand, suppose Fred did not think he owned the diamond. Suppose Fred deduces that there is an owner out there somewhere, and tells Bart that he has only possession to sell. Bart and Fred still have a contract of sale, though not one within the *Sale of Goods Act* definition.[70] Call this transaction *contract # 3*. As we saw, the common law transfer rules were similar for sale of ownership and barter of ownership. Neither reason nor precedent suggests they are different for contracts to sell or barter possession. There is, however, one important distinction. Ownership can be transferred by the parties' intent; possession can't. Possession can not be transferred under Rule 1, which gave the buyer ownership by *contract # 1* as of the time of contracting. But right to immediate possession can. Did B, by *contract # 3*, become the holder of right to immediate possession before transfer of possession occurred?

It is difficult to find judicial answers to these questions. The answers emerge from a comparative analysis of what Fred and Bart hoped to achieve by each of these three contracts.

In each transaction Fred wanted money, and was willing to transfer to Bart by contract whatever property Fred held in the diamond. Bart paid money. We might say that: (i) Bart wanted (and got) ownership by *contract # 1*, where Fred was the owner of the diamond by discovery; (ii) Bart wanted (but didn't get) ownership by *contract # 2*, where Fred possessed and thought he owned it; and (iii) Bart wanted (and got) possession by *contract # 3*, where possession was what Fred claimed to be selling. However, those are lawyers' distinctions. Realistically, Bart wanted to achieve three simple objectives by each of these transactions. First, Bart wanted to acquire possession of the diamond. Second, Bart wanted to be able to keep Fred from regaining possession. Third, Bart wanted protection against interference by others as soon as and for as long as possible.

The first two of Bart's objectives were achieved in all three transactions.

As to Bart's third objective, he got varying degrees of protection against third party interference. Under the 1st contract he was protected for as long as possible when he got ownership. Under the 3rd contract he was protected for as long as he bargained for when

---

which he contracted to receive - namely, the property and right to possession - and that being so, there has been a total failure of consideration": *per* Atkin LJ at 507. Alternatively, the bargain may have been that Bart would buy whatever property Fred held, accepting the risk that he didn't own the diamond. That happened in *Chapman v Speller* (1850) 14 QB 621, 117 ER 240 (Eng), where "the true consideration was the assignment of the right, whatever it was, that the defendant had acquired by his purchase at the sheriff's sale; and that this consideration has not failed": *per* Patteson J at 241.

[70] The Commonwealth sale of goods statutes cover only contracts to sell ownership: see above, "Sale of Goods Statutes". However, sales of possession fall within the *Uniform Commercial Code*: see Art 2-403.

he got possession. Under the 2nd contract he was protected for as long as possible in the circumstances (though less than he bargained for) as he paid for ownership but got only possession.

What about the other aspect of Bart's third objective? Bart wanted protection as soon as possible against third party interference with the diamond. Property in the diamond would give him this protection; Fred's contractual obligation would not do.[71] We know that in *contract # 1*, Bart got ownership immediately and acquired right to immediate possession upon discharge of the unpaid seller's lien. The common law cases base these times of transfer on the parties' intent. In the other two contracts Fred did not have ownership to sell, but in each of them Fred intended to sell and Bart intended to buy all Fred's property in the diamond. Do we need a portfolio of precedents? Surely Bart acquired right to immediate possession upon discharge of the unpaid seller's lien because of the parties' intent in *contract # 2* and *contract # 3*.

Unless B acquired right to immediate possession before transfer of possession he would have no claim against third party interference.

D   SUMMARY: BUYING A SELLER'S PROPERTY

Purchase and sale involves a contractual transfer of property in things. The only property questions are what form of property was transferred and when the transfer took place. Some transactions are covered by statute; some are left to the common law. There are two statutory models in the common law system.

The American *Uniform Commercial Code* substantially modifies the common law approach. Transactional details tend to be emphasized; who held property at various times during the course of a transaction is rarely the key to dispute resolution. Under the *UCC* it is less crucial to know exactly when a buyer acquired ownership or right to immediate possession, though transfer of possession remains an important concept.

The Commonwealth *Sale of Goods* statutes, with only minor variations, reproduce the common law so far as what property is transferred when. The basic transfer rules are simple. Ownership, right to immediate possession, and possession are transferred in a purchase and sale transaction as follows:

> *ownership* of a thing was transferred by contract of sale when the terms of transfer fixed by the contract were met;

---

[71] The contractual claim is enforceable between the contracting parties, but not against others in the common law system. Ownership provides grounds for action against anyone who damages the ownership value, for example by destroying the thing. Where a third party interferes with temporary possession, only the possessor or the holder of right to immediate possession can sue.

right to immediate possession of a thing was transferred by contract of sale when the terms of transfer fixed by the contract were met;

possession of a thing was transferred by contract of sale upon delivery.

The property transfer rules in a "sale of goods" transaction are easy. The difficult questions involve the often artificial process of interpreting the contract to find the parties' intent.

CHAPTER 9

GIFT

A   DEFINITION OF GIFT

Gift is a transaction. Colloquially, a thing is often called a gift ("this necktie was a gift from my grandmother"), but the term is used in law to describe a non-contractual transfer of a form of property from one person to another. The rules determining what property is transferred when by gift are not the same as in transfer by purchase and sale.

Gift is a specific type of common law transaction. Other transactions - transfer by deed, statutory assignment, trust, and equitable assignment - are similar to gift only in that they are ways of transferring property without the consideration necessary to contracts of sale or barter. Each method of transfer has its own peculiar prerequisites. A transfer of property can be proved by proving any one of them. The definition of one of them must be satisfied in order to prove that a transfer took place. Our legal system displays a healthy scepticism toward allegations that someone gave away his property. This was clearly expressed in *Milroy* v *Lord*:[1]

> [the transferor] must have done everything ... necessary to be done in order to transfer the property and render the settlement binding upon him. He may of course do this by actually transferring the property to the persons for whom he intends to provide [but] it will be equally effectual if he transfers the property to a trustee, or declares that he himself holds it in trust ... [If a transfer] is intended to be effectuated by one of the modes to which I have referred, the Court will not give effect to it by applying another of those modes. If it is intended to take effect by transfer, the Court will not hold the intended transfer to operate as a declaration of trust, for then every imperfect instrument would be made effectual by being converted into a perfect trust.

A brief description of the more common alternative methods demonstrates the point.

A *deed* is a document under seal. The common law recognized two types of contracts, agreements upon consideration and agreements under seal. If an intent to transfer property is expressed in a deed it constitutes a contract to transfer that property and the common law rules of bargain and sale apply.[2] By contrast, if a document (i) expresses a present intention to transfer property in a thing, and the document is (ii) sealed and (ii) delivered[3], it then becomes a deed, whereupon the property is transferred.[4]

---

1 *Milroy* v *Lord* (1862) 4 De G F & J 264, 45 ER 1185 (Eng) *per* Turner LJ at 1189-1190.

2 For transfers by deed in particular, see *Ramsay* v *Margrett* [1894] 2 QB 18 (Eng CA) and *French* v *Gething* [1922] 1 KB 236 (Eng CA). The rules governing contractual transfers of property by contract are covered above, under "Purchase and Sale".

3 A document must be sealed before delivery, in order to become a deed: *Goddard's Case* (1584) 2 Co Rep 4b (Eng) and *Tupper* v *Foulkes* (1861) 9 CBNS 797 (Eng). The details of sealing and delivery are explained in Youdan, "The Formal Requirements of a Deed" (1979) 5 Bus LR 71 (Ont).

4 This proposition appears to be uncontroversial. When mentioned at all, it is usually said in an offhand

A *trust* is not a common law transaction. It is an Equitable transaction. A holder of common law property (the trustee) retains the form of property, but assumes a personal obligation to use it for the benefit of someone else (the beneficiary). If a holder of property declares himself to be a trustee there is no transfer of property at all at common law. A holder of common law property who wants to make someone else a trustee must first transfer the property to that other person.[5]

A *statutory assignment* is a transfer of property effected by compliance with a formula set out in a statute, usually enacted for particular types of property. An example is the written assignment of a "chose in action" - property other than property in things - accomplished by statutory assignment in most common law jurisdictions.[6] An *equitable assignment* is, like a trust, not a transfer of common law property at all, but an assignment that results in the common law property holder becoming obliged to use the property for the assignee's benefit.

The fact that authors and judges have often called all of these transactions "gifts" in the past is no excuse for perpetuating terminological inexactitude.

Gift is a transaction "without consideration". This is unrelated to the mythical concept economists call free lunch. The economic assumption is that everything a person does is in anticipation of personal gain, though not always monetary and often illusory: even gamblers plan to make money, though they usually don't. What motivates people to transfer property is of little consequence in legal analysis. The issues are (i) whether property has already been transferred or (ii) whether there are grounds for ordering a future transfer. The former can be proved by evidence of one of the known forms of transfer. The timing of the transfer will vary with the method. A future transfer can be ordered if the holder contracted to transfer the property, but evidence of consideration is required to prove the contractual obligation. If the property holder's promise to transfer

---

way: see, for example, *McIntyre v Royal Trust Co* [1945] 3 DLR 71, affmd [1946] 1 DLR 655 (Man CA). Deeds are commonly used to transfer property in land. Deeds were used more frequently for other transactions before high literacy rates and familiarity with simple contracts rendered them unfashionable. Today's lawyers and clients would find it cumbersome to prepare, seal and deliver formal documents when property in a dog, a car, or a piece of furniture can more easily be transferred by a contract of sale.

5 The distinction between property transfers and declarations of trust was noted by Sir George Jessel MR in *Richards v Delbridge* (1874) LR 18 Eq 11 (Eng) at 15. Analysts in the 19th and 20th centuries made property law seem complex by trying to take short cuts, rather than analyzing legal obligations and equitable obligations as separately evolved and still distinct concepts.

6 See, for example, the Ontario *Conveyancing and Law of Property Act* RSO 1980 C 90 s 53 (1): any "absolute assignment ... by writing under the hand of the assignor ... of any chose in action of which express notice in writing has been given to the ... person from whom the assignor would have been entitled to ... claim such ... chose in action is effectual in law ...". Ontario copied the *Judicature Act (UK 1873)* s 25(6), re-enacted by the *Law of Property Act (UK 1925)* s 136 (1). Other types of property, such as corporate shares, patents, and bills of exchange, are subject to assignment rules found in more particular statutes.

was not under seal and without consideration, there is no legal obligation to enforce. This, as we shall see, is why delivery is critical. If the transfer has not yet been completed, there was no gift.

Gift is a common law transaction that transfers property in a thing [7] from donor to donee by intent and delivery.

B   THE THREE ELEMENTS OF GIFT

Three distinct elements - donor intent, delivery, and donee lack of rejection - are required to prove gift. They fit together in a precise pattern. A plaintiff attempting to prove a gift must prove the existence of donor intent *at the time of or after delivery*, but can be thwarted by proof of donee rejection after that time.

1   Donor Intent

Everyone agrees that there can be no gift without proof of donor intention. However, there is little judicial or academic discussion as to what that means.[8] What exactly must the donor intend?

There are three key factors. It must be proved that the donor intended an immediate (not future) transfer, without consideration, of a form of property in a thing.

First, the intent must be to transfer the property now. A litigant must allege a time of transfer in the past and must prove that the donor then wanted the donee to acquire the property at that time. Proof of an intent to transfer property at some future time is

---

7 Property other than property in things can not be transferred by gift. This is because the definition of gift includes the requirement of delivery, and delivery is proved by a transfer of possession of the thing in which property is held: see "Delivery".

8 The donor must have capacity to form the requisite intent. That rules out gifts by insane people. See, however, *Cory* v *Cory* (1747) 1 Ves Sen 19, 27 ER 864 (Eng) in which the donor appears to have been drunk, but property was transferred by gift. There is also the problem of "undue influence", often treated as a separate topic but surely a question of capacity to make an autonomous decision in the circumstances.

[T]he doctrine of undue influence ... arises out of the fact that ... if the evidence on each side be evenly balanced ... equity will presume that the parent who puts property in a child's name intends to make a gift or give a benefit to the child, while on the other hand money or property passing from the child to the parent cannot be retained by the latter because it is assumed that so unnatural a transaction would have been brought about by undue use of the natural influence that a parent has over a child ... . Both presumptions may be rebutted; each is in truth a convenient device in aid of decisions on facts often lost in obscurity, whether owing to the lapse of time or the death of the parties. [*Re Pauling's Settlement Trusts* [1964] Ch 303 (Eng CA) *per* Willmer J at 336; he then surveyed precedent cases.]

These days, gifts to a child are as likely to be motivated by tax avoidance as enriching the child.

insufficient. An intending donor is at liberty to change his mind before delivery.[9] Of course, what a donor was thinking can be proved by circumstantial evidence: proof that the donor once said "I plan to give you that dog next Tuesday" and subsequent transfer of possession of the dog are likely to be taken as proof of intent to give ownership of the dog at the time of delivery. The donor may recall that he changed his mind before delivery, but a judge is unlikely to believe him.

A gift can also be made by forming the intent to transfer after delivery.[10]

> Suppose a man lent a book to a friend, who expressed himself pleased with the book, whereupon the lender, finding that he had a second copy, told his friend that he need not return the copy he had lent him: it would be very strange if in such a case there were no complete gift, the book being in the possession of the intended donee.

In such a case the transfer would have occurred when the intent was formed, both the intent and delivery requirements then being met. The key question is whether the donee was intended thenceforth to be able to repel interference by the donor as well as by strangers.

The requirement of a present intent to transfer makes gifts subject to condition precedent impossible.

Consider the promise, "I shall give you ownership of my bicycle if it rains next Tuesday". The promise can be withdrawn anytime before Tuesday, in which case there will be no

---

9 "An incomplete gift can, of course, be revoked by the donor at any time": *Standing* v *Bowring* (1885) 31 Ch D 282 (Eng CA) *per* Lindley LJ *obiter* at 290 (legal assignment of government stock into joint names of plaintiff and defendant). "There is no case in which a party has been compelled to perfect a gift, which in the mode of making it he has left imperfect": *Antrobus* v *Smith* (1805) 12 Ves 39, 33 ER 16 (Eng) *per* Grant MR at 18 (no delivery). Without a contract there is no basis for a legal obligation to carry out the announced intention.

10 The quote is from *Cain* v *Moon* [1896] 2 QB 283 (Eng) *per* Wills J at 289. The owner of a "deposit note", a document required to withdraw money from a bank, had transferred possession to the defendant. The purpose of the transfer was for safekeeping. The owner later expressed the intent to "give" the deposit note to the defendant. The defendant was held to be owner of the document by gift. See also *Winter* v *Winter* (1861) 4 LT (NS) 639 (Eng) (gift of ownership of barge, possession previously held by donee as agent of donor). American law is similar. In *Caylor* v *Caylor's Estate* 52 NE 465 (Ind 1899), W told H she was giving ownership of a thing to her nephew. H already held possession of the thing and agreed to hold it for the nephew's benefit. H thereby became owner and trustee.

> Suppose the gift had been made to Daniel [H] himself; it certainly could not be contended with any show of reason that, to constitute a delivery to him while the property was in his possession, it would have been necessary for him to have turned it over to Mary [W], and for her to then have made a manual delivery to him: [Wiley J at 468]

Each of these cases involved *donatio mortis causa*, but the delivery requirements are identical: see later "Gift in Contemplation of Death". An *inter vivos* gift can be proved where the donee has control over the thing by virtue of a power of attorney and expression of intention to donate occurs later: *MacDonald* v *Lobsinger Estate* (1987) 27 ETR 88 (QB).

gift. If it is not withdrawn, there will be no gift without delivery.

If it rains and delivery is made - whether before, on or after Tuesday - your strongest case would be that I expressed an intent to transfer and that the intent remained current until the later of Tuesday and delivery. The rain factor would be an irrelevant complication in your otherwise straightforward presentation, and would not serve me in defence.

If it does not rain, you are clearly out of luck without delivery. You might also be out of luck, even if you can prove delivery, if I deny that on Tuesday I felt inspired to give.

So you see, the fact of rain or no rain on Tuesday might become part of the evidence of what I was thinking at the time of the alleged gift (Tuesday or the subsequent delivery time), but it isn't accurate to describe the transaction itself as a conditional gift.

Second, the intent must be to transfer without consideration. The reason is simple: a proposed transfer upon consideration is an offer to contract, covered by quite different rules.[11] An exchange of promises, a property transfer, performance of a service, or suffering a quantifiable detriment qualify as consideration,[12] but only if rendered in return for an offer. There is a gray area between contract and gift. It is often difficult to determine whether a feat was performed in return for an offer to contract, or whether the person who undertook the performance is now trying to collect in reliance on a gift proposal. "I will give you $500 if you accidentally break your leg" is a promise without consideration, even if a broken leg ensues.[13] By contrast, "I will give you $500 if you deliberately break your leg" would appear to be a contractual offer that could be accepted by undertaking the performance.[14]

The requirement that the donor's intent be to transfer without consideration suggests to

---

11 See "Purchase and Sale". An attempted transfer that fails for lack of consideration is no transfer at all. It might transfer possession temporarily, but a dealer who allowed a potential buyer to test-drive a car would be surprised if a judge converted the transaction into a gift: so would the Court of Appeal.

12 A traditional definition is "valuable consideration, in the sense of the law, may consist in some right, interest, profit, or benefit accruing to the one party, or some forbearance, detriment, loss, or responsibility given, suffered, or undertaken by the other": *Currie* v *Misa* (1875) LR 10 Ex 153 (Eng) at 162 *per* Lush J. The adjective "valuable" was included because it was conventional during the 19th century to describe property transfers as being either "upon good consideration" or "upon valuable consideration". "Good" meant that the transferor was motivated by some emotion called "natural love and affection", which was not sufficient to prove a contract; "valuable consideration" meant precisely what we now call consideration in contract law. The clarity is enhanced and nothing substantial is lost by dropping the adjectives.

13 The example is a commonly attributed to *Shadwell* v *Shadwell* (1860) 9 CBNS 159 (Eng) *per* Byles J at 177.

14 Unless it is legally unacceptable because of a so-called "public policy" against self-mutilation, which would be the conventional analysis of a promise of $500 to break someone else's leg. These examples must not be confused with contracts of insurance, where premiums are paid in advance by the insured party who collects if he breaks his own, or someone else's leg. Luckily, contracts is a separate subject, so we can leave it there.

me that few so-called "conditional gifts" are not gifts at all. A condition precedent would disprove the requirement of present intent. Conditions subsequent pass the intent test. A condition subsequent contemplates an immediate transfer of property that might be undone later upon violation of the condition.

An example of gift subject to condition subsequent is said to have occurred in *Scot* v *Haughton*.[15] F invested in lottery tickets. She distributed them to her servants "upon condition if 20s or more should come up, her daughter should have a moiety". The ticket in the houseboy's possession won £1000. F won a judicial order for payment of half to her daughter. The reasons for judgment are not clear, but it takes little imagination to see that this transaction was not a gift at all. Assume that they were bearer tickets and that the intent was to transfer ownership.[16] There is no suggestion in the case that either F or her daughter was to regain ownership or possession of the ticket if the winning number came up. Instead, the houseboy, by accepting the offer of ownership and possession of the ticket, indicated his agreement that he would pay the daughter money should a certain event over which he had no control occur. That was a contract. The houseboy was ordered to fulfill his contractual obligation to pay half the winnings to the daughter.

Similarly, most other so-called conditional gifts that require any kind of performance - "I'll give you $500 if you join the army (or promise to say a mass for me, or contract a marriage with X)" - are not gifts at all, but contractual transfers (*ie*, bribes).[17] Contrast, "I give you ownership of my bicycle now but ownership reverts to me if it rains next Tuesday". The transaction is a gift subject to condition subsequent only where the expressed condition can not be interpreted as consideration. Such gifts must be rare.

Third, the intent must be to transfer a particular form of property in a thing.[18] A vague purpose to transfer some sort of rights will not do. This is primarily a question of proof. Lending things - temporarily transferring possession - creates evidence sufficient to satisfy the delivery requirement of gift and non-commercial loans of pencils, petty cash, and even cars occur among friends upon the vaguest of terms. That's why, when a

---

15 *Scot* v *Haughton* (1706) 2 Vern 560, 23 ER 963 (Eng).

16 If the winnings were not payable to the possessor ("bearer") of the ticket F must have been registered as the purchaser, in which case it is difficult to see why she had to sue the houseboy. If F intended to transfer only possession of the ticket and retain ownership, then whether classified as a gift or a contractual transfer, the transaction would transfer only that property intended to pass. The houseboy would then have converted F's ownership into _1000, would be liable to pay F the ownership value, and would have to plead contract to retain half.

17 Engagement rings are a traditional example. A disappointed suitor might still recover possession of the ring even though his action for damages for breach of promise to contract a marriage has been abolished. See, however, 7 St John's L Rev 325 (1933) and 3 U Detroit LJ 38 (1939).

18 The holder of property other than property in a thing (examples are corporate shares, bonds, contractual obligations, patents; the category is commonly labelled "choses in action") may well intend an immediate transfer without consideration, but the transfer of this form of property by gift is impossible. The reason is rooted in the definition of gift, which requires delivery, proved by transfer of possession of the thing in which property is held. See the next heading, "Delivery".

dispute arises as to whether a gift took place, the transferee is put to the strict proof that the transferor intended to transfer whatever property in the thing the transferee claims.[19]

Most analysts assume that gifts transfer ownership of things.[20] This is so when an owner intends to transfer ownership and also transfers possession of the thing to a seemingly willing donee. But what of someone who does not hold ownership? A possessor by finding can obviously transfer possession to someone else. If he intends to transfer all property he holds in the thing and the other person takes control and manifests intent to exclude others, the transfer of possession has been effected. It would have been a sale of possession had there been consideration; if there was no consideration, is there any reason for not calling the transaction a gift?[21]

Intent is not much discussed by judges. Plaintiffs are likely to drop cases before the litigation stage, absent unequivocal evidence that a gift was what the defendant had in mind.[22] The controversial issue in most gift cases is the delivery requirement.

---

19 This is a simple extension of the quote from *Milroy* v *Lord* (1862) 4 De G F & J 264, 45 ER 1185 (Eng) set out earlier. The judicial function is to judge what kind of transfer took place; courts have no power to convert one type of transfer into another. See, for example, *Douglas* v *Douglas* (1869) 22 LT 127 (Eng), rejecting a claim that ownership of a sword had been transferred by gift. Chief Baron Kelly said at 129: "[t]he words are these ... . You shall have charge of the sword', that merely is `You are to have possession of the sword'."

20 See, for example, *Crossley Vaines Personal Property* 5th ed at 299: "gift is a gratuitous transfer of the ownership of property [sic]", citing *Blackstone's Commentaries*. See also *Re Price* [1928] Ch 579 (Eng) at 590. "At law only an absolute interest in chattels can be given inter vivos, and a grant of chattels for life vests the whole legal interest in the grantee." Isn't this just a matter of using the wrong form to effect the desired purpose? Would a gratuitous transfer of possession of a thing to X intended to last for his lifetime give X ownership?

21 There are certainly consequences of calling it a gift. If it was a gift the donor can not recover possession from the donee, despite being a prior possessor, because the donee can raise the terms of the transfer as a defence. If it was not a gift, the transferee is a "gratuitous bailee" and the transferor (bailor) is at liberty to seize possession at any time. But what if the transferor announced his intent to transfer possession for one week, delivery occurred, and the transferor sought to recover possession before the week was over? If calling it a gift makes the terms of the transaction a defence, why isn't the same defence available to a gratuitous bailee for a week? We'll explore these issues in Chapter 10 "Bailment: a Separate Transaction?".

22 The normal judicial scepticism was expressed by Mulock J in *Kinsella* v *Pask* (1913) 12 DLR 522 (Ont CA) at 526: "where a person, to his own advantage, but to the prejudice of the giver, obtains by donation some substantial benefit, he is bound to prove clearly, not only that the gift was made, but that it was the voluntary, deliberate, well understood act of the donor, and that the donor was capable of fully appreciating and did fully appreciate its effect, nature, and consequence". The plaintiff was alleged to have given away a large proportion of her money. After surveying relevant cases, the Court concluded that she hadn't. Similarly, see *Doyle* v *Doyle* (1920) 47 NBR 45 (NB). Even cases where the expression of intent is equivocal tend to be decided on the delivery requirement where possible. An example is *Re Cole* [1963] 3 All ER 433 (Eng CA), in which a man took his wife into their new house, showed her the articles of furniture, and said "it is all yours": held, no delivery and therefore no gift.

2   Delivery

Delivery is a necessary part of the proof of every gift.

The law was settled in *Cochrane* v *Moore*.[23] B owned a racehorse. Moore rode the horse in a race. B told Moore "by words of present gift" that Moore was to have "one undivided fourth part of this horse". There was no evidence to prove delivery. B subsequently signed a bill of sale to transfer ownership of the horse to Cochrane. Moore claimed part of the proceeds.

The case reviewed the authorities from the earliest times, when "tradition of seisin" was a necessary part of all transfers of property in things and property in land. Clear points of departure from the old rule were found in cases of deeds and contracts, but none in the case of gifts. The law had always been that there could be no transfer by gift without delivery. Lord Justice Fry summarized.[24]

> This review of the authorities leads us to conclude that according to the old law no gift or grant of a chattel was effectual to pass it whether by parol or by deed, and whether with or without consideration, unless accompanied by delivery: and that on that law two exceptions have been grafted, one in the case of deeds, and the other in that of contracts of sale where the intention of the parties is that the property shall pass before delivery: but that as regards gifts by parol, the old law was in force when *Irons* v *Smallpiece* was decided: that that case therefore correctly declared the existing law ... .

Lord Esher MR had a simple explanation why that was the law. A gift can not transfer property without proof of delivery because delivery is part of the definition of the word gift:[25]

> actual delivery in the case of a "gift" ... is not a piece of evidence to prove the existence of the proposition; it is a necessary part of the proposition, and, as such, is one of the facts to be proved by evidence. ... Short of [delivery by the donor] the donee could not get possession without bringing an action against the donor to force him to give the thing. But if we are to force him to give, it cannot be said that he has given.

Delivery is a constituent element of gift in the same way as offer, acceptance, and

---

23 *Cochrane* v *Moore* (1890) 25 QBD 57 (Eng CA).

24 25 QBD 57 at 72-73: Bowen LJ concurred. The review indicated that a deed could transfer ownership of things "without livery" as early as 7 Edw 4 (1467). In the case of transfer by contract ("bargain and sale"), delivery was generally thought to be a prerequisite until sometime "in the reigns of the early Tudors" (after 1485). The point was still argued in losing causes as late as the reign of Elizabeth (1558-1603). For gifts, *Irons* v *Smallpiece* (1819) 2 B & Ald 551, 106 ER 467 (Eng) upheld the delivery requirement and no great deviation from this view could be was found in other 19th century cases.

25 25 QBD 57 at 75-76. Note the typical 19th century confusion between property and things. The penultimate sentence makes it clear that by "give the thing" Lord Esher meant "transfer *possession of* the thing". Is that also what he meant by delivery?

consideration are necessary components of contract. In a contractual case, we do not begin by saying that two parties have a contract and then proceed to determine whether consideration was provided. Rather, having determined that the two have reached an agreement, we withhold the conclusion that they have a contract until consideration is proved. Likewise, in gift, a consensus[26] that one party will dispose of property and the other will acquire it is necessary, but not sufficient. Without consideration there can be no contract; without delivery there can be no gift.[27]

There is, however, room for argument as to what facts suffice to prove delivery.

Transfer of possession of the thing is sufficient.[28] An interesting case of delivery by transfer of possession is *Thomas v Times Book Co Ltd*.[29] Dylan Thomas had lost the manuscript of "Under Milk Wood" the night before embarking on a tour of America. C, a BBC producer, was able to provide copies which he took to Victoria Air Terminal for Thomas. The poet was understandably grateful and told C "if I could find it [the original] I could keep it. He told me the names of half a dozen pubs and said if he had not left it there he might have left it in a taxi."[30] The manuscript was indeed in one of those Soho pubs and C took possession of it there. Dylan Thomas died some three weeks later. Caitlin, his widow, disputed C's claim of gift and sued for possession of the manuscript.[31]

---

26 I refrain from using the word agreement because, as we'll be see under the next heading, it is possible to prove a gift without evidence that the donee was willing to acquire the property: lack of evidence of unwillingness will suffice.

27 *Re Ridgway* (1885) 15 QBD 447 (Eng) is a good example of the necessity of delivery even where the donor's intent is present and perfectly clear. R purchased ownership of a pipe of port to celebrate the birth of his son, intending it to mature for the boy. It lay in the cellar for 19 years, and then ownership was claimed by R's creditors. Despite the fact that it had always been known as the son's port, there had been no delivery and thus no gift. Similarly, in *Nolan v Nolan & Anor* [2003] VSC 121, the plaintiff alleged that Sidney Nolan had transferred ownership of three paintings to her mother by gift. Both alleged donor and donee were dead and could not testify to the donor intention. The plaintiff relied on statements in documents written by Sidney Nolan, referring to the paintings as "Cynthia's" or as part of "Cynthia's collection". Justice Dodds-Streeton held that at best, such statements satisfied only the first requirement of gift, donative intention. Delivery had not been effected and there was no gift. The case was affirmed on other grounds [2004] VSCA 109, special leave to appeal to the High Court refused [2004] HCA Trans 555.

28 This is one of those legal propositions that is "trite law". Where a transfer of possession has occurred there is usually no argument that it was insufficient to prove delivery, so the point is most often made *obiter*: see, for example, *Irons v Smallpiece* (1819) 2 B & Ald 551, 106 ER 467 (Eng) (possession retained by donor; no delivery). The sufficiency of a transfer of possession is, however, *ratio decidendi* in *Winter v Winter* (1861) 4 LT (NS) 639 (Eng) (gift of ownership of barge, possession previously held by donee as agent of donor). Similarly, see *Cain v Moon* [1896] 2 QB 283 (Eng) and *Caylor v Caylor's Estate* 52 NE 465 (Ind 1899). All three cases held that gifts could be made by effecting delivery and subsequently forming the intent to transfer ownership.

29 *Thomas v Times Book Co Ltd* [1966] 2 All ER 241 (Eng).

30 *Ibid* at 243 *per* Plowman J reviewing the evidence.

31 She sued as Dylan Thomas' administratrix. The defendant claimed ownership of the original manuscript of "Under Milk Wood" by sale from C. The only issue was whether Dylan Thomas had transferred ownership to C by gift.

Justice Plowman, having concluded that intent was proved, turned his attention to the question of delivery. His analysis was surprisingly cursory.[32]

> Mr Cleverdon got possession of this manuscript from the Soho public house in which it had been left by Dylan Thomas, and he got that possession with the consent of Dylan Thomas. That, in my judgment, is sufficient delivery to perfect a gift in Mr. Cleverdon's favour.

Now that leaves some intriguing questions unanswered. Was it the fact that the donor had told him where to look that turned the donee's acquisition of possession into delivery? What if no directions had been provided, but the donee managed to find the manuscript either (i) by deduction from his experience with the donor's lifestyle and likely whereabouts, or (ii) by serendipity? Suppose C had not acquired possession until after the donor died (presumably, there would then be no gift because dead former people don't have present intent to transfer).[33] Why are we missing so many details concerning C's acquisition of possession of the manuscript? Having followed the directions to the right pub, did he find the publican in possession? What would have happened if the publican had refused to relinquish possession? C had no claim to ownership except by gift and there could be no gift until delivery. He did not hold possession if the publican did, so delivery by transfer of possession could not then be proved. Nor did C hold right to immediate possession: even if we construe Dylan Thomas' intent as being to transfer right to immediate possession of the manuscript, the only evidence that such property in the thing had been transferred was again the attempted gift, which required proof of delivery.

The Dylan Thomas case applies the rule that delivery is proved by transfer of possession of the thing. "Possession of the thing" in this context means precisely what it means elsewhere in this book.[34] However, the case extends the concept of "transfer" about as far as the ordinary meaning of the word will bear. A transfer is the conceptual movement of property by transaction. Thus, a transfer of possession describes two concepts - an acquisition of possession by one person and a disposition of possession by another - but

---

32 [1966] 2 All ER 241 at 246. The bulk of the reasons for judgment is on the intent point. The delivery question is disposed of in a mere 13 lines.

33 However, see *Re Bayoff Estate* [2000] 3 WWR 445 (QB), a puzzling decision. Mr Bayoff suffered from terminal cancer. He transferred possession of the key to his safety deposit box to Ms Simard in the presence of his lawyers, saying "everything there is yours". Mr Bayoff died before signing authorization papers to allow Ms Simard access to the box. Justice Krueger held that delivery of the contents of the box was not proved by transfer of possession of the keys. However, he ruled that the *inter vivos* gift was perfected once Ms Simard became Mr Bayoff's executrix, as that role allowed her to take possession of the contents of the box. How could Mr Bayoff's intent to transfer ownership of the contents have outlived him?

34 Thing means a material object, a body, a being or entity consisting of matter, or occupying space. This would include the manuscript of "Under Milk Wood". Possession is a form of property and is thus a relationship between the holder of possession and any other person. Possession of a thing is proved by the coexistence of (i) physical control and (ii) manifest intent to exclude others from interfering with the thing. See Chapter 1 "Property and Things Contrasted" and Chapter 2 "Possession".

focuses our attention on the interaction between the two people that brought about the change. Contrast theft by a pickpocket. We don't call the thief's acquisition of possession a transfer, despite the simultaneity of acquisition and disposition. The reason is that the victim did not voluntarily participate. Consider lost and found things. We don't describe taking possession upon finding as a transfer from loser to finder. The reason is the lack of interaction between loser and finder. Mutually voluntary interaction characterizes transfers of property, whether by contract, by gift, or by other legal transaction. Mutually voluntary interaction is missing in discovery, creation, escape, destruction, losing, and finding things - and all other methods of *unilaterally* acquiring or disposing of property. C's acquisition of possession of Dylan Thomas' manuscript was in the transfer category. The borderline must lie not far beyond.

Having established that a transfer of possession of the thing is sufficient to prove delivery, we now proceed to one of the most difficult questions in gift. Is transfer of possession of the thing *necessary*?[35]

Dictionaries suggest that delivery is fundamentally a physical act. In sale of goods transactions, delivery is said to be defined as "voluntary transfer of possession from one person to another".[36] However, is that what delivery is, or is that the evidence that proves delivery? The meaning of the word "delivery" might be different for gifts, but it is difficult to see why it would be. A brief survey of four problematical situations shows that, for most gifts of property in things, delivery is proved by transfer of possession.

Transferor as agent of transferee. A donor in possession who has formed the intent to transfer ownership of a thing can effect delivery by constituting himself the agent of the donee. This requires an agreement between the parties. The essence of agency is that acts done vis-à-vis third parties by an agent within the scope of the agency agreement are treated at common law as the acts of his principal.[37] The donor held possession: by

---

35 This could only be established by a ruling that there had been no delivery because possession of the thing was not transferred. Descriptions of delivery abound – "the donor must not retain any dominion or control over the subject matter of a gift": *Slager* v *Allen* 220 SW2d 752 (Mo 1949); "the donor must be absolutely deprived of his control": *Foster* v *Reiss* 112 A 2d 560 (NJ 1955) - but definitions are hard to find.

36 *Sale of Goods Act (1893)* s 62(1), *Sale of Goods Act (UK 1979)* s 61(1), Ontario *Sale of Goods Act* s 1(1). These statutory definitions reproduced the common law. According to Blackburn, *A Treatise on the Effect of the Contract of Sale on the Legal Rights of Property and Possession in Goods, Wares, and Merchandise* (William Benning and Co London 1845) at 37, "to constitute [delivery] the possession must have been parted with by the owner, so as to deprive him of the right of lien", citing *Bill* v *Bament* (1841) 9 M & W 37, 152 ER 16 (Eng) See, however, *Benjamin's Sale of Goods* 3rd ed (Sweet & Maxwell London 1987) paras 566-567, expressing doubt whether a transfer of possession is required, despite the definition. The *Uniform Commercial Code* defines delivery in the same way in Art 1-201, though only "with respect to instruments, documents of title, chattel paper or certified securities". Perhaps "instruments" is intended to include the thing in which the property being sold is held.

37 This is different from a trust situation, in which the trustee interacts with third parties as a principal under common law rules, but owes equitable obligations to the beneficiary.

definition, this means that the donor had control of the thing and manifest intent to exclude others. The agency agreement has the effect of attributing the agent's (donor's) acts of control and manifestation of intent to the principal (donee). The donee thereby acquires possession of the thing.

The possibility of delivery by this method was explained in *Irons* v *Smallpiece*.[38] The plaintiff claimed ownership of two colts against his father's executrix. He proved that his father expressed his intent to transfer ownership by gift some 12 months before his death. However, the colts had not been moved from the father's farm. The only other evidence presented suggested that the father had agreed to furnish any hay the colts might require at a set price to be paid by the son. They had been grazing, so no hay was provided. Justice Holroyd summarized the legal situation.[39]

> In order to change the property by a gift of this description there must be a change of possession: here there has been no change of possession. If, indeed, it could be made out that the son was chargeable for the hay provided for the colts, then the possession of the father might be considered as the possession of the son.

It appears that the judge did not believe the son's evidence that he had agreed to pay for hay, though he did acknowledge the possibility of delivery by agency. Delivery can also be effected by transferring possession to a third party who has agreed to act as an agent: if the third party is the donee's agent, the transfer of possession proves delivery.[40] If, however, the third party is the agent of the donor, the agent's possession remains the donor's possession at common law. There is no delivery and no gift.[41] In all cases, proof of an agency agreement between principal and agent is required. Passive acquiescence

---

38 *Irons* v *Smallpiece* (1819) 2 B & Ald 551, 106 ER 467 (Eng).

39 106 ER 467 at 468. Delivery by agency without an apparent change of possession was proved in *Elmore* v *Stone* (1809) 1 Taunt 458, 127 ER 912 (Eng), a sale of goods case. The plaintiff was a horse trader who also kept a livery stable. The defendant contracted to purchase ownership of two horses, but directed the plaintiff to "keep them at livery for him". The plaintiff moved the horses from his sale stable to his livery stable. The issue was whether the plaintiff had a seller's lien, which depended on whether he retained possession. Chief Justice Mansfield held that possession had been transferred to the buyer.

> They were in fact put into another stable, but that is wholly immaterial ... . [A]fter the Defendant had said that the horses must stand at livery, and the Plaintiff had accepted the order, it made no difference whether they stood at livery at the vendor's stable, or whether they had been taken away and put in some other stable. The Plaintiff possessed them from that time, not as owner of the horses, but as any other livery stable keeper might have them to keep.

Was their removal to another stable "wholly immaterial"? Could the plaintiff have proved the livery agreement without it?

40 Note that the possessor can't be the donee's agent except by prior arrangement with the donee's consent. Possession can, of course, be held as a trustee. In that situation analysts tend to call the transaction a gift without clarifying that the gift is made to the trustee who holds the property at common law and is subject to equitable obligations.

41 *Walker* v *Foster* (1900) 30 SCR 299 (NS SCC). Compare *Re Craven's Estate* [1937] 3 All ER 33 (Eng), in which a power of attorney given to the donor's son enabled the son to effect delivery to himself. In such a situation separate proof of the donor's intent to make the gift is required.

on the part of the donee will not do, as that would lead to all statements of intention to transfer ownership by gift being interpreted as including a unilateral declaration of agency.[42] To summarize, possession by the donor as agent for the donee is simply a set of facts that, because of the legal consequences of an agency agreement, proves a transfer of possession to the donee.

Delivery for "ponderous" things. Some things are not easily picked up and handed over to another person. Few of us can manhandle a piano without several friends or a fork-lift. Yet donors can hardly be expected to plan their gifts like military exercises. The courts acknowledge these facts of life and have made it possible to prove delivery of heavy and bulky things without risking a hernia. An example is *Rawlinson* v *Mort*[43]. The owner of an organ lent the organ to church officials, possession being transferred by installation in the church but ownership clearly being retained. The owner subsequently decided to give ownership to the organist. In the presence of the donee and a witness he placed his hand on the organ and stated his intention. It was held that delivery had been made.[44] Similarly, in *Kilpin* v *Ratley*,[45] the furniture in a house occupied by the donee and her husband was owned by the donee's father. The father stood in a room with her and spoke words of present gift, then left the house. This was held to prove a gift of ownership of the furniture.

By contrast, a similar gesture was insufficient to prove delivery in *Re Cole*[46]. H had acquired a leasehold interest in a house and furnished it. He took his wife to the new home and led her around various rooms where she touched some of the furniture. H then said "it is all yours". When H became bankrupt his creditors successfully claimed that he still owned the furniture. Though she had the use of the furniture, such use was normal

---

42 This is one of the critical distinctions between a statement of intention to transfer property by gift and a unilateral declaration of trust. The statement "I want to transfer to X all my property in that thing" expresses an intent make a gift and is ineffective without delivery. The nearly identical statement "I want to transfer to X all my *equitable* property in that thing" is a declaration of trust, effective immediately to constitute the property holder a trustee who retains the property at common law but must use it for the benefit of X. Of course, ordinary people can not be expected to consider such nuances before they speak, but where the evidence proves an intent to give, it cannot be re-interpreted as a declaration of trust should proof of delivery fail: see *Milroy* v *Lord* (1862) 4 De G F & J 264, 45 ER 1185 (Eng), set out earlier. Nor is a subsequent "ratification" of the donor's actions by the donee sufficient to make the donor an agent, as ratification operates only to forgive an agent who has exceeded the scope of authority already set by an agency agreement. "Omnis ratihabitio retrotrabitur et mandato priori aequiparatur" [all retroactive ratifications require a prior mandate]: *Kelner* v *Baxter* (1866) LR 2 CP 178 (Eng) per Byles J.

43 *Rawlinson* v *Mort* (1905) 93 LT 555 (Eng).

44 It was referred to as "symbolical" delivery. See below, concerning the use of such adjectives to describe delivery.

45 *Kilpin* v *Ratley* [1892] 1 QB 582 (Eng).

46 *Re Cole* [1963] 3 All ER 433 (Eng CA). This case inferentially supports the proposition that a transfer of possession of the thing is necessary to prove delivery. What if the father in *Kilpin* v *Ratley* had also lived in the house? Compare *Lock* v *Heath* (1892) 8 TLR 295 (Scot), in which the formal transfer of possession of one chair was held sufficient to deliver all the furniture in the house.

for a wife living with her husband. In effect, the court saw no transfer, rejecting the argument that the furniture had become possessed by the wife and no longer possessed by the husband.

These cases interpret delivery as a transfer of possession. Recall that the definition of possession involves control over the thing and manifest intent to exclude others. In a transfer of possession the focus is usually on whether control has passed from transferor to transferee. Apparent control is measured to a large extent by proximity.[47] Control can be shifted by a re-arrangement of the spatial orientation among the two people involved and the thing possessed. This is most commonly done by moving the thing - handing it to the other person, mailing it, and hiring a delivery boy are mundane examples. But moving the people relative to the thing will achieve the same result.

The father in *Kilpin v Ratley* left the house: his daughter and the furniture stayed and she had control. The husband in *Re Cole* continued to live in the house and, one assumes, to use the furniture: his wife's control was equal to his at best and there was no transfer of possession. In *Rawlinson v Mort* there was no reference to a dramatic exit from the church by the donor, but it seems likely in the circumstances that subsequent events showed the organist in control of the organ. Nor is this approach peculiar to ponderous things. Consider the conventional author, who delivers manuscripts to editors by courier. It takes a more exotic personality to send an editor on a pub crawl, but if the editor finds and takes possession of the manuscript, delivery has occurred.

Keys to locked things. Locking things is a way of exercising control over them. Except for animals, control means restricting other people's access: unchained bicycles are immune to the call of the wild. A bicycle owner exercises control by possessing the key to the lock. Others can touch the bicycle, or admire it as a work of art, but its most popular use is inhibited. Suppose the owner decides to give someone ownership of the bicycle. It is not clear that expressing his intent and lifting it into the donee's arms will suffice. A donee in possession of a bicycle chained to a tree may or may not be able to prove delivery. He certainly manifests less than the usual control. But what if the donor simply transfers possession of the key? Will that do, or is delivery delayed until the unlocking ceremony? If the essence of delivery is the transfer of practical control to a donee intending to possess, possession of the key will do. Some judges have seen it that way.[48]

---

47 It helps to keep in mind Holmes' pictorial example of possession. "A powerful ruffian may be within equal reach and sight when a child picks up a pocket-book; but if he does nothing, the child has manifested the needful power as well as if it had been backed but a hundred policemen": Holmes *The Common Law* at 185.

48 *Ward v Turner* (1752) 2 Ves Sen 431, 28 ER 275 (Eng) *per* Lord Hardwicke *obiter* at 282. The case involved a failed attempt to transfer bonds by transferring possession of the certificate. The plaintiff proposed a rather strained analogy between the certificate as symbol of the bond and a key as symbol of the contents of a locked box. Lord Hardwicke was having none of this. His statement concluded "and therefore the key is not a symbol, which would not do". The notion of "symbolic" delivery is further considered

delivery of the key of bulky goods, where wines, etc, are, has been allowed as delivery of the possession, because it is the way of coming at the possession or to make use of the thing ... .

Other judges have held delivery proved by keys, but haven't explained how. Mystification is preferred to hard facts.[49] There seems a general reluctance to interpret possession of the key as possession of the locked up things, though all the cases are consistent with that interpretation.[50]

Delivery for bulk and fungibles. Finally, transfers of property in large numbers of similar things can pose delivery problems. In sale of goods transactions there are numerous cases holding that possession of a portion of a bulk is sufficient to deliver the whole.[51] However, the role of delivery is different in sale of goods. It usually determines whether the seller's lien has been discharged. Property in most sales transactions is transferred according to the parties' intent, not by delivery. In gift, delivery proves the transaction itself. Thus, where a donor expressed his intent to give a university ownership of his extensive coin collection, but transferred possession of only part of the collection during his lifetime, it was held that he had retained ownership of all the coins in his possession immediately before he died.[52] The issue may be academic. Most people resort to more formal means of transfer when dealing with bulk items.

All the above gift cases are consistent with the proposition that ownership of a thing cannot be given without a transfer of possession of the thing itself. However, judges

---

below. Delivery in a sale of goods case was effected by possession of a key in *Gough* v *Everard* (1863) 2 H & C 1, 159 ER 1 (Eng): "the key of the wharf had been delivered to him and he had manual control over the timber" [*per* Bramwell B at 5]. Similarly, see *Ryall* v *Rowles* (1749) 9 Bli (NS) 377, 5 ER 1338 (Eng). In *Watt v Watt Estate* [1988] WWR 534 (Man CA), transfer of possession of a duplicate set of keys to a boat was found insufficient to prove delivery. The donee could not prove control over the boat to the exclusion of others - specifically, the donor.

49 "[T]here need not be actual delivery, but it may be done by that which is tantamount, such as delivery of the key of a warehouse in which the goods are lodged": *Mclean* v *Mcghee* [1920] 53 DLR 14 (Man CA).

50 See *Lucas* v *Lucas* (1738) 1 Atk 270, 26 ER 172 (Eng) (jewellery in locked chest); *Re Lillingston* [1952] 2 All ER 184 (Eng) (jewels in safe deposit at Harrods). Where possession of the key does not transfer effective control over the things, there is no delivery: *Dublin City Distillery Ltd* v *Doherty* [1914] AC 823 (Ir HL) and *Re Johnson* (1905) 92 LT 357 (Eng) (possession of one of two keys). Transfer of possession of a locked box does not transfer possession of the contents if the transferor retains possession of the key: *Reddel* v *Dobree* (1839) 10 Sim 244, 59 ER 607 (Eng). Transfer of possession of the key a to locked trunk with the words "I give my cousin ... this hair trunk and all that is contained in it" does not transfer ownership of things eventually found in the trunk but not proved to have been there at time of the gift: *Jones* v *Selby* (1891) Prec Ch 301, 24 ER 143 (Eng).

51 *Sluby* v *Heyward* (1795) 2 H Bl 504, 126 ER 672 (Eng) (sales contract; delivery of part of wheat shipment held delivery of whole). *Chaplin* v *Rogers* (1800) 1 East 190, 102 ER 75 (Eng) (sale; delivery of part of stack of hay). See also *Tanner* v *Scovell* (1845) 14 Mee & Wels 37, 153 ER 375 (Eng) and the sales cases reviewed there.

52 *In Re Churchill* [1917] 1 Ch 206 (Eng).

deciding such cases are reluctant to say so and analysts don't analyze them in that way. Instead, they resort to adjectival analysis, suggesting that "symbolic" delivery was made by giving the donee "constructive" or "apparent" possession. Why do people talk that way? Consider "apparent possession": "as possession is itself a thing which appears, I don't see how the 'actual possession' and 'apparent possession' can be in different persons".[53] Compare "symbolic delivery": does it mean literally transfer of possession of a symbol of something - a matchbox replica of a vintage touring car for example - or does it mean something symbolic of delivery, such as a grand gesture in front of witnesses? It isn't clear what those who use the term are getting at.[54] Affixing adjectives to otherwise clear words like delivery and possession causes more confusion than it resolves.

Cheques are a common way of donating to charitable and personal causes. Such contributions are often referred to as gifts. Technically, they are not gifts at all. They are wealth transfers by negotiable instrument. A negotiable instrument is a thing, usually (though not necessarily) a pre-printed piece of paper on which the "drawer" has written a payment order.[55] Ownership of cheques and other negotiable instruments passes to whoever acquires possession through "negotiation" (ie, voluntary transfer), unless the transferee knows at the time of acquisition that the transferor's claim of ownership is defective. The value to the recipient arises by virtue of a contract between the drawer of a cheque and the issuing institution whereby the institution has agreed to exchange possession of banknotes and coins for possession of the cheque from any properly identified payee. To say that the drawer of the cheque has made a gift of money will do for everyday speech. However, it mis-describes the legal transaction that has taken place.[56] A gift is a form of transfer of property in a thing. Money is not a thing, it is a

---

53 *Gough* v *Everard* (1863) 2 H & C 1, 159 ER 1 (Eng) *per* Pollock CB (key to private wharf gave buyer "manual control" over timber locked up there and thus possession). Contrast *Rushak* v *Tuba* [1986] 5 WWR 727 (Sask), in which a father signed and transferred possession of a car registration certificate to his daughter, but retained possession of the car. After the father's death, intent was conceded but delivery was in dispute. A gift was held proved by the daughter's "constructive possession" of the car. This is surely wrong, as it seems to treat delivery as if it were merely part of the proof of intention, a position clearly ruled out in *Cochrane* v *Moore* (1890) 25 QBD 57 (Eng CA).

54 "[D]elivery of the key of bulky goods, where wines, etc, are, has been allowed as delivery of the possession, because it is the way of coming at the possession or to make use of the thing, and therefore the key is not a symbol, which would not do": *Ward* v *Turner* (1752) 2 Ves Sen 431, 28 ER 275 (Eng) *per* Lord Hardwicke *obiter* at 282 (the case involved a failed attempt to transfer bonds by delivery of the certificate). Compare *Crookshank* v *White* (1841) 3 NBR 367 (NB) (sales contract; buyer's agent marks timber as sign of delivery).

55 A 1970 cheque to AP Herbert, author of *Uncommon Law* and *Misleading Cases*, from the editor of *Punch* magazine consisted of payment directions painted on the side of a cow. The bank paid.

56 In *Tate* v *Hilbert* (1793) 4 Bro CC 286, 29 ER 895 (Eng), a dying man wrote a cheque with the plaintiff as payee and gave the plaintiff possession. The cheque not presented for payment before death. On the assumption that death cancels a cheque, the plaintiff tries to prove a gift of the face value in cash: the plaintiff lost. Is a cheque cancelled by death? Books on Bills of Exchange say that a cheque is good until notice of death is given to the bank, citing *Kendrick* v *Dominion Bank* (1920) 47 OLR 372 (Ont). However, that case merely applied the *Bills of Exchange Act* RSC 1906 C 119 s 165 and is no authority for the proposition outside the scope of that Canadian statute. See also *Jenkins* v *Public Trustee* (1914) 33

concept; banknotes and coins are things. Ownership and possession of the banknotes and coins were transferred from the institution, not the cheque-writer. He transferred possession of the cheque to the payee, and that was by the usual method of putting the payee in control of the thing. Ownership of the cheque was transferred by "negotiation", not gift, as it did not depend upon evidence that the transfer was without consideration. The payee got richer by dealing with the institution. The drawer got poorer as a result of the transaction. Only confusion results from trying to analyze what happened in gift terms.[57]

Property other than property in things (commonly called "choses in action") can not be transferred by gift. Delivery is a necessary part of the proof of every gift.[58] If delivery is proved by possession of the thing in which the donor held property, which seems to be the general rule, then proving delivery for property other than property in things is impossible. A patent, a corporate share, or an author's copyright cannot be possessed: they are ideas, not things. If delivery could by proved by some other means - the possession of some thing like a share certificate for example - it might be possible to prove a gift. Many judicial decisions have been explained as if this were a rule. The reasons for judgment don't withstand rigorous analysis.

A 1949 case, *In Re Rose,*[59] is often cited for the proposition that a gift of corporate shares can by proved by transfer of possession of the share certificate. R wanted to transfer 5000 shares to H. He endorsed a share certificate. Under the statute and the corporate constitution, share transfers were not effective until approved by the board of directors. The board approved the proposed transfer to H, but not until after R died. R left a will saying "I bequeath 5000 shares to [H] if such preference shares have not been transferred to him previously to my death". The only issue was whether, in the circumstances, that phrase meant that H got another 5000 shares. The conclusion was that the testator meant for H to get 5000 shares under the will only if the earlier attempted transfer failed: the earlier transfer having been successful, even if not known to be so at the time of death, H

NZLR 1202 (NZ).

57 The courts have also made some serious analytical errors in cases involving "passbooks" and bank accounts. In *Re Kuyat* (1962) 33 DLR 2d 153 (BC) an account-holder transferred possession of a savings account passbook, intending that the transferee should "have the money in the account". This was an attempted gift in contemplation of death (see below), but the main argument was about delivery. Blithely ignoring the facts of the case - bank accounts don't "have money in them" in the way that strongboxes contain banknotes; the holder of a bank account has a contract with the bank and holds no property in any particular banknotes in the bank's possession - the court ruled that a gift had been made since "the delivery of the passbook was in fact the delivery of a document sufficient to pass title to the funds on deposit". It is true that what the account-holder did enabled the transferee to get money from the bank, but the reasons for judgment are nonsense. Compare *Brown* v *Rotenburg* [1946] 4 DLR 139 (Ont CA), which also wrongly describes the transaction, but at least imposes more stringent conditions on enriching others by transferring possession of bank passbooks.

58 *Cochrane* v *Moore* (1890) 25 QBD 57 (Eng CA), explained earlier.

59 *In Re Rose; Midland Bank Executor and Trustee Company Limited* v *Rose* [1949] Ch (Eng).

got no shares under the will.[60] In short, the case decided the interpretation of a will, was indirectly involved with a statutory assignment of corporate shares, but had nothing whatever to do with gifts. The decision would have been the same if the judge had concluded that gifts of corporate shares were impossible, or if the word gift had not even been mentioned. The lawyers and the judge simply misused the term gift to describe the share transfer.

A 1952 case, coincidentally named *In Re Rose*,[61] has been similarly misinterpreted. On 30 Mar 1943 R endorsed share certificates to transfer his corporate shares to W. The directors eventually approved the transfer and W was registered as shareholder on 30 Jun 1943. In the meantime, on 10 Apr 1943, a new tax on share transfers had been enacted. The only issue was whether the transfer from R to W was taxable. The answer was no. The analysis had to do with trusts and the taxation of trustees.[62] The reasoning was that the shares were transferable only by registration and were thus transferred after the new tax law, but that the equitable obligations of the trustee became effective before the tax law did and the beneficiary, not the trustee, was taxable. Here we have a statutory assignment of property and the creation of a trust. Again, the judges spoke of the transaction in gift terms. Again, the decision would have been the same if the judge had concluded that gifts of corporate shares were impossible, or if the word gift had not even been mentioned. There was no gift involved here at all, except in the colloquial sense that there was a transfer of property for which the transferee paid nothing.

In *Birch* v *Treasury Solicitor* an attempt was made to explain how delivery could be effected by transferring possession of a document evidencing the property.[63]

> [A] mere symbolic delivery will not suffice. It might, therefore, be supposed that there could be a valid *donatio* only of such subject matters as were capable of actual manual delivery. This, however, is clearly not the law. ... For reasons which we have attempted to give, we think that the real test is whether the instrument handed over is the essential

---

60 "The real position, in my judgment, is that the question here is one of construction of the will. The testator says '[I bequeath 5000 shares to H] *if* such preference shares have not been transferred to him previously to my death' ... . It cannot, in my judgment, be held that by using those words the testator intended the efficacy of the provision to depend on whether the act of third parties, namely, the directors, necessary to complete the legal title in Mr. Hook by registration should have been performed before or after his death." [1949] Ch 78 at 89-90 *per* Jenkins J.

61 *In Re Rose; Rose* v *Inland Revenue Commissioners* [1952] Ch 499 (Eng CA).

62 See [1952] Ch 499 at 513 *per* Evershed MR ("as long as, pending registration, the legal estate remains in the donor, he was, by the necessary effect of his own deed, a trustee of that legal estate") and 515-518 *per* Jenkins LJ ("he had not transferred the full legal title, nor could he do so by the unaided operation of any instrument of his [and] ... pending registration, the deceased [R] was in the position of a trustee of the legal title in the shares").

63 *Birch* v *Treasury Solicitor* [1950] 2 All ER 1198 (Eng CA) *per* Evershed MR at 1205-1207. The Oxford English Dictionary defines "symbol" in three main ways: it can be one thing representing another thing, a thing representing an abstract concept, or a written character conventionally evoking the image of some thing or concept. Allowing delivery by symbol would reduce the role of delivery in gifts to empty formalism.

indicia or evidence of title, possession or production of which entitles the possessor to the money or property purported to be given, so that delivery of the instrument "amounts to a transfer".

The case had been argued as a gift in contemplation of death. The plaintiff's argument was that a transfer of possession of bank account deposit books gave the transferee access to the account and thus "delivered" the credit balance. But why call this transaction a gift?[64] Imagine a similar, technologically updated transaction. A transfers possession of a bank card to B and whispers in his ear his personal identification number. B visits an automated teller machine. It dispenses some banknotes. All of the issues that might come up - A v Bank, Bank v B, A v Pickpocket, even theft charges against B - can be resolved without talking about gifts. Indeed, the only reason gift might be brought up is if B asserts that A assured him that no compensation would be demanded for what he did, but A denies it. A would then be claiming that they had a contract. B might say that the transaction was a gift, not a contract, but that would be an alternative argument, not a defence. B's defence, properly pleaded, would be "no contract".

Analyses of "gifts" of "choses in action" are full of confusing (and confused) terminology.[65] If we went back to the traditional theory that only property in things can be transferred by gift,[66] the results in most cases would be the same, although judges and

---

64 See the earlier comments on cheques.

65 Several examples are set out above. Even in *Cochrane* v *Moore* (1890) 25 QBD 57 (Eng CA), the case that confirmed the delivery requirement in gifts of property in things, we find the following example of judicial jabberwocky (*per* Fry LJ at 73).

> But assuming delivery to be necessary in the case of the gift of an ordinary chattel, two questions would remain for consideration in the present case - the first, whether the undivided fourth part of the horse admits of delivery, or whether on the other hand it is to be regarded as incorporeal and incapable of tradition; the other, whether the letter written by Benzon to Yates was either a constructive delivery of this undivided fourth part of the horse, or an act perfecting the gift of this incorporeal part so far as the nature of the subject matter of the gift admits.

Perhaps the judge was merely having a little joke. When the donor told Moore "by words of present gift" that Moore was to have "one undivided fourth part of this horse", what the donor pictured as the subject matter of his bounty is impossible to know. But the legal issue is what effect his words had. Plainly, the legal interpretation is that the donor proposed to transfer ownership of the horse from himself to himself and Moore as either joint tenants or tenants in common. The property was ownership, the thing owned was a horse, and the proposed gift would have split ownership (not the horse) 3/4 -1/4 between the donor and Moore.

66 See Costigan "Gift Inter Vivos of Choses in Action" (1911) 27 LQR 326, reviewing the theory of Prof Ames to the effect that "as a matter of historical development and of accurate scientific analysis" the assignment of a *chose in action* created only a power of attorney to be exercised by the assignee. "The English cases ... talk of ... incomplete gifts ... [but what they mean is] that the power given the assignee was revocable and has been revoked by the death of the assignor or otherwise; and when they say that the gift is complete, they mean that the power was irrevocable". Cases suggesting that only property in things could be transferred by gift include *Ward* v *Turner* (1752) 2 Ves Sen 431, 28 ER 275 (Eng) (because a gift must be complete "according to the nature of the thing", Lord Hardwicke opined that there could be no transfer by gift of a simple debt or of arrears of rent because there is nothing to deliver); *Miller* v *Miller*

lawyers would be forced to describe the technical processes of legal assignment, equitable assignment, declarations of trust, and negotiation of instruments in explaining how they reached their conclusions. It is true that some cases would have to be categorized as wrongly decided. This would not be a bad thing. The old reports are full of cases that are never cited because they are universally regarded as wrong. There is little merit in continuing to cite and apply the reasoning in other cases merely because their flaws have not previously been exposed.[67]

Mis-labelling other forms of property transfers as "gifts" is a deep-seated lawyerly habit. Over the past 200 years it has relieved claimants of the burden of proving the formal prerequisites of those other transactions in cases that might otherwise have been successfully defended. It has also distorted the meanings of gift and delivery, two simple common law terms.

3   Donee Lack of Rejection

Individual liberty incorporates self-determinism. People in the common law system are not obliged to put up with what other people conceive to be good for them. Economic enrichment - whether through cash injections or gifts of ownership of tarantulas, eskimo artlessness, and other things lacking universal appeal - cannot be forced upon an unwilling donee. This can be phrased in positive or negative terms.

The positive postulation is that there is no gift unless the donee accepts. This suggests that some evidence of acceptance is required, which is not so. Absent evidence of donee rejection, acceptance is said to be "presumed".[68]

The negative postulation is that there is no gift if the donee rejects the proposed transfer. This relates directly to the libertarian principle underlying the rule: if the donee refuses to become a property holder, no one can force him to be one. If there is no evidence to prove donee rejection, the proposed transfer was not rejected and, if the other elements of gift were proved, property passed to the donee. Putting the rule this way has the

---

(1735) 3 P Wms 356, 26 ER 1099 (Eng) (promissory note); and *Tate* v *Hilbert* (1793) 4 Bro CC 286, 29 ER 895 (Eng) (promissory note and cheque). "Apart from the much criticized case of *Lawson* v *Lawson* (1718) 1 P Wms 441, there seems to be no instance of a thing in action other than a bond or deed passing as a *donatio mortis causa* until after *Duffield* v *Elwes* (1827) 1 Bli.NS 497": Winder "Notes of Cases" (1939) 3 Mod LR 310.

67 "It is revolting to have no better reason for a rule of law than that it was laid down in the time of Henry IV. It is still more revolting if the grounds upon which it was laid down have vanished long since, and the rule simply persists from blind imitation of the past ...": Holmes, *The Common Law*.

68 "The law presumes that every grant is for the benefit of the grantee, and therefore, till the contrary is shown, supposes an agreement to the grant": *Butler* v *Baker* (1591) 3 Co Rep 25a, 76 ER 684 (Eng). "[A] benefit conferred upon a man is presumed to be accepted by him until the contrary is proved": *Cook* v *Lister* (1863) 13 CBNS 543, 143 ER 215 (Eng) *per* Willes J at 595.

advantage of focusing our attention upon the evidence rather than inviting us to "presume" to read the donee's mind.

C GIFT IN CONTEMPLATION OF DEATH

1 The Concept Donatio Mortis Causa

Donatio mortis causa (*DMC*) is an ancient form of property transfer. Picture the patriarch's deathbed. "I'm dying" he gasps, "and I want you to have this", handing his sword or some other thing to his son. Then, with the hope that springs eternal, he cautions: "but if the gods spare me, I want it back". Such transfers originated in days when written wills were less common than they are today. It has outlived what former usefulness it had.[69] Nevertheless, it seems destined to linger on until laid to rest by legislation, so we must assess its nature.

DMC can be defined as a gift made in contemplation of imminent death, but subject to a condition subsequent of the donor's recovery. This definition is not entirely in conformity with conventional opinion[70]. However, it captures the essence of a gift in contemplation of death and accurately describes its scope.

2 The Elements of *DMC*

There are three parts to a *DMC*. First, it is a gift. Second, the donor must have been contemplating death when he intended to transfer property. Third, the gift must be made conditional upon death and is undone if the donor recovers.

Because it is a sub-species of gift, a *DMC* must have all the characteristics of a gift. The donor must intend to transfer a particular form of property, without consideration, delivery is required,[71] and donee rejection will prevent the transfer. The intent must be to

---

69 People on their deathbeds remain at liberty to dictate wills, declare themselves trustees, sign documents assigning property, and transfer property by gift *inter vivos*. We could do without further complications. "Improvements in the law, or some things which have been considered improvements, have been lately proposed; and if, among those things called improvements, this *donatio mortis causa* was struck out of our law altogether, it would be quite as well": Lord Eldon in *Duffield* v *Elwes* (1827) 1 Bli NS 497 at 530, 4 ER 959 at 971 (Eng HL).

70 There is a perfectly clear definition set out in *Tate* v *Hilbert* (1793) 2 Ves Jun 111 at 119, 28 ER 552 (Eng) by Lord Eldon. Unfortunately, it is not written in English. The most controversial point in my definition will be that recovery is a condition subsequent. We'll explore that, and other particulars, under the next heading. In general, the prerequisites in America have remained the same as in the early English cases: see *Welton* v *Gallagher* 630 P 2d 1077 (Hawaii 1981); *McCarton* v *Estate of Watson* 693 P 2d 192 (Wash 1984).

71 The delivery requirement is the same as for gifts *inter vivos*. As such, delivery can precede intention:

transfer the property now, not in the future. The requirement of present intent makes gifts subject to conditions precedent impossible.[72] Delivery plus the words "I shall give you ownership of my bicycle if it rains next Tuesday" creates no gift at all until Tuesday, and no gift on Tuesday unless the donor's intent is proved to have remained unchanged until then. It is difficult to see how changing "if it rains next Tuesday" to "if I die of this fever" would make any difference. In fact, making death the condition precedent probably makes it more difficult to prove that the intent to transfer continued until the condition was satisfied. Will a judge believe that the donor's last thought was "I'm certainly glad we got that bicycle thing settled"? These problems are avoided if the property transfer is immediate, but subject to a condition *subsequent* of donor recovery.

The second point, that the donor must have been contemplating death, is admitted by all analysts. However, there is substantial difference of opinion as to what it means. Life is a terminal disease, yet philosophical reflection upon the inevitability of death will not do. At the other extreme, no one would restrict *donatio mortis causa* to classic deathbed scenes. What is required is probably accurately described as[73]

> contemplation, though not necessarily expectation of death [but more than] a vague and general impression that death *may* occur from one of those ordinary risks that attend all human affairs.

Descriptions like that are helpful, but are notoriously difficult to apply in particular cases. *Thompson* v *Mechan* illustrates the point. The donor was afraid of flying. Before flying to Winnipeg he transferred possession of his car to the defendant with the clear intent that she was to be the owner if he died. The flight was uneventful, but he died of a heart attack before returning home. In assessing the donor's contemplation of death, Roach JA introduced the concept of "in extremis".[74]

---

see *Woodward v Woodward* [1995] 3 All ER 980 (CA). A son was in possession of his ill father's car. During a hospital visit, the father told his son, "you can keep the keys, I won't be driving it anymore." Lord Justice Dillon held that ownership of the car was transferred to the son by DMC (at 40): "[t]he words of gift in such circumstances can operate to change the nature of the possession from possession as bailee to possession as donee, albeit in the present case as donee under a *donatio mortis causa* rather than under an immediate gift." Some have suggested that less evidence of delivery is sufficient for a DMC: see, eg. *Union of London and Smith's Bank Limited v Wasserbery* [1915] 1 Ch 195 (Eng) (bearer bond certificates in locked box; transfer of possession of key). In *Re Bayoff Estate* [2000] 3 WWR 445 (QB), Mr Bayoff transferred possession of a key to his safety deposit box to a friend, attempting to transfer to her ownership of the contents. The evidence was insufficient to prove delivery under a gift *inter vivos* but was held to prove gift in contemplation of death. It isn't clear why. If anything, more evidence might be required for a *DMC*, given that the donor is unavailable to give his side of the story.

72 See above "Donor Intent".

73 *Thompson* v *Mechan* (1958) 13 DLR 2d 103 (Ont CA) per Roach JA.

74 *Thompson* v *Mechan* (1958) 13 DLR 2d 103 (Ont CA) per Roach JA at 108. He said this *obiter*, having decided that the donor had recovered from the peril he was contemplating, thus invoking the condition subsequent and undoing the gift; see "Recovery by the Donor", below.

A *donatio mortis causa* is only valid when made in near contemplation of death from a cause that is proximate, either an existing or immediately impending peril, placing the donor *in extremis*. A person cannot be said to be *in extremis* from a cause that exists only in his fancy or imagination and where in fact, he is exposed to no more than the ordinary risks that affect mankind in his ordinary and natural movements and pursuits. The risks attendant upon air travel come within that class.

That would subject the donor's contemplation to two tests. One requires a degree of urgency, an apprehension of imminent death. The other imposes an objective assessment of the peril.

As to the first test, there is clearly some outer limit required, but *in extremis* may be a bit too restrictive. In one case a donor decided to make a gift *mortis causa* after learning that he was dying of cancer. He died a month later from pneumonia, having got a chill while coming home from market on a bus. The gift was upheld.[75] Contemplation of imminent death is probably an adequate description of the requirement, keeping in mind that recovery by the donor will undo the transaction and that post-contemplation longevity suggests recovery.[76]

As to the second proposed test, there is no reason to require the donor to think like most other people. If a donor tried to make a *DMC* before falling off the Empire State Building, why can't we take his pathological fear of edges into account?[77] An objective assessment of the peril may be appropriate in assessing whether the expressed apprehension was genuine, but fear of flying (for example) is no less genuine for being slightly weird. Normalcy reflects fashion, not diagnostic skill.[78] If the donor genuinely contemplated imminent death because of some phobia, and if the question is whether the gift was made in contemplation of imminent death, the fact that the reasonable man does not share his phobia is a red herring.

---

75 *Wilkes* v *Allington* [1931] 2 Ch 104 (Eng). See McGarry "Case Note" 81 LQR 21 (1965) recommending that the standard be "real and substantial apprehension of premature death". What is an unreal but substantial (or a real but insubstantial) apprehension? See also on "in extremis" *Canada Trust* v *Labadie* [1962] OR 151 (Ont); "Case Note" 2 Osgoode Hall LJ 520 (1963); "Note - Apprehension of Death in Gifts Mortis Causa" 32 Columbia L Rev 702 (1932).

76 See, for example, *Fendly* v *Laster* 538 SW 2d 555 (Ark 1976), in which the donor contemplated death after a heart attack. He lived more years, conducting business affairs on a part-time basis. It was decided that there was no gift because the donor had recovered. This seems correct: his recovery tells us nothing about the sincerity or urgency of his thoughts while contemplating death. We'll deal with recovery later.

77 Fear of heights is a misnomer. No one is afraid of falling off Denver.

78 "It was considered a sign of particular renown and bravado for the [French] King's son, the Duc d'Orleans [to enter a house infected with the Black Death and slash up the bed-clothes with his sword]. He was dead within three days, but a mistake in judgment in no way lessened the honour of his action." Smith *Henry VIII: The Mask of Royalty*. In a more modern setting, Yossarian in *Catch 22* was considered peculiar because he thought the Germans were trying to kill him.

It was probably a similar notion of acceptable, normal behaviour that once made contemplation of suicide inadequate grounds for a *DMC*.[79] Such gifts are now generally allowed.[80]

The third point, that the gift must be made conditional upon death and is undone if the donor recovers, is also variously interpreted. If no such condition was imposed and if a gift *inter vivos* cannot be proved, there is no gift at all. This requires an interpretation of the donor's expressed intentions.[81] If the evidence proves the condition was imposed, the more difficult question is exactly what it means. Whether the donor recovered is a separate topic, dealt with under the next heading. Here, the issue is not the determination of recovery, but the interpretation of the recovery rule itself. Is recovery a condition subsequent or is death a condition precedent. The distinction is important: it determines, among other things, when a gift *mortis causa* occurred.[82]

I suggest that recovery is a condition subsequent which retroactively undoes the attempted gift. The reasoning is simple. Gifts in contemplation of death are a sub-species of gifts. Gifts are proved by the coincidence of present intent and delivery. A condition subsequent contemplates an immediate transfer of property that might be undone later upon the happening of the condition. Here, the condition is recovery. Consider an example.

> Casey, contemplating major surgery, says "I want Yogi to have my baseball card collection if I don't survive the operation". He transfers possession of the cards to Yogi.

Before delivery, Casey owned the cards. Eventually we shall know whether Casey died during the operation or recovered. If Casey died, Yogi will subsequently be viewed as having owned the cards since the time of delivery. If Casey recovered, Yogi will subsequently be regarded as never having owned the cards at all, although he will have possessed them with Casey's permission for a time. Nor are there major analytical problems in the interim. Yogi has at least a possessor's remedies against third parties. He

---

79 See *Agnew v Belfast Banking Co* [1896] 2 Ir 204 (Ir CA); *Re Dudman* [1925] Ch 553 (Eng); *Re Fanning* [1923] 3 DLR 925 (Ont). The reasoning was probably based on criminal laws proscribing attempted suicide.

80 *Scherer v Hyland* 380 A 2d 698 (NJ 1977).

81 For example: "I am going to give you all my jewellery. I am giving you my key to the safe deposit at Harrods and when I am gone you can go and get the jewellery". This was held to prove that the donor intended that she would "resume complete dominion" should she recover: *Re Lillingston* [1952] 2 All ER 184 (Eng). There is often scant evidence of precisely what the donor said and a glance through the digests will uncover an amazing variety of accepted evidence.

82 If recovery is a condition subsequent, the gift took place before death when delivery and intent coincided, but will be retroactively undone should the donor recover from the peril. If death is a condition precedent, there is no gift until the donor dies within the peril. Different tax consequences might follow if intent and delivery occurred near the end of one tax year and the donor died after the new tax year started. Also, where the donee died before the donor, the donee's heir would get the property under the condition subsequent interpretation, but not if the donor's death were a condition precedent.

can pass his own precarious ownership to buyers at common law and might even transfer more under a sale of goods statute.[83] As to disputes between Casey and Yogi, how likely are they while Casey is languishing within the peril? Any such disputes are unlikely to require judicial resolution before adequate evidence of death or recovery is available; if they do, they must be dealt with according to the evidence available at that time. It is worth keeping in mind that the concept of a condition subsequent is not unique to *donatio mortis causa*. That conditions subsequent retroactively change history is a minor problem in a system where conditions subsequent abound and retrospective analysis of what happened is the norm.

An alternative analysis is that death of the donor is the event that completes the gift. Cases usually cited for this proposition do not really it.[84] A property transfer at the time of death is difficult to reconcile with the requirement of present intent, particularly where the expression of intent and delivery occurred some days or weeks earlier. It is incredible to suggest that the donor was thinking of the specific gift at a time when his mind was likely on other things. Moreover, if there is a will, the will speaks as of the time of death and would therefore be better evidence of the donor's last intentions regarding property not disposed of by gifts that took effect before death. If death is the time of transfer, *donatio mortis causa* begins to look like a partial, unwritten will in which delivery has replaced the usual statutory requirements of a signature and witnesses. It looks even more like an unwritten will if cases suggesting *obiter* that the donor can revoke the gift before death are correct.[85] I have found no case decided on this point.[86] I suggest that the

---

83 See Chapter 8 "Sale of Goods Statutes" and "The Uniform Commercial Code".

84 *Duffield* v *Elwes* (1827) 1 Bli NS 497, 4 ER 959 (Eng HL) is commonly cited as the English authority. It is not a gift case. The issue was whether a dying person had transferred mortgages and bonds - not property in things - to the plaintiff. Lord Eldon concluded, at ER 976, that the executors held the mortgages and the bonds as trustees for the plaintiff. This is consistent with a transaction whereby the dying person made himself a trustee for the plaintiff, but utterly inconsistent with a transfer of the property by gift. Contrast *Christiansen* v *Rumsey* 429 P 2d 416 (Idaho 1967), which suggests that a *DMC* immediately passes a "defeasible title", but was decided on the failure to prove present intent. Three other cases, suggesting that property given in contemplation of death remains subject to the donor's debts, are commonly cited in support of the proposition that the gift occurs at death. *Ward* v *Turner* (1752) 2 Ves Sen 431, 28 ER 275 (Eng) says no such thing: it was a case where there was no delivery, so no gift was proved. In *Tate* v *Leithead* (1854) Kay 658, 69 ER 279 (Eng), such a statement was made, but it was not even said *obiter*: the plaintiff's lawyer argued that a donor's creditors could claim against the donee, citing *Smith* v *Casen*; Sir Page Wood VC interjected "I think that is so settled now". No argument was heard on the other side and the case was decided on other grounds. *Smith* v *Casen* itself consists of a two sentence "memo" recited by the reporter at (1718) 1 P Wms 406, 24 ER 447 (Eng). It suggests that allowing the donee to keep the property might be a "fraud upon the creditors". Insufficient detail is provided to permit much elaboration on this point, but if it means that a donor and donee cannot get away with conspiring to practice a deliberate fraud upon creditors then it tells us something we already knew, but nothing at all about when a *DMC* takes effect.

85 See on this point Schouler "Oral Wills and Death-Bed Gifts" (1886) 2 LQR 444. It is one thing to say that if the donor retakes possession after delivery the gift is revoked, but quite another to propose that the donor has the power to revoke the gift by retaking possession. If the donee surrendered possession, the gift may have been undone by mutual consent. But suppose the donee refuses to give up possession. The intent

donor does not hold right to immediate possession. Both ownership and possession have already been transferred to the donee, subject only to the condition subsequent of donor recovery.

3   Recovery by the Donor

No one here gets out alive. Yet we have a rule that if the donor recovers, a *donatio mortis causa* is retroactively undone. What does donor recovery mean? The answer is almost certainly that it means survival of the peril that inspired the donor to contemplate death.

Contemplation of death from a specific peril was the thought that triggered the gift. Recovery from that peril is the condition that undoes it. We know from common law cases how to assess the perceived peril and determine whether the attempt to give failed at the outset.[87] The same cases establish that the donee retains the property only if the donor dies *within* (though not necessarily from) that peril.

Wilkes v *Allington*[88] illustrates the rule. T he donor was told he was dying of cancer and made a gift in contemplation of death. A month later, while coming home from market on a bus, he got a chill and developed pneumonia, from which he died. It was held that he had not recovered and the gift was upheld. Similarly, in *Ridden* v *Thrall*,[89] the donor's gift was made before a serious operation. Though the surgery appeared successful, he died of a heart attack two weeks later. It was held that he was still within the contemplated peril. By contrast, in *Thompson* v *Mechan* the donor's attempted gift while leaving on a business trip was prompted by his fear of flying.[90] The flight was uneventful, but the trip was not. He died of a heart attack while in Winnipeg. It was held

---

to make a gift conditional upon death having been expressed, and delivery having been made, isn't the donor trapped by his own voluntary actions? By what authority does he propose to dispossess the donee?

86 In *Bunn* v *Markham* (1816) 7 Taunt 224, 129 ER 90 (Eng) the keys to a locked chest were "to be delivered to" donee after the donor's death: held, no delivery and therefore no gift. The judge speculated that a donor could retake possession after delivery, and referred to counsel's argument to that effect in another case, but made no decision on the point. *Cant* v *Gregory* (1894) 10 TLR 584 (Eng CA) referred to the notion, but the case was again decided on the ground that there had been no delivery at all. In *Edwards* v *Jones* (1836) 1 My & Cr 226, 40 ER 361 (Eng) the evidence showed that the donor intended to make a present assignment, not a gift in contemplation of death. In *Atkins* v *Parker*, 173 SE2d 38 (NC 1970) the judge assumed that there was such a rule, although it was not invoked. The ratio (at 41) was "the fact that [the donor] told [the possessor] he would let him know if he wanted the certificates back would not defeat the gift mortis causa". *Spiller* v *Herpel* 357 So 2d 572 (La 1978) suggested that there may well be such a rule in the *Civil Code* of Lousiana.

87 See above "The Elements of DMC".

88 *Wilkes* v *Allington* [1931] 2 Ch 104 (Eng).

89 *Ridden* v *Thrall* 26 NE 627 (NY 1891).

90 *Thompson* v *Mechan* (1958) 13 DLR 2d 103 (Ont CA). Recovery also undid an attempted *DMC* in *Staniland* v *Willot* (1852) 3 Mac & G 664, 42 ER 416 (Eng) (fit of apoplexy or epilepsy with subsequent recovery before lapsing into lunacy).

that there was no gift because he did not die "either from or while within the alleged peril".[91] The question to be asked is whether the donor recovered from the peril, not whether he anticipated the cause of his death.

D SUMMARY: THE RESULT OF GIFT

1 What Property is Transferred

Gift is a common law transaction that transfers common law forms of property in things. Either ownership or possession of a thing can be transferred, depending on the donor intent and what property the donor holds. Right to immediate possession could also be transferred by gift, so long as delivery could be proved without a transfer of possession of the thing.[92]

Judges and lawyers habitually call all voluntary transfers without consideration "gifts". Transfers of other forms of property - security interests in things, equitable interests and property other than property in things - can be achieved by statutory and equitable assignment or through negotiable instruments. Each of these transactions has its own formal prerequisites. Calling them gifts does not excuse litigants from proving those prerequisites. They are not gifts at all.

2 When and How Property is Transferred

Property in a thing is transferred by gift when a present intent to transfer and delivery coincide. This is usually proved by an expression of donor intent and a transfer of possession of the thing, but may be disproved by subsequent donee rejection. Conditions precedent are impossible. A donor must intend to transfer the property now, not in the future. Conditions subsequent are possible, although the transaction is not a gift if the condition can be interpreted as consideration. A gift in contemplation of death (*donatio mortis causa*) is the most common example of a gift subject to condition subsequent. The property transfer takes place immediately, but may be retroactively undone by the condition.

---

91 He was afraid of flying, not of Winnipeg. Similarly, see *Fendly* v *Laster* 538 SW 2d 555 (Ark 1976) (donor contemplating death after heart attack; lived five more years and conducted business affairs on part-time basis; donor had recovered, so no gift)

92 This is an alternative explanation of a gift of possession of a car by a donor who does not own it. Delivery could be proved by a transfer of possession of the keys. Maybe this transfers right to immediate possession to the donee, who must take possession of the car to complete the ownership transfer.

CHAPTER 10

BAILMENT: A SEPARATE TRANSACTION?

Bailment is a transaction. It consists of an agreement and a transfer of property. The property transferred is possession of a thing. The agreement proposes a future transfer of possession of the thing, either to a third party or back to the transferor.

Bailment has long been treated as a separate category.[1] This probably does little harm, though as we shall see all bailments can be analyzed as either sales, barters, or gifts. Often, however, bailment is used to describe virtually any situation in which one person holds possession of a thing while another person holds ownership or right to immediate possession. Judges and lawyers habitually misuse the term in this way.[2] The practice has led to much confusion, particularly about a bailee's remedies.

Relationships create remedies. Property in a thing is the type of relationship created by a bailment transaction. The bailment (*ie*, transactional, not property) issues are whether and upon what terms possession has been transferred.

We begin with the search for a simple definition of bailment.

A   BAILMENT DEFINED

"You may take possession of my car." Thus begins a classic bailment. It does not matter for the moment why the speaker (the bailor) proposed the transfer, or what might motivate the other party (the bailee) to take possession of the car. The bailor may be transferring possession of the car to a ship as transatlantic cargo, to a mechanic for

---

1 Not everyone agrees that it should be. See McMeel "The Redundancy of Bailment" [2003] LMCLQ 169 at 171: "[m]y thesis is that all the alleged distinctive hallmarks of bailment are better explained in terms of general principles of contract, tort, unjust enrichment or property". He goes on to explain his point (at 199).

> Bailment at best is useful shorthand for all those situations where there is a transfer of possession of tangible personal property short of outright sale. In the commercial context there is almost invariably a contractual regime spelling out in detail the rights and obligations of the parties *inter se*. Outside the commercial context the law of tort supplies the default rules which apply when there is such a transfer, which is occasionally reinforced by reference to unjust enrichment, for example where a bailee recovers in respect not just of his own interest but also in respect of his bailor's interest.

2 One exhaustive (1013 pages!) work on the topic does not even give a clear definition. Palmer *Bailment* (Law Book Company Limited Sydney 1979) at 2 says that "a bailment comes into being whenever one person is knowingly and willingly in possession of goods which belong to another". He claims this enjoys "the general support of judicial authority". But what is bailment? Is it a form of property? Is it a way of acquiring property? Is it very like a whale (or a snark)? Palmer's description implies that one can possess a thing other than willingly, which is contrary to the definition of possession (control and intent to exclude others). Is bailment simply possession? If so, the term is redundant.

routine maintenance, or to his teenage son for a night on the town. The bailee may be a tourist seeking possession of a rental car, a neighbour keeping the car safe while the owner is on vacation, a friend who has offered to rotate the tires, or even a thumb-breaker securing payment of a loan. All of these are bailment transactions. It is useful to identify what they have in common before focusing on their differences.

Bailment, like sale and gift, is a transaction that creates property relationships. In a typical bailment situation the bailor holds ownership of the thing while possession has been transferred to the bailee.[3] There are then two relationships - ownership and possession - between bailor and bailee. They have obligations to one another because of those relationships.[4] The bailment transaction may have added other obligations, for example some contractual terms. However, the primary obligations of each arise from the property the other holds; bailment is simply the transaction by which the bailee came to hold possession of the thing.[5]

Lawyers and judges often talk of some mysterious "bailment relationship" between a bailor and a bailee. This leads to confusing mental gymnastics. *Morris v CW Martin and Sons Ltd* provides an example.[6] The plaintiff had sent a mink stole to a furrier for cleaning. With the plaintiff's consent, the furrier had sent the stole to the defendant, a specialist cleaner. The employee assigned to do the cleaning work stole the fur from the defendant's premises. The defendant's liability was analyzed as follows by Diplock LJ.[7]

> Duties at common law are owed by one person to another only if there exists a relationship between them which the common law recognizes as giving rise to such duty.

---

3 It is, of course, not necessary that the bailor hold ownership. A possessor can transfer possession to a bailee. The transaction is identical; the *relationship* between bailor and bailee is different, but only because the bailor does not hold ownership of the thing.

4 Third parties have obligations to the owner: their obligations are based on the fact of his ownership, not on the irrelevant circumstance that he was the bailor in a bailment transaction. Third parties also have obligations to the possessor: these obligations are based on the fact that he holds possession. That he acquired possession by being a bailee in a bailment transaction is irrelevant to the possessor - third party relationship, except to the extent that the transaction may fix the period of his projected possession and thus limit the damages he might collect. This issue is covered later under "Bailee v Third Party: Possession, Tort, and the Assessment of Damages".

5 See Tay, "The Essence of a Bailment: Contract, Agreement or Possession" (1967) 5 Sydney LR 239. She approved of what she perceived as a "growing tendency to distinguish contractual and consensual elements surrounding a bailment from the bailment itself" [at 240]. After conducting a careful search of the roots of *detinue sur bailment* and *detinue sur trover*, and examining several cases on the degree of "negligence" in each category, she drew the following conclusion.

> The primary duty of the bailee ... arises from his entering into a relationship with a chattel; it requires neither an agreement, nor any knowledge of the person of, a particular bailor.

If only she had left out the words "with a chattel".

6 *Morris v CW Martin and Sons Ltd* [1966] 1 QB 716 (Eng CA).

7 [1966] 1 QB 716 at 731.

One of such recognized relationships is created by the voluntary taking into custody of goods which are the property of another. By voluntarily accepting from Beder [the furrier] the custody of a fur which they knew to be the property of a customer of his, they brought into existence between the plaintiff and themselves the relationship of bailor and bailee by sub-bailment. The legal relationship of bailor and bailee of a chattel can exist independently of any contract.

It is true that a bailment transaction can be accomplished without a contract. Bailment without consideration (and thus without contract) occurs when the owner of a book lends it to a friend. But there must be some interaction between the parties, either personally or by agency. Otherwise, there is no bailment transaction between the parties because there is no transaction at all. There was neither contract nor contact between Morris and C.W. Martin and Sons Ltd.[8] All they had was a property relationship: the defendant held possession of a fur owned by the plaintiff. Suppose the defendant had acquired possession of the fur by finding, or even by theft, had assigned an employee to clean it, and subsequently discovered that the employee had stolen the fur. Would there be any doubt about the defendant's tort liability to the plaintiff for the value of ownership of the fur?[9] Why did the English Court of Appeal think it necessary to concoct an artificial bailment transaction in this case?[10]

The second key ingredient in a bailment transaction is an agreement between the parties

---

8 Although the plaintiff authorized Beder the furrier to send the fur to the defendant for cleaning, none of the judges concluded that Beder did so as the plaintiff's agent.

9 The answer, as explained in the next footnote, is yes there is still some doubt. See, however, *Frost* v *Plumb* 16 Am Rep 18 (Conn 1873), in which a bailee was held responsible for injury to a horse in his possession through a Sunday agreement. It being against the law at the time to contract on a Sunday, the defendant sought to impugn the transaction. He failed.

> All that the plaintiff is required to prove is title in himself, and a conversion by the defendant. ... It is quite immaterial how the horse came to be in the defendant's possession. Whether lawfully or unlawfully is not of the slightest consequence. He may have found him in the highway; he may have hired him of a stranger; he may have taken him from the plaintiff's stable, with or without leave, upon a weekday or upon the Sabbath; it is all the same.

10 The problem, as we shall see later, lies in a not quite yet definitively overruled (though largely discredited) line of precedent suggesting that a bailee's duty of care in tort varies depending on the nature and purpose of the bailment transaction. These cases suggest that a "bailee for reward" is responsible on a general negligence standard whereas a "gratuitous bailee" is liable only for "gross negligence". Most writers equate the obligations of a possessor by finding with those of a "gratuitous bailee": see *eg.* Palmer *Bailment* (Law Book Company Limited Sydney 1979) at 873; Raushenbush *Brown on Personal Property* 3rd ed (Callaghan & Company Chicago 1975) at 30. In *Morris v CW Martin and Sons Ltd* itself, none of the three judges was inclined to comment on possible liability outside the facts of the case, which they all classified as "bailment for reward". Diplock LJ said at 737.

> I should add that we are not concerned here with gratuitous bailment. That is a relationship in which the bailee's duties of care in his custody of the goods are different from those of a bailee for reward. It may be that his duties being passive rather than active, the concept of vicarious performance of them is less apposite. However this may be, I express no views as to the circumstances in which he would be liable for conversion of the goods by his servant.

We'll explore later whether "bailment for reward" and "gratuitous bailment" are meaningful distinctions.

concerning a future disposition of possession of the thing. The most common agreement is that possession will be retransferred to the bailor at some specified time.[11] Less common, though still a bailment agreement, is a proposal that the bailee retain possession for a time and then transfer possession to a third party.[12] The key factors are that the bailee's possession is agreed to be for a limited time and that possession of the same thing, not some different thing, is to be relinquished after that time.[13] How the time of projected possession is limited does not matter. Thus, "keep this til I want it back" describes a bailment term to end on demand by the bailor. "Keep this for a week" describes a bailment term projected to last one week. It is implicit in each case that the speaker means "keep [possession of] this" for the specified term.[14]

Agreement is an important part of the bailment transaction because it must be proved that the bailee assented to the transfer of possession proposed. "A man cannot be made a bailee of goods against his will".[15] Cases involving car parks illustrate the point. An estate holder in land who permits a car owner to park his car on the land is not necessarily a bailee in possession of the car. If the terms of the transaction do not show that the estate holder accepted possession, the owner of the car is a licensee who is accorded the privilege of using the land.[16] There are dozens of car park cases. Factors such as security

---

11 A bailee who fails to return possession of the thing to the bailor can be liable for the costs arising from the bailor having to retrieve possession. In *Laflamme v Howard* (1996) 185 AR 151 (Prov Ct), the bailees left the bailor's truck in a different municipality than that agreed to by the parties. The bailees were liable for the costs of having the truck picked up.

12 See, for example, *Biddle v Bond* (1865) 6 B & S 225 (Eng.); *Harding v Commissioner of Inland Revenue* [1977] 1 NZLR 337 (NZ), and Pollock and Wright, *Possession in the Common Law* (1888) 161.

13 If the possessor has the option of returning possession of some other thing, the transaction is an "exchange", not bailment: *Austin v Seligman* 18 F 519 (US 1883). Complications may be introduced in the case of fungibles, like wheat: see *Schindler v Westover* 99 Ind 395 (Ind 1882). Fungibles are dealt with in some detail in Chapter 4 "Accession, Mixing and Fixtures"; we'll consider the possibility of a bailment of fungibles later under this heading. Quite radical changes in the character or external appearance of things may be contemplated - leather to be made into shoes in *Mansfield v Converse* 8 Allen (Mass) 182; logs to be sawn into lumber in *Gleeson v Beers* 10 A 86 (Vt); milk to be made into cheese or butter in *Bank v Schween* 20 NE 681 (Ill.); even grapes to be made into wine - yet the possessor is a bailee of the raw material and then of the finished product.

14 Although it is unsettled whether the bailee in a non-contractual bailment can retain possession if the bailor changes his mind and demands possession part way through the term: more on this later, under "Possession by Gift". In many bailment transactions most of the terms are implicit. A neighbour who seeks permission to "borrow your lawnmower" is likely without a defence if he refuses to return possession fairly promptly.

15 *McCutcheon v Lightfoot* [1930] SCR 108, [1930] 1 DLR 995 (SCC).

16 *Ashby v Tolhurst* [1973] 2 All ER 837 (Eng). The essential question is whether the transaction is a transfer of possession of a thing to be stored or the rental of a place in which to store it? See *Zweeres v Thibault* 23 A 2d 529 (Vt 1942) (storage of furniture). In the latter situation, the licensor does not acquire possession and is mainly responsible only to honour the particular terms of the license. Whether there was a transfer of possession depends on whether the operator of the car park has dominion and control over the car: *Motor Ins Corp v American Garages Inc* 414 NYS2d 841 (NY 1979).

arrangements,[17] signs,[18] whether instructions are followed,[19] and whether the keys are left behind[20] are balanced in them to prove the terms of the parties' transaction. The keys are important. They are the instruments by which one gains access to the normal usage of the car. We saw in gift transactions that a transfer of possession of the keys to a car might be interpreted as transfer of possession of the car.[21] In the car park cases, the driver's retention of possession of the car keys is strong evidence that the parties did not agree to a transfer of possession of the car.[22]

Lack of agreement to accept possession is also the reason why unsolicited delivery does not make the recipient a bailee. *Cowen v Pressprich*[23] is an example. The defendant had contracted to purchase a particular corporate bond from the plaintiff stockbroker. The plaintiff's delivery boy pushed through the defendant's mail slot a negotiable certificate for a different bond. The defendant's clerk spotted the error almost immediately. He opened the door and called the plaintiff's name, not having seen the boy. A rogue boy appeared, passed himself off as the plaintiff's boy, and disappeared with the certificate. The plaintiff lost a conversion action against the defendant. Though the defendant was referred to as an "involuntary bailee", the conclusion was that he was not liable without some "exercise of dominion ... some act inconsistent with the complete right of dominion

---

17 The extent to which the exit is guarded may suggest a bailment situation. See *Council of the City of Sydney v West* (1964) 82 WN (NSW) 139, affm'd (1965) 114 CLR 481, in which it was proved that the parking lot attendant would not release possession of a car unless the appropriate ticket was produced. Similarly, see *Walton Stores Ltd v Sydney City Council* [1968] 2 NSWR 109. The opposite decision was influenced by the lack of such security in *Palmer v Toronto Medical Arts Building Ltd* (1960) 21 DLR 2d 181 (Ont) and *BG Transport Services Ltd v Marston Motor Co Ltd* [1970] 1 Lloyd's Rep 371 (Eng).

18 Clear notices posted or printed on a parking receipt to the effect that "charges are for use of parking space only" point toward a licence situation. This seems to have been the deciding point against the bailment contention in *Bata v City Parking Canada Ltd* (1973) 43 DLR 3d 190 (Ont CA). The plaintiff had parked his car in a downtown parking lot and left the keys on the seat as instructed by the attendant, receiving a ticket with the printed notice. The car was stolen and damaged, but the plaintiff failed to collect damages from the operator of the lot who successfully argued that possession had not been transferred. Compare, however, the later case *Heffron v Imperial Parking Co Ltd* (1974) 46 DLR 3d 642 (Ont CA). The two cases are difficult to reconcile.

19 A bailment transaction was proved where the plaintiff complied precisely with the instructions of the defendant's Service Manager who designated the manner in which the plaintiff's truck was to be delivered: *Letourneau v Otto Mobiles Edmonton (1984) Ltd* [2003] 3 WWR 389. Similarly, in *Munroe v Belinsky* (1995) 103 Man R (2d) 12 (QB) at para 13, the judge concluded that the defendant was a bailee of the plaintiff's truck because (among other reasons) "the defendant told the plaintiff ...where to leave the truck".

20 Bailment is suggested, though not necessarily proved, when the owner of the car is required to leave the keys with an attendant. This was probably the most important factor in *Heffron v Imperial Parking Co Ltd* (1974) 46 DLR 3d 642 (Ont CA).

21 See Chapter 9 "Delivery".

22 By contrast, where a person gains entry by ticket machine, chooses his own parking space, and retains possession of the keys there is no bailment: *Central Parking System v Miller* 586 SW2d 262 (Ky 1979); *Allright Auto Parks Inc v Moore* 560 SW2d 129 (Tex 1977); *Mather v Carnes* 551 SW2d 272 (Mo 1972); *Ashby v Tolhurst* [1973] 2 All ER 837 (Eng).

23 *Cowen v Pressprich* 194 NYS 926 (NY 1922).

of the ... owner".[24] This can only mean that the defendant never held possession of the certificate, that he was no bailee at all. The defendant's actions were described as "an honest attempt to restore possession to the ... owners". Does that matter? Would the defendant have incurred liability if he had flung the unwanted piece of paper into the street? Maybe so, but not on the basis that was a bailee when the evidence clearly showed that he had refused to take possession.[25]

Many sources, including Halsbury's, say that finders are bailees. "This expression is not etymologically accurate, because the word 'bailee' is derived from the French 'bailler' meaning to deliver or hand over, and there is no delivering or handing over to a finder."[26] The sole justification advanced for calling a finder a bailee appears to be that a possessor by finding, like a possessor by bailment, owes certain non-contractual obligations to the owner of the thing possessed.[27] But a careless driver owes substantially the same

---

24 This was the dissenting view of Lehman J at trial, but his analysis was specifically adopted when the majority view was overturned on appeal, 194 NYS 926 (1922).

25 In *Lethbridge* v *Phillips* (1819) 2 Stark 544, 171 ER 731 (Eng) an unsolicited miniature sent to the defendant was damaged by being placed near a stove. The defendant was not liable. In *Neuwith* v *Darwen Co-operative Society* (1894) 63 LJNS 290 (Eng) a violin left behind after an orchestra rehearsal was damaged by an employee of the estate holder. The estate holder was not liable. In *Stewart* v *Gustafson* [1999] 4 WWR 695 (Sask) the plaintiff left some things in the farmyard of the defendants without informing the defendants of their existence or whereabouts. The things were damaged. The plaintiff brought an action for conversion and lost. Similarly, in *Luider* v *Nguyen* [1994] AJ No 494 (Prov Ct) the plaintiff left his heifer at the defendant's slaughterhouse without informing the defendant. The carcass of the former heifer was not available for pick-up the next morning because the heifer had escaped. The plaintiff lost in an action for damages against the defendant. In *Marcq* v *Christie Man & Woods Ltd* [2002] 4 All ER 1005 the plaintiff argued that an auctioneer, once in possession of his stolen painting, should be thought of as his "unconscious" bailee and should be liable in conversion for having permitted a third party to take possession. The argument was unsuccessful. In *Elvin & Powell Ltd* v *Plummer Roddis Ltd* (1933) 50 TLR 158 (Eng) a rogue requested that the plaintiff send some coats to the defendant's premises, then wired the defendant saying they were sent in error and that he would pick them up for the plaintiff. The defendant was not liable for allowing the rogue to take possession. There was no decision on whether the defendant had become a bailee, but Hawke J noted, *obiter*, at 159: "[i]f persons were involuntary bailees and had done everything reasonable they were not liable to pay damages if something they did resulted in the loss of property. There was an obligation on the part of an involuntary bailee to do what was right and reasonable". So he says, and so say most other analysts: see, for example, Palmer, *Bailment* 393. But on what basis can the courts require "reasonable" behaviour from someone who returns home to find that some uninvited caller has pushed an unwanted object through the mail slot? Isn't he like the finder of a lost or discarded thing who is not obliged to take possession of it and incurs no liability if he simply leaves the thing where it lies. Indeed, isn't he simply a victim of trespass? Can't he fling it in the street, or in the garbage, with impunity? See to that effect, *obiter*, *Forster* v *Juniata Bridge Co* 55 Am Dec 506 (Pa 1851) (bridge carried onto plaintiff's land by flood).

26 Lord Pearson in *Gilchrist Watt and Sanderson Pty Ltd* v *York Products Pty Ltd* [1970] 3 All ER 825 at 831, [1970] 1 WLR 1262 (NSW JCPC) at 1262. We need not look far for judicial misuse of the term.

> The obligation is at any rate the same as that of a bailee, whether or not it can with strict accuracy be described as being the obligation of a bailee. ... In the English courts the word 'bailment' has acquired a meaning wide enough to include this case. It may not have acquired such a wide meaning in the Australian courts: Lord Pearson, in the same case, at WLR 1270.

27 Palmer *Bailment* (Law Book Company Limited Sydney 1979) at 26: "cases of finding give rise to a

common law duty of care to the owner of a dog crossing the highway. We don't call the driver a bailee of the dog merely because he owes tort damages for interference with property in the dog. Nor does it make any sense, whatever a possessor's obligations may be, to try to accommodate possession by finding into the category of transfer of possession by bailment. Bailment is just a method of acquiring possession. So is finding. Possessors by finding are not bailees because the way they acquired possession lacks the identifying characteristics - transaction and agreement - of bailment.

Sales transactions are also excluded as all conventional definitions classify bailment as a transfer of possession and sale as a transfer of ownership.[28] Which form of property has been transferred is determined by the intention of the transacting parties. What they intended is not, however, always obvious from what they said. People are not in the habit of specifying "I agree to transfer to you ownership [or possession] of this thing upon the following terms". Other factors usually determine whether an ownership transfer was what the parties had in mind.[29]

The issue has often arisen when the transaction involved fungibles deposited in a storage or processing facility.[30] The courts have settled upon the following distinctions. First, where the operator of the facility is at liberty to either re-deliver possession of an equivalent portion of the bulk or to pay the depositor the market value of ownership of that portion, the original transfer was a sale of ownership.[31] Second, where the operator is obliged to retransfer possession of an equivalent quantity and quality of the fungibles if demanded by the depositor, the transaction may be interpreted as a bailment.[32] The latter

---

bailment, at least to the extent that the finder owes substantially the same common law duties in relation to the chattel as an ordinary consensual bailee". Cases saying that possessors by finding owe the owner the duties of a "gratuitous bailee" include *Newman v Bourne and Hollingsworth Ltd* (1915) 31 TLR 209 (Eng); *Helson v McKenzies (Cuba St.) Ltd* [1950] NZLR 878 (NZ); *Grafstein v Holme and Freeman* (1958) 12 DLR 2d 727 (Ont); *Kowal v Ellis* (1977) 76 DLR 3rd 546 (Man CA). As might be expected, these and other cases vary in phrasing those duties in terms of "gross negligence" or reasonable care, with most recent authorities tending toward the latter. We'll explore these distinctions later under "Bailor v Bailee: Liability in Tort and Contract".

28 See Chapter 8 "Purchase and Sale". Later, under the heading "Possession by Contract" a case is presented that all contractual bailments could be more simply analyzed as sales of possession.

29 Insurance is sometimes thought to be a factor. The party paying for and benefiting from insurance in the thing is more likely to be the owner of the thing. See, for example, *Coro (Canada) Inc (Re)* (1997) 36 OR (3d) 563 (Registrar) or *Busse v Edmonton Grain & Hay Co* (1932) 26 Alta LR 83 (CA).

30 As to what sorts of things judges (as opposed to linguists) are likely to construe as fungibles, see the comments in Chapter 4 "Mixing: Things Confused".

31 *Lawlor v Nicol* (1898) 12 Man R 224 (Man CA) (wheat deposited in a grain elevator; wheat or money returnable; sale of ownership). *South Australian Insurance Co v Randell* (1869) LR 3 PC 101 (S Austr JCPC) (corn deposited with miller who may use it "as part of the current consumable stock or capital of the miller's trade"; corn or money returnable; sale of ownership). "The distinction is, can the depositor .by his contract compel a delivery of wheat, whether the dealer is willing or not? If he can the transaction is a bailment. If the dealer has the option to pay for it in money or other wheat, it is a sale": *Lyon v Lenon* 7 NE 311 (Ind 1886).

32 *Burke v Boulder Milling and Elevator Co* 235 P 574 (Col 1925); *Kimbell Milling Co v Greene* 170

interpretation depends upon the various depositors being legally regarded as "tenants in common" (*ie*, sharing ownership in undivided shares proportional to the amount each deposited) of the stored bulk[33] and upon each deposit being factually construed as a unit of fungible mass, rather than discrete items of fungibles. Otherwise it would be impossible to conclude that the depositor held property in the same thing before, during, and after the bailment transaction. If that conclusion is impossible, the transaction was not bailment.[34]

Bailment can be defined as follows.

> *Bailment is a transaction whereby possession of a thing is transferred upon agreement that possession of the same thing, perhaps in an altered state, will be transferred back to the transferror or on to someone else as agreed.*[35]

SW 2d 191 (Tex 1943); *Dier v Thompson Chemicals Corp* 281 SW 2d 572 (Mo 1955); *Mohoff v Northrup King Co* 380 P 2d 983 (Ore 1963).

    33 *Rice v Nixon* 49 Am Re 430 (Ind 1884):

> the course of business in this great branch of commerce ... leads to the presumption that both the warehouseman and the depositor intended that the grain should be placed in a common receptacle and treated as common property. ... If the warehouseman is not bound to place grain in a separate place for each depositor, then the fact that he puts it in a common receptacle with grain of his own and that of other depositors does not make him a purchaser, and if he is not a purchaser then he is a bailee. In all matters of contract the intention of the parties gives character and effect to the transaction, and in such a case as this the circumstances declare that the intention was to make contract of bailment and not a contract of sale.

The risk of loss fell on the depositors as owners. See, to the same effect, Art 7-207 of The *Uniform Commercial Code* which is explained in some detail in Chapter 8. Doubts were expressed about this interpretation in *South Australian Insurance Co v Randell* (1869) LR 3 PC 101 (S Austr JCPC) at 111.

    34 Mixing of fungibles is sometimes seen as a sales transaction and not a bailment, despite the fact that the possessor is obliged to re-deliver an equivalent quantity and quality of fungibles if demanded by the depositor. In *Re Delta Smelting & Refining Co* (1989) 33 BCLR (2d) 383 (BC SC), McLachlin CJ held (at para 18): "where the material delivered is mixed with other material, on the basis that an equivalent quantity of the same type of material will be returned, the contract is one of sale, not bailment.".

    35 This is not the way bailment transactions are traditionally described. But if one takes a disciplined approach, considers what words like "relationship", "transaction", "property", "possession", and "thing" mean, and attempts to define categories to describe how property law is structured, this is the type of definition one comes up with. Compare Tyler & Palmer (eds) *Crossley Vaines' Personal Property* 5th ed (Butterworth's London 1973) at 70: "[b]ailment eludes precise definition because the term covers a host of legal relationships which have as a common denominator only that one is in possession of another's chattel". Does that mean bailment is possession, or possession plus any number of additional factors? Does it mean anything at all? Contrast two more traditional attempts at judicial definition. In *Lesser v Jones* (1920) 47 NBR 318 (NBCA), Hazen CJ said:

> bailment is a delivery of something of a personal nature by one party to another to be held according to the purpose and object of the delivery, and to be returned or delivered over when that purpose is accomplished [and] there shall be a delivery of the chattel according to the purpose or object of the delivery, and another condition is that it is to be returned or re-delivered when the purpose for which it is delivered is accomplished.

A more compact description is found in *State v Chew Muck You* 25 P 355 (Ore 1890): "[a] bailment takes place when any article of personal property is put into the hands of one for a special purpose, and it is to be

I said earlier[36] that my objectives in classifying sales, gifts, and bailments were to describe in each category (i) what forms of property are the parties dealing with and (ii) when does an acquisition or disposition take place. Acceptance of the above definition would nearly complete that task in the bailment category. However, there are two problems. One is that most property lawyers will reject the definition as too narrow. I want to deal with their reservations. The other problem is whether we need a separate category called bailment in the common law. As we shall see, all bailment transactions and the legal obligations flowing from them can be explained in terms of three concepts of common law property (ownership, possession and right to immediate possession) and two transactions (sale and gift).

I therefore propose to review and reorganize the traditional sub-categories of bailment and to analyze the legal obligations of bailors, bailees, and third parties in terms of the property they hold rather than the way those property holdings came about. This allows a simpler organization of the existing law.

B   TRADITIONAL CATEGORIES OF BAILMENT

There are some cases that all law students are forced to ruminate. Many are fundamentally indigestible. *Coggs v Bernard*[37] is one.

In *Coggs v Bernard*, Chief Justice Holt ordered bailments into six categories that he imported into 1703 England from Roman law. Paraphrased, his categories were:[38]

(i)   for guarding by bailee, without reward (deposit);
(ii)   for use by bailee, without reward (loan);
(iii)   for use by bailee, bailor rewarded (hire);
(iv)   to secure a debt owed by bailor (pawn);
(v)   for carriage or servicing, bailee rewarded;
(vi)   for carriage or servicing, without reward.

Note the basis of the classification. First, the motivation of one of the parties to the transaction is set out. The bailor wants the thing guarded (i), wants a loan (iv), or wants something done to the thing (v and vi); the bailee wants to use the thing (ii and iii). Second, we are told whether the other party to the transaction paid or received a "reward".[39] Looked at in terms of motivation and reward, Holt's CJ categories can be re-

---

returned by the bailee to the bailor, or delivered to some third person, when the object of the trust is accomplished".

36 See Chapter 8 "Purchase and Sale".

37 *Coggs v Bernard* (1703) 2 Ld Raym 909, 92 ER 107 (Eng).

38 92 ER at 109.

39 Chief Justice Holt used the word "reward" rather than "paid" (which would have been simpler) or

arranged as follows:

> guarding by bailee,
>> (a) without reward,
>> (b) with reward (seemingly forgotten by Holt CJ)
>
> use by bailee,
>> (a) without reward,
>> (b) with reward;
>
> security for debts,
>> (a) n/a (the loan being a reward),
>> (b) with reward;
>
> carriage or servicing,
>> (a) without reward,
>> (b) with reward;

Most modern analysts regard the categories of Holt CJ as too narrow. Their objection is that non-consensual bailments are left out. As will be obvious from my definition, I do not think that an acquisition of possession without agreement can be a bailment at all. I shall deal with their objections later, in analyzing a bailee's liability to his bailor.[40] For the moment, let's see where our re-arranged categories lead us.

The motivation of one of the parties is easy to imagine in each category. Some of us prefer not to leave plants, pets and jewellery in an empty house when we go on vacation, so we temporarily resort to friends, pooch hotels and safety deposit boxes. Those of us who do not own a car sometimes want to acquire possession of one owned by someone else for a week, a day, or a trip downtown. Most of us have wanted loans from time to time. We've all owned things that we wanted transported somewhere, or repaired. What of the other party in each of these transactions? How do we classify what motivates the guard, the bailor of a car, the lender of money, the carrier and the fixer?

The usual legal response is that these people agree to enter such transactions either with or without "consideration". Consideration is a law word, with purely legal implications.

"consideration" (which would have been more precise, if that is what he meant). Nor was his terminology consistent. He described the sub-categories as (i) "a *bare naked* bailment of goods", (ii) "when goods ... are lent to a friend *gratis*", (iii) "when goods are left ... *for hire*", (iv) when goods ... are delivered [as] security *for money borrowed*", (v) "when goods or chattels are delivered to be carried, or something is to be done about them *for a reward*", and (vi) "delivery of goods or chattels to somebody, who is to carry them, or do something about them *gratis, without any reward*". [Emphasis added] Other analysts, as we shall see, have concluded that "reward" is different from "legal consideration" or "payment", and that "gratis" means something different from "without consideration". These distinctions make little sense in modern economics or law.
40 See "Bailor v Bailee: Liability in Tort and Contract".

There will be no contract between the parties without consideration; there will be a contract if there was consideration.[41] Whether a bailment transaction was accomplished by contract will determine whether there are contractual obligations between the parties. If there are contractual obligations, they may include terms fixing the standard of performance or degree of care expected of the bailee. If there is no contract, the bailee's performance and degree of care will be governed by property and tort rules. Thus, the presence or absence of consideration might enhance or restrict either party's ability to enforce terms of their agreement and might determine the bailee's liability, should the thing be damaged while in his possession.

All of the above categories now become more manageable or more complex, depending on the meaning of "reward". Either *[Meaning A]* reward means something different from consideration, or *[Meaning B]* reward means consideration. Taking as an example the situation in which the bailee wants possession (and temporary use) of someone else's car, we have the following possibilities.

BAILMENT FOR USE BY BAILEE

Meaning A	*Meaning B*
(a) without reward	(a) without consideration
(i) and without consideration	
(ii) but with consideration	
(b) with reward	(b) with consideration
(i) but without consideration	
(ii) and with consideration	

Each of the above categories of bailment could be described on a similar chart. Obviously, things are much simpler if a "reward" in the context of bailment is always consideration in contract law and if "without reward" (or "gratis") means simply without consideration.[42]

---

41 Not exactly. There might be a contract, even without consideration, if the parties had formally concluded a written agreement "under seal". This is unlikely in most bailment situations, but if it occurs, the parties are contractually bound. There might be no contract, even with consideration, if the agreement was for an illegal purpose, if the parties lacked the intention to contract, if no offer or acceptance can be discerned, or if any of the other prerequisites to contract are missing. However, my purpose here is simply to point out that "reward" in a bailment transaction might mean consideration as we understand that term in contract law, or it might mean something else.

42 The Supreme Court of Canada came close to equating "reward" and "consideration" in *Seaspan International Ltd* v *The Ship Kostis Prois* [1974] SCR 920 (BC SCC). Justice Ritchie said the following:

> It is sometimes said that a bailment involves the existence of a contract expressed or implied, and the appellants' contention that the circumstances here disclose a bailment for reward *presupposes a duty of care was assumed by the respondents for valuable consideration* as part of the contract of carriage. As I have indicated, not only was there no consideration passing between either of the appellants and the respondents, but there was no contractual relationship whatsoever between them, and I am accordingly of

However, that is not what judges, lawyers, and other writers are getting at when they talk of bailments for reward. Understanding what they mean requires some review of the standard of care bailees owe their bailors, as that was the context in which the traditional categories were created. We shall see that common lawyers' understanding of the standard of care has evolved since 1703, and that evolution calls into question the premises underlying the traditional organization of bailment. Following that, I'll propose some modernized categories.

C   BAILOR v BAILEE: LIABILITY IN TORT AND CONTRACT

"In order to show the grounds, upon which a man shall be charged with goods put into his custody, I must shew the several sorts of bailments. And there are six sorts ... ."[43] This is how Chief Justice Holt introduced the traditional common law organization of bailment in 1703. His view was that some bailees were required to exercise greater care than others. The American jurist Story agreed, and clarified the degrees of care for bailees in 1878.[44]

> When the bailment is for the sole benefit of the bailor, the law requires only slight diligence on the part of the bailee, and of course makes him answerable only for gross neglect. When the bailment is for the sole benefit of the bailee, the law requires great diligence on the part of the bailee and makes him responsible for slight neglect. When the bailment is reciprocally beneficial to both parties, the law requires ordinary diligence on the part of the bailee, and makes him responsible for ordinary neglect.

That is the traditional view. It holds that the duty of care owed by bailees is variable, that the degree of carelessness tolerated depends on how the parties are judicially perceived to have benefited from the transaction. If the bailee got no benefit (eg, guarding or repairing a thing without reward), the standard of care is low; if the bailee got all the benefit (eg, borrowing a thing), the standard of care is high; if both parties benefited (eg, renting a car), the standard of care is in the middle. This makes no sense in terms of modern economics and is probably not the modern law.

---

opinion that the contention of the appellants that the respondents were in the position of *bailees for reward* and thus seized with the burden of proving that the barge and cargo were damaged without their negligence must fail. [Emphasis added]

43 *Coggs* v *Bernard* (1703) 2 Ld Raym 909, 92 ER 107 (Eng) at 109 *per* Holt CJ.

44 Story *Bailments* 9th ed (1878) at 27. Chief Justice Holt had overruled *Southcote's Case* (1601) 4 Co Rep 83b, 76 ER 1061 (Eng), which held that a bailee was responsible whether at fault or not "because the plaintiff delivered the goods to be safe kept, and the defendant had took it upon him by the acceptance of such delivery, and therefore he ought to keep them at his peril, although in such case he should have nothing for his safekeeping". For a judicial summary of the law in Story's categories, see *Hanes* v *Shapiro & Smith* 84 SE 33 (NC 1915).

The easiest situation to deal with is a bailment "reciprocally beneficial to both parties". Consider a contractual car hire or the rental of a safety deposit box. If the contract includes terms detailing the bailee's liability for particular incidents or requiring a specific degree of care, the contractual obligations prevail.[45] To the extent that no standard of care is specified in the contract the bailee is held to a standard of reasonable care, the classic negligence test.[46]

Compare bailment "for the sole benefit of the bailee", classically the loan of a thing for the bailee to use. According to the traditional test "the borrower is bound to the strictest care and diligence ... because the bailee has a benefit by the use [and] if the bailee be guilty of the least neglect, he will be answerable".[47] This test has gone through three stages of evolution. Early cases may well have applied the traditional standard.[48] Later judges adopted the habit of reciting it, but then explaining what it means in terms that sound suspiciously like the standard of ordinary care from the previous category. How else is one to interpret the following?[49]

> The borrower must exercise the utmost diligence in his use of the chattel borrowed and is liable for the least degree of negligence. This does not mean that [in an accidental fire the bailee] must save the borrowed chattel though he lost his own; but he must show that there was no negligence on his part occasioning the loss.

---

45 Subject to consumer protection legislation or other statutes to the contrary in the particular jurisdiction. If one party got fleeced in the negotiations, that is a problem for the law of contracts, not for a book on property: see a contracts text on "unconscionability" or "inequality of bargaining power".

46 There is no shortage of authority for this proposition. See, for example: *Ludgate v Lovett* [1969] 1 WLR 1106 (Eng); *British Crane Hire Corporation Ltd v Ipswich Plant Hire Ltd* [1975] 1 QB 303 (Eng); *A-1 Rentals, Sales & Service Ltd v Alberta Arches and Beams Ltd* (1966) 60 DLR 2d 4 (Alta); *Fairley & Stevens (1966) Ltd v Goldsworthy* (1973) 34 DLR 3rd 554 (NS); *Sumich v Auckland Rental Cars Ltd* [1955] NZLR 1131 (NZ); *Loeb v Ferber* 30 A 2d 126 (Pa 1943); *Alamo Airways Inc v Benum* 374 P 2d 684 (Nev 1962); *Haidinger-Hayes Inc v Marvin Hime & Co* 206 Cal App 2d 46 (Cal 1962); *Mason v Westside Cemetaries Ltd* (1996) 135 DLR 4th 361 (Ont). Most of those cases refer to a host of others. Additional authorities to the same effect can be found in the standard digests.

47 *Coggs v Bernard* (1703) 2 Ld Raym 909, 92 ER 107 (Eng) at 111.

48 Although *Vaughan v Menlove* (1837) 3 Bing (NC) 468, 132 ER 490 (Eng) likely did not. It was not a bailment case. A hay rick spontaneously ignited and fire spread to a neighbour's house. Somehow the factual question became whether the defendant had been "grossly negligent", so Chief Justice Holt's comments were cited and the case became a digest entry under bailment. The real issue was whether the defendant could be held to the standard of "a man of ordinary prudence" (this being early days for tort law). It is interesting reading because it leaves the impression that the lawyers and judge used the term "gross negligence" to mean nothing more than a greater degree of carelessness than would have been exhibited by the ordinarily prudent person in the circumstances. As to the American situation, see *Brown on Personal Property* 3rd ed (Callaghan & Company Chicago 1975) at 264, where it is noted that "there is seldom any adequate discussion of the precise significance of the phrase employed".

49 *Riverdale Garage Ltd v Barrett Bros* [1930] 4 DLR 429 (Ont CA) *per* Latchford,CJ at 430. Similarly, see *AR Williams Machinery Co Ltd v Muttart Builders' Supply (Winnipeg) Ltd* (1961) 30 DLR 2d 339 (Man), affmd (1961) 31 DLR 2d 187 (Man CA); *Smith v Moats* (1921) 56 DLR 415 (Sask CA); *Gibson v Wilson* (1922) 67 DLR 410 (BC); *Anderson v Royer* [1928] 3 DLR 248 (Sask CA).

More recently, there has been a discernible judicial trend toward disavowing or ignoring the traditional wording and holding borrowers to the standard of reasonable care.[50] There don't seem to be many cases of bailment in the "sole benefit of the bailee" category. This may be because neighbourly lenders aren't litigious. More likely, as we shall see, judges find the law easier to apply if the evidence discloses any possible indication that the bailment was in the "reciprocally beneficial" category. Nevertheless, the trend toward requiring reasonable care for borrowers is there and is likely to continue.

Similar things have happened in bailments "for the sole benefit of the bailor". The classic examples in this category are guarding, transporting, or servicing things without reward. The traditional test required only slight diligence by the bailee and made him liable only if "gross negligence" was proved.[51] As early as 1868, however, English judges began assimilating the traditional test to the standard of reasonable care. In *Giblin* v *McMullen*,[52] railway debenture certificates were stolen from a bank strong room box by the bank's cashier. Oddly, the case proceeded on the basis that the bank was a gratuitous bailee. After deciding that "gross negligence" was an apt phrase to describe the gratuitous bailee's standard of care, Lord Chelmsford described the standard as follows.[53]

---

50 In *Fairley & Stevens (1966) Ltd* v *Goldsworthy* (1973) 34 DLR3d 554 (NS) at 568, Dubinsky J indicated (*obiter*) that the bailee's duty of care would have been the same even if he had found the bailment to be "solely for the benefit of the bailee" (car test driven by potential purchaser). *Walker* v *Watson* [1974] 2 NZLR 175 (NZ) leans this way. Compare *Clott* v *Greyhound Lines Inc* 180 SE 2d 102 (NC 1971) (leather bag containing cash missing while passenger changing buses; new trial ordered) at 107:

> the terms slight negligence, gross negligence, and ordinary negligence are convenient terms to indicate the degree of care required, but in the last analysis, the care required by the law is that of the man of ordinary prudence. This is the safest and best rule and rids us of the technical and useless distinctions in regard to the subject; ordinary care being that kind of care which should be used in the particular circumstances and is the correct standard in all cases.

Similarly, see *Edwards* v *CN Investment Co* 272 NE 2d 652 (Ohio 1971). A few cases say that the three standards of care remain unchanged: see, eg, *Ferrick Trucking and Grading Co* v *Senger Trucking Co* 484 A 2d 744 (Pa 1984) (high lift damaged during transport by defendant) urging that "the common sense of the matter is that ... a person who has borrowed another's goods without payment of a fee should be required to take greater care for the preservation of those goods than he would under normal circumstances for his own goods". Other judges suggest the traditional test still applies, but tend to find (somehow) that they are dealing with facts which do not require that the test be applied: see *Chapman* v *Robinson and Ferguson* (1969) 71 WWR 515 (Alta) and *Morris* v *CW Martin and Sons Ltd* [1966] 1 QB 716 (Eng CA), dealt with later.

51 We saw this phrase used earlier, in *Vaughan* v *Menlove* (1837) 3 Bing (NC) 468, 132 ER 490 (Eng). Two other English cases in the first half of the 19th century attempted to define the term: see *Beauchamp* v *Powley* (1831) 1 M & Rob 38, 174 ER 14 (Eng) ("great and somewhat extraordinary negligence"); *Doorman* v *Jenkins* (1834) 2 A & E 256, 111 ER 99 (Eng) ("a great and aggravated degree of negligence"). Note how these early descriptions suggest that liability is being imposed because the bailee has fallen far below the required standard of care, rather than indicating that a relatively low standard of care was expected but not met. As we shall see, imprecise use of the word "negligence" continues to hinder analysis in this area.

52 *Giblen* v *McMullen* (1869) LR 2 PC 317 (Vict JCPC).

53 LR 2 PC 317 at 337, 339. The case came to the Judicial Committee on appeal from a non-suit and the issue was (at 336): "[d]id the Plaintiff, then, give any evidence of the Bank having been guilty of that

It is clear, according to the authorities, that the Bank in this case were not bound to more than ordinary care of the deposit intrusted to them, and that the negligence for which alone they could be made liable would have been the want of that ordinary diligence which men of common prudence generally exercise about their own affairs. ... No one can fairly say, that the means employed for the protection of the property of the Bank, and of the Plaintiff, were not such as any reasonable man might properly have considered amply sufficient.

He analyzed the bank's performance in terms of the classic negligence standard despite his support for the "gross negligence" test. While paying lip service to the old idea that the duty of care varied with the category of bailment, the Judicial Committee applied the same test to a "gratuitous bailee" as governs a "bailee for reward". Other early cases simply ignored the traditional wording.[54]

Late 20th century courts have came round to the position that bailees in this category owe their bailors a duty of reasonable care. In *Gaudreau v Belter*[55] a gratuitous bailee left the bailor's golf clubs in an unlocked warehouse. They were stolen. To determine liability, Justice Acton was adamant: "[a] test that focuses on what is reasonable in the circumstance is more appropriate than trying to force facts into pigeon hole classifications and more practical than trying to determine what category of a fool a defendant comes within".[56]

That might be the Canadian position.[57] It appears to be the rule in England.[58] In America

---

degree of negligence which renders a gratuitous Bailee liable for the loss of property deposited with him?" For a similarly downgraded description of gross negligence, see *Brown* v *National Bank of Australasia Ltd* (1890) 16 VLR 475 (Vict).

54 *Nelson* v *Macintosh* (1816) 1 Stark 237, 171 ER 458 (Eng) (gratuitous carrier); *Ronnenburg* v *Falkland Islands Co* (1864) 17 CBNS 1, 144 ER 1 (Eng) (gratuitous storage of gunpowder). Both cases held the bailee to a standard of reasonable care. For a criticism of both the history and future of the "gross negligence" test, see Wright "Gross Negligence" (1983) 33 U Toronto LJ 184.

55 *Gaudreau v Belter* (2001) 290 AR 377 (Alta).

56 *Ibid* at para 10.

57 The Canadian cases are, well, Canadian: they are wishy-washy and have long been all over the map. Several cases support the gross negligence test, though they tend to be self-contradictory when they try to describe what it means: see *Palin* v *Reid* (1884) 10 OAR 63 (Ont CA) (gratuitous bailee loses box of books; gross negligence means "actual clear negligence"); *Green Fuel Economizer Co* v *Toronto* (1915) 8 OWN 541 (Ont) (gross negligence found, but no explanation); *Ginsberg* v *Vanstone Motors Ltd* [1949] OWN 345 (Ont) at 346 (theft from gratuitous bailee; term "gross negligence" used, but degree of care required described as "that degree of negligence [sic] which men of common prudence generally exercise about their own affairs"); *Martin* v *Town 'n' Country Delicatessen* (1963) 42 DLR 2nd 449 (Man CA) at 453 (no bailment in free customer parking lot; alternatively, if gratuitous bailment, test would be gross negligence); *Martin v Stephens*, 2002 BCPC 196, (Prov Ct) (gratuitous bailee loses boxes; damages only for compelling evidence of gross negligence). A popular quote has been that a gratuitous bailee is liable only for "a failure to take the same care ... as a reasonably prudent and careful man may fairly be expected to take of his own property of the like description": see *Brewer* v *Calori* (1921) 29 BCR 457 (BC); *Munn* v *Wakelin* (1944) 17 MPR 447 (PEI); *Sutherland* v *Bell & Schiesel* (1911) 18 WLR 521 (Alta); *McCowan* v

"[a] bailee without reward is responsible for such care as a prudent man takes of his own property; in other words, for ordinary care. ... An increasing number of the modern authorities have adopted this standard".[59] As Fleming notes "there is but scant modern authority for the view that, in bailments solely for the benefit of the bailor, the bailee is liable only for gross negligence".[60]

In part, this is because there are not many modern cases on gratuitous safekeeping and

---

McColloch [1926] 1 DLR 312 (NS); *Mumford v Northern Trusts Co* [1924] 2 WWR 745 (Sask CA); *Seaspan International Ltd v The Kostis Prois* (1973) 48 DLR3d 1 (BC SCC) at 5 *obiter*; *Letourneau v Otto Mobiles Edmonton (1984) Ltd* [2003] 3 WWR 389 at para 46; *Skakun v A.J. Equipment Sales Ltd* (2004) 2004 CarswellOnt 6331 (SCJ) at para 50. Compare *Cosentino v Dominion Express Co* (1906) 4 WLR 498 (Man CA) at 505-508 (test said to be gross negligence; reasonable diligence required) and *Piper v Geldart* [1954] 2 DLR 97 (NBCA) at 105 (gratuitous transport case supporting the ordinary diligence test). Perhaps the most Canadian of all is *Fairley & Stevens (1966) Ltd v Goldsworthy* (1973) 48 DLR 3rd 554 (NS) at 568, where there are alternative findings that the defendant was "negligent" and "grossly negligent [meaning] a very marked departure from the standards by which responsible and competent people in charge of motor vehicles habitually govern themselves". The future was previewed (*obiter*) in the *Fairley and Stevens case*, quoting from Paton *Bailment in the Common Law* (1952) at 110.

> Presumably the criterion of reasonable care will win the day - the tendency is more and more against the retention of gross negligence as a test in the common law. So long as the gratuitous bailee is judged only by the standard of what could reasonably be expected of him in the circumstances (and the fact that the bailment is gratuitous is one of those circumstances) no great harm will be done. Case will then have triumphed over the vestiges of Roman law.

Compare the rather definitive sounding summary of the Canadian position in Palmer, *Bailment* (Law Book Company Limited Sydney 1979) at 302. Unfortunately, his survey is flawed: of the 18 cases cited, one (*Holmes v Moore* (1867) LCR 143) is from Quebec which is not a common law jurisdiction, two (*Wright v Standard Trust Co* (1916) 29 DLR 391 (Man) and *Ferguson v Eyer* (1918) 43 OLR 190 (Ont)) are contracts cases, three (*Stevenson v Toronto Board of Education* (1919) 49 DLR 673 (Ont), *Palmer v Toronto Medical Arts Building Ltd* (1961) 20 DLR 2nd 181 (Ont CA), and *Seaspan International Ltd v The Kostis Prois*(1973) 48 DLR3d 1 (BC SCC)) are negligence cases where there was no bailment and which say virtually nothing about a gratuitous bailee's standard of care, and several others are classified under different categories on the basis of functionally identical quotes.

58 *James Buchanan & Co Ltd v Hay's Transport Services Ltd* [1972] 2 Lloyd's Rep 535 (Eng): "I am quite satisfied that this sub-bailment was a gratuitous one, but I take the view that the standard of care is the same. It is that which a reasonable man would take of his own goods in similar circumstances". Similarly, see *Blount v War Office* [1953] 1 All ER 1071 (Eng); *Birch v Thomas* [1972] 1 All ER 905 (Eng) and *Houghland v RR Low (Luxury Coaches) Ltd* [1962] 1 QB 694 (Eng CA) (coach passenger's suitcase lost; coach operator held gratuitous bailee; no liability because "all reasonable care had been exercised").

59 *National Broadcasting Company Inc v Rose* 215 A 2d 123 at 126 (Conn 1965). Compare *Koennecke v Waxwing Cedar Products Ltd* 543 P 2d 669 (Ore 1975) at 673 *per* Bryson J.

> Although a majority of the states adhere to the common law rule that a gratuitous bailee is liable only for gross negligence, courts frequently circumvent this rule by altering the definition. ... A substantial number of jurisdictions have completely abandoned the concept of divisibility of diligence and negligence into degrees and, consequently, apply only one standard of care, that of the ordinary prudent men [*sic*] under the particular circumstances [citing 8 Ark L Rev at 504]. ... We conclude that the standard of care required of a gratuitous bailee is such reasonable care as the particular circumstances of the bailment demand.

This view was cited and adopted in *Christensen v Hoover* 643 P 2d 525 (Col 1982).

60 Fleming *The Law of Torts* 7th ed (The Law Book Company Limited 1987) at 112 fn 39

even fewer on gratuitous carriage or service. Judges tend to avoid the varying standards of liability by juggling the facts to find that the terms of a bailment were mutually advantageous to both parties. By this process the case is shifted into a category where the traditional rule imposes a standard of reasonable care on the bailee. The judicially perceived mutual advantage is often minimal,[61] but that is a question of fact and the judge (or the civil jury, where applicable) is the sole arbiter of fact. Thus, it has been found to be mutually beneficial to the parties when a bus line or railway transported passengers' luggage without extra charge,[62] when hotel staff took possession of guests' things for safekeeping,[63] when a coat was hung up in a retail services establishment,[64] when lawyers or accountants possessed clients papers,[65], when a customer was given possession of car while his car was being repaired,[66] and when a customer parked his car at a dealer's lot while test driving a new car[67]. Oddly, banks were often held to be gratuitous bailees when they kept possession of things without levying a specific fee. However, *Kahler* v *Midland Bank Ltd*[68] probably overruled the 19th century cases. Generally it seems that it "is not essential ... that the bailee actually receive compensation ... so long as the bailment is an incident of the business in which the bailee makes a profit, or was accepted because of the benefits expected to accrue".[69]

---

61 See, for example, *Bainbridge* v *Firmstone* (1838) 8 A & E 743, 112 ER 1019 (Eng), in which the defendant for some reason wanted to weigh the plaintiff's boilers. He borrowed them, took them apart, and refused to return possession. Somehow, the lawyers chose to argue about whether there had been consideration for the transaction. "The consideration is, that the plaintiff, at the defendant's request, had consented to allow the defendant to weigh the boilers. I suppose the defendant thought he had some benefit; at any rate, there is a detriment to the plaintiff from his parting with the possession for even so short a time." (Patteson J at 1020) "The defendant had some reason for wishing to weigh the boilers." (Lord Denman CJ at 1020)

62 *Cohen* v *SE Railway Co* (1877) 2 Ex D 258 (Eng) at 258; *Burnet* v *Ritter* 276 SW 347 (1925). Similarly, see *Cairns* v *Robins* (1841) 8 M & W 258, 151 ER 1934 (Eng) (carrier keeps possession of things for a year when not retrieved).

63 *Peet* v *Roth Hotel Co* (1934) 253 NW 546 (1934) ("ring ... accepted in the ordinary course of business by defendant in rendering a usual service for a guest"); *White* v *Burke* 197 P 2d 1008 (Wash 1948) (possession of banknotes left for safekeeping; plaintiff frequent guest who had previously recommended hotel to others); *Daniel* v *Hotel Pacific Pty Ltd* [1953] VLR 447 (Vict); *contra, Dalton* v *Hamilton Hotel Operating Co* 206 NYS 272 (NY 1924).

64 *Murphy* v *Hart* (1919) 46 DLR 36 (NS) (restaurant); *Webster* v *Lane* 212 NYS 298 (NY 1925) (dentist); *Timaru Borough Council* v *Boulton* [1924] NZLR 365 (NZ) (swimming pool); *Fidelman-Danziger Inc* v *Statler Management* 136 A 2d 119 (Pa 1957) (hotel). *Contra*, see *Martin* v *Town 'n' Country Delicatessen Ltd* (1963) 42 DLR 2nd 449 (Man CA) (car in restaurant parking lot; but were defendants bailees?). In *Helson* v *McKenzies (Cuba St) Ltd* [1950] NZLR 878 (NZ) a shopkeeper was said to be a bailee for mutual reward, though the handbag was lost and found.

65 *Woodworth* v *Conroy* [1976] 1 All ER107 (Eng).

66 *Sanderson* v *Collins* [1904] KB 628 (Eng CA); *Queens' Sales & Service Ltd* v *Smith* (1963) 48 MPR 364 (NS). *Contra*, see *Riverdale Garage Ltd* v *Barrett Bros* [1930] 4 DLR 429 (Ont CA).

67 *Sampson* v *Birkeland* 211 NE 2d 139 (Ill 1965). Compare *Fairley & Stevens (1966) Ltd* v *Goldsworthy* (1973) 48 DLR 3rd 554 (NS), as to the liabilities of the test driver.

68 *Kahler* v *Midland Bank Ltd* [1948] 1 All ER 811 (Eng CA). A similar prejudice in favour of banks can be seen in the earlier American cases: see Raushenbush *Brown on Personal Property* 3rd ed (Callaghan & Co Chicago 1975) at 261.

69 *Global Tank Trailer Sales* v *Textilana-Nease Inc* 496 P 2d 1292 (Kan 1972).

When judges in modern cases find themselves within the category of bailments for the sole benefit of the bailor, they are reluctant to apply the traditional interpretation of the bailee's standard of care. I have already chronicled the tendency away from "gross negligence". However, it is rarely made clear what the required standard of care is. The reason is the chronic misuse of the term "negligence" by lawyers, academics and judges. Negligence means tortious conduct, not merely careless conduct. To say that a defendant in a case was negligent is to make three distinct statements of fact: (i) that he owed a duty of care to the plaintiff; (ii) that his conduct fell below the standard of care required, and; (iii) that his conduct was the proximate cause of some injury to the plaintiff. In short, negligence is a conclusion of liability, not a type of behaviour. A driver who meanders all over a country road after the bars have closed is exhibiting careless behaviour, but he is not negligent unless he hits someone or something. A medical doctor or a lawyer may well be more careful than most ordinary people, yet be negligent if he causes injury while using less care than the average doctor or lawyer.

Yet judges do not always use the term "negligent" in this way. This causes problems. When a neighbour takes possession of a pet budgie for a week, returns possession of a dead former budgie, and is found liable as "a negligent gratuitous bailee", which of the following conclusions are we to draw?

> *Possibility 1* The defendant was negligent, in the sense that he failed to observe the standard of ordinary care. Even a gratuitous bailee is obliged to take ordinary care (the modern standard?). The defendant's negligent conduct caused injury to the plaintiff and he must pay.

> *Possibility 2* A gratuitous bailee is obliged to take minimal care (the traditional standard). The defendant failed to take even minimal care of the budgie. Injury to the plaintiff was caused by that failure. The defendant was therefore negligent and he must pay.

> *Possibility 3* Even a gratuitous bailee is obliged to take ordinary care (the modern standard?). The defendant took minimal care of the budgie, but less than ordinary care. His failure to meet the required standard of care caused injury to the plaintiff. The defendant was therefore negligent and he must pay.

The judge might mean any of the above. *Possibility 1* involves misuse of the technical term "negligent", yet it is conventional judgespeak. *Possibilities 2* and *3* both involve technically proper use of the term, yet they impose quite different standards of care. The problem is that anyone who causes injury to someone through failure to meet a standard of care owed to that person in the circumstances is, by definition, negligent. Saying so discloses nothing about the standard of care except that it was violated. What standard of care is to be required of gratuitous bailees is a preliminary issue. Because of the small number of cases in the category and the ambiguity of judicial terminology, this is probably an open question in the common law today.

The real issue, then, is what do we want the standard to be? Are we committed to the traditional view that the degree of carelessness tolerated in a bailee depends on how the parties are judicially perceived to have benefited from the transaction? Are we intent upon keeping bailment unique, with latin-labelled categories and Roman rules, or are we prepared to develop modern bailees' duties by analogy to the rest of 21st century tort law? The analogies are available. Consider the liability of someone who gives free advice. Like a gratuitous bailee, he could once afford to be careless. Indeed, he was better off, for it was thought until 1964 that free bad advice carried no liability at all. Carelessly undertaking a non-contractual service was recognized as grounds for a negligence action in *Hedley Byrne & Co Ltd* v *Heller & Partners*, where Lord Devlin ventured the following generalization.[70]

> A promise given without consideration to perform a service cannot be enforced as a contract by the promisee; but if the service is in fact performed and done negligently, the promisee can recover in an action in tort. This is the foundation of the liability of a gratuitous bailee.

In sum, a promise without consideration to keep a neighbour's budgie for a week is unenforceable. Keeping the budgie for a week, and doing it badly, is actionable in negligence. The standard of care in *Hedley Byrne* was the familiar reasonable care in the circumstances.[71] The traditional position before that case was that less care was demanded of free advisors (none, so long as they were honest) than unrewarded bailees (slight care). After *Hedley Byrne*, free advisors had leapfrogged to a rule requiring greater (reasonable) care than was traditionally required of unrewarded bailees. Is taking care of a budgie, or carrying a package to another city, so different from the giving of advice that it is outside the scope of the *Hedley Byrne* ruling? Isn't taking temporary possession of a thing for the purpose of unrewarded guarding or carriage just the undertaking of another non-contractual service in which reasonable care in the circumstances can be expected?[72]

---

70 *Hedley Byrne & Co Ltd* v *Heller & Partners* [1964] AC 465 (Eng HL) at 526 *per* Lord Devlin. Compare, "if a person undertakes to perform a voluntary act, he is liable if he performs it improperly, but not if he neglects to perform it": *Skelton* v *North Western Railway Co* (1867) LR 2 CP 631 (Eng) at 636 *per* Willes J.

71 One of the circumstances was that the defendant was a specialist in the area of the advice given and was thus held to a higher standard than an amateur advisor. The same would apply to doctors, lawyers, and professional budgie keepers within their own fields of expertise. As it turned out, there was no liability in *Hedley Byrne*, but only because of a disclaimer issued before the advice was given. Did the advisor contract out of his tort liability?

72 Liability arises in the

> sort of relationship which gives rise to a responsibility towards those who act upon information or advice and so creates a duty of care towards them. [It is not] a responsibility imposed by law upon certain types of persons or in certain types of situations. It is a responsibility that is voluntarily accepted or undertaken, either generally where a general relationship, such as that of solicitor and

There is another way of looking at gratuitous bailees that is even simpler. *Donoghue* v *Stevenson*[73] summed up modern tort law in the proposition that one must take reasonable care to avoid an act which could forseeably injure one's neighbour. Taking possession of a thing owned by someone else is a classic neighbourly act. Sometimes neighbours contract - they hire possession of things, they send things for professional repairs, they ship them elsewhere - and the party in possession must exercise reasonable care or otherwise as prescribed by the contract. Sometimes they do not contract - they borrow things, they fix one another's things without charge, they carry one another's things when making a trip - and the party in possession must exercise some degree of care. Chief Justice Holt and Story long ago invited us to fix the degree of care only after assessing whether the transfer of possession was for the sole benefit of the bailor, for the sole benefit of the bailee, or reciprocally beneficial to both parties. That was before modern economics was summed up in the phrase "there is no free lunch". The economic assumption is that everything one neighbour does for another is in pursuit of some self-interest, some reward however small or speculative. Compare this to the bailment cases cited above, in which judges find the bailment reciprocally beneficial to both parties "so long as the bailment is an incident of the business in which the bailee makes a profit, *or was accepted because of the benefits expected to accrue*".[74] Judges concluded that there were not many bailments for the sole benefit of one party in 20th century cases. Economists would have told them there were none.

It is odd that this message seems not to have reached the English Court of Appeal. Two of the three judges in *Morris* v *CW Martin and Sons Ltd* thought that a "gratuitous bailee" might not be liable in negligence.[75] All three tried to explain how a sub-contractor hired

---

client or banker and customer is created, or specifically in relation to a particular transaction. *Hedley Byrne & Co Ltd* v *Heller & Partners* [1964] AC 465 (Eng HL) at 529 *per* Lord Devlin. Taking possession of a thing which someone else owns creates such a relationship, based on ownership and possession. Thus is the possessor by finding required to take reasonable care. So, surely, is the possessor by transaction (bailee), unless there is a contract saying otherwise.

73 *Donoghue* v *Stevenson* [1932 AC 562 (Eng HL).

74 *Global Tank Trailer Sales* v *Textilana-Nease Inc* 496 P 2d 1292 (Kan 1972). [Emphasis mine] This is not to be confused with the issue whether the parties have a contract. There, the courts measure *the sufficiency, but not the adequacy of consideration*, which is a fancy way of saying that the courts look for some objective benefit accruing to one party, or objective detriment suffered by the other: see *Currie* v *Misa* (1875) LR 10 Ex 153 (Eng) at 162 *per* Lush J. Transfer of possession of a peppercorn, or a specific promise in return for performance, is sufficient because it is an objective benefit, and it makes no difference whether the judge thinks that either he or the contracting party would ever have thought it *adequate* payment. Note the distinction in traditional bailment analysis, where the judge is assessing whether the bailor or bailee "expected" some benefit to accrue.

75 *Morris* v *CW Martin and Sons Ltd* [1966] 1 QB 716 (Eng CA). Lord Denning suggested (at 725) that a gratuitous bailee is not liable for his servant's theft "because he was not under any duty to prevent it being stolen, but only to keep it as his own. ... [S]ee *Giblen* v *McMullen* (1869) LR 2 PC 317 (Vict JCPC) where it was assumed, rightly or wrongly, that the bank was a gratuitous bailee." Lord Justice Diplock said (at 737):

by a furrier to clean the plaintiff's fur could be sued as the plaintiff's bailee for reward.[76] That was a nonsensical rendering of the facts. The furrier had transferred possession to the defendant subcontractor with the plaintiff's consent, but not as the plaintiff's agent, so there was no transaction at all between plaintiff and defendant. The defendant was unable to return possession of the fur because the employee assigned to do the cleaning work had stolen it. Liability was established on the following ground:[77]

> Morrissey [was] the servant through whom the defendants chose to discharge their duty to take reasonable care of the plaintiff's fur. ... A bailee for reward is not answerable for a theft by any of his servants but only for a theft by such of them as are deputed by him to discharge some part of his duty of taking reasonable care.

It is inconceivable that a classic "gratuitous bailee", or even a possessor by finding, would not be held liable for a theft by the very servant he designated to guard the thing, whatever general duty of care he owed. This ratio of this case tells us nothing we didn't already know about a bailee's liability. Unfortunately, the *obiter dicta* read like Schweik's anabasis and one is left with the impression that the traditional categories of bailment may not yet be dead.[78]

---

we are not concerned here with gratuitous bailment. That is a relationship in which the bailee's duties of care in his custody of the goods are different from those of a bailee for reward. It may be that his duties being passive rather than active, the concept of vicarious performance of them is less apposite. However this may be, I express no views as to the circumstances in which he would be liable for conversion of the goods by his servant.

Lord Justice Salmon simply said the defendants were bailees for reward (citing two cases that say nothing of the kind) and gave no indication whether he thought the rules were different for gratuitous bailees.

76 A "sub-bailee" is said to owe to the original bailor the same non-contractual duties as did the original bailee. These were described in some detail in *Moukataff* v *BOAC* [1967] 1 Lloyd's Rep 396 (Eng) at 414-415 *per* Browne J. Assuming that the original bailee was the owner, the list of duties looks remarkably like the duties owed by any possessor to an owner, regardless how possession was acquired, subject of course to any contractual defences the possessor may have.

77 [1966] 1 QB 716 at 738 *per* Salmon LJ. Compare Diplock LJ at 737:

> [the defendant company] put Morrissey as their agent in their place to clean the fur and to take charge of it while doing so. The manner in which he conducted himself in doing that work was to convert it. What he was doing, albeit dishonestly, he was doing in the course of his employment in the technical sense of that infelicitous but time honoured phrase. The defendants as his masters are responsible for his tortious act.

78 The reasoning of the English Court of Appeal was applied in *Pioneer Container (The)* [1994] 2 AC 324 (HK JCPC), in which the defendant got the benefit of a contractual term between two other people. The strange conclusion was said to be based, not in contract, but on "the law of bailment". The Judicial Committee said, at 342:

> a person who voluntarily takes another person's goods into his custody holds them as bailee of that person (the owner); and he can only invoke, for example, terms of a sub-bailment under which he received the goods from an intermediate bailee as qualifying or otherwise affecting his responsibility to the owner if the owner consented to them.

There must be a less complicated way of reaching this commercially sensible solution.

As noted at the beginning of this section, the purpose of the traditional categorization was to classify the differing standards of care applicable to different bailees. Many analysts now think that one standard of care is appropriate for all.[79] If this is so, there is no particular reason to maintain the categories as they were described in 1703. To the extent that we want to determine the liability of a possessor by bailment in a particular situation, the "so-called distinction between slight, ordinary, and gross negligence over which courts have quibbled for a hundred years can furnish no assistance".[80]

D MODERNIZED CATEGORIES OF BAILMENT

There is no purpose in creating categories of bailment unless doing so helps us organize some useful information about bailors and bailees. The traditional categories no longer do this: they are based on varying degrees of bailees' liabilities that probably don't exist. The tort liability of a possessor to an owner (or holder of right to immediate possession) doesn't depend on how possession was acquired.

Bailment is merely a way of acquiring possession on agreed terms.[81] Sometimes the terms are enforceable. Sometimes they may not be enforceable. A useful categorization would be one that tells us something about whether and how a bailor or a bailee can enforce the terms of the transaction by which possession was transferred. One obvious category is contract. Another category, less obvious perhaps, is gifts of possession. Contracts are enforceable; gifts, once made, cannot be undone. Maybe all bailment transactions are either contracts or gifts.

1 Possession by Contract

Many bailment transactions involve transfers of possession of things in return for consideration. A car rental is a familiar example: the bailee contracts with the bailor, takes possession, and is contractually entitled to retain possession of the car for the

---

79 See, for example, Palmer *Bailment* (Law Book Company Limited Sydney 1979) at 302 ("Depositum"), at 338 ("Mandatum") and at 361-362 ("Commodatum"). Compare Raushenbush *Brown on Personal Property* 3rd ed (Callaghan & Company Chicago 1975) at 256: "[i]t would be more understandable and easier to administer if, regardless of the nature of the bailment, the bailee were held to a standard of 'ordinary care in the circumstances' ... Some courts have so held".

80 *Koennecke v Waxwing Cedar Products Ltd* 543 P 2d 669 (Ore 1975) at 673 *per* Bryson J. Similarly, see *Houghland v RR Low (Luxury Coaches) Ltd* [1962] 1 QB 694 (Eng CA) *per* Ormerod LJ at 697: "to try and put a bailment, for instance, into a watertight compartment - such as gratuitous bailment on the one hand, and bailment for reward on the other - is to overlook the fact that there might well be an infinite variety of cases which might come into one or the other category".

81 Bailment is a transaction whereby possession of a thing is transferred upon agreement that possession of the same thing, perhaps in an altered state, will be transferred back to the transferor or on to someone else as agreed: see above "Bailment Defined".

duration of the rental period. Other bailments involve a transfer of possession under a contract for repairs or other service to be performed by the bailee. In a bailment contract for car repairs the bailee is paid for the service performed. Acquisition of possession is not the main objective in the latter type of transaction, but there is still a transfer of possession by contract.[82]

It isn't difficult to determine whether a transaction is in this category. First, there is the contract issue: did the parties contract, or did they merely agree without concluding legally binding contractual terms? This usually reduces to the question whether "consideration"[83] passed between the parties. There will be no contract between the parties without consideration; there will be a contract if there was consideration.[84] Second, if the parties contracted, was a proposed temporary transfer of possession of a thing one of the contractual terms?[85] Third, did the proposed transfer of possession take place? If so, the bailee acquired possession by contract.

How long and upon what conditions the bailee can retain possession will depend on the terms of the contract. The parties are at liberty to include any kinds of terms they like, though the terms will usually reflect the planning and bargaining position of one party as anyone who has ever read and tried to change a car rental form will recall. There may also be terms "implied" by virtue of statutes or common law to fill in the blanks left ambiguous by the parties.[86]

---

82 These transactions could be thought of as sales contracts where possession is sold for a limited time. The word "sale" was traditionally used to describe transfers of ownership of things in exchange for money, "barter" being used where money was not the consideration paid: see Chapter 8 "Purchase and Sale". However, the word sale is often applied to transfers of other forms of property such as corporate shares and leasehold interests in land. I have avoided using the word as it will offend the conventional and doesn't really add much to the point being made.

83 A traditional definition is "valuable consideration, in the sense of the law, may consist in some right, interest, profit, or benefit accruing to the one party, or some forbearance, detriment, loss, or responsibility given, suffered, or undertaken by the other": *Currie* v *Misa* (1875) LR 10 Ex 153 (Eng) at 162 *per* Lush J. The adjective "valuable" was included because it was conventional during the 19th century to describe property transfers as being either "upon good consideration" or "upon valuable consideration". "Good" meant that the transferor was motivated by some emotion called "natural love and affection", which was not sufficient to prove a contract; "valuable consideration" meant precisely what we now call consideration in contract law. The clarity is enhanced and nothing substantial is lost by dropping the adjectives and using the noun "consideration" only in the old sense of "valuable consideration".

84 The issue is slightly more complex than that. There might be a contract, even without consideration, if the parties had formally concluded a written agreement "under seal". There might be no contract, even with consideration, if the agreement was for an illegal purpose, if the parties lacked the intention to contract, if no offer or acceptance can be discerned, or if any of the other prerequisites to contract are missing.

85 Contrast a sale of ownership. If the possessor has the option of returning possession of some other thing, the transaction is an "exchange", not bailment": *Austin* v *Seligman* 18 F 519 (US 1883). Note, however, the complications that may be introduced in the case of fungibles, like wheat: see *Schindler* v *Westover* 99 Ind 395 (Ind 1882) and other cases dealt with above in "Bailment Defined".

86 See, for example, Palmer *Bailment* (Law Book Company Limited Sydney 1979) at 721-744 on the types of implied terms one is likely to find in contracts for the "hire of chattels". He notes throughout the

Apart from those types of details, each party's position can be summarized as follows.

A contractual bailor is unable to compel a re-transfer of possession from the bailee during the term of the contract.[87] The bailee has a contractual defence, having contracted for possession during the term specified. This means, by definition, that the bailor does not hold right to immediate possession during the term of the contract.[88] Consequently, the transferor had no common law action in trover against third parties.[89] The bailor acquires right to immediate possession upon expiry of the contractual term,[90] or upon breach of the contract during its term.[91]

Property is acquired under a contractual bailment according to simple rules. The bailee acquires right to immediate possession when intended by the parties, which will usually mean at the earliest time for delivery under the contract. Possession is acquired upon delivery, which means when the bailee is in a position to prove both physical control over the thing and manifest intent to exclude others.[92] Ownership remains with the bailor, if he held ownership,[93] or with whoever else held ownership if the bailor did not.

---

similarities between such contracts and contracts for the sale of goods.

87 *Brierly* v *Kendall* (1852) 17 QB 937, 117 ER 1540 (Eng) (possession seized by bailor during term of contractual bailment; bailee wins damages for loss of possession for remainder of term).

88 Right to immediate possession of a thing is a form of property in the thing. The holder of right to immediate possession can invoke state assistance in gaining possession of the thing from its possessor. See Chapter 2 "Right to Immediate Possession".

89 *Pain* v *Whittaker* (1824) R & M 99, 171 ER 956 (Eng) (bailor of hired piano loses trover action against sheriff who seized possession from bailee). *Ferguson* v *Cristall* (1829) 5 Bing 305, 130 ER 1078 (Eng) (ship chartered, possession of ship seized for seamen's wages; owner had no right to possession before charter ended). Of course, an owner may claim damages to the extent that the ownership value is diminished: see the later heading "Bailor v Third Party: Ownership, Right to Immediate Possession, and Tort". This was the situation in *Morris* v *CW Martin and Sons Ltd* [1966] 1 QB 716 (Eng CA), despite the reasons for judgment.

90 *Manders* v *Williams* (1849) 4 Exch 479, 154 ER 1242 (Eng) (brewer supplies porter in casks; contract permits recovery of possession of casks as soon as empty; brewer wins trover action against sheriff who seized possession of empty casks from customer).

91 Thus, where a possessor by contract of hire violates the contract by purporting to sell ownership to a third party, the hirer may recover possession from the third party: *Bryant* v *Wardell* (1848) 1 CB 685, 154 ER 580 (Eng) ("action for trover is maintainable for the conversion"); *Fenn* v *Bittleston* (1851) 7 Exch 152, 155 ER 895 (Eng). Note that seizure and sale by the holder of a statutory security interest will terminate the bailor's claim: see Chapter 2 "Security Interests".

92 That is, when the definition of possession is met.

93 The bailor need not hold ownership of a thing in order to transfer possession of it. A person who acquires possession of a thing for two weeks can immediately transfer possession to someone else for one week. So long as possession is to be restored to the transferor at the end of the week, or transferred to someone else according to the transferor's instructions, the one week transfer is a bailment transaction.

2   Possession by Gift

Bailment without consideration transfers possession without contractual obligation. Classic examples abound. Friends borrow books, clothes and gardening tools. Sellers give temporary possession for potential buyers to test drive cars. A pen is loaned to complete a customs form. The obligation to return possession does not evolve from the transaction: it exists because of the property held by the lender in the thing loaned.

Where there is no consideration for the transfer of possession, the bailee does not have a contractual defence to the bailor's demand for repossession. Many cases involving various categories of non-contractual bailors have concluded that the bailors had access to the possessory remedies at common law both against the bailees and against strangers.[94] These remedies are available only to a possessor (*ie*, the bailee) or to a holder of right to immediate possession.[95] Each of these cases therefore must stand for the proposition that the bailor retained right to immediate possession during the term of the bailment.[96] If this is so, it follows by definition[97] that the bailor could retake possession at any time from the bailee.

That would surely be the rule where the bailor transferred possession upon agreement that possession was returnable on demand. If the bailee agreed to "keep this until I want it back", right to immediate possession is obviously retained by the bailor.[98] Even if consideration had been paid the result would be the same because the agreement specified a term that ended in the mind and at the whim of the bailor.

However, the law is less obvious where the parties agreed that the bailee was to have possession for a specified period of time. What if the bailee wanted possession of a car

---

94 See Pollock and Wright, *Possession in the Common Law* (Clarendon Press Oxford 1888) at 166 fn 2, citing 13 cases on the point.

95 See eg. *Johnson v Diprose* [1893] 1 QB 512 (Eng CA) at 516 *per* Bowen LJ: "[a] person who brings an action for trespass to goods must either be in possession of them at the time of the alleged trespass or entitled to the immediate possession".

96 "Under English law, where there is a simple contract of bailment [he meant bailment at will; there was no contract] the possession of the goods bailed passes to the bailee. The bailor has in such a case the right to immediate possession and by reason of this right can exercise those possessory remedies which are available to the possessor The person having the right to immediate possession is, however, frequently referred to in English law as being the 'possessor' - in truth the English law has never worked out a completely logical and exhaustive definition of possession": *USA v Dollfus Mieg et Compagnie S.A. and Bank of England* [1952] AC 582 (Eng HL) (gold bars held by Bank of England after war, owned by foreign government; litigation blocked by sovereign immunity). Similarly, see *Burton v Hughes* (1824) 2 Bing 173, 130 ER 272 (Eng) (possessor of furniture who put it in house occupied by wife of bankrupt recovers in trover against bankrupt's creditors).

97 Right to immediate possession is a form of property in a thing which gives the holder access to state assistance in gaining possession of the thing from its possessor. See Chapter 2 "Right to Immediate Possession".

98 *Nicholls v Bastard* (1835) 2 Cr M & R 659, 150 ER 279 (Eng) (loan of a cow; trover against third party by lender).

for a week, was contemplating a rental car, but was assured by a friend that he could use a car owned by the friend "until Saturday"? Must he relinquish possession if the bailor demands it on Friday?

If we *assume* that a non-contractual bailor retains a right to immediate possession, the answer is yes. But that seems an unwarranted extrapolation. Various cases have held that particular non-contractual bailors have common law possessory remedies against third parties. No cases support the proposition that *all* non-contractual bailments are revocable at will.[99] It is thus open for speculation that possession for an agreed term is enforceable by the bailee, even without a contract. The question is, how?

One way, an unlikely one, is that there may be a cause of action called "breach of terms of bailment". The argument would be historical. Bailment is generally conceded to be an ancient concept which predates the rise of contract. I don't know whether there was ever such a remedy: a search of the Year Books might reveal one I suppose. At any rate, I doubt that one could win a case by pleading such a cause of action today.

Another way to enforce an agreed term of possession is to stretch the commonly accepted boundaries of gift.

Gift is a common law transaction that transfers property in a thing from donor to donee by intent and delivery.[100] Most people assume that only ownership can be transferred by gift. I don't see why. Consider the following transactions.

Gifts transfer ownership by intent and delivery. Assume A owns a thing and decides to transfer ownership without consideration to D. This is a classic gift from donor A to donee D. Ownership of the thing is transferred by gift when A intends to transfer ownership and "delivers". Delivery is effected and proved by a transfer of possession of the thing.[101] The promise to transfer ownership by gift is not enforceable by the donee,

---

99 The following passage on bailors' remedies against strangers was often quoted by 20th century writers. Note that it does not say that all non-contractual bailees hold right to immediate possession.

> [T]he bailor by reason of his right to possession may retain ... a sufficient right to maintain trespass and theft against strangers. This seems to be the case wherever the bailment is revocable by the bailor at his pleasure either unconditionally or upon a condition which he may satisfy at will. But if the bailment is for a term certain (as in the case of goods let to the tenant of furnished lodgings) or determinable only after notice or after a default by the bailee or upon any other occurrence which does not depend on the will of the bailor, then until the term has expired or been determined or become determinable at will it seems that the bailor is excluded and cannot maintain either trespass or theft or trover even against a stranger": Pollock and Wright *Possession in the Common Law* (Clarendon Press Oxford 1888) at 166.

100 See Chapter 9 "Definition of Gift".

101 See Chapter 9 "Delivery". D is, of course, at liberty to refuse to accept ownership, in which case the attempted gift fails.

but a transfer of ownership by gift, once completed, cannot be revoked by the donor.[102]

Some attempted gifts of ownership transfer only possession. Sometimes a person holds possession of a thing under the mistaken impression that he owns it. Consider B, an unwitting buyer from a thief. B paid for ownership but acquired only possession, which was all the thief had to sell. Suppose B subsequently attempts a gift to D. Such a transaction clearly would not be enforceable before delivery. But would it be irrevocable once made? Would B's intent and delivery be effective to transfer to D all the property B held in the thing? Cases on the point are hard to find, perhaps because a donor's lack of ownership never emerges unless the owner appears and demands possession. Of course the owner could recover possession from D who has no better claim than B had. There seems, however, no reason to support a repossession claim by B against D, his donee.[103] Such a failed gift of ownership probably operates as an effective gift of possession and leaves the donor without right to immediate possession.

A transfer of possession by a non-owner who does not intend that possession will ever be returned operates as a gift of possession. Suppose C finds and takes possession of a lost watch. Things found and not abandoned are possessed but not owned by the finder. C makes enquiries, but the owner does not appear. C doesn't particularly desire long term possession of the watch, but C's friend D does. C transfers possession to D, saying "if I owned this watch I'd give it to you anyway, so keep it, I don't want it". So far, no owner has showed up. Ignore the prospect of C's potential liability to the owner. I expect that C can not recover possession from D.[104] If we call the transaction between C and D a gift of possession we can apply the rule that a donor may not revoke a completed gift. If we do not call it a gift, we must invent some other rule or concede that C may change his mind and recover possession.

A transfer of possession by an owner who does not intend that possession will ever be returned is a more problematical case. Examples will be rare for two reasons. First, ordinary people are not usually precise as to what property they are transferring. Words such as "I want you to keep my antique forever" are likely to be judicially construed as intended ownership transfers. Second, there are not many obvious incentives for retaining ownership of a thing without expectation of future possession, except where rent is being collected.[105] The only situation that springs to mind is a parent who holds

---

102 *Mackintosh* v *Stuart* (1864) 36 Beav 21, 55 ER 1063 (Eng) (gift to sisters; banknotes and promissory notes); *Coleby* v *Coleby* (1866) LR 2 Eq 803 (Eng) (heir pays funeral expenses, intending gift; subsequently changes mind; too late).

103 Unless the donor appears as the agent of the owner and seeks repossession on the owner's behalf.

104 Unless, as above, C appears as the agent of the owner and seeks repossession on the owner's behalf. C can not impose himself on the missing owner by unilaterally declaring his agency: a principal gets to choose his agents.

105 Equipment suppliers make money by renting long term possession of things like fleets of trucks. The possessors (bailees) gain tax and cash flow advantages in avoiding the capital expenditure of ownership. There may be, among such transactions, some that specify that the owner will never regain

ownership of a car intended for exclusive use by a high cost teenage insurance risk. Arguably, once the transfer of possession had occurred, the parent could not recover possession because her right to immediate possession was given away by gift.[106]

Note that the above transfers are not bailment transactions. None of them meets the definitional requirement for an agreement that possession of the same thing will be transferred back to the transferor, or on to someone else. My point was to illustrate that some transfers of possession could be analyzed as gifts of possession. Anyone who adheres to the view that the word "gift" can only be applied to ownership transfers could refrain from calling them gifts on grounds of linguistic purity. Those willing to adopt the broader definition of gift will have no reason for not including these types of transfers.

The next question is whether the same analysis can be applied to non-contractual bailment situations.

Let's go back to the example of the bailee who wanted possession of a car for a week, was contemplating a rental car, but was assured by a friend that he could use a car owned by the friend "until Saturday"? The non-contractual promise to transfer possession is not enforceable should the friend change his mind before possession is transferred. That is the same rule as in gifts. What happens, however, once the bailee gets possession of the car? Must he relinquish possession if the bailor demands it on Friday? The answer is no, if we construe the transaction as a gift of possession for the time stipulated. The answer is probably yes, if we don't.

I don't see that any major problems are created if we decide that such transactions are gifts and thus irrevocable once delivery occurs. It simply means that the donor can't change his mind and recover possession before the due date. That is the situation in gifts of ownership, the principal difference being that there the due date is never. I doubt that casual lenders will suddenly be caught in an invidious legal trap. Where no return date is specified, a reasonable period of time can be implied in the circumstances: for how long would an ordinary neighbour be willing to extend the casual loan of a lawnmower? Where the parties specify a return date, there is still room for interpretation as to whether the bailor said that the bailee could definitely keep possession of the thing until then, or whether the parties understood at the time of the agreement that the bailor might require repossession before that time, although he did not anticipate that he would. In the latter case, the bailor would be viewed as having said "keep it until I want it back, or until Saturday at the latest", and the transfer of possession would be revocable at the bailor's whim. In the former case, the bailor is simply stuck with the arrangement he voluntarily

---

possession during the projected useful life of the equipment. However, these are contractual bailments.

106 An interesting question would arise if the parent transferred ownership to a third party. Could the third party owner reclaim possession from the teenager? The standard legalist retort, that the third party is a "bona fide purchaser for value without notice", is no answer. That is a defence to Equity-based claims. The teenager's property (possession) is legal, not equitable.

made once delivery of possession takes place. There may be some persuasive argument against enforcing such a rule, but I can't think of one.

In sum, a non-contractual bailment can be construed as a gift of possession for the term agreed by the parties

3 Other Bailments?

If the above two categories are classified as (i) "contractual bailments" and (ii) "non-contractual bailments", they cover the range of possibilities and there could be no other bailments. I have suggested that all non-contractual bailments can be construed as gifts of possession for whatever time the parties have agreed. If so, there are only two categories of bailment and they can be designated (i) "possession by contract" and (ii) "possession by gift".

The two categories subsume the six traditional categories of *Coggs* v *Bernard*[107] and the three categories of Story.[108] *There are no other kinds.*

E THIRD PARTY INTERVENTION

Every bailment transaction makes the bailee possessor of a thing. Intervention by a stranger may result in interference with that possession. Interference may consist of dispossession or may lower the value of possession, perhaps by defacing the thing possessed. The usual possessor's remedies are available.

The bailor may or may not hold property in the thing while the bailee possesses it. Whether the bailor does will depend on whether the bailor was owner of the thing or retains right to immediate possession during the bailment term.[109] If the bailor retains property in the thing and a stranger destroys that property (through destruction of the thing) or lowers the value of the bailor's property, the bailor will also have a property-based action against the stranger.

These are elementary propositions. They have been forgotten in a few controversial cases in which bailors or bailees sued third parties for damages. This has led to logical inconsistencies, particularly in calculating the amount of damages owed.

---

107 Chief Justice Holt described six categories of bailment in *Coggs* v *Bernard* (1703) 2 Ld Raym. 909, 92 ER 107 (Eng). They are set out above, under "Traditional Categories of Bailment".

108 These were: bailments for the sole benefit of the bailor; bailments for the sole benefit of the bailee; and bailments reciprocally beneficial to both parties. They are explained above, under "Bailor v Bailee: Liability in Tort and Contract".

109 The bailor will not hold right to immediate possession of the thing in a contractual bailment during the term of the contract. Nevertheless, the bailor may suffer injury to the value of the property he will hold (*ie*, possession) in the future when the bailee's possession ends.

1   Bailor v Third Party: Ownership, Right to Immediate Possession, and Tort

The old law reports contain many cases in which a bailor out of possession sued someone other than the bailee for interference with the thing. Usually the bailor lost. The stumbling block was standing to sue. The reasons had to do with the common law causes of action. For example:[110]

> to maintain trover it is necessary that the plaintiff should have either an absolute or a special property in the goods which are the subject of the action. He who has an absolute or general property [*ie*, ownership] may support this action, although he has never had the actual possession; for it is a rule of law, that the *property* of personal chattels draws to it the *possession*, so that the owner may bring either trespass or trover at his election against any stranger who takes them away. ... However there must exist a *right of possession*, as well as of property, to support this action; therefore, where a man let a house and furniture for a term, and the furniture was wrongfully taken in execution pending the term, it was holden that the lessor could not maintain trover, because, during the term, he had parted with *the right of possession*.

The common law causes of action are fascinating, but much misunderstood. They worked as follows. In *trover* the plaintiff alleged that the defendant had been found in possession and sought damages on the ground that the defendant was depriving the plaintiff of the value of holding possession.[111] In *detinue*, which evolved before trover, the plaintiff alleged wrongful detention and sought possession of the thing.[112] *Conversion*, in which the plaintiff sought damages and alleged that the defendant had "converted [the thing] to his own use", developed later and usurped the roles of trover and detinue. *Trespass* "was the appropriate remedy [for] direct invasion of a right by force ... while case lay [if] one of those elements was lacking".[113] *Replevin* tested whether a distraint had been warranted and was therefore only available against defendants like landlords and sheriffs who had levied distress (seized possession as security). The remedy was damages, but this was because the plaintiff would have already applied to the sheriff, promised to sue upon the illegality of the original distress and to retransfer possession should he lose, and had the thing *replevied* before

---

110 See *Wilbraham* v *Snow* (1669) 2 Wms Saunders 47, 85 ER 624 (Eng) at 626. What appear to be the reasons for judgment are, rather, notes written many years later by one Sergeant Williams, a highly regarded authority on the topic of standing to sue. I have deleted the extensive footnotes, but I recommend that anyone interested in common law standing to sue in property actions read the notes (at 636-645).

111 See R Sutton *Personal Actions at Common Law* (Butterworths, London 1929) at 49. This is a marvellous little book, containing the best overview I have seen of the common law causes of action (at 46-71).

112 Although the defendant could "wage his law" and "was at liberty to satisfy the judgment by paying the value of the property and keeping it": Sutton at 50.

113 Sutton at 57.

commencing the action. Thus, the plaintiff held possession and sought damages for temporary dispossession.[114]

Many jurisdictions now have less rigid rules of practice and allow actions to be commenced without using the old technical labels.[115] However, the key to who can sue whom still revolves around basic property concepts. The key to analyzing a bailor's standing to sue a third party is not the fact that the plaintiff is a bailor. The issue is either what property the plaintiff is trying to protect or what loss of value the plaintiff is seeking to recover.[116] The key fact is that the plaintiff (bailor) was out of possession at the time the third party interfered. The plaintiff therefore does not hold possession and was not deprived of possession by the third party.

A person who did not hold possession at the time of a third party's interference with a thing has two possible claims. First, the plaintiff may prove and sue on the basis of right to immediate possession of the thing. Second, the plaintiff may sue on the basis of a so-called "reversionary interest".

(a)   Claims Based on Right to Immediate Possession

The first possible claim requires that the bailor prove right to immediate possession. An action may be brought against the third party by any plaintiff who holds right to immediate possession of a thing.[117] Like any other holder of property, the holder of right

---

114 Sutton at 66.

115 Such statutory rules invite the plaintiff to specify alternative remedies, and leave the selection of remedies to judicial discretion. In my own jurisdiction, Ontario, this is the general approach of the *Courts of Justice Act* SO 1984 C11 s 117 and of Rule 44.01 of the *Rules of Practice*, subordinate rules relating to the conduct of legal actions and of interest chiefly to the Ontario bar. This is not the place to go into detail concerning these unhappily worded rules or similar ones in other jurisdictions. Statutes like this do not generally give standing to sue in situations where no remedy at all was available due to lack of standing under the common law actions.

116 This is nothing revolutionary or peculiarly modern about this suggestion. Lots of old cases were decided this way. See, for example, *Ferguson* v *Cristall* (1829) 5 Bing 305, 130 ER 1078 (Eng) (ship chartered, possession of ship seized for seamen's wages; owner lost; owner had no right to possession before charter ended; noted (*obiter*) that plaintiff could have recovered if the ownership value was lowered) and *Pain* v *Whittaker* (1824) R & M 99, 171 ER 956 (Eng) (bailor of hired piano loses trover action against sheriff who seized possession from bailee).

117 See, for example, *Johnson* v *Diprose* [1893] 1 QB 512 (Eng CA) at 516 *per* Bowen LJ: "[a] person who brings an action for trespass to goods must either be in possession of them at the time of the alleged trespass or entitled to the immediate possession." See also *Wilson* v *Lombank Ltd* [1963] 1 All ER 740 (Eng). There is no shortage of authority for this proposition. For an example of this principle as *ratio*, see *Dunwich Corp* v *Sterry* (1831) 1 B & Ad 831, 109 ER 995 (Eng). The plaintiff was a "grantee of wreck". This meant that the King had granted the plaintiff corporation a proprietary claim to all things washed ashore from shipwrecks in the area. The plaintiff was authorized to take possession of any such wreck, but could be dispossessed should the owner show up and make a claim. In short, the plaintiff, though neither an owner nor a prior possessor, held *right to immediate possession* of all wreck. A cask of whiskey floated ashore; the defendant found and took possession of it. The plaintiff sued for possession and won. This simply confirmed that the holder of right to immediate possession of a thing prevails over a possessor by

to immediate possession can invoke state assistance or use self-help. The objective here is to gain possession of the thing from its possessor.[118] Not all bailors hold right to immediate possession. It is up to the plaintiff seeking to rely on a form of property to prove that he holds it.[119] Whether a bailor holds right to immediate possession depends upon the terms of the transaction by which he became a bailor.

This takes us back to the terms of the transfer of possession between bailor and bailee. As I pointed out earlier,[120] the outcome may depend on whether the bailment transaction was or was not a contract.

If the bailment transaction was a contract between bailor and bailee, the bailor does not hold right to immediate possession during the term of the contract.[121] Consequently, the bailor had no common law action in trover against third parties.[122] The bailor could sue if the interference occurred after the contractual term had expired,[123] or after a breach of the

---

finding. The result would be the same where right to immediate possession arises through prior possession and dispossession rather than by state grant.

118 Right to immediate possession is a form of property in things. A holder of right to immediate possession is at liberty to seize possession of the thing and has standing to invoke state assistance in gaining possession. See Chapter 2 "Right to Immediate Possession".

119 The essence of the plaintiff's claim is "the defendant interfered with *my* property in the thing". The classic defence is "the general issue", which essentially means "no I didn't interfere with *your property*, and I put you to the strict proof of your claim". The plaintiff must prove the property alleged, or lose. Consider a case in which I assert that you owe me money for trespassing at Buckingham Palace. If you did trespass there, maybe you owe *someone* money. However, I can't collect by simply making the claim, waiting for you to move for a non-suit, then pointing out that you lose because you failed to prove that Buckingham Palace wasn't mine. Bellowing "*jus tertii*" (as to which, see later) does not shift my burden of proof to you.

120 See above, "Possession by Contract".

121 The bailee has a contractual defence, having contracted for possession during the term specified. A contractual bailor is unable to compel a re-transfer of possession from the bailee during the term of the contract: *Brierly* v *Kendall* (1852) 17 QB 937, 117 ER 1540 (Eng) (possession seized by bailor during term of contractual bailment; bailee wins damages for loss of possession for remainder of term).

122 *Pain* v *Whittaker* (1824) R & M 99, 171 ER 956 (Eng) (bailor of hired piano loses trover action against sheriff who seized possession of it from bailee) . *Ferguson* v *Cristall* (1829) 5 Bing 305, 130 ER 1078 (Eng) (ship chartered, possession of ship seized for seamen's wages; owner had no right to possession before charter ended). Of course, an owner may claim damages to the extent that the ownership value is diminished. This, I suggest, was the situation in *Morris* v *CW Martin and Sons Ltd* [1966] 1 QB 716 (Eng CA), despite the reasons for judgment.

123 See, for example, *Manders* v *Williams* (1849) 4 Exch 479, 154 ER 1242 (Eng) (brewer supplied porter in casks; contract permitted recovery of possession of casks as soon as empty; brewer won trover action against sheriff who seized possession of empty casks from customer). In an Australian case, *Followmount Transport P/L v Premier Group P/L* [1999] QCA 232, possession of things was transferred in three separate bailment contracts from A to B to C to D. The Queensland Court of Appeal held that B could maintain an action in detinue against D because once B had "demanded the goods back" from C, the bailment contract between B and C terminated. Consequently, B acquired right to immediate possession, which was sufficient to justify proceedings in detinue against someone who held only possession (D). Note that the chain of bailment transactions must be irrelevant to the result. B had no contact or contract with D. B was successful because of the property relationship between B and D.

contract during its term.[124] However, while the contract remained in force, the bailor's action failed because his allegation - that the defendant had interfered with *his* right to immediate possession of the thing - was not true.

If the bailment transaction was not a contract between bailor and bailee, it is less clear whether the bailor holds right to immediate possession and can sue the third party. One possibility is that such a bailor always can because the bailee would have had no contractual (or other) defence to his demand for retransfer of possession.[125] This possibility is explored above, under the heading "Possession by Gift". I suggested there that the cases were not conclusive on the point and that non-contractual bailments could be analyzed as gifts of possession. A bailee who proved a gift of possession for a day, a week, or a year would have proved a transaction whereby he acquired possession for that period of time. During that period of time the bailor would not hold right to immediate possession because to claim it would be inconsistent with the terms of his own gift.[126] On that analysis, non-contractual bailors have no claim based on right to immediate possession against third parties who interfere with or take possession of the thing.

Common law analysis in this area have rarely been expressed with precision. The following view is typical. "The person having the right to immediate possession is ... frequently referred to in English law as being the 'possessor' - in truth the English law has never worked out a completely logical and exhaustive definition of possession".[127] Is this the reason why authority rooted in principle seems so difficult to find?

(b) Claims Based on Plaintiff's "Reversionary Interest"

A bailor may be able to prove that his "reversionary interest" has been devalued. Two types of bailors may use this approach - owners, and non-owners who will become possessors after the bailment term expires. The term reversionary interest is commonly

---

124 This is because the bailor can treat the breach of contract as terminating the contract. Thus, where a possessor by contract of hire violates the contract by purporting to sell ownership to a third party, the hirer may recover possession from the third party: *Bryant* v *Wardell* (1848) 1 CB 685, 154 ER 580 (Eng) ("action for trover is maintainable for the conversion"); *Fenn* v *Bittleston* (1851) 7 Exch 152, 155 ER 895 (Eng).

125 Many cases involving non-contractual bailors have concluded that the bailors had access to the possessory remedies at common law both against the bailees and against strangers: see Pollock and Wright *Possession in the Common Law* (Clarendon Press Oxford 1888) at 166 fn 2, citing 13 cases on the point. These remedies are available only to a possessor (*ie*, the bailee) or to the holder of right to immediate possession: see eg. *Johnson* v *Diprose* [1893] 1 QB 512 (Eng CA) at 516 *per* Bowen LJ. Each of these cases, therefore, must stand for the proposition that the bailor retained right to immediate possession during the term of the bailment. See *Burton* v *Hughes* (1824) 2 Bing 173, 130 ER 272 (Eng) (possessor of furniture who put it in house occupied by wife of bankrupt recovers in trover against bankrupt's creditors).

126 A donor who transfers ownership of a thing by gift has no subsequent claim to ownership or possession: see Chapter 9 "Gift". If it is possible to transfer possession by gift, the same rule would apply.

127 *USA* v *Dollfus Mieg et Compagnie SA and Bank of England* [1952] AC 582 (Eng HL).

used by analysts, but is somewhat euphemistic here, as owners sue on the basis of ownership (which is a current, not a reversionary interest), while non-owners who use this approach are claiming thwarted expectations regarding property to be held in the future (which may be reversionary, but is not an "interest" in the proprietary sense).

A bailor who holds ownership of the thing can sue if the value of ownership has been diminished by what the third party did.[128]

This approach would appear to have been available to the plaintiff in *Chapman* v *Robinson and Ferguson*.[129] The owner of a car let her daughter have possession. The daughter transferred possession to the defendant, who let a drunk friend drive. The car was wrecked. Why the case was decided on the basis that there was a "contract [*sic*] of sub-bailment" is mystifying. The simpler claim was surely that the defendant gave possession to a drunk without the owner's permission and was responsible to the owner for the foreseeable wreck caused by the drunk.

Similarly, in *Morris* v *CW Martin and Sons Ltd*,[130] the plaintiff's ownership value was lowered and the defendant was held liable, but the analysis was remarkably complicated. The plaintiff had sent a mink stole to a furrier for cleaning. With the plaintiff's consent, the furrier had sent the stole to the defendant, a specialist cleaner. The employee assigned to do the cleaning work stole the fur from the defendant's premises. The plaintiff continued to hold ownership of it, assuming it had not been destroyed, but the market value of her ownership was substantially reduced by virtue of her inability to locate and take possession of the mink stole.[131] All three judges found the defendant liable, but expressed themselves differently.

Lord Denning viewed the case as an opportunity to expound upon "the important question of how far a master is liable for theft or dishonesty by one of his servants".[132]

---

128 *Mears* v *London and South Western Rail Co* (1862) 11 CB (NS) 850 (Eng). The plaintiff owned a barge possessed by a bailee. The defendant's employees dropped a boiler through the bottom. Chief Justice Earle explained the problem, and the obvious solution.

> The question is whether the owner of the barge has a right to maintain an action for the injury. In my opinion he has that right, the mere temporary outstanding interest in the hirer of the barge amounting to nothing. That trover will not lie for the conversion of a chattel out on loan is clear. But ... an action for a permanent injury done to the chattel while the owner's right to the possession is suspended may be maintained.

129 *Chapman* v *Robinson and Ferguson* (1970) 71 WWR 515 (Alta). Justice Belzil noted that the plaintiff "could have rejected the sub-bailment and sued him for interference with her ownership". It appears to have been the plaintiff's lawyer who was confused.

130 *Morris* v *CW Martin and Sons Ltd* [1966] 1 QB 716 (Eng CA).

131 The thief was convicted of another theft. No one seems to have discovered what happened to the fur. Note that anyone who paid her for a transfer of ownership could find and dispossess the thief or his transferee, but few would pay much for the opportunity to embark on this adventure unless similar fur coats were in short supply.

132 [1966] 1 QB 716 (Eng CA) at 723. "If the master has himself been at fault in not employing a

He compared hypothetical facts, in which a car owner left his car for repairs at a garage and the car was taken for a "joyride" by an employee of the garage keeper. He said that the authorities supported the proposition that the garage keeper was responsible to the owner if the employee wrecked the car. Lord Denning seems to have thought this was because of the bailment transaction between owner and garage keeper. But unless the bailment transaction was a contract, which it need not be,[133] it is unclear how the owner could sue *on the transaction*. There is no cause of action in the common law system called breach of terms of bailment. The cause of action is in tort, for diminishing the ownership value.

The other two judges stuck to the issue: was the defendant liable for theft by the very employee assigned by the defendant to clean the fur? This caused both of them to focus on the relationship between the parties to the action, and the liabilities arising from that relationship. What each of them said can be simplified by applying some of the conclusions established under earlier headings. Lord Justice Diplock said the following.[134]

---

trustworthy man, of course he is liable. But what is the position when the master is not at fault at all. ... On this question the cases are baffling."

133 The cases seemed to suggest that (i) the garage keeper was responsible for his employee's acts because he was a "bailee for reward", but that (ii) he could be a "bailee for reward" even without a contract. According to Palmer *Bailment* at 286,

> [a]ny benefit or advantage, however prospective or conjectural, will suffice to make the intended recipient a bailor or bailee for reward, provided that it was with such advantage in mind that he entered into the bailment, or continued that relationship where it could otherwise have been determined.

This suggests that the fact of reward is not the *source* of the cause of action. By contrast, the Supreme Court of Canada equated "bailment for reward" with a contractual transfer in *Seaspan International Ltd* v *The Ship Kostis Prois* [1974] SCR 920 (BC SCC) *per* Ritchie J.

> It is sometimes said that a bailment involves the existence of a contract expressed or implied, and the appellants' contention that the circumstances here disclose a bailment for reward *presupposes a duty of care was assumed by the respondents for valuable consideration* as part of the contract of carriage. As I have indicated, not only was there no consideration passing between either of the appellants and the respondents, but there was no contractual relationship whatsoever between them, and I am accordingly of opinion that the contention of the appellants that the respondents were in the position of *bailees for reward* and thus seized with the burden of proving that the barge and cargo were damaged without their negligence must fail.

I suggest that the English Court of Appeal in *Morris* v *CW Martin & Sons Ltd* effectively destroyed any meaningful distinction created by the characterization "bailment for reward". I have already argued that "bailees for reward" and "gratuitous bailees" owe the same standards of care: see above "Bailor v Bailee: Liability in Tort and Contract".

134 [1965] 1 QB at 731-737. Just before the last sentence, Diplock LJ noted (at 737) "[w]hat he was doing, albeit dishonestly, he was doing in the scope or course of his employment in the technical sense of that infelicitous but time-honoured phrase". My purpose here is to explain the basis upon which an owner sues a third party. The defendant in this case was such a third party - someone with whom the owner had not transacted: none of the judges concluded that Beder the furrier sent the fur to the defendant as the plaintiff's agent. An employer's vicarious liability for an employee's torts and crimes is a quite separate topic.

By voluntarily accepting from Beder [the furrier] the custody of a fur which they [the specialist cleaners] knew to be the property of a customer of his, they brought into existence between the plaintiff and themselves the relationship of bailor and bailee by sub-bailment. The legal relationship of bailor and bailee of a chattel can exist independently of any contract. ... Beder was authorized by the plaintiff ... to create between her and them the common law relationship of bailee for reward to do work upon the fur [and] the mere existence of the common law relationship of bailor and bailee for reward gave rise to common law duties owed by the defendants to the plaintiff in respect of their custody of her fur. They put ... their agent in their place to clean the fur and to take charge of it while doing so. The manner in which he conducted himself in doing that work was to convert it. ... The defendants as his masters are responsible for his tortuous act.

This analysis can be explained more succinctly, using property terms. There was a property relationship between plaintiff and defendant, the defendant having taken possession of a fur owned by the plaintiff.[135] A possessor of a thing owes a duty of care to the owner.[136] The defendant breached that duty through the acts of an employee and must compensate the owner for the value of ownership of the fur. Lord Justice Salmon's reasoning can be similarly rendered as (i) the defendants voluntarily took possession of a fur owned by the plaintiff, (ii) the fur was stolen by the employee assigned by the defendants to clean it, and (iii) the defendants "must be answerable for the manner in which that agent has conducted himself in doing the business which it was the act of the master to put him in".[137]

---

135 Lord Justice Diplock was no doubt of the school that describes bailment as the mere state of affairs in which possession and ownership are held by different people. I have defined bailment as a transaction whereby possession of a thing is transferred upon agreement that possession of the same thing, perhaps in an altered state, will be transferred back to the transferror or on to someone else as agreed: see above, "Bailment Defined". According to this definition, there was no bailment transaction between plaintiff and defendant in this case, just as there is no bailment transaction in a finding case: there was merely the fact of possession of a fur owned by someone else.

136 See Chapter 7 "Owners' Claims [Against Possessors by Finding]" in support of the propositions:

(i)   that possessors by finding and possessors by bailment transaction owe the same duties of care to owners, and

(ii)   that the duty is based on each defendant's having taken possession of the thing owned, not on whether possession was taken by transaction or otherwise.

See particularly, under the latter heading, the comparison with other common tort obligations based on "a responsibility that is voluntarily accepted or undertaken, either generally where a general relationship, such as that of solicitor and client or banker and customer is created, or specifically in relation to a particular transaction." *Hedley Byrne & Co Ltd* v *Heller & Partners* [1964] AC 465 (Eng HL) at 529 *per* Lord Devlin. Taking possession of a thing which someone else owns creates such a relationship, based on ownership and possession. Thus, the possessor by finding is required to take reasonable care. So is the possessor by transaction (bailee), unless the transaction is a contract that says otherwise.

137 [1965] 1 QB 737-740.

Punch v Savoy's Jewellers Ltd got it right.[138] The plaintiff (Punch) received ownership of a ring from her aunt. She sent it to a jeweller (Savoy) for repair. Savoy, unable to perform the necessary repair, sent it to another jeweller. The other jeweller repaired the ring and contracted with Canadian National Railways (CN) to return possession to Punch. CN lost the ring. A clause in the shipping contract exempted CN's liability to $100 dollars. Realizing that there was no contract between the plaintiff and CN, Cory JA analyzed CN's liability to Punch in tort.[139]

> Obviously Lenore Punch, who knew nothing of the clause, the contract of carriage or the carrier, cannot be bound by it. C.N. is liable to her for the full value of the ring since its contract of carriage specifically contemplates the existence of an owner to whom a duty of care is owed.

The duty of care arose out of the property relationship between an owner (the plaintiff) and a possessor (CN).

The other type of bailor who can use this approach is a non-owner who will become possessor of the thing after the bailment term expires. Such a plaintiff must prove either that his acquisition of possession was thwarted or that it was made less valuable by what the third party did.

The major problem faced by a plaintiff in this category is that he did not hold property in the thing at the time of the third party's interference. An example will assist in explaining the theoretical difficulties with such a plaintiff's claim.

> Plaintiff leased possession of a car for a year from Owner. Halfway through the year, Plaintiff transferred possession of the car to Bailee by contractual bailment. The contract said that possession would be held by Bailee for one week and then returned to Plaintiff. Defendant carelessly smashes into the car, leaving it dented and unsightly.

Plaintiff will be contractually entitled to possession of a dented and unsightly car at the week's end, but holds no property in the car until then. The issue is whether Plaintiff can sue and recover damages from Defendant.[140]

---

138 *Punch v Savoy's Jewellers Ltd* (1986) 54 OR (2d) 383.

    139 *Ibid* at para 34.

    140 This is an important theoretical question. There may, of course, be other ways to proceed so that Plaintiff is indirectly compensated. For example, cases suggest that Owner can recover damages and must then pay some of the money to Plaintiff (who is Owner's contractual bailee). Other cases - criticized under the next heading - suggest Bailee can recover the diminished *ownership* value and will be accountable to Plaintiff and Owner.

This falls within the evolving area of "economic negligence",[141] and involves how far one can pursue claims of "economic loss". Professor Feldthusen defined "pure economic loss" as "a financial loss which is not causally consequent upon physical injury to the plaintiff's own person or property".[142] In our terminology, the last point would require proof of physical injury to a thing in which the plaintiff held property - which is precisely what Plaintiff can not prove in our example. It appears that there are at least two conflicting tests. One theory would allow for compensation for "economic loss ... [that] is the direct reflection of [physical] damage".[143] The other theory would restrict such claims to those who prove damage to property and "precludes recovery for relational economic loss".[144] Which of the two theories will prevail is beyond me; the question is outside the field of property in things.

Our plaintiff in the above example held no property in the car, but had a contractual claim for future transfer of possession. Surely another plaintiff in a similar position, but without even a contractual claim against the possessor would be in no better position. Thus, if Plaintiff leased possession of a car from Owner, *loaned* the car to Bailee for a week (a non-contractual bailment transaction), and received at the end of the week possession of a car dented by Defendant's carelessness, Plaintiff would seem less likely to recover. First, there is a "foreseeable plaintiff" issue. The plaintiff in the previous example was claiming on the basis of a contract with the possessor and probably was foreseeable; the non-contractual plaintiff may well be unforeseeable under tort rules. Second, recovery is clearly precluded by the narrower of the two "pure economic loss" theories, while the broader theory is probably restricted to cases in which the plaintiff can prove, by contract or otherwise, an existing right to future possession.[145]

Some readers may think that the Latin term *jus tertii* is applicable when third parties defend these actions by bailors. I am sure that it is not. Even if it were, it would make no difference, for the reasons detailed under the next heading, to which sceptics are referred.

---

141 The leading authority in this field is my colleague Bruce Feldthusen.

142 See Feldthusen *Economic Negligence: the Recovery of Pure Economic Loss* 4th ed (Carswell Toronto 2000) at 1.

143 *Schiffahrt und Kohlen GmbH v Chelsea Maritime Ltd; The Irene's Success* [1982] QB 481, [1982] 1 All ER 218 (Eng) *per* Lloyd J. A similar result was reached in *Rockaway Blvd Wrecking & Lumber Co v Raylite Elec Corp* 29 NYS 2d 926 (NYCA 1960) (plaintiff had contract to demolish building and salvage the materials; building burned down by defendant's carelessness; plaintiff collected damages from defendant for the lost salvage). Professor Feldthusen points out (at 247) that "the *Rockaway* decision also demonstrates that the exception [allowing the plaintiff's claim] is limited to situations in which the plaintiff has a right to future possession ...".

144 Feldthusen at 247, citing *Leigh & Sillivan v Aliakmon Shipping Co* [1986] 2 WLR 902, [1986] 2 All ER 145 (Eng HL).

145 See Feldthusen at 247. Ironically, a non-contractual bailor might end up in a better position than a contractual bailor if all non-contractual bailors can revoke the proposed term and demand repossession at any time. This possibility is canvassed above, under the heading "Possession by Gift", and invokes the unsettled (and no doubt unsettling for some) question whether all non-contractual bailment transactions are gifts of temporary possession.

2   Bailee v Third Party: Possession, Tort, and the Assessment of Damages

A third party who interferes with a bailee's possession may be sued in tort. Temporary or permanent dispossession is actionable interference. So is physical impairment of the thing itself, as it lowers the value of possession. As possession is a form of property and the bailee held possession, one would expect to find a simple rule authorizing the possessor to sue and collect the amount by which his possession was devalued. That, I shall argue, is the state of the law.

However, that is not the state of the precedents. The common law cases are confused in this area. The confusion revolves around two quite separate points. The first involves the bailee's standing to sue: does he sue as a possessor or by virtue of his status as bailee?[146] The second, and more controversial point, involves the assessment of damages for interference with property held by a bailee. Here, an analytical error in high places has led to a widely cited, but thoroughly irrational rule.

It is not clear what the earliest law was. It is commonly said that "medieval law" required possession with an assertion of title.[147] This, however, may well be too narrow, for there is another way of making sense of the old law. The famous note by Sergeant Williams set out at *Wilbraham* v *Snow* is frequently cited as the root of the modern law on the point.[148] Sergeant Williams said something quite interesting.

---

146 *Richard* v *Nowlan* (1959) 19 DLR 2d 229 (NBCA) illustrates the point. The plaintiff was driving his mother's car without permission. The defendant ran into and damaged the car. The trial judge concluded that the plaintiff could not sue because he was not a bailee. The Court of Appeal saw through this confusion, recognized that the plaintiff held possession of the car and could therefore sue in negligence, and ordered a new trial.

147 "Medieval law" (possession with assertion of title) and "Winkfield law" (possession alone sufficient) are aptly contrasted in a clearly written article by Warren, "Qualifying as Plaintiff in an Action for a Conversion" 49 Harvard L Rev 1084 (1936). Professor Warren said (at 1088): "[p]ossession under a claim of ownership was title against a wrongdoer in medieval times. The twentieth century doctrine is that *any* possession is title against a wrongdoer." He went on to say that if the thing was destroyed by third party interference, the possessor claiming title in the old days (and any possessor nowadays) could sue the third party and collect "the full value of *the thing*". Note once again how confusing property and things may have helped bring about an absurd result. Prof Warren also (at 1088) took the position that the formula "possession is title against a wrongdoer" evolved from the "real property" remedy available to one who claimed to have acquired an estate in land by tortiously "desseising" the estate holder in occupation. He may or may not be correct on the "real property" point, but there is little evidence that the trover and conversion remedies evolved by that analogy.

148 *Wilbraham* v *Snow* (1669) 2 Wms Saunders 47, 85 ER 624 (Eng). The case was decided in 1669, but it is generally conceded that the note was written much later. Professor Warren cites the note as the foundation of the modern law, but disputed its accuracy as to the state of the "Medieval law" of standing in trover.

So possession with an assertion of title, or even possession alone, gives the possessor such a property as will enable him to maintain this action against a wrongdoer, for possession is *prima facie* evidence of property.

Sergeant Williams clearly saw possession as one form of property, despite the somewhat anomalous last clause. Which types of possessors had standing to sue for third party interference may have been controversial at the time. Sergeant Williams suggested that any possessor did.[149]

Holmes Jr agreed. More than 100 years ago he reviewed the possessor's standing in *The Common Law*.[150]

It has been supposed, to be sure, that a "special property" was necessary in order to maintain replevin or trover. But modern cases establish that possession is sufficient, and an examination of the sources of our law proves that special property did not mean anything more.

Holmes maintained that possession was always the ground of the common law actions and that to think ownership had anything to do with it was an 18th or 19th century misinterpretation.[151]

I do not propose to enter the antiquarians' debate as to whether Holmes was right about the early law. Maybe he was wrong. Maybe only a possessor who also claimed ownership could sue.[152] If so, the 1722 decision in *Armory* v *Delamirie* must have

---

149 It does not follow from that statement alone that any particular amount of damages could be collected. The issue was simply the possessor's standing to sue.

150 Holmes *The Common Law* Howe ed (Harvard U Press 1963) at 190. Holmes traced the error to the fact that bailees sued on the ancient writ "*bona et catella sua*", rather than the more technically proper phrase "*bona in custodia sua exestentia*", because the chancery clerks were unwilling to frame a writ in the latter form.

151 Holmes was fond of noting, often persuasively, how common lawyers had got their logic twisted. "The inverted explanation of Beaumanoir will be remembered, that the bailee could sue because he was answerable over, in place of the original rule that he was answerable over so strictly because only he could sue": *The Common Law* at 135, citing a judicial quote from YB 11 Henry IV 23 (1410) as an early example of the error.

152 There is no shortage of opinion that Holmes overstated his case. Pollock and Wright in *Possession in the Common Law* at 91 took the position that "a plaintiff in an action founded on right to possess, whose case would be good if he relied on his own possession, may spoil it if he shows the badness of his own title by setting out the previous history", citing *Doe* v *Barnard* (1849) 13 QB 945 (Eng). See also *Asher* v *Whitlock* (1865) LR 1 QB 1 (Eng) at 6 and *Beaudoin* v *Brown* [1961] OR 429 (Ont). In *USA* v *Dollfus Mieg et Compagnie SA and Bank of England* [1952] AC 582 (Eng HL), Evershed MR went further (*obiter*) at 345: "there is neither logic nor authority for the view that a bailor [he meant possessor] who can, and does, assert no title of any kind to the goods bailed (eg, a thief or a mere finder) [his words] may bring an action for trespass against a third party who has either acquired physical possession of the goods, or threatens to do so, or claims the goods as his own". As we shall soon see, there is substantial logic and plenty of reputable authority for the view he so casually dismissed.

changed the common law.153 *Armory* v *Delamirie*[154] was a pure possessor by finding *versus* stranger dispute. The plaintiff, finder of a jewel, complained that the jeweller whom he had asked to appraise it refused to return possession. He sued in trover and won.[155] The modern acceptance of that approach, and a suggested rationale for it, were summarized in 1982 by Donaldson LJ: "[the rule in *Armory*] must be right as a general proposition, for otherwise lost property would be subject to a free-for-all in which the physically weakest would go to the wall".[156]

That *possession alone gives standing to sue a third party* has thus been settled since 1722. Unfortunately, 19th century judges fell into the habit of mystifying this simple proposition. Lord Campbell complicated matters with the following comment in 1856.[157]

> A person possessed of goods as his property has a good title as against every stranger and ... one who takes them from him having no title in himself is a wrong-doer and cannot defend himself by showing that there was title in some third person: *for against a wrong-doer possession is title...*

The emphasized words are superfluous. Against a wrong-doer, possession gives sufficient standing to sue. Moreover, it seems obvious that the defendant cannot defend himself by showing some third person holds some other form of property in the thing. The plaintiff's claim might fail if the defendant held right to immediate possession,[158] or if the defendant interfered as agent of a holder of right to immediate possession.[159] However, the mere fact that someone else held ownership does not affect the plaintiff's standing, so evidence that someone else did is irrelevant to the standing issue. An 1892

---

153 *Quo warranto?* Where in the British constitution does it say that judges have power to make or change law?

154 *Armory* v *Delamirie* (1722) 1 Str 505, 93 ER 664 (Eng).

155 The ruling was uncomplicated: "the finder of a jewel, though he does not by such finding acquire an absolute property or ownership, yet he has such a property as will enable him to keep it against all but the rightful owner".

156 *Parker* v *British Airways Board* [1982] 2 WLR 503 (Eng CA). Similarly, see *Daniel* v *Rogers* [1918] 2 KB 228 (Eng CA) *per* Scrutton LJ at 234: "[s]ince the case of *Armory* v *Delamirie* it has been well established that mere possession is enough to entitle a person to sue in trover and that he need not show the manner in which possession was obtained". An American case, *Anderson* v *Gouldberg* 53 NW 636 (Minn 1892) put it even more clearly.
> One who has acquired the possession of property, whether by finding, bailment, or by mere tort, has a right to retain that possession as against a mere wrongdoer who is a stranger to the property. Any other rule would lead to an endless series of seizures and reprisals in every case where property had once passed out of the possession of the rightful owner.
See also *Bird* v *Town of Fort Frances* [1949] OR 292, [1949] 2 DLR 791 (Ont HC), explained in detail in Chapter 6 "Finders on Offence".

157 *Jeffries* v *The Great Western Railway Co* (1856) 5 El & Bl 802, 119 ER 680 (Eng) *per* Lord Campbell CJ at 805. (Emphasis added)

158 Claims by a holder of right to immediate possession are surveyed under the previous heading. For more detail see above "Bailor v Bailee: Liability in Tort and Contract" and Chapter 7 "Prior Possessors' Claims". It would make no difference how right to immediate possession was acquired.

159 The agency defence is analyzed later, as part of the damages issue.

case, *Claridge* v *South Staffordshire Tramway Company*, clarified that point.[160] The plaintiff was an auctioneer who had acquired possession of a horse by bailment and had the owner's permission to use the horse until the auction was conducted. The horse was frightened by defendant's train, fell, and was injured. A County Court found the defendant had been carelessly driving at excessive speed, but denied recovery for the horse's injuries. On appeal, Hawkins J. explained why.

> It is true that if a man is in possession of a chattel, and his possession is interfered with, he may maintain an action, but only for the injury sustained by himself. The right to bring an action against the wrongdoer is one thing; the measure of the damages recoverable in such action is another. And here the plaintiff has suffered no loss at all.

That seems simple enough. There were two quite distinct issues in the case. First, did the plaintiff have standing to sue for interference with his possession of the horse? The answer was clearly yes. Second, could such a plaintiff collect damages for that interference: again, the answer was yes. However, this plaintiff, having proved no damages, collected none. The "possession gives standing" aspect of *Claridge's* case is generally accepted as correct and is unaffected by judicial rethinking of the damages issue in *The Winkfield*[161] and other 20th century cases. The cases on the damages issue are dealt with below.

Thus, a possessor by bailment (or any other possessor) has standing to sue a third party for interference with possession. It is, of course, always open to the defendant to disprove a lying plaintiff's claim. Proof that some third party held possession at the time of the interference is one way of proving the plaintiff a liar. But apart from the factual determination of the plaintiff's possession, the right of any third party - the so called "*jus tertii* defence"[162] - is of no relevance to the standing issue.

The damages issue is more complicated,[163] because of some 19th and 20th century cases. Before examining them, let's consider two perfectly ordinary damages claims, separated by some 286 years.

---

160 *Claridge* v *South Staffordshire Tramway Company* [1892] 1 QB 422 (Eng).

161 *Winkfield (The)* [1902] P 42 (Eng CA).

162 The defence of "*jus tertii*" looms large in textbooks and reasons for judgment in this area, usually on the damages issue. When writers and judges resort to Latin, truth and logic evaporate. It is the plaintiff's *lack of property*, not that some other person holds property, that the defendant wants to prove. A defendant can't be stopped from proving that.

163 Again, it is hard to say what the early law was. In *Heydon* v *Smith* (1610) 13 Co Rep 67, 77 ER 1476 (Eng), Coke CJ opined at 1478: "clearly, the bailee, or he who hath a special property, shall have a general action of trespass against a stranger, and shall recover all in damages, because that he is chargeable over". He seems to have made the same error that Holmes Jr referred to as "the inverted explanation of Beaumanoir ... that the bailee could sue because he was answerable over, in place of the original rule that he was answerable over so strictly because only he could sue": *The Common Law* at 135, citing a judicial quote from YB 11 Henry IV 23 (1410) as an early example of the error.

A real damages claim arose in 1722 in *Armory* v *Delamirie*,[164] dealt with above. The plaintiff found a jewel, asked the defendant jeweller to appraise it, was denied repossession, sued, and won. The report tells us that,

> the Chief Justice directed the jury, that unless the defendant did produce the jewel, and shew it not to be of the finest water, they should presume the strongest against him, and make the value of the best jewels the measure of their damages: which they accordingly did.

That makes almost perfect sense. As to quality, the plaintiff was in no position to classify the jewel. The jeweller was. Neither proved its quality, so the jury was told to estimate the high-quality end of the spectrum of possibilities. As to value, the direction is ambiguous. The Chief Justice fell into the familiar trap of confusing property with things. Things don't have value; property does.[165] The Mona Lisa is often said to be "priceless", but possession of it for a week could no doubt be arranged for a price and ownership might even be procured for a larger, but still finite number of dollars.

In the above quote "the value of the best jewels" is probably a colloquial reference to the ownership value. The ownership value was to be used as "the measure" of the damages. Did that mean the amount of damages was the ownership value or that the ownership value of the best quality jewels was a benchmark against which the plaintiff's loss was calculated? The plaintiff had been deprived of property and was entitled to damages equal to the full value of that property. That property was possession, not ownership. There was probably an owner out there who might have dispossessed the plaintiff at any time. However, there being no evidence predicting the chimney sweep's imminent dispossession, the jury (or the market) might value his possession at or near the ownership value.[166]

Nearly 286 years later a similar, but hypothetical damages claim arises often in my life. When I hire a car for a day I routinely pay less than 1% of the ownership value of the car. In exchange, I acquire possession of the car for one day. Suppose I park the car somewhere and someone blows it up. I have lost the value of possession for that day. I may also incur public transit or hotel expenses. Twentieth century cases said that the rule

---

164 *Armory* v *Delamirie* (1722) 1 Str 505, 93 ER 664 (Eng)

165 Again, would you pay more for possession of the Mona Lisa (say for 15 seconds) than for ownership of the Mona Gorilla; more to rent (*ie*, acquire possession of) a new Lincoln for a day than to buy (*ie*, acquire ownership of) a new Diet Chevy?

166 The defendant seems not to have brought up such key questions as where the jewel was found, which might have helped the jury determine whether the owner was likely to appear. We don't really know how the jury proceeded or what their conclusion was. They probably relied on the law given to them by the judge, who relied on the law argued by the parties' lawyers, who are unlikely to have dwelt on the distinction between ownership value and possession value. Common law analysts sometimes make too much of the reasons for judgment, forgetting that they tend to be a product of the arguments presented rather than a thoughtful overview of the area in dispute.

is perfectly clear, that I can sue my dispossessor, and that I will collect the ownership value - 100 times my loss - in damages. That is absurd.[167]

Cases supporting such a rule must be wrong. A sensible rule could be explained by the following series of statements, uncontroversial but for the last. Possession is a form of property. Interference with property is actionable. Dispossession is interference with possession. Dispossessors pay. They pay the value of the plaintiff's possession.

Some key 19th and 20th century cases made a major *faux pas* at the last step.

Jeffries v *The Great Western Railway Co*[168] was decided in 1856. The facts were not particularly complicated, but they require some elaboration as there were two issues at stake. The case began at the Gloucester Summer Assizes. The plaintiff was found in possession of some railway trucks and was dispossessed by the defendant. The plaintiff sued in trover. Two defences were argued. The first - that the assignment by which the plaintiff had acquired possession and claimed ownership "was fraudulent and void against the defendants" - failed for lack of evidence. The second defence was that the plaintiff's assignor was a bankrupt at the time of the assignment. This was interpreted as an allegation that someone else, the assignees in bankruptcy, held ownership of the trucks before the plaintiff acquired possession. The Assizes judge ruled that even if this were true, ownership by a third party was no defence to the plaintiff's claim of dispossession, so that evidence was excluded.

During Michaelmas Term, the defendant obtained a rule *nisi* in two parts. First, a new trial was ordered on the basis of some new evidence that the assignment was fraudulent. Second, it was concluded that the evidence as to the assignor's bankruptcy and third party ownership due to the assignor's bankruptcy was improperly excluded and a new trial was ordered on that issue as well. The plaintiff challenged the rule *nisi*. We find that challenge before the full court in the English Reports.

The full court made short work of the appeal on the fraud point, ordering a new trial in one line.[169] The rest of the reasons for judgment focused on the third party ownership issue, which would appear by then to have been *obiter* on the parties' dispute.

---

167 It also strikes me that I wouldn't get 100 times my loss because none of the local judges I know would apply so-called rules like that. Supporters of the rule say that I collect the ownership value, but that I hold all except my own loss "in trust" for the owner. They forget that owners willing to rent possession of insured and easily traceable cars might entertain a healthy scepticism about entrusting the likes of me with a briefcase full of cash, unless all the planes to Las Vegas are fully booked that week.

168 *Jeffries* v *The Great Western Railway Co* (1856) 5 El & Bl 802, 119 ER 680 (Eng).

169 "On the affidavits, however, a new trial must be granted" was all Lord Campbell CJ said on the issue. Neither of the other two judges is even reported as having commented on the issue, though the reporter's summary (119 ER 682) confirms that a new trial was indeed ordered on that point. The reporter also noted that the argument on the fraud point was omitted from the report.

Lord Campbell CJ, whose analysis is most often quoted from this case, explained fairly clearly why he thought the evidence was properly excluded.[170]

> I am of opinion that the Chief Baron did right in refusing to admit evidence to impeach the title of the plaintiff. The defendants were strangers to the title which they proposed to set up; and the plaintiff had been for some time in possession, when the defendants seized the goods, claiming them as their own, but having, as we must now take it, no right to the goods; and I think that, under such circumstances, the *jus tertii* could not be set up, by the defendants averring that they themselves were mere wrongdoers at the time of the conversion, but that there were strangers who then had a right to take the goods. I am of opinion that the law is that a person possessed of goods as his property has a good title as against every stranger, and that one who takes them from him, having no title in himself, is a wrong-doer and cannot defend himself by shewing that there was title in some third person: for against a wrong-doer possession is title. The law is so stated by the very learned annotator in note (1) to *Wilbraham* v *Snow* 2 Wms Saund 47; and I think it most reasonable law, and essential for the interests of society, that peaceable possession should not be disturbed by wrongdoers.

The original order issued at the Gloucester Assizes was that the defendant pay damages of £470. That appears to have been the amount the plaintiff had paid for the allegedly fraudulent assignment by which the plaintiff had acquired possession and claimed ownership. Thus, it represented a presumed market value for *ownership* of the railway trucks.[171] The plaintiff, having been tricked by someone else into paying too much for possession, was now trying to trick the court. Ownership by a third party was clearly relevant to the amount of the plaintiff's loss. A third party owner who was known, nearby, and aware of the plaintiff's possession might testify that he would have

---

170 *Ibid* at 681. Justice Wightman gave a shorter version of the same analysis, concluding (at 681), "I can find no case where the person in actual possession has been defeated in an action of trover because the defendant was permitted to set up the *jus tertii*". Raising the third party's ownership in response to an outrageous damages claim would not "defeat" the plaintiff; it would merely clarify that the plaintiff was not the owner and limit the plaintiff's damages to the value of what the plaintiff was deprived of - possession. Contrast *Barwick* v *Barwick* 33 NC 80 (1850), decided around the same time.

> The bare possession is sufficient to maintain an action of trespass against a wrong doer, for the gist of that action is any injury to the *possession*, and the measure of damage is not the value of the property, but the injury done to the plaintiff by having his possession disturbed. It is true, that when nothing appears, but the fact that the defendant took the property out of the possession of the plaintiff and converted it to his own use, trover will lie. For the possession of personal property is prima facie evidence of title, and in the absence of any proof to rebut this presumption, the person in possession is taken to be the owner and can recover the full value. But, if it appears on the trial that the plaintiff, although in possession, is not in fact the owner, and that the property belongs to a third person, the presumption of title, inferred from the possession, is rebutted: and it would be manifestly wrong to allow the plaintiff to recover the value of the property.

171 This information can be found in an alternative report of the case, (1856) 25 LJ (CL) NS 107. Note that if the defendant had been ordered to return possession of the trucks to the plaintiff, third party ownership would have been irrelevant, as standing and dispossession were proved. Similarly, if only nominal damages were sought, or if the amount had been agreed by the parties, ownership was a red herring.

236

dispossessed the plaintiff within a few days had the defendant not interfered. A plaintiff in those circumstances who claimed a loss greater than the value of a few days' possession – *ie*, the rental value of those trucks for that time - would be either an incurable optimist or a liar and a cheat. Evidence to prove that the plaintiff was either seems clearly admissible if the issue is the amount of the plaintiff's loss.

Justice Crompton was the only one of the three judges who even mentioned the damages issue. This is what he said.[172]

> We are now to decide *whether a wrongdoer in actual possession of goods, the property of a stranger, can recover their value in an action of trover against a wrongdoer who takes the goods from him.* My impression has always been, like that of the rest of the Court, that he can do so; but that is a question on which there has been considerable doubt, and which has never been expressly decided. ... It is now necessary to decide that point; for in this case the defendant is a wrongdoer, and he has not been permitted to give in evidence the title of a third person against whom he is himself a wrongdoer. The question is, should he be permitted to do so? My impression has always been that the better opinion was that stated in note (1) to *Wilbraham* v *Snow* 2 Wms Saund 47; and I therefore think that the Chief Baron ruled rightly when he rejected this evidence. [Emphasis added]

Note the traditional confusion between property and things in the emphasized portion of the quote. Thus phrased, it invites a rhetorical question - an actual possessor can get the goods back from a wrongdoer, so why can't the actual possessor get the value of the goods? Only when we translate from duckspeak to the language of property do we see that the question is fatuous. The plaintiff was not deprived of goods: he was deprived of possession of goods. He is entitled to an order for possession. Alternatively, the plaintiff may claim damages equal to the value of his loss. The value of the plaintiff's loss is the value of the *property* taken by the defendant, not the value of someone else's property. Whether someone else held property is relevant *because it tells us something about the value of the plaintiff's property in the trucks.* The issue is the value of the plaintiff's

---

172 119 ER at 681-682. Only the following sentence is deleted from the reasons for judgment, to make the quote shorter.

I find that Parke B, in delivering the considered judgment of the Court of Exchequer in *Elliot* v *Kemp* 7 M & W 306, 312, says: 'It is unnecessary, in this case, to decide the question, whether, in an action of trespass or trover for personal property, the simple fact of possession, which is unquestionably evidence of title, is conclusive evidence, and constitutes a complete title, in all cases, against a defendant who is a mere wrongdoer, as it does in actions of trespass to real property, and in those actions for injuries to personal chattels, in which the plaintiff had a special property in such chattels.'

The report also quotes the appellant's barristers as having argued as follows.

The right of the mere [possessor] to maintain trespass against a person unjustifiably depriving him of his possession seems clear enough on principle; but whether he can in trover recover as damages for the conversion the whole value of the property has not been, I think, as yet decided. It seems hard if the person converting goods is to pay the full value both to the [possessor] and to the true owner, of whose title, it may be, he was ignorant till after the conversion.

possession, and that is a function of how long his possession would have lasted. Evidence that someone else owned and held right to immediate possession of the trucks is probative of that issue.

In 1892, property analysis was put back on the rails. It was not to stay there long.

Claridge v *South Staffordshire Tramway Company*[173] was a simple damages case. I have already dealt with it on the standing issue. The plaintiff was an auctioneer who had acquired possession of a horse by bailment and had the owner's permission to use the horse until the auction was conducted. The horse was frightened by defendant's train, fell, and was injured. A County Court found the defendant had been carelessly driving at excessive speed, but denied recovery for the horse's injuries. On appeal, Hawkins J clearly explained why.[174]

> It is true that if a man is in possession of a chattel, and his possession is interfered with, he may maintain an action, but only for the injury sustained by himself. The right to bring an action against the wrongdoer is one thing; the measure of the damages recoverable in such action is another. And here the plaintiff has suffered no loss at all. ...If both the bailee and the bailor have suffered damage by the wrongful act of a third party, I think that each may bring a separate action for the loss sustained by himself. I cannot understand why a bailee should be allowed to recover damages beyond the extent of his own loss simply because he happened to be in possession.

We don't know whether the plaintiff had incurred any expenses. It is likely that the rental of horses was less of an everyday practice in 1892 than car rental is today. Perhaps the auctioneer simply did without, or used his own horse after the accident. What the case tells us is that the plaintiff had proved no loss attributable to his deprivation of possession of a healthy horse and that, of course, he could not expect a windfall in the form of damages for someone else's loss of ownership value.

That eminently sensible analysis was overruled 10 years later. The English Court of Appeal ruled in *The Winkfield*, "that *Claridge's Case* was wrongly decided, and that ... in an action against a stranger for loss of goods caused by his negligence, the bailee in possession can recover the value of the goods".[175]

---

173 *Claridge* v *South Staffordshire Tramway Company* [1892] 1 QB 422 (Eng).

174 *Ibid*. Justice Wills concurred: "cases that have been cited relate only to the right of a bailee to maintain an action; they have nothing to do with the measure of damages recoverable in such action."

175 *Winkfield (The)* [1902] P 42 (Eng CA) *per* Collins MR at 54. Note yet again the one to one correspondence between confusing property with things and producing questionable legal analysis. Interestingly, the *Winkfield* court completely misread *Claridge*. "The ground of the decision in *Claridge's Case* was that the plaintiff in that case, being under no liability to his bailor, could recover no damages" noted Collins MR. That is not so. The trial judge in *Claridge* is said to have thus directed the jury, but both judges on appeal made it plain that the plaintiff would have won had he proved some personal loss.

The Winkfield was a ship. It was carrying troops to South Africa when it ran into the good ship *Mexican*, carrying mail home from the Cape Colony. *The Mexican* went down with the mail. The owners of *The Winkfield* admitted liability: the question was, liability for what? The agreed facts were that the Postmaster General held possession of the mail by bailment from the various owners thereof *and* that the Postmaster General was not liable to the bailors for their losses. The lower court ruled, following *Claridge*, that the Postmaster General had standing but no losses, and awarded no damages.

On appeal, things got confused. There are five analytical steps in the reasons for judgment. Each of the five steps raises some troublesome questions.

First, Collins MR noted the position of a possessor by finding who is dispossessed by a stranger, grounding his analysis on the rock of *Armory*. Unfortunately, he overstated the case. "It cannot be denied that since the case of *Armory* v *Delamirie* ... a mere finder may recover against a wrongdoer the full value of the thing converted", he said.[176] The problem is that it *can* be denied: as demonstrated earlier, a dispossessed finder collects the value of *his property in the thing*.

Second, the by now familiar annotation from *Wilbraham* v *Snow* was recited.[177] This time the concluding words of Sergeant Williams' quote - "*for against a wrong-doer possession is title*" - were *emphasized*. Those words were superfluous. Sergeant Williams was explaining that any possessor had standing to sue a third party. Like most of the 19th century judges, Collins MR was fixated on ownership. He wrongly viewed the concluding words as the key to the common law analysis

Third, having reviewed various authorities, Collins MR set out a post-19th century summary of the common law position.[178]

> Therefore ... the root principle of the whole discussion is that, as against a wrongdoer, possession is title. The chattel that has been converted or damaged is *deemed* to be the chattel of the possessor and of no other, and therefore its loss or deterioration is his loss, and to him, if he demands it, it must be recouped. ... As between bailee and stranger possession gives title - that is, not a limited interest but absolute and complete ownership, and he is entitled to receive back a complete equivalent for the whole loss or deterioration of the thing itself. [Emphasis added]

---

176 [1902] P 42 (Eng CA) *per* Collins MR at 55.

177 "A person possessed of goods as his property has a good title as against every stranger and ... one who takes them from him having no title in himself is a wrong-doer and cannot defend himself by showing that there was title in some third person: *for against a wrong-doer possession is title* ... :" [1902] P 42 at 55 *per* Collins MR. (Emphasis his).

178 *Ibid* at 60.

Possession is *not* title. Possession and ownership are different forms of property. Judges do not have the power to "deem" possession to be ownership. "Deem" is a word most of us know from our student days in tax class. The legislature sometimes statutorily "deems" facts to be other than what they are, or seem to be from the evidence. The effect is that the facts are what the legislature says they are. No amount of evidence to the contrary - no common knowledge, no matter how notorious - can change what the legislature has "deemed" to be.[179] Legislatures have that kind of constitutional power to fiddle with reality. Judges don't. Judges must determine what the facts are from the evidence presented. The evidence presented in *The Winkfield* was that the Postmaster General possessed, but did not own, the mail. The disappearance of anything in the mail may have cost the sender or the addressee dearly, but at worst it slightly diminished the reputation of the Postmaster General. That was no great loss.

Fourth, Collins MR set out (as if it were a rule) an assumption that any plaintiff suing for dispossession and collecting the ownership value in damages would hold the ownership value as trustee for the owner.[180]

> As between bailor and bailee the real interests of each must be inquired into, and, as the bailee has to account for the thing bailed, so he must account for that which has become its equivalent and now represents it. What he has received above his own interest he has received to the use of his bailor.

That may be so in most situations, but there are two problems with it. I noted one earlier: owners who trust the likes of you and me with possession of an insured and easily traceable car might think twice about trusting us with its ownership value in cash. The other is that it isn't true that the plaintiff is always accountable to the owner. The parties to a rental contract are at liberty to contract away such accountability. Equipment renters don't usually do so, but a bailee by contract with more bargaining power than most renters might insist on the inclusion of such a term. That bailee would have a contractual defence to a claim by the bailor, yet would still collect the ownership value for third party interference, according to reasoning in *The Winkfield*.

---

179 See, for example, the *Income Tax Act* of Canada s 69 (1)(b)(ii): "where a taxpayer has disposed of anything to any person by way of gift *inter vivos* the taxpayer shall be deemed to have received proceeds of disposition therefor equal to [the] fair market value". Thus might capital gains tax be payable on a transaction whereby, but for the section, two friends could have generated a tax deductible capital loss.

180 [1902] P 42 (Eng CA) at 60-61. Fourteen years before *Claridge's case*, a New Zealand court had awarded ownership damages to the bailee of a horse and carriage smashed by a third party. The reasoning, vaguely similar to the *Winkfield* point, was unconvincing.

> If it were otherwise, as moveable property can be readily destroyed or made away with, the bailor would have to follow the bailee, and be always at hand to protect his interests against possible wrongdoers. The application of the rule may give rise to difficulty and inconvenience in certain cases, but I think on the whole that the balance of convenience is in its favour: *Mangan* v *Leary* (1877) 3 NZ Jur (NS) 10 (NZCA).

Finally, *The Winkfield* would create a new rule of civil procedure. "The wrongdoer, having once paid full damages to the bailee, has an answer to any action by the bailor."[181] Is that so? What if the bailee grossly underestimated the ownership value? The bailee as plaintiff may win the full amount demanded in the statement of claim, but it is the bailor who has lost the ownership value and ends up short-changed by the supposed rule. What if the bailee demands the ownership value, but agrees to less in a settlement which saves litigation expenses and court time? Even without collusion on the part of bailee and third party, the bailor loses. Moreover, the scope of the pretended rule is unclear. If the wrongdoer has an answer to the bailor upon losing to and paying the bailee, why doesn't the wrongdoer also have an answer upon defeating the bailee's claim? What if the bailee hires a lesser lawyer than the bailor could have afforded, and the lawyer botches the case? The analysis looks like some twisted version of *res judicata*. If so, it would turn on the fact that the issue had been ruled upon, not on what the ruling was. These are but a sampling of the consequences of the so-called rule whereby the owner is non-suited by the bailee's recovery of damages. It is small consolation to the owner that alternative remedies may be available against the bailee or someone else.

The *Winkfield* analysis was accepted as gospel for most of the 20th century.[182] Most academics cite and do not question it. Students express surprise when I do. Judges are commonly said to apply it,[183] though on occasion they don't.[184] Despite all that support,

---

181 *Ibid* at 60.

182 See, for example, *Wilson v Lombank Ltd* [1963] 1 WLR 1294 (Eng). Possession of a car passed through a chain of buyers and sellers who mistakenly thought they were transferring ownership. The plaintiff, the last in the chain, left the car at a garage for repairs. The defendant, who apparently had not been paid by his transferee, seized possession at the garage. The defendant subsequently discovered the flaw in his own claim and restored possession to the owner. The plaintiff sued the defendant in trespass. The judge concluded that the plaintiff had held right to immediate possession, there being no mechanics lien because of a monthly credit arrangement at the garage. Contradicting himself, the judge also concluded that the plaintiff held possession when the seizure occurred. He therefore awarded damages, which he assessed as "the full value of the article wrongfully taken", plus the repair costs incurred . The "full value", for no apparent reason, was calculated as the amount the plaintiff had paid when he thought he bought ownership. *That makes no sense.* It was not the defendant's fault that the plaintiff was fleeced by some intermediate possessor who claimed to be selling ownership, but lied.

183 Many American, English and Canadian authorities (2 full pages of citations, some against the proposition) on this point can be found in a lengthy annotation at 150 ALR 163 at 174 (1944). The point is summarized:

> where the defendant is shown to have seized the goods while they were in the plaintiff's possession under claim of ownership he is not permitted to question the plaintiff's title or to show title in a third person unless to justify his seizure by authority of that title.

I have not checked all the cases looking for plaintiffs who were neither liable nor accountable to the owners, though I'd be interested to know if there are any.

184 See, for example, *West v Palmer* [1943] 3 DLR 400 (NS). The plaintiff borrowed a car. It was struck by a careless driver. He sued and won one dollar as "compensation for the loss of the use of the car for the comparatively short period of time in which he was delayed by the collision" [at 406]. See also *Terminal Warehouse v JH Lock & Sons Ltd* (1958) 12 DLR 2d (Ont CA) and *Courtenay v Knutson* (1951) 32 WWR 481 (BC).

The Winkfield is wrong.[185]

We can now summarize the bailee *versus* third party analysis. A third party who interferes with a bailee's possession may be sued in tort. Temporary or permanent dispossession is actionable interference; so is physical impairment of the thing itself, as it lowers the value of possession. The bailee collects damages equal to the amount by which his possession was devalued.[186] That, I have argued - notwithstanding precedent to the contrary - is the state of the law.

F SUMMARY: SALES AND GIFTS OF POSSESSION

This analysis of acquisition and disposition by transaction began with two relatively uncontroversial propositions. First, I identified the three best known categories of transactions - *purchase and sale*, *gift*, and *bailment* - which transfer property in things in common law jurisdictions. Second, I suggested that the main *property* issues in each category are (i) what forms of property are the parties dealing with and (ii) when does an acquisition or disposition take place.

Sales transactions and gifts were defined and explained under separate headings.[187]

---

185 Like many misguided English precedents, it is unlikely to be judicially reversed there due to statutory change. In the United Kingdom, an action for wrongful interference with goods may now be defended by showing third party title: *Torts (Interference with Goods) Act* 1977 C 32 s 8. The effect, I assume, is to limit the damages to the value of the plaintiff's property.

186 This calculation may be speculative, but so what? Courts have no difficulty estimating a value for other types of property that may turn out to have no value at all. Consider pension entitlements under an employment contract. They sometimes have to be valued long before it can be ascertained whether any pension will ever be paid to the particular employee. For example, when a contract of marriage doesn't work out the courts may be called upon to value the property held be each party in order to calculate "net family property" under the Ontario *Family Law Act* SO 1986 c 4. In *Flynn v Flynn* (1989) 68 OR 2d 129 (Ont) this included an employer funded pension to which the employee (husband) had no present claim and which might never accrue to him unless he remained in his present employment more than ten years. The court had no difficulty valuing it (at 132) *per* Flinn DCJ.

> The employee's entitlement under a pension plan that has not yet vested is an existing right the benefit of which is accruing to him. As a right it has a value to him contingent though it may be in realization. ... One can envisage many contingencies occurring which might prevent the vesting of this pension right. It is a weighing of these contingencies as applied to an as-if-vested value which gives rise to the valuation of the property by the court. ... Here the husband's pension was little more than two months away from vesting. He was secure in his employment in that termination for any number of reasons was remote. He was of middle age with no evidence of poor health. The discount to the valuation given on an as-if-vested basis would not be substantial. Accordingly, I would value the husband's pension at the date of separation at $4,836 and include that value in the property of the husband.

187 See Chapter 8 "Purchase and Sale" and Chapter 9 "Gift".

BAILMENT: A SEPARATE TRANSACTION?

This heading – "Bailment: a Separate Transaction?" - posed the question whether every bailment was just an example of either sale (or barter)[188] or gift. I define bailment as a transfer of possession of a thing upon agreement that the transferee would in the future transfer possession of the thing to a third party or back to the transferor.[189] Using that definition, I have tried to show that bailment is not a separate transaction at all and that some bailments are transfers of possession by contract (sales), while the rest are transfers of possession by gift. This view of bailments might change a few minor rules, but mostly it would do away with some centuries-old categorizations whose time is long past. It would also help to demonstrate that simple property questions in the common law too often become confused with the details of the transactions by which the property was acquired.

The familiar categories will, no doubt, continue to be used in our law. The distinctions are based more on terminology than substance.

And … that's all she wrote.

---

188 Barter is, in effect a sale. It is not so called because the word sale has been artificially restricted in common law jurisdictions to contractual transfers *for a money consideration*: see Chapter 8 "Background: the Codification of Sales Law".

189 This does not conform to the conception of bailment espoused by many other analysts.

INDEX